MIGRATING MEMORIES

Romanian Germans, mainly from the Banat and Transylvania, have occupied a place at the very heart of major events in Europe in the twentieth century, yet their history is largely unknown. This east-central European minority negotiated their standing in a difficult new European order after 1918, changing from uneasy supporters of Romania, to zealous Nazis, tepid Communists, and conciliatory Europeans. *Migrating Memories* is the first comprehensive study in English of Romanian Germans and follows their stories as they move across borders and between regimes, revealing a very European experience of migration, minorities, and memories in modern Europe. After 1945, Romanian Germans struggled to make sense of their lives during the Cold War at a time when the community began to fracture and fragment. The revolutions of 1989 seemed to mark the end of the German community in Romania, but instead Romanian Germans repositioned themselves as transnational European bridge-builders, staking out new claims in a fast-changing world.

JAMES KORANYI is Associate Professor of Modern European Cultural History in the Department of History at Durham University. He has published widely in three languages on cultural memory in Germany, Romania, and Hungary, on east-central European minorities, and on transnational history.

T0371048

MIGRATING MEMORIES

Romanian Germans in Modern Europe

JAMES KORANYI

University of Durham

Shaftesbury Road, Cambridge CB2 8EA, United Kingdom

One Liberty Plaza, 20th Floor, New York, NY 10006, USA

477 Williamstown Road, Port Melbourne, VIC 3207, Australia

314–321, 3rd Floor, Plot 3, Splendor Forum, Jasola District Centre, New Delhi – 110025, India

103 Penang Road, #05–06/07, Visioncrest Commercial, Singapore 238467

Cambridge University Press is part of Cambridge University Press & Assessment, a department of the University of Cambridge.

We share the University's mission to contribute to society through the pursuit of education, learning and research at the highest international levels of excellence.

www.cambridge.org
Information on this title: www.cambridge.org/9781009048446

DOI: 10.1017/9781009047449

First published 2022
First paperback edition 2023

A catalogue record for this publication is available from the British Library

ISBN   978-1-316-51777-2   Hardback
ISBN   978-1-009-04844-6   Paperback

To Nora, Clara, and Nina

Contents

Figures

Acknowledgements

This book has been a long time in the making. What started as a naïve enterprise in oral history went through various migrations of its own before becoming *Migrating Memories*. First and foremost, I owe thanks to all the Romanian Germans I have encountered along the way. Those encounters began much earlier than any research on my thesis. Growing up in suburban Munich, I had a number of teachers with 'funny accents' in German at my grey, functionalist *Gymnasium*. One was a *Sudetendeutscher*, Günter Elgner, who really captured my enthusiasm for history. The other was Margot Seiler, a middle-class Transylvanian Saxon whose family, according to her stories, had lost their fortune thanks to the Communists. One of my friends at school (and still a close friend today), also a German from Transylvania, sided with the Communists on that matter, in a way that only self-important teenagers could. I had no idea back then that Hans Bergel, a big name for Romanian German literature and politics who features throughout this book, lived in a neighbouring Munich suburb, nor did I know who he was. Perhaps, then, it was in the *Münchner Umland* that this book project began.

Migrating Memories was never trapped in Munich's suburbia, though I returned there time and again to interview Romanian Germans, to conduct research at the IKGS (Institut für deutsche Kultur und Geschichte Südosteuropas), and to spend time at the *Landsmannschaften*, the homeland societies, of both the Transylvanian Saxons and the Banat Swabians. The *Landsmannschaften*, though dealt with critically here in this book, were nothing but supportive and helpful. The archivists, librarians, editors, and historians who helped me in archives and institutes, often tucked away from the glamorous international spotlight that big, well-known archives enjoy, deserve a particular mention. The Siebenbürgen Institut, in Gundelsheim in the south-west of Germany, formed one such important focal point for this book despite all the financial difficulties it has had to navigate over the past decade. Christian Rother, Ingrid Schiel,

Michaela Adam (for her patience with my payments), Harald Roth, and Jutta Fabritius (for pointing me to surprising archival finds) made my research at the institute pleasant and smooth. Though I often darted in for just a day or two, they were always welcoming and prepared to help in the short space of time I had. Siegbert Bruss at the Landsmannschaft der Siebenbürger Sachsen in Munich was also a great ally for my research, as were friends and colleagues at the IKGS in Munich. Input from them – Florian Kührer-Wielach, Mariana Hausleitner, Enikő Dácz, Peter Motzan – was invaluable. Hannelore Baier, a journalist and historian based in Sibiu, has been a constant source of feedback on my work, as have Cristian Cercel, Gaëlle Fisher, Michaela Nowotnik, and Thomas Şindilariu in their own supportive and critical ways. I remain indebted to: Herwig Horn, who helped with the sourcing of images; Sergiu Dema, the director of the Casa de Cultură in Jimbolia; Camelia Boca, from the Biblioteca Centrală Universitară Mihai Eminescu in Iaşi; Florin Popa, from the Romanian Academy Library in Bucharest; Lucian Popa, from the National Library of Romania; and Nina May, the editor-in-chief of the *Allgmeine Deutsche Zeitung für Rumänien*.

Migrating Memories has been read, seen, and heard by so many people. My thanks go to Jonathan Kwan for reading an earlier (and perhaps unrecognisable) draft of sections of this book. James Mark, Martin Thomas, Bill Niven, and Richard Overy also read, commented on, and dissected early attempts. Special thanks go to Nora Goldschmidt, who constantly challenged the text beyond its content. I would also like to thank my colleagues at Durham, not just in general for the supportive environment in my department, but also specifically for reading earlier versions of this work: Sarah Davies, Rachel Johnson, Len Scales, and Jo Fox as well as Kay Schiller and Christian Liddy for super advice on packaging this book. Ruth Wittlinger was also a huge pillar of support, and I am deeply sorry that she will not get the opportunity to see the final version of *Migrating Memories*. The north-east of England has been a fantastic hub of academic solidarity, and I am very grateful to colleagues for allowing to introduce my work in different settings in the region: André Keil, Tom Stammers, Daniel Laqua, Charlotte Alston, Delphine Doucet, and many others. Beyond my world at Durham and in the north-east of England, the Society for Romanian Studies provided a wonderful forum for presenting and exchanging views on my work. Margaret Beissinger, Alex Drace-Francis, Roland Clark, and Irina Livezeanu have all helped me along the way.

This book would not have been possible without some very serious support and architecture around it. I owe special gratitude to the two anonymous reviewers of my manuscript. Their detailed, insightful comments – the product of an unstinting effort – helped to shape this book in very significant ways. I would also like to thank Liz Friend-Smith for her guidance and encouragement throughout the entire process of publication and my wonderful copy-editor, Karen Anderson. But, most importantly, I would like to thank my family for propping me up and, occasionally, putting everything into perspective: this book is for you, Nora, Clara, and Nina.

A final word on my research encounters: in Romania I became immersed in a world of stories, heritage, and claims on German traces. Alina Hughes and Tom Hughes accompanied me around the villages of central Transylvania on a very instructive research trip. Staff at archives in Sibiu, Timișoara, Arad, and elsewhere guided me throughout my research, as did the people working in the German Democratic Forum in Sibiu and the members of staff at the Colegiul Național 'Samuel von Brukenthal' in Sibiu. Anca Fleșeru helped me map out Sibiu in ways that crucially informed some of the granular material in *Migrating Memories*. While on research trips in Romania and Germany, I encountered a great deal of generosity, interest, and hospitality. And, in a curious way, my Munich suburb never seemed that far away. While waiting for a night train at Mediaș station in Transylvania, I struck up a conversation with a German-speaking family. We quickly established that we were from neighbouring Munich suburbs and that the family's best friend was a teacher at my former school. I knew that teacher, Melitta Dörner, although she never taught me. But she was another one of those Germans with 'funny accents', a German from central Transylvania who, like many others in this book, made up the tapestry of Romanian Germans and their stories.

Note on the Text

Names are political. In east-central Europe, the choice of language and name can trigger intense discussions about place and belonging. In *Migrating Memories*, I have not been able to dodge that issue. I have tried to use place names according to their context. I have, for instance, insisted on Sibiu – and not Hermannstadt or Nagyszeben – when referring to the city after 1918. There are, however, additional complexities. If the city's name appeared in the original source as Hermannstadt, I have still used Sibiu unless there was an important cultural and political significance attached to the German (or other) name. When first mentioning a place in the book, I have included its name in its other dominant languages in brackets. Throughout the book, where they have appeared in German or Romanian, I have provided translations of names of organisations and institutions, ideas, and concepts. In only a very few instances have I left a word or expression in its original language. Any inconsistencies in language politics in this book are not intended as political statements.

Stories, Identities, Memories

'A barren land': that is how a charter described the land bestowed forever upon the chosen people (*vocati*), a land where they would be their own masters, a desolate land without people, a land unspoilt and untouched by the plough, with forests growing unchecked and water flowing unfettered. This was the scene the wanderers encountered.[1]

At some point in the twelfth century, a group of people went in search of a new homeland 'beyond the forest'. On their journey, they encountered aurochs still roaming freely and bears looking for honey. Eventually, they reached the land they were looking for: Transylvania. On arrival, two of the men drew their swords and rammed them into the ground, swearing allegiance to their new homeland. They then separated, each taking their sword to a different place: one to Broos/Orăștie in western Transylvania, and the other to Draas/Drăuşeni in eastern Transylvania, where the swords would remain as symbols of their attachment to the wondrous new land. The new settlers worked the land, enduring hardship and wars in the centuries that followed. The union with their land was finally broken in 1944, when the sword in Draas disappeared as the local Germans were evacuated with the retreating Wehrmacht.[2]

This canonical foundation narrative is told by the Romanian German historian and folklorist Carl Göllner (1911–95) in his *Heimatbuch*, published in Romania in 1973, *Am Rande der Geschichte* (*On the Edge of History*). Göllner's story recounts one of most prominent episodes in the foundation story which Romanian Germans in the twentieth century told about the origins and ending of their community, a story that combined

---

[1] Original: 'Eine Öde – so nennt eine Urkunde das den "Gerufenen" (*vocati*) für ewig verliehene Land, auf dem sie ihre eigenen Herren sein sollten, eine Öde ohne Menschen, ein urhaftes Land, noch nie von der Pflugschar aufgerissen, wild wuchernder Wald und Gewässer, die fluteten, wie sie wollten. In eine solche Wüste traten die Wanderer.' See Heinrich Zillich, 'Achthundert Jahre', in Hans Bergel and Walter Myß (eds.), *Wir Siebenbürger* (Innsbruck: Wort und Welt Verlag, 1986), p. 60.
[2] Carl Göllner, *Am Rande der Geschichte* (Bucharest: Kriterion, 1973), p. 12.

and embellished different phases in the community's past. Reportedly following the call of King Géza II of Hungary (1130–62), Germans – or Saxons as they were more commonly known – first arrived in Transylvania in the twelfth century, bolstering the frontier zone with fortified churches. Later, throughout the eighteenth century, Swabians settled in the Banat, which at the time was a war-torn and depopulated borderland. Both German groups arrived in the area in the hope of a better life, land, and opportunities. By the beginning of the twentieth century, the two groups had fused into the Romanian German minority in the Romanian state, newly enlarged after 1918. Their combined experiences of the upheavals of the twentieth century spurred them on to another exodus, to a new 'Promised Land' in Germany.

This book is about Romanian Germans making sense of modern Europe through their stories and memories. As a group, they experienced major developments and events in Europe in the twentieth century: the reordering of the European map after the First World War, inclusion in the Romanian state, National Socialism, the Second World War, deportation, Cold War division, post-communist uncertainty, and migration. Their exposure to many of the major currents of modern European history forced them continually to reconsider and refashion their identity as a group, processing and reprocessing their collective identity in response to the shifting socio-political pressures that encroached on their community. As this book argues, the greatest challenge Romanian Germans faced throughout the twentieth century was to justify their existence vis-á-vis Germans in Germany and Romanians, as well as other groups and institutions. Defensive 'people's stories' were flexibly remoulded as offensive tactics in their embrace of and commitment to National Socialism. After 1945, Romanian Germans were constantly in search of explanations for their role in National Socialism and communism, as well as their place in Europe more broadly as the Cold War drew to a close.

Romanian Germans came to exist as a group under the pressure of political circumstances: following the end of the First World War, the Romanian state increased its territory and incorporated the former Habsburg regions of Transylvania, Bukovina, and parts of the Banat. In the east, it gained Bessarabia and consolidated its claim on the Dobruja region in the south. Distinct German groups became compatriots almost overnight. The two main groups of greatest interest to us are Transylvanian Saxons (*Siebenbürger Sachsen*) and Banat Swabians (*Banater Schwaben*), as well as the Landler from southern Transylvania. Although the German minority in Romania after 1918 also included Bukovina Germans,

Bessarabian Germans, the Germans in Bucharest, and Sathmar Swabians, this book focuses mainly on Banat Swabians and Transylvanian Saxons for a number of reasons. By sheer strength of numbers – 250,000 and 230,000 respectively in the 1930 census in Romania – they dominated Romanian German politics.[3] At the same time, Swabians, and particularly Saxons, were also the most prolific writers in all areas: from personal correspondence to newspaper publishing to literary work. After 1945, they were neither expelled, nor was their territory incorporated into a new state, as was the case for the Bessarabian Germans and most Bukovina Germans. Instead, a sizeable Romanian German community remained in Romania during the Cold War, and Romania would play a key role in debates on identity both before and after 1989. In practice, then, Romanian Germans were mainly defined by Banat Swabians and Transylvanian Saxons, and it is among these two groups that Romanian German history was constructed.

The term 'Romanian German' has been a contested one. It has been argued that regional identities prevailed over any sense of Romanian German identity, or that their different confessional identities – Banat Swabian Catholics and Transylvanian Saxon Protestants – undermined adherence to a 'Romanian German' group. Much of the resistance to the term has come from Romanian German writers for whom it evokes the minorities policies of the Romanian state in the twentieth century, and Romanian German literature conventionally rejected the term 'Romanian German' as 'artificial'.[4] For Romanian German writers and intellectuals, the label Romanian German has frequently been viewed as a threat to what many feel are the 'authentic' regional identities of Transylvanian Saxons and Banat Swabians. This book does not contest the importance of other kinds of constellations of group identities; rather, it operates on the premise that identities exist on different levels and thus coexist even when they appear to be mutually exclusive. Though Swabians and Saxons (and other German groups in Romania) each made attempts to defend their 'unique' identity, almost in spite of this a shared sense of community emerged very quickly, and myths of origin and identity were

---

[3] For an overview of interwar Romanian demographics, see Irina Livezeanu, *Cultural Politics in Greater Romania: Regionalism, Nation Building, and Ethnic Struggle, 1918–1930* (Ithaca, N.Y.: Cornell University Press, 1995), pp. 8–11. A more detailed history of Transylvanian Saxons and Banat Swabians follows in Chapter 1.

[4] See, for instance, Annemarie Weber, *Rumäniendeutsche? Diskurse zur Gruppenidentität einer Minderheit (1944–1971)* (Cologne: Böhlau, 2010), and Mathias Beer, Dietrich Beyrau and Cornelia Rauh (eds.), *Deutschsein als Grenzerfahrung: Minderheitenpolitik in Europa zwischen 1914 und 1950* (Essen: Klartext, 2009).

fused, giving voice to a common experience of Romanian Germans through the twentieth century and beyond.

A sense of a shared Romanian German identity was nascent at the very outset of the enlarged Kingdom of Romania at the end of the First World War. Faced with shared challenges as a minority in interwar Romania, Germans learned to use a common language as a way of making sense of the new political situation. Radicalisation and alignment with Nazi Germany firmly cemented the idea of them being first and foremost Germans in Romania. The language of belonging to a *Schicksalsgemeinschaft* – a so-called community of fate – gave Saxons and Swabians a grammar with which to explain their shared experiences in Romania, which had the effect of beginning to level out regional particularities.

What set Romanian Germans apart from most other German and other east-central European minorities are their experiences at the end of the Second World War and during the Cold War. While it is true that many Germans from Romania were dispersed across Europe during the 1930s and 1940s, a majority of Romanian Germans ended up 'back' in Romania by the early communist period. They were the only German group in east-central Europe to suffer repercussions against Germans at the end of the war without facing large-scale expulsions.[5] Even Germans in Hungary, some of whom remained in Hungary after 1945, experienced serious dislocation by various forms of flight and expulsion as the war ended.[6] Others, like Silesian Germans, faced a sudden and violent end to their hybrid identity by comprehensive expulsion as the Second World War drew to a close.[7] The Romanian German community thus gives a unique insight into life under communism as a previously victimised German group. Their experiences after the war and during communism defined them as outsiders, as they were associated with National Socialism despite their official rehabilitation in the 1950s. This meant that Romanian Germans simultaneously had to re-examine their previous links with Nazi Germany and think about how to live in a state that had defined them, temporarily at least, as untrustworthy.

---

[5] See Georg Weber et al. (eds.), *Die Deportation der Siebenbürger Sachsen in die Sowjetunion 1945–1949: 3 Volumes* (Cologne: Böhlau, 1996).

[6] See John C. Swanson, *Tangible Belonging: Negotiating Germanness in Twentieth-Century Hungary* (Pittsburgh: University of Pittsburgh Press, 2017), pp. 228–344. For a historical overview of Germans in Hungary, see Gerhard Seewann, *Geschichte der Deutschen in Ungarn, Vol. II, 1860 bis 2006* (Marburg: Verlag Herder-Institut, 2011).

[7] See Gregor Thum, *Uprooted: How Breslau Became Wrocław* (Princeton: Princeton University Press, 2011).

Yet the communist period was not only framed by Romanian German memories of fascism and their subsequent victimisation. Romanian Germans were part of a transnational network in which they were torn between isolation within Romania, association with Romania, and the increasing drive to leave Romania for (West) Germany. Further afield, trans-Atlantic connections would also play an important role. Unlike most other German speakers in east-central Europe, Romanian Germans remained part of their homeland on a scale unparalleled elsewhere, and as a result they developed a complicated relationship with their imagined homeland, Germany.[8] Yet a growing number of Romanian Germans continued to disassociate themselves from Romania by leaving for Germany with increasing urgency during the Cold War. Very little work has been done on the link between earlier experiences in twentieth-century Romania and the subsequent decision to emigrate. While prominent Romanian German authors of prose fiction such as the Nobel Prize laureate Herta Müller (1953–) have found Romanian German experiences a fascinating subject for literature, studies have largely steered clear of explaining the evolution of a minority identity over the course of a century, which resulted in the virtual dissolution of the community by the 1990s.[9]

At the end of a fraught century, most of the Romanian German community had migrated to Germany. But far from being the end of Romanian German history, the processes of Europeanisation – political and cultural – exposed Romanian Germans to developments that confronted them yet again with the need to make sense of their transnational existence. The dwindling community in Romania and émigrés in Germany responded differently to the late Cold War and post-communist period; yet, more recent developments within the Romanian German community show a convergence of identity towards a more confident Romanian German self-understanding, embodied most clearly in the figure of Klaus Iohannis (1959–), the Romanian German who was elected president of Romania in 2014.

---

[8] Germans in Hungary are the closest parallel to Romanian Germans, though their numbers dwindled considerably after the Second World War, leaving behind a splintered and rump community that does not compare to the lively German community in Romania. See Swanson, *Tangible Belonging*, and Sebastian Sparwasser, *Identität im Spannungsfeld von Zwangsmigration und Heimkehr: Ungarndeutsche Vertriebene und die Remigration* (Vienna: New Academic Press, 2018).

[9] Herta Müller, *Hetztier* (Munich: Carl Hanser Verlag, 2007); Dieter Schlesak, *Visa: Ost–West Lektionen* (Frankfurt am Main: S. Fischer, 1970).

Framing Identities and Memories

The growing body of literature on German diasporas, comprehensive in many areas, has opened up avenues for studying identity formation, 'transnational Germans', and memory, but it has only begun to take Romanian Germans seriously.[10] Much of the focus has been on Poland, Bohemia, and the Baltic region, as well as the burgeoning interest in Germans overseas in the Americas.[11] In scholarship from east-central Europe, there has been a tendency to focus on 'their' minorities: Romanian-language scholarship on Germans and Jews in Romania, Hungarian scholarship on Hungarians abroad, Polish scholarship on Silesian diversity, and so on.[12] Specifically, work on Romanian Germans has often focused on circumscribed periods in Romanian German history,

---

[10] See, for instance, Andrew Demshuk, *The Lost German East: Forced Migration and the Politics of Memory, 1945–1970* (Cambridge: Cambridge University Press, 2012), R. M. Douglas, *Orderly and Humane: The Expulsion of the Germans after the Second World War* (New Haven: Yale University Press, 2012), Ulrich Merten, *Forgotten Voices: The Expulsion of the Germans from Eastern Europe after World War II* (New Brunswick: Transaction, 2012), Winson Chu, *The German Minority in Interwar Poland* (Cambridge: Cambridge University Press, 2013), Bill Niven (ed.), *Germans as Victims: Remembering the Past in Contemporary Germany* (Basingstoke: Palgrave Macmillan, 2006), Panikos Panayi (ed.), *Germans as Minorities during the First World War: A Global Comparative Perspective* (Farnham: Ashgate, 2014), and Peter Polak-Springer, *Recovered Territory: A German–Polish Conflict over Land and Culture, 1919–1989* (New York: Berghahn, 2015). Much of the focus has tended to be directed at German groups that *de facto* ceased to exist after 1945. In this way, Germans from Poland and Czechoslovakia have received much attention. For a refreshing attempt to break the view that 1945 represents a cut-off point for studies on German minorities in east-central Europe, see Bill Niven, 'On a Supposed Taboo: Flight and Refugees from the East in GDR Film and Television', *German Life and Letters* 65/2 (2012), pp. 216–36. Another exception to this is Cristian Cercel's work on the afterlives of Romanian Germans in post-communist Romania. See Cristian Cercel, *Romania and the Quest for European Identity: Philo-Germanism without Germans* (London: Routledge, 2018); see also Gaëlle Fisher, *Resettlers and Survivors: Bukovina and the Politics of Belonging in West Germany and Israel, 1945–1989* (New York: Berghahn, 2020).

[11] Alongside the work mentioned in n. 10, there are a growing number of works on German migrants to the Americas, including H. Glenn Penny, 'From Migrant Knowledge to Fugitive Knowledge? German Migrants and Knowledge Production in Guatemala, 1880s–1945', *Geschichte und Gesellschaft* 43/3 (2017), pp. 381–412, Tammy Proctor, 'Patriotic Enemies: Germans in the Americas, 1914–1920', in Panayi (ed.), *Germans as Minorities*, pp. 213–34, Alexander Freund, *Aufbrüche nach dem Zusammenbruch: Die deutsche Nordamerika-Auswanderung nach dem Zweiten Weltkrieg* (Göttingen: Vandenhoeck & Ruprecht, 2004).

[12] For Czechoslovakia, see Jiří Pešek, *Německé menšiny v právních normách 1938–1948: Československo ve srovnání s vybranými evropskými zeměmi, Vol. I* (Brno: Doplněk, 2006); for Hungary see Ágnes Tóth, *Rückkehr nach Ungarn 1946–1950* (Munich: Oldenbourg, 2012), and Tibor Zinner, *A magyarországi németek kitelepítése* (Budapest: Magyar Hivatalos Közlönykiadó, 2004); and for Romania see, for instance, Corneliu Pintilescu, 'Problema "Naționaliști Germani" în activitatea Securității (1948–1964)', in Cosmin Budeancă and Florentin Olteanu (eds.), *Identități sociale, culturale, etnice și religioase în comunism* (Iași: Polirom, 2015), pp. 269–83, as well as Mathias Beer, Sorin Radu and Florian Kührer-Wielach (eds.), *Germanii din România: migrație și patrimoniu cultural după 1945* (Bucharest: Editura Academiei Româna, 2020).

and most of this has been done in German.[13] As in much of the work on German diasporas and migrant communities, the Second World War has figured as a dividing line between scholars where German diasporas before the rise of fascism are dealt with in migration history, while German diasporic communities after 1945 have tended to be included in the history of flight and expulsion.[14] As a result, much of the scholarship on east-central European German minorities, including Banat Swabians and Transylvanian Saxons, implicitly distinguishes between Germans as 'doers' before the Second World War and Germans as victims after. Work in east-central European languages on Germans in east-central Europe, and Romania specifically, has been more focused on the topic of expulsion, victimisation, and emigration.[15] German 'doers' as migrants, by contrast, have often coalesced around German history as global history.[16] This book addresses that tension between a parochial post-1945 and a global history of German migration by explaining how these themes are in fact connected.

[13] Such studies are hugely valuable for our understanding of Romanian German history, though they are limited in their scope. See, for instance, Hannelore Baier, 'Arbeitslager für die deutsche Bevölkerung im Innern Rumäniens nach 1945', *Südostdeutsche Vierteljahreshefte* 54/4 (2005), pp. 379–87, and Weber et al. (eds.), *Die Deportation der Siebenbürger Sachsen*, vols. I–III. Annemarie Weber has attempted to conceptualise the question of Romanian German identity in the Cold War period, although her study falls somewhat short of offering a comprehensive picture due to its chronological focus. See Annemarie Weber, *Rumäniendeutsche?*. Other illuminating studies on Romanian Germans include Cristan Cercel, 'The Relationship between Religious and National Identity in the Case of Transylvanian Saxons, 1933–1944', *Nationalities Papers* 39/2 (2011), pp. 161–80, Cercel, *Romania and the Quest for European Identity*, and Tudor Georgescu, 'Ethnic Minorities and the Eugenic Promise: The Transylvanian Saxon Experiment with National Renewal in Interwar Romania', *European Review of History/Revue Européenne d'Histoire* 17/6 (2010), pp. 861–80.

[14] More broadly, there are some exceptions to this, most notably Panayi (ed.), *Germans as Minorities*. For examples of this divide for Romanian Germans and other east-central European German minorities, see, for instance, Mathias Beer and Dittmar Dahlmann (eds.), *Migration nach Ost- und Südosteuropa vom 18. bis zum Beginn des 19. Jahrhunderts: Ursachen, Formen, Verlauf, Ergebnis* (Munich: Franz Steiner Verlag, 1999), Mathias Beer (ed.), *Krieg und Zwangsmigration in Südosteuropa 1940–1950: Pläne, Umsetzung, Folgen* (Munich: Franz Steiner Verlag, 2019), Stefan Manz, *Constructing a German Diaspora: The 'Greater German Empire', 1871–1914* (New York: Routledge, 2014), and John Eicher, *Exiled among Nations: German and Mennonite Mythologies in a Transnational Age* (Cambridge: Cambridge University Press, 2020), which also only goes up to 1945.

[15] See, for instance, Dan Popa, *Naționalitatea ca vină: deportara etnicilor germani din România în URSS* (Bucharest: Editura Mica Valahia, 2015), and Lavinia Betea et al. (eds.), *Lungul drum spre nicăieri: Germanii din România deportați în URSS* (Bucharest: Cetatea de Scaun, 2012); on the Bărăgan deportations in 1951, see Smaranda Vultur, *Istorie trăită – istorie povestită: deportarea în Bărăgan (1951–1956)* (Timișoara: Amarcord, 1997).

[16] See, for instance, Sebastian Conrad, *Globalisation and the Nation in Imperial Germany* (Cambridge: Cambridge University Press, 2010), and Werner Abelhauser et al., *German Industry and Global Enterprise. BASF: The History of a Company* (Cambridge: Cambridge University Press, 2004).

In scholarship on Romanian Germans, there have been some important studies on specific topics, often with 1944/5 as the pivot on which they turn.[17] Other work in the field, though fundamental for comprehending the Romanian German community and how they have constructed their history, has had a distinct parochial edge.[18] A holistic approach, which deals with the wider developments throughout the twentieth century up until the present, has been largely absent.[19] While much existing work remains invaluable, it has not been transferred into an international arena. The larger implications of that work for modern European identity debates are often marginalised by an absence of international dialogue.[20] This book positions Romanian German identities and narratives in a broader framework by interrogating scholarship on minorities, identity, nationalism, and myth, while also situating itself in what is now a vibrant body of literature concerned with memory and groups with multiple identity layers, including its transnational dimension.[21]

---

[17] The excellent series of edited volumes published by the publishing house IKGS (Institut für deutsche Kultur und Geschichte Südosteuropas) is a good example of this. See, for instance, Mariana Hausleitner and Harald Roth (eds.), *Der Einfluss von Faschismus und Nationalsozialismus auf Minderheiten in Ostmittel- und Südosteuropa* (Munich: IKGS Verlag, 2006), Mariana Hausleitner (ed.), *Deutsche und Juden in Bessarabien: 1814–1941* (Munich: IKGS Verlag, 2005), and Krista Zach and Cornelius Zach (eds.), *Deutsche und Rumänen in der Erinnerungsliteratur: Memorialistik als Geschichtsquelle* (Munich: IKGS Verlag, 2005). The latter book is a unique exception that cuts across the nineteenth and twentieth centuries.

[18] See, for instance, Georg Hromadka, *Kleine Chronik des Banater Berglands* (Munich: Südostdeutsches Kulturwerk, 1993).

[19] A good example of a study on a minority group in the region is the book by Gaby Coldewey et al. on the life stories of Jewish émigrés from Chernivtsi/Czernowitz in the Bukovina; see Gaby Coldewey et al. (eds.), *Zwischen Pruth und Jordan: Lebenserinnerungen Czernowitzer Juden* (Cologne: Böhlau, 2003). The same applies to studies that try to tell a longer story of the identity of a place; see Thum, *Uprooted*. A recent edited volume tried to cover the twentieth century more holistically, but there are lacunae in its coverage. See Ottmar Traşcă and Remus Gabriel Anghel (eds.), *Un veac frământat: Germanii din România după 1918* (Cluj-Napoca: Institutului pentru Studierea Problemelor Minorităţilor Naţionale, 2018). For an excellent study on Transylvanian Saxon self-image as shaped in the diaspora, see Sacha E. Davis, 'Reflecting on the Diaspora: The Transylvanian Saxon Self-Image and the Saxons Abroad', *Siebenbürgische Landeskunde* 35/2 (2012), pp. 150–70.

[20] Two recent studies incorporate Romanian Germans into broader studies on Transylvania as a European problem and on population transfers of minorities in Europe, even though Romanian Germans are not the subject of these two books; see Holly Case, *Between States: The Transylvanian Question and the European Idea during World War II* (Stanford: Stanford University Press, 2009), and Matthew Frank, *Making Minorities History: Population Transfer in Twentieth-Century Europe* (Oxford: Oxford University Press, 2017).

[21] This book fits with broader studies on diaspora; see, for instance, Vijay Agnew, *Diaspora, Memory, and Identity: A Search for Home* (Toronto: University of Toronto Press, 2006), Claire Sutherland and Elena Barabantseva (eds.), *Diaspora and Citizenship* (Abingdon: Routledge, 2011), and a study on Romanian migrant diasporas by Ruxandra Trandafoiu, *Diaspora Online: Identity Politics and Romanian Migrants* (New York: Berghahn, 2013).

Rogers Brubaker's work has played a crucial role for understanding minorities in east-central Europe.[22] His concept of 'groupness' and his model of the 'triadic nexus' have deeply influenced east-central European studies on minorities to such an extent that they have almost become gospel in the field.[23] Brubaker's model of a 'triadic nexus', which allowed him to differentiate between 'nationalising nationalisms' and 'transborder nationalisms',[24] has been applied to Slovak–Hungarian relations, to Hungarian migrants to Hungary, to Ceauşescu's 'Nationality Policy' in 1970s Romania, and to local identities in Transylvania.[25] Applied to Romanian Germans, this model would connect the minority group (in our case Romanian Germans), its actual homeland (Romania after 1918), and its external homeland (varieties of Germany). Yet if, as Brubaker argues, 'groupness' is something that is 'unstable' and can be mobilised only at particular moments, Romanian Germans present an exceptionally rich and challenging case study.[26] One way to account for that richness has been explored by Cristian Cercel, whose work on the post-war Romanian German community expands Brubaker's model to a 'quadratic nexus' by seeing the émigré community as a fourth component.[27] While the idea of the émigré community acting as a fourth component is appealing, it does not fully do justice to the complex case that Romanian Germans pose. The

---

[22] See, for instance, Rogers Brubaker, *Nationalism Reframed: Nationhood and the National Question in the New Europe* (Cambridge: Cambridge University Press, 1996), Rogers Brubaker, *Ethnicity without Groups* (Cambridge, Mass.: Harvard University Press, 2004), Rogers Brubaker et al., *Nationalist Politics and Everyday Ethnicity in a Transylvanian Town* (Princeton: Princeton University Press, 2006), and Rogers Brubaker, *Grounds for Difference* (Cambridge, Mass.: Harvard University Press, 2015), esp. chapter 5.

[23] See, for instance among many, László Kürti, *The Remote Borderland: Transylvania in the Hungarian Imagination* (Albany: SUNY Press, 2001), esp. p. 185, and Vello Pettai, 'Explaining Ethnic Politics in the Baltic States: Reviewing the Triadic Nexus Model', *Journal of Baltic Studies* 37/1 (2006), pp. 124–36.

[24] Brubaker, *Nationalism Reframed*, pp. 4, 5; see also Brubaker et al., *Nationalist Politics*.

[25] See Katarína Lezová, 'The Notion of Kosovo as a Precedent and the Impact of the Hungarian Minority Issue on Slovakia's Policy towards Kosovo's Independence', *Europe–Asia Studies* 65/5 (2013), pp. 965–91, Jon E. Fox, 'From National Inclusion to Economic Exclusion: Transylvanian Hungarian Ethnic Return Migration to Hungary', in Tsuda Takeyuki (ed.), *Diasporic Homecomings: Ethnic Return Migration in Comparative Perspective* (Stanford: Stanford University Press, 2009), pp. 186–207, Monica Andriescu, 'Identity Politics under National Communist Rule: The Rhetoric Manifestations of Nicolae Ceauşescu's Nationality Policy in 1970s Romania', *Studia Politica: The Romanian Political Science Review* 9/1 (2009), pp. 105–17, and Brubaker et al., *Nationalist Politics*.

[26] Brubaker, *Ethnicity without Groups*, pp. 3, 4.

[27] Cristian Cercel, 'Postwar (West) German–Romanian Relations: Expanding Brubaker's Analytical Triad', *Nationalism and Ethnic Politics* 23/3 (2017), pp. 297–317. This is also true of other studies that have played with the idea of a 'quadratic nexus'; see David J. Smith, 'Framing the National Question in Central and Eastern Europe: A Quadratic Nexus?', *Global Review of Ethnopolitics* 2/1 (2002), pp. 3–16.

Romanian German émigré community was too diverse to fit the categories of 'entrepreneurs' and 'enactors' or even to present a uniform relationship to their 'home' in Germany.[28] But Brubaker's work is indispensable to the understanding of how the Romanian German community functioned. Crucially, it allows us to take terms such as 'diaspora', 'group', and 'identity' not as fixed analytical categories, but as categories of *practice*.[29] In the sources this book draws on – essays, newspaper articles, interviews, adverts, letters, poems, visual material – we see, in practice, what it meant to be Romanian German at certain moments in history.

How then might we understand Romanian German identity? This book places the vernacular articulation and understanding of identity by Romanian Germans at the centre of its analysis. Drawing on Brubaker's model of 'ethnopolitical entrepreneurs', who evoke a group when invoking the stories around that group, this book focuses on episodes when Romanian German identities were contested and reshaped by 'entrepreneurs'. These entrepreneurs are visible in this book: cultural activists, National Socialist enthusiasts, emigration advocates, and homeland associations in Germany, as well as writers and intellectuals.[30] Then there are those Romanian Germans – 'ordinary' Romanian Germans – who practised a performative identity, but were not necessarily 'entrepreneurs'. What united these two categories is their experiences as a group – or 'groupness' using Brubaker's term – at certain moments in time. For Romanian Germans, this meant performing Germanness after the political contours shifted in 1918 or responding to rapid political and ideological realignments from the 1930s through to the end of communism. And, while Romanian German ethnopolitical entrepreneurs have an important role to play in this book, the distinction between them and 'ordinary people' is fuzzy.

Studies of 'banal nationalism' and heritage culture can help to further clarify the ways in which identities have been mobilised in politically charged and uncertain settings.[31] Concerned with the agency of 'ordinary people' in the construction of their own narratives, 'banal nationalism' has stood accused of lacking evidential backing.[32] But this book addresses that

---

[28] See Smith, 'Framing the National Question', and Cercel, 'Postwar (West) German–Romanian Relations'.

[29] See Brubaker, *Ethnicity without Groups*, and Brubaker, *Grounds for Difference*, pp. 128, 129.

[30] Rogers Brubaker, 'Ethnicity without Groups', *Journal of European Sociology* 43/2 (2002), pp. 163–89.

[31] The idea of 'banal nationalism' dates back to Michael Billig's book from 1995; see Michael Billig, *Banal Nationalism* (London: Sage, 1995).

[32] A special issue of *Nations and Nationalism* from 2018 tried to tackle the methodological issues around banal nationalism. See Jon Fox and Maarten van Ginderachter, 'Introduction: Everyday

point by including 'ordinary voices': interviews, private letters, unpublished poems, and other 'fugitive sources'. With its focus on migrants and migration – one of the main experiences for Romanian Germans in the twentieth century – 'banal nationalism' has also opened up ways for scholars to explore the relationship between national frameworks (though not always national) and the behavioural patterns of 'ordinary people'.[33] But, beyond behaviour and nationalism explicitly, the idea of 'banal nationalism' allows us to blur the distinction between 'producers' and 'consumers' of identity. John Swanson's study of Germans from Hungary, for instance, examines everyday voices in detail and thus anchors articulations of 'banal nationalism' in the present.[34] Equally, Cercel's work on German heritage in post-socialist Romania lays bare the machinations of entrepreneurs of 'Germanness' – politicians and cultural activists in Romania – as a political tool.[35] For Romanian Germans, their 'banal nationalism' was constantly performed in their obsessive interest in collecting and celebrating their local *Volksgeschichten*, in nostalgic reminiscing about a communal past during moments of crises, and – later, in West Germany – in re-enactments of local traditions and festivities.

Romanian Germans were also an integral part of east-central Europe, and their identities were bound up with identity discourses in east-central and south-eastern Europe, including notions of civilisation, mission, and otherness.[36] Romanian Germans articulated and performed such ideas in intervals and particularly at moments of pressure and uncertainty.[37] When crises occurred, the issues of 'civilisation' and 'otherness', which have also been explored elsewhere in studies in east-central Europe, were

---

Nationalism's Evidence Problem', *Nations and Nationalism* 24/3 (2018), pp. 546–52. See also the critical reply to the special issue, Sophie Duchesne, 'Who's Afraid of Banal Nationalism', *Nations and Nationalism* 24/4 (2018), pp. 841–56.

[33] See Michael Skey, '"There Are Times When I Feel Like a Bit of an Alien": Middling Migrants and the National Order of Things', *Nations and Nationalism* 24/3 (2018), pp. 606–23.

[34] Swanson, *Tangible Belonging*.   [35] Cercel, 'Postwar (West) German–Romanian Relations'.

[36] For an excellent collection of contemporary discourses on national identity in east-central Europe, see Balázs Trencsényi and Michal Kopeček (eds.), *Discourses of Collective Identity in Central and Southeast Europe (1770–1945): Late Enlightenment – Emergence of the Modern 'National Idea'*, Vol. I (Budapest: CEU Press, 2006); see also Brubaker et al., *Nationalist Politics*, in particular, chs. 1 and 2.

[37] This book thus adds to work that has challenged ideas of a straight line of identity formation. See, for instance, Jeremy King, *Budweisers into Czechs and Germans: A Local History of Bohemian Politics, 1848–1948* (Princeton: Princeton University Press, 2005), Pieter Judson and Marsha Rozenblit (eds.), *Constructing Nationalities in East Central Europe* (New York: Berghahn, 2003), esp. chs. 9–15, and Nancy Wingfield, *Flag Wars and Stone Saints: How the Bohemian Lands Became Czech* (Cambridge, Mass.: Harvard University Press, 2007).

always a central part of identity debates.[38] For Transylvanian Saxons, bound together by their Lutheranism,[39] religion would continue to play a crucial role in understanding their 'mission' as pioneers of a European civilisation.[40] In particular, the Lutheran Church was crucial for the battle during the interwar period over Romanian German commitment to Nazism, where conflicts over ideas of belonging and civilisation erupted. These debates were often based on crude orientalising stereotypes, documented in studies on Eastern Europe since the 1990s.[41] Yet Romanian Germans are a particularly interesting case to follow, since their stereotypes about civilisation fractured internally with contested and contradictory views of where their future lay. And while Romanian German images of Romania and Romanians often repeated stereotypes about 'Balkan backwardness', there were surprising counter-voices throughout their century that inverted this imagery and projected it westwards.

Myths and the historical imaginary anchor these broader issues about belonging, and they thus appear throughout this book. East-central European studies are replete with research on myth-making, though such studies often assume an oppositional relationship between 'myth' and 'reality'.[42] Born out of deep loathing for the myth-making of communist regimes, several studies in the first two decades after 1989 deconstructed

---

[38] In this case, modernity is crucial to Romanian German identity formation, as this identity was constructed against purportedly 'backward' others. See Maria Todorova, 'The Trap of Backwardness: Modernity, Temporality, and the Study of Eastern European Nationalism', *Slavic Review* 64/1 (2005), pp. 140–64.

[39] Krista Zach, Joachim Bahlcke, and Konrad G. Gündisch, *Konfessionelle Pluralität, Stände und Nation: Ausgewählte Abhandlungen zur südosteuropäischen Religions- und Gesellschaftsgeschichte* (Berlin: LIT Verlag, 2004), p. 158.

[40] Daniela Mârza, 'Aspects de l'enseignement roumain confessionnel en Transylvanie', *Transylvanian Review* 15/2 (2006), pp. 36–44.

[41] On eastern Europe, see Larry Wolff, *Inventing Eastern Europe: The Map of Civilization on the Mind of the Enlightenment* (Stanford: Stanford University Press, 1994). Larry Wolff's work has been revised and critiqued since its publication, but its central role in framing an entire body of literature is undisputed. For a more recent collection of essays specifically on the 'German East' and orientalism, see Rita Aldenhoff-Hübinger, Catherine Gousseff and Thomas Serrier (eds.), *Europa vertikal: Zur Ost-West-Gliederung im 19. und 20. Jahrhundert* (Göttingen: Wallenstein, 2016). On the Balkans and stereotypes, see Maria Todorova, *Imagining the Balkans* (Oxford: Oxford University Press, 1997), Maria Todorova, *Scaling the Balkans: Essays on Eastern European Entanglements* (Leiden: Brill, 2019), and Vesna Goldsworthy, *Inventing Ruritania: The Imperialism of the Imagination* (New Haven: Yale University Press, 1998).

[42] See, for instance, Lucian Boia, *Istorie şi mit în conştiinţa românească* (Bucharest: Humanitas, 1997), Pål Kolstø (ed.), *Myths and Boundaries in South-Eastern Europe* (London: Hurst, 2005), and Alexander Wöll and Harald Wydra (eds.), *Democracy and Myth in Russia and Eastern Europe* (London: Routledge, 2008).

historical myths in east-central Europe.[43] Work in this field has covered a lot of ground by focusing on specific case studies, often nation by nation, in much detail.[44] *Migrating Memories* adds to that literature by examining, among other aspects, the fraught relationship between official myths during communism and the Romanian German community. It also breaks with much of that field by understanding myths not in opposition to reality, but as constitutive of historical experience. The focus on national frameworks of myth-making is also a straitjacket which this book resists by placing myth-making in a transnational framework in which historical myths and narratives were constantly changing and not always according to the wishes of 'nation-builders'. In this view, myths are not national orthodoxies that constrain identity, but part of the performative element of identity. Romanian Germans in communist Romania, for instance, often worked within the political framework to articulate deeply held ideas of belonging. People's stories of a deep past were not hidden away, but articulated within those Cold War paradigms.

Migrating Memories also engages with recent work in the field of transnational history when using Brubaker's model.[45] Transnational history foregrounds the importance of different scales in historical analysis, going beyond, but not against, the nation-state to include both 'big' and 'small' scales of history.[46] One of the main applications of transnational history is therefore to appreciate that the differences between 'ethnopolitical entrepreneurs' and those who perform identity are mainly a matter of

---

[43] In addition to the works cited in n. 42, other notable names involved in attempting to puncture holes in historical myths include Vladimir Tismăneanu and György Schöpflin. Their studies have been criticised for being overtly political in their approach. See, for instance, Vladimir Tismăneanu, *Fantasies of Salvation: Democracy, Nationalism and Myth in Post-Communist Europe* (Princeton: Princeton University Press, 2008), and Geoffrey Hosking and György Schöpflin (eds.), *Myths and Nationhood* (London: Hurst, 1997).

[44] See, for example, Anamaria Dutceac Segesten, *Myth, Identity and Conflict: A Comparative Analysis of Romanian and Serbian Textbooks* (Lanham, Md.: Lexington Books, 2011).

[45] See, for instance, Bernhard Struck, Kate Ferris and Jacques Revel, 'Introduction: Space and Scale in Transnational History', *International History Review* (Special Issue: 'Size Matters: Scales and Spaces in Transnational and Comparative History') 33/4 (2011), pp. 573–84. For a very succinct summary of transnational history, see Patricia Clavin, *Defining Transnationalism* (Cambridge: Cambridge University Press, 2005), Pierre-Yves Saunier, *Transnational History* (Basingstoke: Palgrave Macmillan, 2013), Akire Iriye and Pierre-Yves Saunier (eds.), *The Palgrave Dictionary of Transnational History* (Basingstoke: Palgrave Macmillan, 2009), and Pierre-Yves Saunier, 'Learning by Doing: Notes about the Making of *The Palgrave Dictionary of Transnational History*', *Journal of Modern European History* 6/2 (2008), pp. 159–79.

[46] On the question of different levels in transnational history, see Struck, Ferris, and Revel, 'Introduction', and Kiran Klaus Patel, 'Transnational Geschichte', *EGO: Europäische Geschichte Online* (2010), at http://ieg-ego.eu/de/threads/theorien-und-methoden/transnationale-geschichte (accessed 28 Aug. 2019).

scale (though they may often operate on the same scale). Romanian Germans were not simply caught between two states (Romania and Germany), but they articulated and remoulded their notions of belonging on various levels: in different communities (families, professional identity, national identity, in public, in private) and through different ideas (politics, ideology, cultural ephemera, national identity, competing community voices). Romanian Germans, like many other Germans and various minorities in east-central Europe, were thus embedded in European, even global, networks that complicate the notion of 'Germanness', which made 'Germanness' fluid, usable, and difficult at the same time.[47] Likewise, examining these different scales of Romanian German actors adds a further layer to Brubaker's idea of a triadic nexus.

Crucially, though, this book also builds on literature from the burgeoning field of 'memory studies' and enriches it by including a transnational lens in the analysis. Particularly since the 1980s, the focus of cultural and social history has shifted towards a study of memory cultures, though the picture of how memory has been approached is diffuse.[48] By looking at the memorial practices of particular groups, and the ways in which they tell and retell narratives about their shared past in order to reinforce or change aspects of their identity, it is possible to get at the 'glue' that holds identities together. As such, *Migrating Memories* takes for granted the view that all

---

[47] See, for instance, an edited volume on German migrants to the British Empire, John R. Davis et al. (eds.), *Transnational Network: German Migrants in the British Empire, 1670–1914* (Leiden: Brill, 2013), and Swanson, *Tangible Belonging*. See also H. Glenn Penny's vast work on 'global' Germans: H. Glenn Penny, 'From Migrant Knowledge to Fugitive Knowledge? German Migrants and Knowledge Production in Guatemala, 1880s–1945', *Geschichte und Gesellschaft* 43/3 (2017), pp. 381–412, H. Glenn Penny, 'Material Connections: German Schools, Things, and Soft Power in Argentina and Chile from the 1880s through the Interwar Period', *Comparative Studies in Society and History* 59/3 (2017), pp. 519–49, and H. Glenn Penny and Stefan Rinke, 'Germans Abroad: Respatializing Historical Narrative', *Geschichte und Gesellschaft* 41/2 (2015), pp. 173–9 6; see also Manz, *Constructing a German Diaspora*.

[48] On the difficulty of Pierre Nora's reception and forgotten east-central European traditions of memory studies, see Maciej Górny and Kornelia Kończal, 'The (Non-)Travelling Concept of *Les Lieux de Mémoire*', in Małgorzata Pakier and Joanna Wawrzyniak (eds.), *Memory and Change in Europe: Eastern Perspectives* (New York: Berghahn, 2016), pp. 59–76. For a study on east-central European memory sites and cultures, see James Mark, *The Unfinished Revolution: Making Sense of the Communist Past in Central-Eastern Europe* (New Haven: Yale University Press, 2010). On the concept of the *lieux de mémoire*, see Pierre Nora (ed.), *Les Lieux de mémoire, Vols. I–III* (Paris: Gallimard, 1997). Other important works include Paul Connerton, *How Societies Remember* (Cambridge: Cambridge University Press, 1989), T. G. Ashplant, Graham Dawson and Michael Roper (eds.), *The Politics of War: Memory and Commemoration* (London: Routledge, 2000), and Iwona Irwin-Zarecka, *Frames of Remembrance: The Dynamics of Collective Memory* (Rutgers: Transaction Publishers, 2007). This memory 'boom' is also reflected in the publishing of journals devoted to the study of history and memory; see *History & Memory* and *Memory Studies*, launched in 1988 and 2007 respectively.

memories of events are only ever shaped in a collective framework,[49] but complicates matters by placing these group memories in a transnational framework. Using Brubaker, it charts the formation of memory cultures among Romanian Germans and, in so doing, further challenges the distinction between those who create memory culture and those who simply adopt it. It is difficult, for example, to categorise former camp internees in the USSR at the end of the Second World War as 'entrepreneurs'. Yet out of the fragments of their sketches, poetry, and other cultural artefacts surfaced Romanian German narratives and memories of the war and its aftermath. By dealing with issues of disruptive and traumatic memories,[50] this book also considers the emotional and moral demands of memory.[51] Among Romanian Germans, their traumatic memories translated into an established sense of victimhood.[52] As this book shows, collective Romanian German memories have often been marked by contestation and opposition within Romanian German memory cultures, which were themselves torn, divided, and uncertain: the contradictory experiences of nationalism, National Socialism, communism, deportation, and migration necessarily muddled these stories.

While there are established literatures on many of the intricate issues of memory and identity, little exists at present about Romanian Germans.[53]

---

[49] Maurice Halbwachs, *On Collective Memory* (Chicago: University of Chicago Press, 1992). There are east-central European counterparts to Halbwachs's work, such as Stefan Czarnowski's interwar work on 'memory sites'; see Górny and Kończal, 'The (Non-)Travelling Concept'.

[50] There is a growing body of literature on trauma and intergenerational memory of the Holocaust. See, for instance, Victoria Aarons, *Third-Generation Holocaust Representation: Trauma, History, and Memory* (Evanston, Ill.: Northwestern University Press, 2017). Romanian Germans used the terminology of 'trauma' only sparingly, which is why the term – trauma – features less prominently in this book.

[51] Jeffrey Blustein, *The Moral Demands of Memory* (Cambridge: Cambridge University Press, 2008), Jeffrey K. Olick (ed.), *The Politics of Regret: On Collective Memory and Historical Responsibility* (New York: Routledge, 2007), and Vladimir Tismăneanu and Marius Stan, *Romania Confronts Its Communist Past: Democracy, Memory, and Moral Justice* (Cambridge: Cambridge University Press, 2018).

[52] On trauma and victimhood, see Didier Fassin and Richard Rechtman, *The Empire of Trauma: An Inquiry into the Condition of Victimhood* (Princeton: Princeton University Press, 2009). Fassin and Rechtman focus mainly on French history, but helpfully consider the equivalence of victimhood as well as its relationship to the way stories are narrated.

[53] The few studies that do exist include Zach and Zach (eds.), *Deutsche und Rumänen in der Erinnerungsliteratur*, Pierre de Trégomain, 'Versperrte Wahrnehmung: Die Auseinandersetzung der evangelischen Kirche A.B. In Rumänien mit dem Nationalsozialismus 1944–1948', in Hausleitner and Roth (eds.), *Der Einfluss von Faschismus*, pp. 331–50, Corina Anderl, 'Siebenbürger Sachsen, Banater Schwaben und Landler als Deutsche in Rumänien: Zur Ambivalenz der kulturellen Funktion von Ethnizität in multiethnischen Regionen', in Wilfried Heller et al. (eds.), *Ethnizität in der Transformation: Zur Situation nationaler Minderheiten in Rumänien* (Vienna: LIT Verlag, 2006), pp. 42–55, and Trașcă and Anghel, *Un veac frământat.*

In a broader view, east-central Europeans have only recently been fore-grounded as agents of their own narratives, Romanian Germans included.[54] Instead, east-central Europeans have frequently been seen as mainly reactive to agendas set elsewhere, often in western Europe. Current scholarly trends that examine, for instance, communist-era memory cul-tures as important in their own right go against the prevalent approach of thinking of east-central European memories as 'liberated' or reactive after 1989.[55] Yet the communist period in Romania has repeatedly been treated as a 'fake' expression of Romanian German (and broader Romanian) self-understanding.[56] Only recent developments in the field have explained communism and memory in a more mutually constitutive way.[57] Romanian Germans' transnational position in Europe makes them an excellent case study for exploring the ways in which memory discourses are framed in different settings. Romanian Germans enable us to examine those elusive carriers of memory, which 'second-generation' memory scholars have looked for in their research.[58] Demands for evidence of 'reception' can be met by examining the moments when narratives are articulated and performed without making totalising claims about

---

[54] See Joanna Wawrzyniak, *Veterans, Victims, and Memory: The Politics of the Second World War in Communist Poland* (Frankfurt am Main: Peter Lang Edition, 2015), Ferenc Laczó and Joanna Wawrzyniak, 'Memories of 1989 in Europe between Hope, Dismay, and Neglect', *East European Politics and Societies and Cultures* 31/1 (2017), pp. 431–8, and Lars Breuer and Anna Delius, '1989 in European Vernacular Memory', *East European Politics and Societies and Cultures* 31/1 (2017), pp. 456–78, Simon Lewis, *Belarus – Alternative Visions: Nation, Memory and Cosmopolitanism* (Abingdon: Routledge, 2018), Alexander Etkind et al., *Remembering Katyn* (Cambridge: Polity, 2012), Pakier and Wawrzyniak (eds.), *Memory and Change in Europe*, and Mark, *The Unfinished Revolution*.

[55] This is an area of research that is still in its infancy. See Maria Bucur, *Heroes and Victims: Remembering War in Twentieth-Century Romania* (Bloomington: Indiana University Press, 2002), pp. 144–93, and Radostina Sharenkova, 'Forget-Me-(-Not): Visitors and Museum Presentations about communism before 1989', in Mihail Neamțu, Corina Doboș and Marius Stan (eds.), *History of Communism in Europe, Vol. I, Politics of Memory in Post-Communist Europe* (Bucharest: Zeta Books, 2010), pp. 65–82.

[56] See Weber, *Rumäniendeutsche*, and Tismăneanu and Stan, *Romania Confronts Its Commuinst Past.*

[57] See, for instance, Monica Ciobanu, *Repression, Resistance and Collaboration in Stalinist Romania 1944–1964: Post-Communist Remembering* (London: Routledge, 2020), and Michaela Nowotnik, *Die Unentrinnbarkeit der Biographie: Der Roman 'Rote Handschuhe' von Eginald Schlattner als Fallstudie zur rumäniendeutschen Literatur* (Cologne: Böhlau, 2017).

[58] The 'second wave' of memory studies refers to the (re-)emergence of memory studies from the 1980s. Pierre Nora, Jan Assmann, Jay Winter, and Paul Connerton are perhaps the best-known of that generation, but the second wave also included a number of edited volumes that sought to explore a plurality of approaches to memory. See, for instance, Katherine Hodgkin and Susannah Radstone (eds.), *Contested Pasts: The Politics of Memory* (London: Routledge, 2003), Susannah Radstone (ed.), *Memory and Methodology* (Oxford: Berg, 2000), Connerton, *How Societies Remember*, Jan Assmann, 'Collective Memory and Cultural Identity', *New German Critique* 65 (1995), pp. 125–33, and Jay Winter, *Sites of Memory, Sites of Mourning: The Great War in European Cultural History* (Cambridge: Cambridge University Press, 1995).

Romanian German memory cultures.[59] Allowing Romanian Germans to tell their own narratives through different media is a powerful way of getting at these moments of memory.

Voices and Stories

This book gives voice to Romanian German stories through a number of different sources. It draws on a diverse range of publications, including 'partisan' literature, memoirs, (auto)biographies, and local histories. Other sources also feature: newspapers, pamphlets, church literature, and publications of the *Landsmannschaften* (homeland societies). These materials often crossed borders and were received and read in different settings. Many of these sources 'travelled' by their very nature: letters, correspondence, gifts, catalogues, travel books, and even newspapers. The sources do not divide neatly into elite and non-elite sources and further blur the distinction between identity 'entrepreneurs' and 'enactors'. Much of the material is held in archives and institutions in both Romania and Germany. Its provenance often reflects the disparate Romanian German experiences of the twentieth century: the Institut für deutsche Kultur und Geschichte Südosteuropas (IKGS) in Munich is home to extensive collections of correspondence between Romanian German public figures and thinkers, while the Siebenbürgen Institut in Gundelsheim, north of Stuttgart, offers the most comprehensive collection of Transylvanian Saxon material available. Both the castle on the hilltop, a former castle of the Teutonic Order, and the modest *Fachwerkhaus* in the town's centre are repositories of Romanian German memory and history. On top of the hill, the castle has been transformed into a combined museum, library (with a sumptuous collection of Transylvanica), and care home for elderly Transylvanian Saxons. Numerous *Nachlässe* (literary remains) – originating from well-known 'celebrities' to obscure private individuals from the last 150 years – form the core of this important centre of Transylvanian Saxon history in Germany. Both the *Landsmannschaften* of the *Banater Schwaben* and *Siebenbürger Sachsen* in Munich and Stuttgart offered crucial access to official documentation of Romanian German émigré life and publications. The Haus des Deutschen Ostens with its library and special collections is also a part of the mosaic of the Romanian

---

[59] See, for instance, Alon Confino, 'Collective Memory and Cultural History: Problems of Method', *American Historical Review* 102/5 (1997), pp. 1386–1403. Here, Confino demanded more focus on *reception* of memory instead of what he saw as simply *describing* political representations of the past.

German community in Germany. In Romania, the Teutsch Haus in Sibiu
and the adjacent Zentralarchiv der Evangelischen Kirche A.B. in
Rumänien hold material on church life in Romania in the twentieth
century along with Romanian German publications (newsletters, short-
lived magazines, and journals). Likewise, the Demokratisches Forum der
Deutschen in Rumänien in Sibiu has been a valuable port of call for
contemporary material on German life in Romania, as have the municipal
archives in Sibiu, the headquarters of the *Hermannstädter Zeitung* in Sibiu,
and the Brukenthalschule in Sibiu. The Biblioteca Judeţeană Timiş in
Timişoara contains otherwise undigitised newspaper archives.[60] Generous
private donations of written material by individuals, in both Germany and
Romania, have added to the complex picture built up here. Finally, this
book incorporates oral history, based on eighty-one interviews collected
between February 2005 and August 2012,[61] which have provided a crucial
way of reaching and documenting the stories told, repeated, and understood by Romanian Germans. Enabling a radical insight into how individuals frame their stories in particular environments, these oral history
sources have furnished new raw material offering insights into the politics
of Romanian German memory.[62] Together, the body of material introduced in this study reveals the narratives that have shaped Romanian
German identities at crucial junctions in history.

   Chapter 1 outlines the history of the two main groups of Romanian
Germans in the twentieth century, Transylvanian Saxons and Banat
Swabians. It begins with an overview of their pre-history, drawing on
the latest research, and moves on to chart the origins of Romanian
German narratives in the twentieth century. Taking three themes from
Transylvanian Saxon and Banat Swabian stories as its starting point, it
expounds upon the ways in which they were woven together to form
a usable past for Romanian Germans after 1918. The themes of Saxon

---

[60] Other important collections of newspapers are digitised by the Austrian National Library on their
portal *ANNO: Austrian Newspapers Online*: http://anno.onb.ac.at (accessed 5 Jun. 2016).

[61] Of the interviewees, thirty-five were women, and forty-four were men. The ages of the respondents
varied between fifty-four and ninety-one at the time of interview, though the vast majority of
interviewees were aged between sixty-three and seventy-five.

[62] For oral history as a vital methodology, see, for example, Paul Thompson, 'The Voice of the Past', in
Robert Perks and Alistair Thomson (eds.), *The Oral History Reader* (London: Routledge, 2012), pp.
22–4, Luisa Passerini, *Fascism in Popular Memory: The Cultural Experience of the Turin Working
Class* (Cambridge: Cambridge University Press, 1987), Kate Fisher, *Birth Control, Sex and Marriage
in Britain, 1918–1960* (Oxford: Oxford University Press, 2006), Alessandro Portelli, *The Death of
Luigi Trastulli and Other Stories: Form and Meaning in Oral History* (Albany: SUNY Press, 1991), and
Alessandro Portelli, *The Order Has Been Carried Out: History, Memory, and Meaning of a Nazi
Massacre in Rome* (Basingstoke: Palgrave Macmillan, 2007).

privilege, the experience of being under siege, and Swabian hardship and ordeal, I argue, became the backbone of Romanian German narratives after 1918, forming a set of motifs that were constantly re-used in various circumstances. By analysing the dynamics of these thematic connections, the chapter illuminates the complexity of Romanian German narratives and memory cultures, which have always operated on different but inter-connected levels: the local (specific Saxon and Swabian stories), the national (incorporating these into a Romanian German framework), and the transnational (the ever-growing importance of being German as opposed to Saxon or Swabian).

Chapter 2 investigates the importance of various ideas of homelands, enemies, and escapes in Romanian German narratives. Engaging with Brubaker's notion of a 'triadic nexus', this chapter analyses the dynamics of Romanian Germans' identity debates in Cold War Europe. It maps out the ways in which Romanian Germans evaluated their role in a complex web encompassing Romania, West and East Germany, his-toric Germany, family ties, and 'Balkan backwardness'. Romanian Germans may have 'ended up', in the main, in (West) Germany, yet their transnational stories have always remained central to Romanian German self-understanding.

Chapters 3 and 4 deal with two fundamental aspects of Romanian German identity that complicate their history: their exposure to and experience of ideology in twentieth-century Europe. Romanian Germans did not simply find themselves 'caught' between national boundaries. Far more, the interaction with ideologies, ideas, and war exemplifies the multifaceted experience of Romanian Germans in twentieth-century Europe. Both chapters trace fundamental historical developments in the twentieth century, National Socialism and communism, and address how Romanian German debates illuminate broader European trends in dealing with the legacies of fascism and communism. Chapter 3 examines the role and meaning of National Socialism in Romanian German history. Heavily committed to interwar fascism and the German war effort during the Second World War, and subject to recriminations after it, Romanian Germans were constantly forced to reconsider this particular facet of Romanian German history. Romanian German radicals from the 1920s to the 1940s understood their role, to varying degrees, as pioneering a new Nazi German spirit. The Second World War, the experience of being denounced as 'Hitlerists', rehabilitation, and the confusing experience of a self-critical (West) German society all contributed to a shaping of Romanian German history that drew on older tropes about besiegement and hardship. As the chapter demonstrates, however, these stories about the Romanian German fascist past and subsequent victimisation were far from fixed. Identity, nationalism, and other forms of belonging remained very fluid throughout the second half of the twentieth century for Romanian Germans, despite a seemingly 'settled' post-war European environment.

At the same time, of growing importance was the experience of living through communism in Romania. Chapter 4, therefore, places Romanian German association with Romanian state and society at its core and in so doing attempts to disrupt approaches that locate the period after the Second World War as the end of German history in east-central Europe. Quite the contrary, Romanian German experiences of life under communism formed an essential part of Romanian German identity contests. Mass emigration towards the end of the Cold War did not change that. Instead, it augmented the status of life in Romania in Romanian German narratives about themselves. An ideal case study of this process in action is the memory of a famous show trial in the late 1950s. Eginald Schlattner's (1933–) novel *Rote Handschuhe* (*Red Gloves*) from 2001 sent ripples through the Romanian German community. Its contrast to a publication in 2008 by another Romanian German, Carl Gibson (1959–), about German opposition to communism, bookends a crucial period – the new millennium – as a turning point in Romanian German memory of the communist period. Charting these controversies over German dissidence during the communist eras in both Germany and Romania also exposes broader debates over the legacy of communism in Europe after 1989: what did collaboration mean? What were opposition and dissidence? How should societies confront issues and individuals associated with an authoritarian past? In that sense, the legacy of communism complicated Romanian German identities with memory contests that broke down allegiances and notions of belonging that had dominated Cold War identity debates.

Finally, Chapter 5 examines life after mass emigration from Romania to Germany after the Cold War. Stories and fears about the end of Germans in Romania, such as the notion of *finis Saxoniae* (the end of the Saxons), have been at the forefront of debates over Romanian German history. The abandonment of their centuries-old homeland coupled with a paradoxical EU rhetoric of an 'ever closer union' unsettled seemingly stable stories even further: local stories had been transformed into a Romanian German narrative and then altered through the complex prism of twentieth-century European history around ideology, war, and migration. The emergence of a pan-European framework at the end of the twentieth century and into the twenty-first upset Romanian German stability further still while also giving it a new lease of life. In the end, from origin stories to identity politics, and from Nazism to communism to EU politics, Romanian Germans tell a dynamic story of minority identity enmeshed in the currents of modern European history.

CHAPTER I

Making Romanian Germans

A people that still has both its history and a Protestant church can never be considered a lost people.[1]

In the beginning, there were no Romanian Germans. There were disparate German groups in various empires and principalities. Older and more narrowly defined ideas of kinship persisted and were only really challenged from the nineteenth century.[2] It was not until much later that the idea of a unified Romanian German identity was to emerge out of shared experiences of living in a unified Romanian state in the interwar period and during the crucial period of the Second World War.[3] In trying to understand their experiences of the interwar period, Nazism, communism, and migration, Germans in Romania continually returned to, revised, and reinvented their histories, picking and choosing from the stories of these component groups according to the circumstances in which they found themselves. As this chapter argues, those stories were not simply made up of the top-down accounts told by historians – the entrepreneurs – but formed a web of long-standing narratives constructed by the communities themselves. Together they made up a 'usable past' that was crucial to Romanian German identity formation in the twentieth century. This chapter maps out the materials from which Romanian Germans constructed their identity from the late

---

[1] Original: 'Ein Volk, das seine Geschichte und eine evangelische Kirche hat, ist niemals als verloren anzusehen.' Georg Friedrich Teutsch quoted in Gerhard Möckel, 'Fatum oder Datum?', in Andreas Möckel (ed.), *Gerhard Möckel: Fatum oder Datum? Aufsätze und Briefe* (Munich: Südostdeutsches Kulturwerk, 1997), p. 23.

[2] See Jonathan Kwan, 'Transylvanian Saxon Politics, Hungarian State Building and the Case of the *Allgemeiner Deutscher Schulverein* (1881–1882)', *English Historical Review* 127/526 (2012), pp. 592–624.

[3] Comparable studies highlight the flexibility of Germanness among a number of German diasporas right up until the 1940s. See, for instance, John Swanson, *Tangible Belonging: Negotiating Germanness in Twentieth-Century Hungary* (Pittsburgh: University of Pittsburgh Press, 2017), John Swanson, 'Minority-Building in the German Diaspora: The Hungarian-Germans', *Austrian History Yearbook* 36 (2005), pp. 148–66, Winson Chu, *The German Minority in Interwar Poland* (Cambridge: Cambridge University Press, 2013), and H. Glenn Penny and Stefan Rinke, 'Germans Abroad: Respatializing Historical Narrative', *Geschichte und Gesellschaft* 41/2 (2015), pp. 173–96.

nineteenth century into the interwar period. It starts with an overview of the history of Germans in the region before engaging in detail with three key identity myths that emerged from and around that history. The final section embeds those identity narratives in a transnational web of reception and affirmation spanning interwar Europe. In making sense of their experiences in the twentieth century, this chapter argues, Germans in Romania used long-standing narratives that had been important to the two communities of Saxons and Swabians, picking and choosing older 'foundation myths' from these groups according to the needs of the circumstances in which they found themselves. Those myths were highly malleable and usable by a variety of actors in the community, not just elites. Romanian Germans thus returned to three key themes time and again: Saxon privilege and superiority, a sense of being under siege, and the Swabian path of ordeal.

Transylvanian Saxon identity rested on 'people's stories', secure – as the chapter epigraph by Georg Friedrich Teutsch (1852–1933) neatly encapsulates – in a strong sense of history and the importance of the Lutheran Church. Banat Swabians, meanwhile, developed a distinct Banat Swabian identity from the mid-nineteenth century.[4] Some commonalities between Saxons and Swabians already existed before the First World War. But it was the unification of Transylvania and the Banat with 'Greater Romania' that brought Saxons and Swabians together, forcing them to reconsider their standing as a national minority – and thus the stories they told – in this new polity. Spurred on by these political developments, a 'usable past' emerged for the newly formed Romanian German community.

Overview: German Arrivals

German settlers arrived across east-central and south-eastern Europe in numerous waves and for different reasons from the eleventh century onwards.[5] The two main areas of German settlement in what is now Romania were Transylvania and the Banat.[6] Yet even the terms used for

---

[4] Márta Fata, 'Migration im Gedächtnis: Auswanderung und Ansiedlung in der Identitätsbildung der Donauschwaben', in Márta Fata (ed.), *Migration im Gedächtnis: Auswanderung und Ansiedlung in der Identitätsbildung der Donauschwaben* (Stuttgart: Franz Steiner, 2013), pp. 7–21.
[5] Some useful guides to this history include Harald Roth, *Kleine Geschichte Siebenbürgens* (Cologne: Böhlau, 2003), Wilhelm Andreas Baumgärtner, *Der Vergessene Weg: Wie die Sachsen nach Siebenbürgen kamen* (Bonn: Schiller Verlag, 2010), and Márta Fata, *Migration im kameralistischen Staat Josephs II: Theorie und Praxis der Ansiedlungspolitik in Ungarn, Siebenbürgen, Galizien und der Bukowina von 1768 bis 1790* (Münster: Aschendorff, 2014).
[6] I will use the present-day countries to explain the location of regions, towns, and groups unless otherwise stated.

these historic regions can cause confusion. Transylvania is often misleadingly referred to as all the territory ceded by Hungary to Romania following the First World War.[7] Historically, Transylvania has only included the central part of the Transcarpathian region of Romania, and not the Hungarian Plains to the west. It is delimited by the Carpathian Mountains to the north, east, and south, and the Trascău Mountains to the west.[8] The Banat, which lies to the west of Transylvania, is now divided between the western Banat in Serbia and Hungary and the eastern Banat in Romania. The Banat region in its entirety lies between the river Danube to the south, the Tisza to the west, the Mureş to the north, and the Trascău Mountains and Southern Carpathian Mountains to the east. Its name derives from its position as a medieval military frontier.[9] Both regions, Transylvania and the Banat, were always linguistically and culturally diverse.[10] Transylvania and the Banat have been home to Romanians, Hungarians, Szeklers, Saxons, Swabians, Serbs, Jews, Armenians, Roma, and Bulgarians, as well as lesser-known groups such as the Protestant Landler who escaped religious persecution in Lower Austria under Empress Maria Theresa in the eighteenth century. The religious landscape has been equally diverse and complex, comprising Roman Catholicism, Protestantism, the Reformed Church, Judaism (both Reformed and Orthodox), Romanian Orthodox, Serb Orthodox, Greek Orthodox, Greek Catholic, Unitarianism, and also, increasingly in the twentieth century, non-religious alignment.[11] Population figures have also varied widely over the centuries.[12] Due to its position as a war-torn border-land, the Banat was less densely populated than Transylvania.[13] Nevertheless,

---

[7] An example of this is Elemér Illyés, *National Minorities in Romania: Change in Transylvania* (Boulder, Co.: East European Monographs, 1982), p. 9.

[8] Lucian Boia, *Romania: Borderland of Europe* (London: Reaktion Books, 2001), p. 23.

[9] On the medieval name, Ban, see Irina Marin, *Contested Frontiers in the Balkans: Ottoman and Habsburg Rivalries in Eastern Europe* (London: I. B. Tauris, 2013), pp. 4–7.

[10] For an examination of the multicultural history of the Banat over the past three centuries, see Victor Neumann, *The Banat of Timişoara: A European Melting Pot* (London: Scala Art and Heritage Publishers, 2019).

[11] For a comprehensive volume on religion in the Banat and Transylvania, see Mihai Spariosu, *Intercultural Conflict in and Harmony in the Central European Borderlands: The Cases of Banat and Transylvania 1848–1939* (Göttingen: V&R Unipress, 2017). For a very good case study analysis of population and religious statistics in the second half of the nineteenth century in Transylvania, see Ioan Bolovan et al., *Legislaţia ecleziastică şi laică privind familia românească din Transilvania în a doua jumătate a secolului al XIX-lea* (Cluj-Napoca: Academia Română, Centrul de Studii Transilvane, 2009). See also Paul Shore, *Jesuits and the Politics of Religious Pluralism in Eighteenth-Century Transylvania: Culture, Politics, and Religion, 1693–1773* (London: Routledge, 2017).

[12] Ioan Bolovan, Crinela Elena Holom and Marius Eppel, 'Ethnicity and Politics: Censuses in the Austro-Hungarian Empire (Case Study: Transylvania, 1869–1910)', *Romanian Journal of Population Studies* 10/2 (2016), pp. 137–52.

[13] See Marin, *Contested Frontiers*, pp. 21–38.

between the eighteenth century and the beginning of the twentieth, its population grew from 400,000 to 1.5 million. Transylvania, by contrast, had a population of just over 5 million by the early twentieth century, 10 per cent of whom were Saxons.[14]

While Saxons and Swabians represented the two biggest German groups in the region, there were also other German communities in present-day Romania.[15] The *Zips* or *Zipser* (Carpathian Germans), for instance, were among the longest-settled Germans in the broader region.[16] They were first mentioned in the thirteenth century and mainly straddled present-day Slovakia into the region of Maramureş and Satu Mare county.[17] Other groups settled much later in the Danubian–Carpathian region. *Bukowinadeutsche* (Bukovina Germans), a small rural group, arrived in the Bukovina (northern Romania) in the eighteenth century.[18] Other groups include *Bessarabiendeutsche* (Bessarabia Germans) in Bessarabia (Moldova, Ukraine), *Dobrudschadeutsche* (Dobruja Germans) in Dobruja (southern Romania and northern Bulgaria), and *Sathmarschwaben* (Sathmar Swabians) around Satu Mare (western Romania) as well as the Landler in southern Transylvania (see Figure 1.1).[19] Settlers were either motivated by a need to escape persecution, such as the Landler, or by new opportunities in response to calls to settle in and fortify parts of the Habsburg Empire, the Russian Empire, and the Kingdom of Hungary.[20] These smaller German-speaking groups had always been fairly insignificant in number in comparison with the Saxons and Swabians, and 'population transfers' and deportations during and after the Second World War diminished these smaller minorities to an even greater degree.[21] Some

---

[14] See Günter Schödl (ed.), *Deutsche Geschichte im Osten Europas: Land an der Donau* (Berlin: Siedler Verlag, 1995).

[15] I will refer to the territory of present-day Romania as Romania unless explained otherwise.

[16] Helmut Protze, 'Die Zipser Sachsen im Sprachgeographischen und Sprachhistorischen Vergleich zu den Siebenbürger Sachsen', *Zeitschrift für Siebenbürgische Landeskunde* 29/2 (2006), pp. 142–51.

[17] Harald Zimmermann, 'Die deutsche Südostsiedlung im Mittelalter', in Schödl (ed.), *Deutsche Geschichte im Osten Europas*, p. 44.

[18] Pieter Judson, 'When Is a Diaspora not a Diaspora? Rethinking Nation-Centered Narratives in Habsburg East Central Europe', in Krista O'Donnell, Renate Bridenthal and Nancy Reagin (eds.), *The Heimat Abroad: The Boundaries of Germanness* (Ann Arbor: University of Michigan, 2005), pp. 235–7.

[19] Image taken from Zimmermann, 'Die deutsche Südostsiedlung im Mittelalter', p. 33. The Landler settled mainly around Sibiu. See Márta Fata, 'Einwanderung und Ansiedlung der Deutschen (1686–1790)', in Schödl (ed.), *Deutsche Geschichte im Osten*, pp. 173–80, and Martin Bottesch, *Landler-Büchlein* (Sibiu: Honterus, 2007), pp. 5–28.

[20] Fata, 'Einwanderung und Ansiedlung', pp. 146–80.

[21] Günter Schödl, 'Lange Abschiede: Die Südostdeutschen und ihre Väterländer (1918–1945)', in Schödl (ed.), *Deutsche Geschichte im Osten*, pp. 455–529. See also Gaëlle Fisher, *Resettlers and*

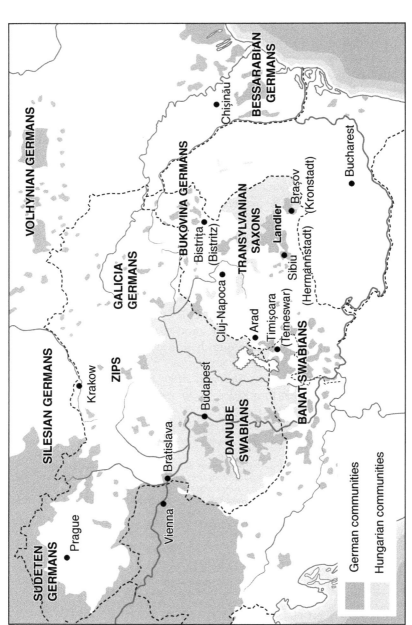

Figure 1.1 Map of historical settlements of Germans and Hungarians in the Danubian-Carpathian region.

groups, such as the *Sathmarschwaben*, were assimilated into Hungarian society, whereas others, such as the *Bessarabiendeutsche* and *Dobrudschadeutsche*, ceased to exist in 1940 as a result of the *Heim-ins-Reich* relocation policy under the Third Reich.[22]

But the two main German communities in Romania with a prominent history in the region were Transylvanian Saxons and Banat Swabians. The *Siebenbürger Sachsen* first arrived in Transylvania in the twelfth century as settlers, mainly from Moselle-Franconia in the western German Lands.[23] As they had similar linguistic traits as to the Moselle-Franconian dialect and Luxembourgish, the provenance of these first Saxon settlers has remained obscure, and theories about their origins emerged and disappeared again over time. Outside the realms of myth-making, most established literature on the topic, however, now suggests that the majority of early settlers colonised the area following a call by the Hungarian King Géza II.[24]

Filling the void created by centuries of wars, the German-speaking settlers began founding urban settlements.[25] From the outset, their primary role was to defend Christendom and, later, the Kingdom of Hungary from invading forces from the south-east.[26] They were given a guarantee of privileges, and the settlement area was declared a *Königsboden* – *fundus regius* or 'Royal Land' – which gave the Saxons a high level of autonomy,[27] enshrined in 1224 in the *Andreanum* charter (*Goldener Freibrief*), a pioneering document for Saxons' legal rights and privileges.[28] These privileges would play a crucial role for Romanian German identity debates in the twentieth century.

A second wave of settlers in the sixteenth century transformed Transylvania into a truly 'modern', urban region. Following the Hungarian defeat by the Turks at Mohács in 1526, Transylvania existed as an independent principality between the Ottoman Empire and the

---

Survivors: Bukovina and the Politics of Belonging in West Germany and Israel, 1945–1989 (New York: Berghahn, 2020).

[22] Schödl, 'Lange Abschiede', pp. 613–26.   [23] Roth, *Kleine Geschichte Siebenbürgens*, pp. 30–3.

[24] See, for instance, Tudor Sălăgean, 'Romanian Society in the Early Middle Ages (Ninth–Fourteenth Century)', in Ioan-Aurel Pop and Ioan Bolovan (eds.), *History of Romania Compendium* (Cluj-Napoca: Romanian Culture Institute, 2006), pp. 162–5.

[25] Roth, *Kleine Geschichte Siebenbürgens*, p. 31.

[26] For an excellent collection of essays on the murky beginnings of the Saxons, the Germans, and the Teutonic Order in Transylvania and indeed the Banat, see Konrad Gündisch (ed.), *Generalprobe Burzenland: Neue Forschungen zur Geschichte des Deutschen Ordens in Siebenbürgen und im Banat* (Cologne: Böhlau, 2012).

[27] Roth, *Kleine Geschichte Siebenbürgens*, p. 32.

[28] Zimmermann, 'Die deutsche Südostsiedlung im Mittelalter', p. 41.

emerging Habsburg Empire.[29] Into this political and military uncertainty, new burghers settled in the region from the mid-sixteenth century onwards. Unlike previous settlers, these were established Hanseatic merchants who had left the Baltic Sea coast following the gradual decline of the Hanseatic League.[30] These German-speaking migrants cemented the Saxons' position in the flourishing financial sector and led to the conversion of Saxons to Protestantism.[31] At the same time, the make-up of Transylvanian society became far more concrete: three distinct groups were recognised as *nationes* or 'pillars', and were thus granted special privileges.[32] The Hungarians (nobility), the Szeklers (administration and military), and the Saxons (economic and financial sectors) were the three 'pillars' of society, while the Romanians remained serfs and were not recognised as a group.[33] There were other pockets of 'privilege', such as the special rights of Greek tradespeople in Transylvanian towns, but they were never a threat to the existing order of the three pillars of Transylvanian society.[34] Saxons, in particular, seemed to benefit from geopolitical changes in the region in the late seventeenth century. The Leopoldinum (1690) became the 'basic law' for Transylvania after the Treaty of Karlowitz (1699) until the revolutions of 1848/9.[35] The period 1690 to 1699 not only confirmed the privileged position of Saxons (and

[29] See James D. Tracy, 'The Habsburg Monarchy in Conflict with the Ottoman Empire, 1527–1593: A Clash of Civilizations', *Austrian History Yearbook* 46 (2015), pp. 1–26, and Teréz Oborni, 'Between Vienna and Constantinople: Notes on the Legal Status of the Principality of Transylvania', in Gábor Kármán and Lovro Kunčević (eds.), *The European Tributary States of the Ottoman Empire in the Sixteenth and Seventeenth Centuries* (Leiden: Brill, 2013), pp. 67–89. For a comprehensive overview of sixteenth- and seventeenth-century overlapping histories of the Habsburg and Ottoman Empires, see Arno Strohmeyer and Norbert Spannenberger (eds.), *Frieden und Konfliktmanagement in interkulturellen Räumen: Das Osmanische Reich und die Habsburgermonarchie in der Frühen Neuzeit* (Stuttgart: Franz Steiner Verlag, 2013).
[30] Balázs A. Szelényi, *The Failure of the Central European Bourgeoisie* (Basingstoke: Palgrave Macmillan, 2006), pp. 43–51.
[31] See ibid., Konrad Gündisch, 'Die "Geistliche Universität" der siebenbürgisch-sächsischen Kirchengemeinden im 15. und 16. Jahrhundert', in Volker Leppin and Ulrich A. Wien (eds.), *Konfessionsbildung und Konfessionskultur in Siebenbürgen in der Frühen Neuzeit* (Stuttgart: Franz Steiner Verlag, 2005), pp. 105–14, and Gustav Binder, 'Die Reformation in Siebenbürgen', *Siebenbürgische Semesterblätter* 1/1 (1987), pp. 37–55.
[32] Roth, *Kleine Geschichte Siebenbürgens*, pp. 49–51.
[33] Chris Hann, *The Skeleton at the Feast: Contributions to East European Anthropology* (Canterbury, UK: Centre for Social Anthropology and Computing Monograps, 1995), p. 78.
[34] See Mária Pakucs-Willcocks, 'Between "Faithful Subjects" and "Pernicious Nation": Greek Merchants in the Principality of Transylvania in the Seventeenth Century', *Hungarian Historical Review* 6/1 (2017), pp. 111–37.
[35] For a definitive collection of essays on political developments from 1690 to 1867, see Zsolt Lengyel and Ulrich Wien (eds.), *Siebenbürgen in der Habsburgermonarchie: Vom Leopoldinum bis zum Ausgleich (1690–1867)* (Cologne: Böhlau, 1999).

Szeklers and Hungarians), but also saw the decline of the Ottoman Empire and the rise of the Habsburg Empire, a development that had significant impact on Transylvania's position in east-central Europe.[36]

Despite this imperial certainty, Transylvania, too, was changing. By the seventeenth and eighteenth centuries, Romanians were the largest group in Transylvania.[37] The region retained its distinctiveness while being integrated into the Habsburg Empire. Under Samuel von Brukenthal (1721–1803), the governor of the Grand Principality of Transylvania, the educational sector flourished in the eighteenth century. Brukenthal enjoyed the close confidence of Empress Maria Theresa, and he was able to give Transylvania, and Hermannstadt in particular, its uniqueness by insisting against the Catholic centre on a curious 'Protestant baroque' architectural makeover.[38] All the while, there were further population movements: persecuted religious groups found refuge in central and southern Transylvania over the course of the eighteenth century, while economic migrants – the Swabians – settled to the west in the Banat. Complex developments after the Napoleonic Wars transformed nationalism into a pivotal force across the wider region and, in so doing, created tensions and claims throughout Transylvania based on new ideas of belonging.[39] The heart of the growing Romanian nationalist movement was in Transylvania, and not the principalities of Moldavia and Wallachia, leading to Romanian demands to be recognised as the fourth constituent nation in Transylvania.[40] Only later, by the early twentieth century, did emancipatory politics metamorphose into territorial demands on Transylvania.[41] While much of the historiography has emphasised Hungarian–Romanian antagonism in nineteenth-century nationalist struggles, Transylvanian Saxons were in fact also caught up in this web of contestation and threatened by the new forces within it.[42] Following the

---

[36] Konrad Gündisch, *Siebenbürgen und die Siebenbürger Sachsen* (Munich: Langen-Müller, 1998), pp. 102–6.

[37] Roth, *Kleine Geschichte Siebenbürgens*, p. 101.

[38] See Lisa Fischer, *Eden hinter den Wäldern. Samuel von Brukenthal: Politiker, Sammler, Freimaurer in Hermannstadt/Sibiu* (Cologne: Böhlau, 2007).

[39] For an excellent history of the Habsburg Empire, see Pieter Judson, *The Habsburg Empire: A New History* (Cambridge, Mass.: Harvard University Press, 2016).

[40] For a history of Romanian nationalism and its relationship to others, see Constantin Iordachi, *Liberalism, Constitutional Nationalism, and Minorities: The Making of Romanian Citizenship, c. 1750–1918* (Leiden: Brill, 2019).

[41] László Kürti, *The Remote Borderland: Transylvania in the Hungarian Imagination* (Ithaca: SUNY Press, 2001), p. 25.

[42] Robert John Weston Evans, *Austria, Hungary, and the Habsburgs: Central Europe c. 1683–1867* (Oxford: Oxford University Press, 2006), pp. 218–25, and Alexander Maxwell, 'Hungaro-German Dual Nationality: Germans, Slavs, and Magyars during the 1848 Revolution', *German Studies Review* 39/1 (2016), pp. 17–39.

revolutions, their special privileges were gradually stripped back. Saxons were on the receiving end of aggressive Hungarian policies towards minorities through the policies of Magyarisation after the Austro-Hungarian compromise of 1867.[43] The long-established self-governing public body *Universitas Saxonum*, which guaranteed Saxon rights, was *de facto* abolished in 1876 by transforming it into a body responsible for managing Saxon landownership. All the while, emigration – one of the chief concerns of the Habsburg Empire – continued to hit the Saxon community hard.[44] The uncertainties and threats to the Transylvanian Saxon community were confounded by strained Saxon–Hungarian relations in the final decades of the Habsburg Empire. The 1890 Saxon–Hungarian Compromise went some way to repairing relations, but, ultimately, the collapse of the empire pushed Saxons towards support for the successor state of Romania.

Banater Schwaben, by contrast, had a much shorter history, yet their origins also became fundamental to Romanian German identity in the twentieth century. German speakers settled all over the Hungarian part of the Habsburg Empire, especially in those areas from which the Ottoman Empire had retreated, which included the frontier zone of the Banat.[45] German settlers came in three main waves, which together made up the *Großer Schwabenzug* or Great Swabian Trek. Under King Karl VI, roughly 14,000 migrants arrived in Hungary in this first wave, the so-called Carolingian migration, between 1722 and 1726, though not all of these were Germans. They settled mainly in the Bačka and the Banat in the south of Hungary, since these areas had been depleted after the Ottoman–Habsburg wars had effectively ended with the Treaty of Passarowitz in 1718.[46] Two subsequent waves of migration, the Maria Theresian colonisation – roughly between 1744 and 1772 – and the Josephine colonisation – from 1782 to 1787 – ensured a strong German-speaking presence in the Banat region.[47] Of 350,000–400,000 inhabitants in the Banat, roughly 43,000 of them were considered German, by the late 1770s.[48] Unlike

---

[43] See Anton Sterbling, 'Minderheitenprobleme und interethnische Konflikte in Siebenbürgen nach 1867', *Siebenbürgische Semesterblätter* 10/2 (1996), pp. 109–24, and Jonathan Kwan, 'Austro-German Liberalism and the Coming of the 1867 Compromise: "Politics Again in Flux"', *Austrian History Yearbook* 44 (2013), pp. 62–87.

[44] See Carl Göllner, 'Bevölkerung: Soziale Struktur 1849–1914', in Carl Göllner (ed.), *Die Siebenbürgen Sachsen in den Jahren 1848–1918* (Cologne: Böhlau, 1988), pp. 37–55. On the Habsburg fear of emigration, see Tara Zahra, 'Travel Agents on Trial: Policing Mobility in Late Imperial Austria', *Past & Present* 223 (2014), pp. 161–93, and Tara Zahra, *The Great Departure: Mass Migration from Eastern Europe and the Making of the Free World* (New York: Norton, 2016).

[45] For a good history of the Banat, see Marin, *Contested Frontiers*.

[46] Fata, 'Einwanderung und Ansiedlung', pp. 146–9.   [47] Ibid., pp. 153–70.

[48] Barta, 'Die Deutsche Einwanderung', p. 33.

Transylvanian Saxons, Swabians never converted to Protestantism, but remained Catholic and were spared the religious persecution widespread in the Habsburg Empire during the seventeenth and eighteenth centuries.

Once Swabians had settled in the Banat, they were chiefly employed in the agricultural sector and later in the mining sector.[49] The special privileges accorded their Saxon counterparts did not extend to Banat Swabians, though, as settlers, they enjoyed other special provisions. Most Swabian settlements were largely rural, though, unlike many other rural peasants, they were not serfs. Similar to other German groups in east-central Europe, their name – *Schwaben* – did not reflect their place of origin, but was simply used as a synonym for 'German'. The Swabian colonisers had originally migrated from a vast area spanning from southern Germany and Austria to Switzerland. Banat Swabians were a rather fragmentary group with no single provenance, common dialect, or set of customs.[50] Nevertheless, the Austro-Hungarian compromise of 1867 posed a threat to *Banater Schwaben*, as they also felt the full force of Magyarisation policies.[51] The Swabians of the Banat shared the same fears of assimilation as other German groups throughout the Hungarian Kingdom.[52] Ostensibly, *Banater Schwaben* were stuck between Hungarian chauvinism directed from Budapest, and growing nationalism from the new Kingdom of Romania (1881), as well as Yugoslav and Serb nationalism from the west.[53] Yet Banat Swabian identity was far more plural and hybrid, and it allowed for a sense of patriotism towards the Kingdom of Hungary. There is much evidence of a greater willingness to assimilate into Hungarian society. During the Hungarian Revolution of 1848, some Swabians fought on the side of the Hungarian revolutionaries against Austrian control.[54]

---

[49] János Barta, "'Pflüg' mir den Boden, wackre Schwabenfaust": Die deutsche Einwanderung nach Ungarn im 18. Jahrhundert und ihre Bedeutung für Staat und Gesellschaft', in Fata (ed.), *Migration im Gedächtnis*, pp. 23–37, and Mariana Hausleitner, *Die Donauschwaben 1868–1948: Ihre Rolle im rumänischen und serbischen Banat* (Stuttgart: Franz Steiner Verlag, 2014), ch. 1.

[50] Franz Gschwandtner, 'Ansiedlung und Landesausbau im Banat des 18. Jahrhunderts', *Transylvanian Review* 14/2 (2005), pp. 44–69.

[51] Carola L. Gottzmann and Petra Hörner, *Verheissung und Verzweiflung im Osten: Die Siedlungsgeschichte der Deutschen im Spiegel der Dichtung* (Hildesheim: Georg Olms Verlag, 1998), pp. 279–81.

[52] Ibid., pp. 280–5.

[53] Gheorghe Iacob, 'Romanians during the Emergence of Nation-States (1859–1918)', in Pop and Bolovan (eds.), *History of Romania Compendium*, pp. 510–13, and Hausleitner, *Die Donauschwaben 1868–1948*.

[54] See James Koranyi, 'The Thirteen Martyrs of Arad: A Monumental Hungarian History', in Dominik Geppert and Frank Müller (eds.), *Sites of Imperial Memory: Commemorating Colonial Rule in the Nineteenth and Twentieth Centuries* (Manchester: Manchester University Press, 2015), pp. 53–69.

Swabians were far more flexible in the identities they assumed and, while a more definite German nationalism became palpable in the late nineteenth century, Swabian identity was marked by accommodation and identity that coexisted despite some tensions.[55] And, while both Swabians and Saxons fought for the Habsburg Empire during the First World War, the disintegration of the empire forced Saxons and Swabians to consider their political future very carefully.

On 1 December 1918, the National Assembly of Romanians of Transylvania and Hungary in Alba Iulia/Karlsburg/Weißenburg[56] voted unanimously in favour of the unification of Transylvania, the Banat, and other regions with what had constituted Romania before the First World War (see Figure 1.2).[57] It was not only the Romanian vote that approved of

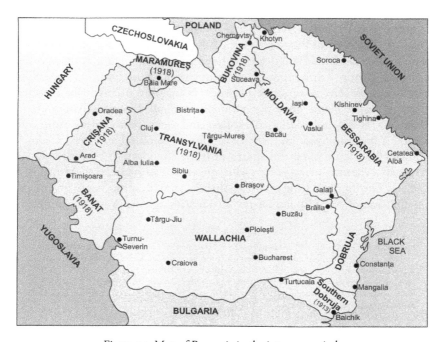

Figure 1.2 Map of Romania in the interwar period.

[55] See Victor Neumann's case study of multicultural Timișoara: Victor Neumann, 'Multiculturality and Interculturality: The Case of Timișoara', *Hungarian Studies* 21/1–2 (2007), pp. 3–18.
[56] The German name of the city has changed over time. Until 1711, it was known as Weißenburg; thereafter its name changed to the current German name Karlsburg.
[57] Roth, *Kleine Geschichte Siebenbürgens*, pp. 121–6.

this new state. Transylvanian Saxons and, in a less exuberant manner, Banat Swabians endorsed breaking away from the dying Habsburg Empire.[58] Banat Swabians had also attempted to create the short-lived multicultural Banat Republic in November 1918 under the social democrat Dr Otto Roth (1884–1956). But this project failed for a number of reasons, including a misunderstanding that a republic had also been declared in Hungary at the same time. The Banat Republic lasted only two weeks and, by mid-November 1918, the Banat was occupied by Serbian troops. In Transylvania, Saxons moved more slowly. They were now represented by a new leadership after 1918 and pledged a common future with Romania.[59] The immediate aftermath of the war ushered in uncertainty and chaos. In Sibiu/Hermannstadt, for instance, Romanian, Saxon, and Hungarian militias guarded the city's streets during weeks of rioting.[60] Their budding cooperation was a sign of things to come. The new heads of the Saxon Central National Committee (Sächsischer Zentralausschuss), President Adolf Schullerus (1864–1928) and secretary Dr Hans Otto Roth (1890–1953) (not to be confused with the Swabian Dr Otto Roth), both elected on 29 October 1918, moved the Saxon community and its politics towards a settlement with Romania.[61] On 2 November 1918, a German-Saxon National Council (Deutsch-sächsischer Nationalrat) met and discussed the immediate future of Transylvania's position in east-central Europe. It decided to lend a supportive voice to the Alba Iulia assembly a month later. Finally, at the beginning of 1919, on 8 January, the Saxon National Assembly backed the unification of Greater Romania and the inclusion of Saxons within this new state:[62] 'Conscious of the importance of this decision, the Saxon people now regard themselves as members of the Romanian Empire [*sic*], and its sons and daughters as citizens of the state', declared Saxon representatives in Mediaş on 8 January 1919.[63] Saxons congratulated Romanians on their achievement of

[58] Research on the short-lived Banat Republic is limited. For a very good overview of this brief interlude, see Marin, *Contested Frontiers*, pp. 101–9.
[59] Conversely, Banat Swabians sent a delegation to the Paris Peace Treaties negotiations, which also suggests they were more active in the early period of the new Romanian state than previous scholarship has assumed. See Anne Delouis, 'Die Delegation der Banater Schwaben bei der Pariser Friedenskonferenz: Hintergrund und Bedeutung eines unbeachteten Memorandums von 1919', *Revue des études sud-est européennes/Journal of South-East European Studies* 53/1–4 (2015), pp. 279–326.
[60] Harald Roth, *Hermannstadt: Kleine Geschichte einer Stadt in Siebenbürgen* (Cologne: Böhlau, 2006), p. 190.
[61] Ibid., pp. 190–1.   [62] Roth, *Kleine Geschichte Siebenbürgens*, pp. 123–4.
[63] See 'Mediascher Anschlußerklärung des erweiterten sächsischen Zentralausschusses', in Ernst Wagner (ed.), *Quellen zur Geschichte der Siebenbürger Sachsen, 1191–1975* (Cologne: Böhlau, 1981), p. 268.

their 'national ideals' and 'extended ... their brotherly greetings'.[64] Eight months later, on 15 August 1919, Banat Swabians followed suit and publicly declared their loyalty to the new Romanian state.[65] Such public avowals were of course motivated by a degree of political pragmatism. Yet these statements also spoke of a commitment to the new order and – unlike many other Germans in east-central Europe – they were, initially at least, not marked by revanchism and right-wing demagoguery.

By 1920, Transylvania and the Banat had officially become part of the Romanian state's territory. This new political reality shifted their politics in a shared direction, which made them 'Romanian Germans' (*Rumäniendeutsche* or *Germanii din România*). There were, by 1930, around 750,000 Germans in Romania. The political and socio-economic developments in the newly unified Romanian state had a major impact on Saxon and Swabian identities and on the cultural functions they fulfilled.[66] The unification of Romania brought *Siebenbürger Sachsen* and *Banater Schwaben* together in a novel political context. Until then, there had been nothing specifically 'Romanian' about *Sachsen* and *Schwaben*, though there were precedents for unifying German groups in the region: Rudolf Brandsch, a leading Transylvanian Saxon politician in the first half of the twentieth century, had called for closer co-operation between different German groups in Hungary as early as 1910. When the Romanian state began referring to the different German-speaking groups in Romania as *Germanii din România*, with centrally structured institutions as representative organs in Romania, it simplified in many ways the ambitions of German actors in Romania. The Verband der Deutschen in Rumänien (Union of Germans in Romania) became the umbrella organisation for all Germans in Romania.[67] In parliament, Germans were represented not by Saxon or Swabian parties, but by the Deutsche Volkspartei in Großrumänien (German People's Party in Greater Romania).[68] The two chairmen of the

[64] Ibid., p. 267.
[65] See Michael Kroner, *Die Deutschen Rumäniens im 20. Jahrhundert: Siebenbürgen, Banat, Sathmar, Bukowina, Bessarabien, Dobrudscha, Altrumänien* (Vienna: Österreichische Landsmannschaft, 2004), p. 29. See also Josef Wolf, 'Selbstrepräsentation und kulturpolitische Neuorientierung der Banater Schwaben 1918–1925', in Walter Engel and Walter Ţonţa (eds.), *Die Banater Schwaben nach dem Ersten Weltkrieg: Kulturelle Kontinuität und neuer Aufbruch* (Stuttgart: Landsmannschaft der Banater Schwaben, 2015), pp. 79–139.
[66] Corina Anderl, 'Siebenbürger Sachsen, Banater Schwaben und Landler als Deutsche in Rumänien: Zur Ambivalenz der kulturellen Funktion von Ethnizität in mulitethnischen Regionen', in Wilfried Heller et al. (eds.), *Ethnizität in der Transformation: Zur Situation nationaler Minderheiten in Rumänien* (Vienna: LIT Verlag, 2006), pp. 42–55.
[67] Ioan Scurtu, 'Beiträge zur Geschichte der Deutschen Parlamentspartei 1919–1937', in Walter König (ed.), *Siebenbürgen zwischen den beiden Weltkriegen* (Cologne: Böhlau, 1994), p. 56.
[68] Ibid.

party, Rudolf Brandsch (1919–22) and Dr Hans Otto Roth (1922–38), were explicitly *German* representatives.[69] Even local savings banks co-operatives (*Sparkassen*) were transformed from Saxon and Swabian into German.[70] After the First World War, debates about identity among German groups intensified: Germans were torn between their local roots, their new Romanian homeland, and Germany, as well as more global ideas about self-determination.

Romania's unification used to be seen as a conclusion to the struggle for national unity in the 'long nineteenth century', relegating issues around minorities to the margins.[71] More recent studies, however, have foregrounded minorities and language politics as a central issue in interwar Romania.[72] Transylvania and the Banat were regions where conflict over language was particularly palpable.[73] By focusing on language provisions in schools and universities, the Romanian state tried to raise a new generation out of the minorities in Romania to become part of a governing elite that would make possible a cohesive Romanian society.[74] Minorities pushed back against such central policies by 'self-organising' into minority islands

[69] Ibid., pp. 55–67. For a biography of Dr Hans Otto Roth, see Thomas Frühmesser, *Hans Otto Roth: Biographie eines rumäniendeutschen Politikers (1890–1953)* (Cologne: Böhlau, 2013).

[70] Attila Gábor Hunyadi, 'National Economic Self-Organizational Models in Transylvania: The Confluences of the Hungarian, German and Romanian Cooperative Movements', in Attila Gábor Hunyadi (ed.), *State and Minority in Transylvania, 1918–1989: Studies on the History of the Hungarian Community* (Boulder, Co.: Atlantic Research and Publications, 2012), p. 33.

[71] See R. W. Seton-Watson, *A History of the Roumanians from Roman Times to the Completion of Unity* (London: Cambridge University Press, 1934), R. W. Seton-Watson, *Roumania and the Great War* (London: Constable and Company Ltd, 1915), and Stefan Fisher-Galaţi, *Twentieth Century Rumania* (New York: Columbia University Press, 1970), as good examples of liberal thought on the conclusion of the struggle for national unity prior to 1918, in particular, Seton-Watson, *History of the Roumanians*, appendix IX, 'The New Frontier and a Just Settlement', pp. 95–7. A prominent Romanian example of this narrative is Nicolae Iorga, *A History of Roumania: Land, People, Civilisation* (London: T. Fisher Unwin Ltd, 1925). For a different approach to the break-up of the Habsburg Empire, see Robin Okey, *The Habsburg Monarchy c. 1765–1918* (Basingstoke: Macmillan, 2001). A further good deconstruction of this thesis is offered by Lucian Boia; see Boia, *Romania: Borderland of Europe*, and Lucian Boia, *History and Myth in Romanian Consciousness* (Budapest: CEU Press, 2001).

[72] See, for instance, Gábor Egry, 'Unholy Alliances? Language Exams, Loyalty, and Identification in Interwar Romania', *Slavic Review* 76/4 (2017), pp. 959–82.

[73] The making of a united Romanian state in 1918 featured as a unifying foundation narrative during the communist period, especially from the 1970s during Nicolae Ceauşescu's national communism, when the focus was on the crucible of Transylvania. See, for example, Ştefan Pascu, *The Making of the Romanian Unitary National State* (Bucharest: Editura Academiei Republicii Socialiste România, 1989), and Constantin C. Giurescu, *Transylvania in the History of Romania: An Official Outline* (London: Garnstone Press Ltd, 1969). Useful studies of the role of Transylvania in this discourse include Sorin Mitu, *National Identity of Romanians in Transylvania* (Budapest: CEU Press, 2001), and Sorin Antohi, *Civitas Imaginalis: istorie şi utopie în cultura română* (Iaşi: Polirom, 1999).

[74] See Gábor Egry, 'Endangered by Alienation? Raising a Minority Elite between Nationalising Higher Education Systems: The New Generation of Hungarians in Interwar Romania', in

with loyalties beyond Romania. The Hungarian-language journal *Hitel*, for instance, was one such example of a minority group quarantining itself, in a right-wing Hungarian milieu, from Romanian central politics.[75] Similar developments of accommodation and resistance, discussed in detail in Chapter 3, occurred within the Romanian German community.[76] Continuity figures such as Dr Hans Otto Roth advocated accommodation with the Romanian state, while the 1930s saw the advent of radical forces around 'self-help' organisers such as Fritz Fabritius (1883–1957) and the illustrious right-wing writer Heinrich Zillich (1898–1988).[77] And, though Romanian unification represented a rupture for the German communities included in the Romanian nation-state after 1918, the multi-layered debates surrounding complex German identities were in place long before the conclusion of the First World War. Out of these histories, Romanian Germans after 1918 pieced together a potent mix of stories of privilege, threats, and hardship.

Telling Stories I: Privilege and Superiority

The interwar period was a confusing time for Germans in Romania. With the exception of the small Dobruja German community, the Bessarabian German community, and the Germans of Bucharest, Germans had for the first time in their history established a formal relationship with Romanians around the newly unified 'Greater Romanian' state. Amid some uncertainty, there was also a buoyant *Aufbruchsstimmung* – an atmosphere of departure – which enveloped the German community.[78] The Romanian state seemed to offer new opportunities and vague hopes of betterment. Saxons, in particular, had hoped that their once privileged social standing and linguistic autonomy, eroded by ever more assertive Magyarisation

Florian Bieber and Harald Heppner (eds.), *Universities and Elite Formation in Central, Eastern and South Eastern Europe* (Vienna: LIT Verlag, 2015), pp. 39–59.

[75] See Zsuzsanna Török, 'Planning the National Minority: Strategies of the Journal *Hitel* in Romania, 1935–1944', *Nationalism and Ethnic Politics* 7/2 (2001), pp. 57–74.

[76] Wilhelm Andreas Baumgärtner, *Eine Welt im Aufbruch: Die Siebenbürger Sachsen im Spätmittelalter* (Sibiu: Schiller Verlag, 2008), Annemarie Röder, *Deutsche, Schwaben, Donauschwaben: Ethnisierungsprozesse einer deutschen Minderheit in Südosteuropa* (Marburg: Deutsche Gesellschaft für Volkskunde, 1998), Gerhard Seewann, 'Siebenbürger Sachse, Ungarndeutscher, Donauschwabe? Überlegungen zur Identitätsproblematik des Deutschtums in Südosteuropa', in Gerhard Seewann (ed.), *Minderheitenfragen in Südosteuropa* (Munich: Südost Institut, 1992), pp. 139–55, and Anton Sterbling, *Kontinuität und Wandel in Rumänien und Südosteuropa: Historisch-soziologische Analysen* (Munich: Südostdeutsches Kulturwerk, 1997).

[77] See Chapter 3 for details.

[78] Roth, *Kleine Geschichte Siebenbürgens*, pp. 122–6, and Engel and Tonța (eds.), *Die Banater Schwaben nach dem Ersten Weltkrieg*.

from the late 1860s, might be re-established.[79] At the same time, a sense of belonging to a greater German community beyond their borders began to emerge.

One of the principal themes that came to define Romanian German identity – a sense of superiority and exceptionalism – was born out of Transylvanian Saxon history.[80] Saxon provenance itself was the stuff of myths.[81] Yet it was precisely these stories that made it possible for Saxons, and later for Romanian Germans, to draw on notions of superiority. According to some, Transylvanian Saxons had been Crusaders led astray as unsuspecting Christian warriors, forced to settle and cultivate the lands of Transylvania.[82] In other stories, they were the children of Hamelin who had been abducted by the Pied Piper.[83] But the most accepted explanation was that they were hired as defenders of Christendom and the Hungarian Kingdom, summoned by King Géza in the eleventh century. Saxon history was a success story. They had built up the characteristic fortified churches of Saxon towns in Transylvania. Seven Saxon fortified churches had turned the region into *Siebenbürgen*, the bastion of Christendom against the ungodly hordes of the East, which was easily transposed into a contemporaneous setting of ideological battles in the twentieth century. All these stories illustrated a wider point that underpinned Saxon, and later Romanian German, identity: Saxons somehow had an 'old home', somewhere in the German Lands, from which they had been coaxed to a far and distant land, their new home of 800 years, Transylvania, where they had set up a durable civilisation. This was a major theme for Transylvanian Saxons in the interwar period. By the 1930s, this foundation story was being thoroughly infused with National Socialism and in this new form made its way into the school system.[84]

---

[79] On the dilemma facing Transylvanian Saxons under Hungarian rule in the late nineteenth century, see Kwan, 'Transylvanian Saxon Politics'.

[80] Sacha Davis argues against a Romanian German commonality in the interwar period. Instead, he contends, the Transylvanian Saxon sense of superiority led them to feel closer to the German *Volksgemeinschaft*, and thus to Germans from elsewhere in Europe, than to their Banat Swabian compatriots. This book argues that both developments took place. Saxons became Greater German enthusiasts while feeling much closer affiliation with Banat Swabians from the 1920s on. See Sacha E. Davis, 'Constructing the *Volksgemeinschaft*: Saxon Particularism and the German Myth of the East, 1919–1933', *German Studies Review* 39/1 (2016), pp. 41–64.

[81] For a good collection of essays on the beginnings of Saxon life in Transylvania, see Gündisch (ed.), *Generalprobe Burzenland*.

[82] That founding story retained its strength into the twenty-first century. See Horst Klusch, *Zur Ansiedlung der Siebenbürger Sachsen* (Bucharest: Kriterion, 2001).

[83] For a wonderful overview of a number of 'conspiracy theories', including the legend of the Pied Piper of Hamelin, see ibid.

[84] See, for instance, the programmatic journal for Transylvanian Saxon teachers in the 1930s: 'Geistige Grundlagen der neuen Erziehung, dargestellt aus der nationalsozialistischen Idee', in

Germans in Romania took their perception of privilege from Saxon heritage and history, and from their association with the global German community. Even in modern-day Romania, they boasted an educated urbanity that seemed to elevate them above others, especially over Romanians from the Old Kingdom on the other side of the Carpathians. This sense of superiority was partly shared with other Transylvanians, namely Hungarians and Romanians, but there was a specifically German dimension to Saxon superiority. The Saxon success story, with its local features, became a German one to which, ultimately, all Germans in Romania could belong. They, in turn, belonged to the wider German community. What the Saxons had built up over 800 years, the Germans had tried to defend in the First World War. In his book, *Deutsche Männer in Siebenbürgen* (*German Men in Transylvania*), writer Fritz Heinz Reimisch commented accordingly:

> These youngsters and men [German soldiers in the First World War] fought for the same cause for which the Transylvanian Saxons have been fighting for nearly 800 years: namely, the worldwide recognition [*Weltgeltung*] of Germanness [*Deutschtum*]. From their blood someday will rise a wonderful seed [*Saat*]!
>
> Today the Balkan floods of dirt are yet again swamping Transylvania. But the unflinching urge of the German people for purity will yet again succeed in removing all stains. Transylvania is part of *Mitteleuropa* – it is not Balkan![85]

Despite Reimisch's protestations, Germans in Transylvania and the Banat found themselves as part of the newly unified Romanian state after the First World War. Romanian German feelings of superiority and difference increased over the course of the twentieth century. Many of their turbulent experiences in Romania were explained as a consequence of an innate quality of Romanian culture, which belonged to the Balkan sphere. The German communities stood in stark contrast to the 'Balkan'

Dr Heinz Brandsch (ed.), *Schule und Leben: Fachzeitschrift des Siebenbürgisch-Sächsischen Lehrerbundes* 6 (1934–5), pp. 266–71.

[85] Fritz Heinz Reimisch, *Deutsche Männer in Siebenbürgen: Aus der Kampf- und Leidenszeit der Siebenbürger Sachsen (Deutsche in Aller Welt)* (Leipzig: Koehler & Amelang, 1925), p. 8:

> Diese Jünglinge und Männer [German soldiers in the First World War] haben für dasselbe gefochten, wie die Siebenbürger Sachsen seit nahezu 800 Jahren, nämlich für die Weltgeltung des Deutschtums. Aus ihrem Blut wird eine herrliche Saat dereinst aufgehen. Wir müssen nur Geduld haben und Vertrauen auf den höchsten Lenker irdischer Geschicke. Heute überspülen die Schmutzfluten des Balkans wiederum Siebenbürgen. Durch des deutschen Volkes unbeirrbaren Drang nach Reinheit wird es auch hier wiederrum gelingen, alle Flecken zu beseitigen. Siebenbürgen ist ein Stück Mitteleuropas – es ist nicht Balkan!

vicissitudes.[86] Saxon and Swabian culture was superior to its Balkan, Romanian surroundings, and it is precisely this notion of particularism that can be traced in older Saxon narratives. As Reimisch claimed in 1925, the battles fought and hardships faced by the Saxons in the Middle Ages were part of a longer struggle of German culture against a primitive 'Balkan' onslaught: be it in the context of the Mongols, the Ottoman Empire, or indeed the German Empire's futile engagement in the First World War. Where they belonged was in a German *Mitteleuropa* as part of the European centre of civilisation.[87]

The notion of Romanian German superiority was embedded in the history of Saxon settlement and heritage, and they had attained special rights and privileges primarily as urban dwellers.[88] Later, in twentieth-century Romania, the story of Saxons as bourgeois Germans acted as a symbol of German success and exceptionalism for all Germans.[89] They had been chosen to settle and defend a land, and had thus become the established group in the region. As founders of the seven main fortresses, they had not only coined the German name of the region – *Siebenbürgen*[90] – but they had also provided Transylvania with a sophisticated urban infra-structure. Coverage of Transylvanian Saxon history in the German press in Germany seemed to confirm their rarefied history and was quoted approvingly in the German-language press in Romania. Other German, non-Saxon groups began to drop their specific names in favour of the word 'German', allowing all Germans to enjoy the Saxons' history of privilege.[91] In a short book on demographics and future prospects for the Banat region

---

[86] This is explored in detail in Chapters 2 and 4.

[87] The idea of *Mitteleuropa* gained currency in the interwar period after its political inception in the late nineteenth and early twentieth centuries. Two of the 'big names' of a *Mitteleuropean* idea are the German geographer Joseph Partsch (1851–1925) and the liberal politician Friedrich Naumann (1860–1919). *Mitteleuropa* around the turn of the century took on a more German nationalist tone, which even a liberal politician like Naumann advocated. See Joseph Partsch, *Central Europe* (London: William Heinemann, 1903), and Friedrich Naumann, *Mitteleuropa* (Berlin: G. Reimer, 1915). For an excellent overview of the historical development of the idea of *Mitteleuropa*, see Peter Stirk, 'The Idea of *Mitteleuropa*', in Peter Stirk (ed.), *Mitteleuropa: History and Prospects* (Edinburgh: Edinburgh University Press, 1994), pp. 1–35, and Tomasz Kamusella, 'Central European Castles in the Air? A Reflection on the Malleable Concepts of Central Europe', *Kakanien Revisited* (July 2011), at www.kakanien-revisited.at/beitr/essay/TKamusella1.pdf (accessed 28 Jun. 2019).

[88] Pál Engel, *The Realm of St Stephen: A History of Medieval Hungary, 895–1526* (London: I. B. Tauris, 2005), pp. 60, 61.

[89] Peter F. Sugar, *Southeastern Europe under Ottoman Rule* (Seattle: University of Washington Press, 1996), p. 146.

[90] The German word *Siebenbürgen* (Transylvania) is derived from *sieben Burgen* (seven castles). These are Bistriţa/Bistritz, Braşov/Kronstadt, Cluj-Napoca/Klausenburg, Mediaş/Mediasch, Sebeş/Mühlbach, Sibiu/Hermannstadt, and Sighişoara/Schäßburg.

[91] Scurtu, 'Beiträge zur Geschichte der Deutschen Parlamentspartei'.

from 1928, Viktor Orendi-Hommenau (1870–1954) referred to Banat Swabians exclusively as German.[92] Written as a complaint about the Treaty of Trianon, the book compared the fate of Germans and German education in the Romanian part of the Banat to their counterparts in Hungary. Orendi-Hommenau is a case in point: as a Transylvanian Saxon publicist and politician, born in 1870 in Dumbrăveni/ Elisabethstadt/Erzsébetváros, he was a specialist and a great publicist for the history of Transylvanian Saxons. But he also strongly championed German language and culture in the Banat as an integral part of Germanness in the region.[93] This was not mere Saxon patronage towards other, perhaps minor, German groups. Orendi-Hommenau regarded Swabians in the Banat as equal Germans and – crucially – took up this cause before the inclusion of the Banat and Transylvania into Romania. In response to the increasing pressure of Magyarisation, Orendi-Hommenau drew attention to the situation of the Swabians and made it his mission to defend German language and culture in the Banat. Both before and after the First World War, Orendi-Hommenau tried to create a defensive castle around the German community of Banat Swabians. He founded the literary journal *Von der Heide* in 1909 in Timișoara/Temesvár/Temeswar, which was at its heart a defence of German literary and cultural life in the Banat under Hungarian rule at the time.[94] His efforts were received approvingly by Germans in Austria who understood his role as a 'lone fighter on the moor for *Deutschtum*' against Magyarisation.[95] In Romania, after the war, Orendi-Hommenau continued to write extensively on Banat Swabian culture and lobbied for the maintenance of language autonomy for German schools in the Banat.[96] By the interwar period, Orendi-Hommenau had become so concerned by all things Swabian in the Banat that he referred to Swabians as 'we' and 'us'.[97] What bothered him most

---

[92] Viktor Orendi-Hommenau, *Gestern und Heute: Eine kleine Statistik* (Timișoara: self-published, 1928).

[93] Gudrun-Liane Ittu, 'Viktor Orendi-Hommenau (1870–1954): Ein Siebenbürger im Dienste der deutschen Sprache und Kultur im Banat', in Wynfried Kriegleder, Andrea Seidler and Jozef Tancer (eds.), *Deutsche Sprache und Kultur im Banat: Studien zur Geschichte, Presse, Literatur und Theater, sprachlichen Verhältnissen, Wissenschafts-, Kultur- und Buchgeschichte, Kulturkontakten und Identitäten* (Bremen: Edition Lumière, 2015), pp. 211–25.

[94] This journal was published in 1909–19, 1922–6, and 1937. See also Christian Marchetti, 'Selbstfindung und Diversität – Kleine Volkskunden in Südosteuropa', in Cornelia Eisler and Silke Göttsch-Elten (eds.), *Minderheiten im Europa der Zwischenkriegszeit: Wissenschaftliche Konzeptionen, mediale Vermittlung, politische Funktion* (Münster: Waxmann Verlag, 2017), p. 92.

[95] Rudolf Bernreiter, 'Literarische Ausblicke', *Unterkärntner Nachrichten*, 16 July 1913, p. 9.

[96] See Orendi-Hommenau, *Gestern und Heute*, and Ittu, 'Viktor Orendi-Hommenau', pp. 223–5.

[97] See, for instance, Viktor Orendi-Hommenau, *Deutsche Dichter aus dem Banat: Literarische Skizze* (Timișoara: self-published, 1921).

were the dangers lurking in and around the Banat that threatened to obliterate this delicate island of German culture.[98] To survive, the Swabians had to emulate what the Saxons had achieved over centuries: to build proverbial fortresses and defend their Germanness.[99]

Yet Saxon heritage not only allowed Germans to feel part of a broader Romanian German community of fate; it also determined the hierarchy among German groups in contemporary Romania. Unlike other groups, Transylvanian Saxons were regarded as a sophisticated, urban, and successful group. This internal hierarchy amongst German groups was, in part, based on Saxon 'bragging rights' due to the sheer length of time they had lived in the region.[100] In this way, they shared similar foundation stories with their German counterparts in other parts of east-central Europe, who had received charters guaranteeing their rights after settling. German settlers in Bohemia, modern-day Poland, and the Baltic coast formed part of a medieval wave of migration, which – for Germans in modern Europe – outshone the histories of later German colonists in the eighteenth and nineteenth centuries.[101] Transylvanian Saxon history was a far longer and more privileged tale, with a long institutional narrative and active minority politics, which other German groups in Romania admired. Saxon success, social standing, and an established history delivered the perfect ingredients for the Saxon success story to form the central theme for all Germans in twentieth-century Romania.

This success story became highly charged in the twentieth century. Transylvanian Saxons' privileged position as part of a central European 'proto-bourgeoisie' had gradually dwindled away:[102] first under the pressure of Magyarisation, and later because of the politics in Greater Romania after 1918. In their attempts to hold on to past glory, there was an outpouring of memories of Saxon greatness in the early twentieth century. The influential Saxon poet Adolf Meschendörfer (1877–1963) insisted on Saxon exceptionalism and greatness in his work in the interwar period. His

---

[98] Ibid., pp. 11, 12.   [99] Ibid., pp. 18–20.
[100] These 'bragging rights' engendered a quasi-class system within the Romanian German community. For an excellent study of this in relation to the appeal of Nazism, see Balázs A. Szelényi, 'From Minority to *Übermensch*: The Social Roots of Ethnic Conflict in the German Diaspora of Hungary, Romania and Slovakia', *Past & Present* 196 (2007), pp. 232–46.
[101] See, for instance, William W. Hagen, *Ordinary Prussians: Brandenburg Junkers and Villagers, 1500–1840* (New York: Cambridge University Press, 2002), Vejas Liulevicius, *The German Myth of the East: 1800 to the Present* (Oxford: Oxford University Press, 2009), pp. 12–43, and Wilfried Schlau (ed.), *Sozialgeschichte der baltischen Deutschen* (Cologne: Wissenschaft und Politik, 2000).
[102] On the early emergence of the 'bourgeoisie' in central Europe and its gradual demise until 1848, see Szelényi, *The Failure of the Central European Bourgeoisie*.

1931 novel, *Die Stadt im Osten*, remembered Saxon urban life from the
perspective of an older Saxon from Brașov/Kronstadt with fictional ego
documents giving a tangible insight into city life as it once was.[103] His
Siebenbürgische Elegie (*Transylvanian Elegy*) from 1927, by contrast, offered
a dreamy glimpse into a rural Saxon world in danger of disappearing:[104]

> Anders rauschen die Brunnen, anders rinnt hier die Zeit.
> Früh faßt den staunenden Knaben Schauder der Ewigkeit.
> Wohlvermauert in Grüften modert der Väter Gebein,
> zögernd nur schlagen die Uhren, zögernd bröckelt der Stein.
> Siehst du das Wappen am Tore? Längst verwelkte die Hand.
> Völker kamen und gingen, selbst ihr Name entschwand.
> Aber der fromme Bauer sät in den Totenschrein,
> schneidet aus ihm sein Korn, keltert aus ihm seinen Wein.
> Anders schmeckt hier der Märzwind, anders der Duft vom Heu,
> anders klingt hier das Wort von Liebe und ewiger Treu.
> Roter Mond, vieler Nächte einziggeliebter Freund,
> bleiche die Stirne dem Jüngling, die der Mittag gebräunt,
> reifte ihn wie der gewaltige Tod mit betäubendem Ruch,
> wie in grünlichem Dämmer Eichbaum mit weisem Spruch.
> Ehern wie die Gestirne zogen die Jahre herauf,
> ach, schon ist es September. Langsam neigt sich ihr Lauf.

Menschendörfer eulogised a Saxon world where time ran differently in the
rural parts of Transylvania. In Meschendörfer's view, the hard-working
German farmer had lived and toiled on the land for centuries. The rapid
political changes since the mid-nineteenth century were merely part of
a coming and going of 'peoples' over the centuries whose names would be
forgotten. The Saxons, pious and honest, remained in place. It is easy to
dismiss this poem as nationalist kitsch, yet it became the standard-bearer
for Saxon self-understanding in the interwar period. And, crucially, it
continued a tradition of economic and political nationalism that, in this
view, set Germans apart from Romanians and Hungarians.[105] More

---

[103] Adolf Meschendörfer, *Die Stadt im Osten* (Sibiu: Krafft & Drotleff, 1931). It is considered the first Romanian German novel.

[104] Michael Markel, 'Adolf Meschendörfers *Siebenbürgische Elegie*: Bausteine zu einer Rezeptionsgeschichte', in Peter Motzan and Stefan Sienerth (eds.), *Deutsche Regionalliteraturen in Rumänien, 1918–1944: Positionsbestimmungen, Forschungswege, Fallstudien* (Munich: Verlag Südostdeutsches Kulturwerk, 1997), pp. 177–222.

[105] See Stéphanie Danneberg, 'Die politischen Beziehungen zwischen Sachsen und Rumänen Siebenbürgens in den Jahren 1900–1914', in Vasile Ciobanu and Sorin Radu (eds.), *Partide politice și minorități naționale din România în secolul XX, Vol. II* (Sibiu: Editura Universității 'Lucian Blaga', 2007), pp. 277–94, and Stéphanie Danneberg, *Wirtschaftsnationalismus lokal Interaktion und Abgrenzung zwischen rumänischen und sächsischen Gewerborganisationen in den siebenbürgischen Zentren Hermannstadt und Kronstadt, 1868–1914* (Göttingen: Vandenhoeck & Ruprecht, 2018).

importantly, the poem was transformed into an identity marker for all Germans in Romania, and it is here the cultural transfer from 'Saxon' to 'German' becomes evident.[106] Bukovina Germans mimicked much of this rhetoric, placing themselves in a line of Saxon, or rather German, privilege. Walter Peter Plajer's *Burzenländer Elegie* quoted much of Meschendörfer's poem.[107] Similarly, the Dobruja German Alida Schielke-Brenner modelled her poem 'Unsre Heimat' ('Our Homeland') on Meschendörfer's supposedly unique Saxon elegy:

> Dort, wo vor hundert Jahren alles noch öde war,
> wo fremde Völker hausten, der Türke und Tatar,
> dort haben unsere Ahnen nach echter deutscher Art
> gepflügt und hart gerungen, gehofft und auch gespart
>
> Dort gründeten sie Dörfer im weiten Steppenland
> und schön gepflegte Felder zeugten von deutscher Hand.
> Sie waren Pioniere mit immer frischem Mut
> und haben sich erschaffen gar manches schöne Gut
>
> Was dieser Boden hergab, war Lohn für ihren Fleiß,
> es war ein hartes Ringen, es kostete viel Schweiß.
> Wir waren dort zufrieden, wir hatten unser Brot,
> es war ja unsre Heimat, wir hatten keine Not.[108]

Written as a retrospective on the tumultuous period of 1940 and beyond, when the German settlers of the Dobruja region were transferred 'back' to Germany as part of the *Heim-ins-Reich* programme,[109] Schielke-Brenner paid tribute to the hard-earned German success and the superior work ethic of Germans in the Dobruja. In these adaptations of Saxon culture

---

[106] See, for example, Claire De Oliveira, '"Autre est le chant des fontaines ... ": Intégration et transformation de l'altérité dans l'*Élégie transylvaine* d'Adolf Meschendörfer', *Études Germaniques* 262/2 (2011), pp. 479–89, and Waldemar Fromm, '"Anders rinnt hier die Zeit." Erinnerung und kollektives Gedächtnis in Adolf Meschendörfers *Siebenbürgische Elegie*: Mit Hinweisen zur Rezeption nach 1945', in Jürgen Lehmann and Gerald Volkmer (eds.), *Rumäniendeutsche Erinnerungskulturen: Formen und Funktionen des Vergangenheitsbezuges in der rumäniendeutschen Historiografie und Literatur* (Regensburg: Verlag Friedrich Pustet, 2016), pp. 47–62.

[107] Markel, 'Adolf Meschendörfers *Siebenbürgische Elegie*', p. 222.

[108] Alida Schielke-Brenner, 'Unsre Heimat', in Landsmannschaft der Dobrudscha- und Bulgariendeutschen e.V. (ed.), *Heimatbuch der Dobrudscha-Deutschen, 1840–1940* (Heilbronn: Heilbronner Stimme, 1986), p. 30.

[109] See, for instance, Rainer Schulze, 'Forced Migration of German Populations during and after the Second World War: History and Memory', in Jessica Reinisch and Elizabeth White (eds.), *The Disentanglement of Populations: Migration, Expulsion and Displacement in Postwar Europe, 1944–1949* (Basingstoke: Palgrave, 2011), pp. 51–70. Chapter 3 of the present book examines identity debates around Nazism and the deportations after the Second World War in detail.

that shifted the emphasis from the urban to the rural, the process of unification of different German groups into Romanian Germans was laid bare. If Saxons could look back on eight centuries of cultural superiority in the form of fortified churches and urban culture, then the rural world of the Banat, Transylvania, the Dobruja, and the Bukovina acted as a common marker of experience and identity.[110] The attention on rural and agricultural life also made possible the *völkisch* turn of the interwar period.[111]

Nostalgic eulogies shaped German understanding of their histories in the region and spoke of a sense of insecurity. While Meschendörfer's *Siebenbürgische Elegie* gained instant popularity in the interwar period, epitomising the need for a strong history and identity among Saxons, there are examples of similar poems from other German groups pre-dating the Saxon elegy. Adam Müller-Guttenbrunn (1852–1923), a Banat Swabian author who lived in Vienna before the First World War, composed the *Banater Schwabenlied* in 1909.[112] In an homage to the Banat Swabians' efforts to work the land, while emphasising the hardships they encountered, Müller-Guttenbrunn praised the Swabians as a German island in the midst of a 'sea of peoples [*Völkermeer*]' drawing on their German virtues to maintain their sense of superiority.[113] Müller-Guttenbrunn, a household name in antisemitic and German nationalist circles, helped to shape a common grammar for an interwar audience receptive to images of a German *Heimat*, which was rural and could also be mobilised as *völkisch*.[114] The nationalist kitsch compiled by Germans in the region from the turn of the century to the interwar period, created a people's history for Romanian Germans after 1918. Saxons, Swabians, Dobruja Germans, and others shared this grammar and used it to express germane themes. That sense of German superiority would play a hugely important role for Romanian German self-understanding, but it was also palpably under threat.

---

[110] For a good overview of the complex history of the wider region of Bessarabia, including Dobruja, see Mariana Hausleitner (ed.), *Deutsche und Juden in Bessarabien, 1814–1941* (Munich: IKGS Verlag, 2005).

[111] See Chapter 3 for further analysis.

[112] See Márta Fata, 'Die Ansiedlungsgeschichte im Gedächtnis: Wie sie Peter Treffil aus Triebswetter/Banat erzählt', in Kriegleder, Seidler and Tancer (eds.), *Deutsche Sprache und Kultur im Banat*, p. 200.

[113] This key theme of Swabian suffering is discussed later in this chapter and then again in Chapter 3.

[114] For an excellent collection of essays on the idea of *Heimat*, see Krista O'Donnell, Renate Bridenthal and Nancy Reagin (eds.), *The Heimat Abroad: The Boundaries of Germanness* (Ann Arbor: University of Michigan Press, 2005).

Telling Stories II: Under Siege

For Romanian Germans, the twentieth century tells the story of ascendancy, war, and demise. The early twentieth century bore some promise of regaining past glory, but these aspirations were stopped in their tracks by the two world wars. Instead, a short period of minority rights – and an interlude of alignment with Nazi Germany – was followed by deportation, expropriation, and obscurity. The sense of being beleaguered by various belligerent and subversive forces had long underpinned the notion of Saxons as guardians of culture and privilege. That feeling of destiny was conjoined to a perception of being under siege and an increasing sense of urgency from the mid-nineteenth century. The threats surrounding them, however, shifted from Hungarian nationalism to Romanian nationalism and later to communism and, to a more limited extent, fascism.[115]

The sense of being under siege and yet resisting successfully was rooted in the wider history of German, or rather Saxon, defensive settlements during the High Middle Ages and in the subsequent waves of attacks and defeats by the advancing Mongols, Tatars, and Turks.[116] As defenders of Christianity and their own particular culture, Saxons maintained their defensive presence very successfully over the centuries.[117] Resistance, then, became a template for successive events and periods in the twentieth century. *Siebenbürger Sachsen* frequently employed the notion of being under siege from outside forces to explain contemporary events. Having been besieged in the run-up to the unification of Romania in 1918 by both Magyar and Romanian nationalists,[118] the Saxons saw the interwar period in which Romania – in particular, Transylvania – was an island surrounded by ideological foes, especially Bolsheviks. What Romanian politicians saw as a problem of minority islands in Romania, Germans interpreted as a calling for the defence of civilisation.[119]

Stories such as the widely known account of the *Rumeser Student* helped make sense of the new world order. The story concerns the siege of Sebeş Alba (Mühlbach) by Sultan Murad II in 1438.[120] Faced with certain defeat by the Turks, a number of defenders valiantly held off the Turks for

---

[115] Szelényi, *The Failure of the Central European Bourgeoisie*, pp. 131–9.
[116] Roth, *Kleine Geschichte Siebenbürgens*, pp. 13, 14, 25–36.   [117] Ibid., pp. 27–30, 41–5, 47–53.
[118] Kwan, 'Transylvanian Saxon Politics', and Gerald Volkmer, *Die Siebenbürgische Frage (1878–1900)* (Cologne: Böhlau, 2004).
[119] Holly Case, *Between States: The Transylvanian Question and the European Idea during World War II* (Stanford: Stanford University Press, 2009), pp. 80–7.
[120] See Ernst D. Petritsch, 'Das Osmanische Reich und Siebenbürgen im Konfessionszeitalter', in Leppin and Wien (eds.), *Konfessionsbildung und Konfessionskultur*, pp. 19–20.

a while, retreating to one of the towers of the city's fortifications. The
student leader proclaimed that 'he would rather die a thousand deaths than
for him, his wife, and children to end up in the hands of the Turks'.[121] In
the end, the act of defiance was broken, and the remaining Saxons in the
tower were either killed or taken prisoner, including the student. *Captivus
septemcastrensis*, as the student was later known (or possibly Frater
Georgius de Unfaria: Brother George), wrote down his experiences,
which would resonate even more strongly among Romanian Germans in
the twentieth century.[122] Besiegement, deportation (or captivity for
Brother George) at the hands of an eastern menace (the Ottoman Turks,
later the Bolsheviks and Russians), and, later envelopment by Germany
(ideological alignment with Nazi Germany and migration to West
Germany) encapsulated the spirit of the twentieth century for Romanian
Germans.

The very make-up of Transylvania, symbolically represented by seven
fortified castles high up in the mountains, laid the foundations for
a paranoid sense of encirclement.[123] Saxons took seriously their role as
a bulwark against enemies whose identities were constantly changing:
Tatars, Mongols, the Byzantine Empire, the Ottoman Empire, and,
later, Muslims. Their religious calling as defenders of Christendom became
very much a key component of Saxon identity. In Transylvania the
Protestant Church's maxim, '*Ein' feste Burg ist unser Gott*' ('A mighty
fortress is our God') taken from the first line of the *Lutherlied*, defined
Transylvanian Saxon self-understanding into the present day. But the
twentieth century saw another layer added to the besiegement of the
community, which made it possible for a once exclusively Saxon narrative
to be adopted by the entire Romanian German community. The ideological framework of fascism on the one hand, and of communism on the
other, represented a mirror image of the histories of confrontations in
medieval and early modern Transylvania. It became a way of categorising
defenders of cultural value and hostile opponents.

The new reality of the interwar period fuelled the conviction of an
eastern menace, communism, threatening all Germans in Romania.

[121] Ibid. See also Carl Göllner, *Am Rande der Geschichte* (Bucharest: Kriterion, 1973), pp. 132–3.
[122] Stefan Sienerth, 'Weltoffenheit und Provinzenge: Die siebenbürgisch-deutsche Literatur von ihren
Anfängen bis zum Ausgang des 19. Jahrhunderts', in Hans Rothe (ed.), *Die Siebenbürger Sachsen in
Geschichte und Gegenwart* (Cologne: Böhlau, 1994), pp. 56–7.
[123] See, for instance, Arne Frank, *Das wehrhafte Sachsenland: Kirchenburgen im südlichen Siebenbürgen*
(Potsdam: Deutsches Kulturforum Östliches Europa, 2007), and Robert Stollberg and
Thomas Schulz, *Kirchenburgen in Siebenbürgen – Fortified Churches in Transylvania* (Cologne:
Böhlau, 2007).

Hermann Plattner, the editor of the *Siebenbürgisch-Deutsches Tagesblatt* in the interwar decades, saw the ideological threat encroaching from all directions, so that just '[l]ike an island Romania stands in the midst of the Bolshevik deluge, which is surging up against its borders from the east, the south, and the west'.[124] The Bolshevik threat may not have been unique to an interwar German imaginary, but it was certainly made more potent by the experience of being a minority in Romania and the sense of besiegement from Transylvanian Saxon history. In this way, Josef Rieß, a Romanian German publicist from the Banat (and therefore explicitly not from Transylvania), noted of the history of Germans in Romania in 1935 that 'those parts of the German *Volk* [*Volksteile*] who had already settled [in the region] became secluded islands of people [*Volksinseln*] in a foreign space; [they became] minority communities of fate'.[125] The political uncertainties of interwar Europe fuelled Romanian German angst that the world they knew could not withstand the threats around them. In his 1923 novel, *Im alten Land*, the linguist and writer Bernhard Capesius (1889–1981) lets his protagonist, Hermann Severinus, transmit the sense of urgency Germans in Romania felt as they witnessed the marginalisation of their community.[126] Severinus, convinced that the Saxons were facing their end of history after a century of erosion of rights, retreats to the village of Coroisânmărtin/Martinsdorf in central Transylvania to escape the threats to German life in Romania – in vain, as it turns out. Panicked by threats to their civilisation, Swabians and Saxons bridged their confessional differences,[127] as Romanian Germans immersed themselves in a narrative of being surrounded by hostile forces.[128] Narratives of siege helped to explain away the rise of National Socialism as merely a 'non-ideological' movement of Germans against the communist onslaught. What mattered, or so the claim went, was less the content of ideology, but its form: namely,

---

[124] Hermann Plattner quoted in Karl M. Reinerth, *Zur politischen Entwicklung der Deutschen in Rumänien 1918–1928: Aus einer siebenbürgisch-sächsischen Sicht* (Thaur: Wort und Welt Verlag, 1993), p. 74.

[125] Original: 'Die bereits vorgeschobenen und angesiedelten deutschen Volksteile wurden zu abgekapselten Volksinseln in fremdem Raum, zu Schicksalsminderheiten'; see Josef Rieß (ed.), *Deutsches Volkwerden im Banat: Reden und Aufsätze Dr Kaspar Muth's* (Timişoara: Ideal, 1935), p. 4.

[126] Bernhard Capesius, *Im alten Land* (Hermannstadt: Krafft & Drotleff, 1923).

[127] Banat Swabians are Roman Catholic, whereas Transylvanian Saxons are Lutheran. For an analysis of the cross-confessional identity of Saxons and Swabians, see László Holló, 'The Clash of Civilisations: Der Fall Siebenbürgen', *Studia Universitatis Babes-Bolyai – Theologia Catholica Latina* 1 (2005), pp. 57–82.

[128] See, for example, Sabine-Else Astfalk (ed.), *Josef Nischbach: Ein Leben für Glaube und Volkstum* (Stuttgart: Landsmannschaft der Banater Schwaben Landesverband Baden-Württemberg, 2000), in particular, pp. 50–60.

being in a perpetual state of besiegement.[129] Any challenges (and supposed solutions to those challenges) that faced Germans in Romania were understood as civilisational clashes, which would continue to set the tone for Romanian German myth-making after 1945. The shared experiences of Romania in the interwar period, and alignment with Nazism, as well as the war and subsequent deportation in 1945, gave Romanian Germans a language with which to express stories of besiegement.[130] Their shared events shaped the community with common narratives and myths derived from older and more regional stories. Romanian Germans caught up in the deportations therefore became *Russlanddeportierte* (deportees to Russia) rather than Saxon deportees or Swabian deportees. These deportees became a German community from Romania united by the theme of being threatened by Romanian nationalism, 'the East', and an overarching communist system.[131]

Telling Stories III: The Swabian Ordeal

If Transylvanian Saxons were able to tell a history of a privilege that was always under threat, *Banater Schwaben* were simply unable to point to a similar level of political sophistication. Unlike the *Schwaben*, the *Sachsen* had enjoyed religious and political autonomy, which had been embodied in institutions such as the so-called Sachsentag, or Saxon Congress, and the autonomous representative body, the Sächsische Nationaluniversität (Universitas Saxonum).[132] Saxons had also enjoyed the benefit of educational independence in primary and secondary education.[133] The church, for Saxons, had been at the centre of their identity as a distinguishing

---

[129] See, for example, Hans Bergel, 'Vorgänge letzter Entkolonialisierung – Aus dem Spannungsfeld des Südostens entlassen: Die Deutschen', in Hans Bergel, *Erkundungen und Erfahrungen: Notizen eines Neugierigen* (Munich: Südostdeutsches Kulturwerk, 1995), pp. 93–4.

[130] An example is Erika Feigel-Burghart, *Mädchenjahre hinter Stacheldraht: Sowjetunion 1945–1949* (Sibiu: Hora Verlag, 2003). The author of this autobiographical work sets the scene by placing the pan-Romanian German experience of the deportations in 1945 in the context of 800 years of Saxon history. See also Emil Sigmeth, *In Krieg und Frieden von Cuenca zum Don: Erlebnisse eines Journalisten aus Siebenbürgen* (Munich: Verlag Südostdeutsches Kulturwerk, 1991).

[131] Joachim Wittstock, '"Lasst uns durchhalten!" Eine Stimme aus der Russland-Deportation', in Joachim Wittstock and Stefan Sienerth (eds.), *'Bitte um baldige Nachricht': Alltag, Politik und Kultur im Spiegel südostdeutscher Korrespondenz* (Munich: IKGS Verlag, 2003), pp. 60–3.

[132] Gábor Egry, 'Ein anderer Ausgleich: Einiges zur Vorgeschichte des Sachsentages 1890', *Zeitschrift für Siebenbürgische Landeskunde* 29/1 (2006), pp. 51–61, and Illyés, *National Minorities in Romania*, pp. 12–14.

[133] Principal examples of independent secondary schools include Stephan Ludwig Roth Gymnasium in Mediaş/Mediasch, Honterus Gymnasium in Braşov/Kronstadt, and the Brukenthal Gymnasium in Sibiu/Hermannstadt, which was only named this in 1921.

marker from other groups. The Catholic *Banater Schwaben*, on the other hand, were almost indistinguishable from other groups, at least on religious grounds. Unlike the *Siebenbürger Sachsen*, Swabians did not possess the same 'bragging rights' either in terms of the length of their history in present-day Romania or of the heritage that they had created. The Saxon-dominated cities of Transylvania exuded an air of erudition, which stood in stark contrast to the more rurally based communities of the *Banater Schwaben*. Saxons were often urban and middle class, while Swabian society was dominated by agriculture and mining.[134]

Class differences had kept the two German groups apart until the early twentieth century.[135] Even the urban parts of the Swabian community were different from the Saxon cities: the two main conurbations of the Banat where Swabians lived, Arad and Timișoara/Temesvár/Temeswar, were too multicultural and too diverse to be regarded as solely German.[136] Even the rural parts of Saxon Transylvania were dominated by the church, while rural Swabian communities were bound together by labour and agriculture. Similar to the Catholic minority of the *Landler* in Transylvania, the Swabians were regarded as more vulnerable to change, and in a specific Swabian way, destined to follow their *Leidensweg* (the path of ordeal). The Swabian past was remembered as modest. The Saxons, however, guarded their culturally urbane heritage.[137] Saxon sophistication was evident in the sheer volume of Saxon art and culture, urban infrastructure, and special legal rights, none of which could be rivalled by Banat Swabians. Only when rural and urban Germans came together as Romanian Germans after the First World War was the rural world elevated to an essential part of Romanian German identity, as Adolf Meschendörfer's poem *Siebenbürgische Elegie* attests. Swabians were becoming a little more Saxon, and Saxons were becoming a little more Swabian, as the burden of the rural world shifted into sharp relief.

---

[134] A wonderful history of the Banat uplands was published by Georg Hromadka, a Romanian German who was loyal to the Romanian communist regime. In it, he foregrounds the hard labour of Swabians in mining and factory work, recounting numerous industrial disasters that befell the hard-working community. See Georg Hromadka, *Kleine Chronik des Banater Berglands* (Munich: Verlag Südostdeutsches Kulturwerk, 1993).

[135] Szelényi, 'From Minority to *Übermensch*'.

[136] For the multicultural legacy of Timișoara, see James Koranyi, 'Reinventing the Banat: Cosmopolitanism as a German Cultural Export', *German Politics and Society* 29/3 (2011), pp. 97–114.

[137] This was a common theme among Saxon memoirs and historical narratives; see, for instance, Gustav Zickeli, *Bistritz zwischen 1880 und 1950: Erinnerungen* (Munich: Verlag Südostdeutsches Kulturwerk, 1989).

While Saxon success acted as a symbol of German ascendancy, Swabian narratives functioned as metaphors of an ordeal and, in some cases, of suffering. Images of German success were juxtaposed with narratives of a German ordeal, or more specifically with the Swabian *Leidensweg*. In stark contrast to the Saxons' success story, the Swabian *Leidensweg* traced the hardships and difficulties *Schwaben* had faced during the three main waves of Swabian settlement in the Banat.[138] The iconic representation of that Swabian foundation myth was found in Stefan Jäger's triptych, *Die Einwanderung der Schwaben* (*The Migration of the Swabians*) from 1910 (Figure 1.3).[139] In its reception, the triptych would come to represent an ordeal with which all Romanian Germans could identify, at least by the time the Second World War was well underway.

Jäger was born a Banat Swabian and died a Romanian German. He was born on 28 May 1877 in Cenei/Tschene in the Banat to the west of Timişoara. He remained a 'local patriot' throughout his life and settled in Jimbolia/Hatzfeld in 1910 until his death in 1962. Jäger focused on agriculture and folklore as motifs for his paintings. His works were exhibited at agricultural and industrial fairs, mainly but not solely in the Banat. While connections to other regions of Europe gave his career a necessary boost, Jäger became a household name in the region, allowing him to rely comfortably on commissions that never really dried up, apart from a fallow period after the First World War.[140] His deep commitment to and interest in Banat Swabian life earned him the name *Schwabenmaler*, an ambiguous title which could mean 'the Swabian painter' or 'the painter of Swabians'. But over the course of the quarter of a century in the interwar period, Stefan Jäger's work outgrew its local, Swabian audience.

While the Banat was part of the Habsburg Empire, Jäger's oeuvre belonged to a rural Swabian world in Hungary. In May 1910, the small town of Cărpiniş/Gertianosch hosted a three-day trade and agricultural

---

[138] Anton Valentin, *Die Banater Schwaben: Kurzgefasste Geschichte einer Südostdeutschen Volksgruppe mit einem Volkskundlichen Anhang* (Munich: Veröffentlichung des Kulturreferates der Landsmannschaft der Banater Schwaben, 1959). See also Christian Glass, 'Die inszinierte Einwanderung: Stefan Jägers Triptychon "Die Einwanderung der Schwaben in das Banat" und seine Wirkungsgeschichte', in Fata (ed.), *Migration im Gedächtnis*, pp. 55–70.

[139] For a brief history and biography of Stefan Jäger, see, for instance, Karl-Heinz Gross, *Stefan Jäger, Maler seiner heimatlichen Gefilde: Aus seinem Leben und Werk* (Sersheim: Hartmann, 1991), Annemarie Podlipny-Hehn, *Stefan Jäger* (Bucharest: Kriterion, 1972), and Landsmannschaft der Banater Schwaben e.V. (ed.), *Stefan Jäger: Maler seiner Banater Heimat* (Munich: Landsmannschaft der Banater Schwaben e.V., 1992); see also Chapter 3.

[140] Walter Tonța, 'Stefan Jäger (1877–1962): Der Lebensweg eines Künstlers am Rande Mitteleuropas', in Peter Krier (ed.), *Hommage an Stefan Jäger* (Munich: Hilfswerk der Banater Schwaben, 2012), p. 131.

Figure 1.3 Stefan Jäger's triptyph *Die Einwanderung der Schwaben* (1905).

fair, which attracted visitors from all over Hungary. The highlight of the event was the unveiling of Stefan Jäger's triptych documenting the migration and arrival of Swabians in the Banat in the eighteenth century. This *Einwanderungs-Triptychon* almost instantly became an important piece for Banat Swabian self-understanding. Jäger managed to capture the Swabian *Leidensweg* – the big foundation myth of a path of ordeal – in his inimitable manner of depicting folkloristic kitsch. The picture was commissioned by Adam Röser, a cultural and political luminary in the Banat, who – along with one Jakob Knopf – conceived of the idea of documenting Banat Swabian history through a monumental painting. When it was finally unveiled on that beautiful May morning in Cărpiniş, it was greeted with much fanfare. Franz Blaskovics, canon and chairman of the local farmers' association, waxed lyrical about the Banat Swabians' historical struggles and troubles as they finally uncovered the painting: 'And now we will gaze upon our past', he told his audience, 'when our ancestors trekked through the desert, just like the Israelites'.[141] The visible changes in infrastructure between what was depicted on Jäger's triptych – ramshackle houses in a barren land, in contrast to an established infrastructure in present-day Banat – were testament to the Banat Swabians' diligence.[142]

Jäger's famous triptych took seriously the *Gründungsmythos* of the Swabians, the so-called *Große Schwabenzüge* of the eighteenth century. The story of their origins as pioneering colonists of a fallow land, which they had helped to transform into a bustling centre of agriculture, mining, and trade, was at the centre of Swabian identity by the late nineteenth and early twentieth centuries. The emergence of a triptych on this theme was part of a wider nation-building process in the Habsburg region (and of course beyond it) which put art, architecture, and culture at the forefront of 'right-sizing' the nation. In 1896, millennial celebrations swept Hungary, including the Banat.[143] Jäger was a student in Budapest in 1896 under the tutelage of the Hungarian artist Bertalan Székely and moved in the very circles that celebrated Árpád Feszty's gargantuan *Arrival of the Hungarians*, produced in 1894 and unveiled in 1896. Similar grand projects continued throughout the period right into the 1920s, as the Racławice Panorama in Lwów/L'viv/Lemberg in 1894 and Alfons Mucha's 1928 *Slav Epic* in Prague exemplify. Likewise, the 1906 Bucharest jubilee exhibition

---

[141] Gross, *Stefan Jäger*, pp. 45–6, Glass, 'Die inszentierte Einwanderung', p. 55, and Krier (ed.), *Hommage an Stefan Jäger*, p. 126.

[142] Gross, *Stefan Jäger*, p. 46.

[143] Maria Bucur and Nancy Wingfield (eds.), *Staging the Past: The Politics of Commemoration in Habsburg Central Europe, 1848 to the Present* (West Lafayette, Ind.: Purdue University Press, 2001).

both celebrated a great national past and looked assertively to a Greater Romanian future across the Carpathians.[144] Banat Swabians were intricately enmeshed in these developments. Jäger's seminal piece should thus be seen as a Swabian attempt to affirm Swabian identity by celebrating the foundation story of migration, hardship, and labour, while reacting to similar developments in Austria-Hungary.

But behind Jäger's painting also lies a deep cultural insecurity. Swabians were not affirming their identity from an equal position. Instead, they were caught between Magyarisation and Romanian and Serbian nationalism. More importantly, the fear of exodus hung over the community. Emigration to the Americas was a concern not just for Habsburg officials, but for entire communities,[145] and the Banat was no exception. The world around Stefan Jäger was in danger of vanishing to the New World. The first recorded official migrant from Cărpiniș/Gertianosch to North America left in 1901. Many followed in the years leading up to First World War. Swabians were stricken by the 'America fever' that raged in east-central Europe.[146] Newspapers carried adverts that lured Swabians and others to Brazil, the USA, Argentina, and other places that seemed to offer so much more promise than their current plight in the Banat and in Hungary. Local bands would play a farewell song at railway stations in the Banat as Swabians left their villages and towns in hope of a better life elsewhere.

A closer examination of the triptych not only reveals Banat Swabian motifs, but also foreshadows key elements of Romanian German self-understanding that developed in the first half of the twentieth century. The triple canvas was impressive in size, at 5 metres wide and 1.5 metres high, with the middle section being slightly bigger (2 metres) than the others. The three sections documented, in order, the 'migration' (*Wanderung*), 'rest' (*Rast*), and 'arrival' (*Ankunft*) of Swabians in the Banat. The first panel depicts the colonists arriving from the west, traipsing through a muddy field under a heavily clouded sky. Some women are bent over, carrying their tired children on their backs. In the middle panel, we see the Swabians resting on the ground. A single leafless tree symbolises the barren land to which they have moved. After the long, gruelling trek, the third and final panel pays tribute to the hard work of the Swabian settlers. Now surrounded by fresh timber, the first basic houses appear in the

[144] Shona Kallestrup, *Art and Design in Romania, 1866–1927: Local and International Aspects of the Search for National Expression* (Boulder, Co.: East European Monographs, 2006).
[145] Zahra, *The Great Departure.* [146] Gross, *Stefan Jäger*, pp. 40–1.

background, while a group of men appear to discuss future plans. The triptych seemed to illustrate perfectly the Swabian story of ordeal, manifesting a Swabian saying about death, hardship, and bread: 'Die Ersten hatten den Tod, die Zweiten die Not, und erst die Dritten das Brot.'[147]

Copies of Jäger's triptych made their way into Banat Swabian classrooms in the 1930s, and the original was wheeled out for a number of anniversaries commemorating the founding of Swabian villages in and around the region.[148] But the painting did not just capture a naïve zeitgeist of Swabian local patriotism. As it grew in popularity, it took on a number of different meanings and grew in prominence. In 1930, the painting went on tour to Yugoslavia and was exhibited in Bečkerek/Zrenjanin before grabbing the attention of *völkisch* Germans in the early 1940s. Its folkloristic style loaned itself to a *völkisch* interpretation during the 1930s and 1940s, when it became famous as a piece of art beyond the rural Banat Swabian world of Jimbolia. Strikingly, it found a new home in the offices of the *Deutsche Volksgruppe* in Timişoara in 1940 and became an integral part of a new National Socialist understanding of Germanness in the region. For National Socialists, Jäger's art formed a bridge between the old rural world – the old masters of 'Alt-Temeschburg', as the *Banater Deutsche Zeitung* put it in October 1941 – and the new, young National Socialist vision.[149] By the 1940s, Jäger's triptych no longer represented a Swabian story, but a German one. The triptych was routinely referred to as the '*Einwanderung der Deutschen ins Banat*' in German-language newspapers. The *Südostdeutsche Tageszeitung* celebrated Stefan Jäger's public appointment to the role of *Kulturrat* (cultural council) in recognition of his role in promoting 'south-east *Deutschtum*'.[150]

Even in the new political environment of communist Romania, Jäger and his work continued to gain recognition. Like other Romanian Germans, he was rehabilitated in the 1950s and was decorated with a second-class Order of Labour medal in 1957.[151] He died in 1962 in Jimbolia, but his afterlife continued to exert influence on the Romanian German imaginary. A posthumous Stefan Jäger boom swept through both West Germany and Romania. Commemorating the 200th anniversary of the founding of

---

[147] Translated: 'The first arrivals found death; the second hardship; and only the third found bread.'
[148] Glass, 'Die inszinierte Einwanderung', p. 66.
[149] 'Deutsche Leistungsschau: Alt-Temeschburg, Kunst und Schrifttum', *Banater Deutsche Zeitung*, 12 October 1941, p. 6.
[150] 'Feierstunde deutscher Kultur: Überreichung der Ehrenurkunde an Otto Alscher, Franz Ferch und Stefan Jäger', *Südostdeutsche Tageszeitung*, 19 January 1943, p. 4.
[151] Tonţa, 'Stefan Jäger', p. 132.

Jimbolia in Ulm in 1966, Banat Swabian émigrés put together the first Stefan Jäger exhibition in Germany. In Romania, the city of Timişoara hosted a major retrospective exhibition of Jäger's work in 1967.[152] Pride of place was given to the triptych, which, after temporarily disappearing from public display as the Second World War drew to a close,[153] had been found in the attic of a farmhouse and held in storage in Timişoara's Banat Museum.[154] Two years later, in 1969, a Stefan Jäger memorial was installed in Jimbolia, Jäger's hometown on the Romanian–Yugoslav border.[155] The painter and his legacy appeared in the public spheres of Romania and Germany time and time again. The *Landsmannschaft* (homeland society) of the Banat Swabians supported a number of commemorative events in Romania. In the other direction, the triptych went on a tour around Germany in 1991 and 1992.[156] The Jäger boom did not abate: various reproductions of the triptych made their way into the public displays of the Adam-Müller-Guttenbrunn-Haus in Timişoara, Haus der Heimat in Stuttgart, and the Danube Swabian Museum (Donauschwäbisches Zentralmuseum) in Ulm as well as onto the front covers of Swabian publications and invitations.[157]

If Jäger's work had once been consumed in the private domain, the legacy of the *Einwanderungstriptychon* became a template for politics. The triptych's motif of the *Leidensweg* was recognisable and powerful, and it was the transnational context of the interwar period that turned the work into an iconic Romanian German piece.[158] After the collapse of the communist regime, Jäger's triptych was moved to the foyer of the Adam-Müller-Guttenbrunn-Haus in Timişoara, where it has since adorned the entrance to the German Democratic Forum. Designed as a central piece of Banat Swabian identity, it transformed into an icon for Romanian Germans in Europe without losing its original regional roots.

Transnational Stories

Romanian Germans were not simply islands of people, as the Romanian interwar politician and prime minister Iuliu Maniu described Romania's minorities.[159] Equally, their identity debates were not conducted in an echo

---

[152] Glass, 'Die inszinierte Einwanderung', pp. 67, 68.   [153] Ibid., pp. 66–8.   [154] Ibid.
[155] Krier (ed.), *Hommage an Stefan Jäger*, p. 126.   [156] Ibid., p. 127.
[157] See Glass, 'Die inszinierte Einwanderung', pp. 67–70.
[158] The second part of the Jäger story is picked up in Chapter 3, which discusses the unfinished sequel to Jäger's triptych, namely the *Tragisches Triptychon* (*Tragic Triptych*) depicting the deportation of Romanian Germans to the Soviet Union in early 1945.
[159] See Case, *Between States*, p. 80.

chamber, but reverberated outside their community. Romanian German experiences were deeply entwined in a transnational network in the interwar period, which became evident in the reception of their narratives in Germany, Austria, Romania, and elsewhere. The stories that came to shape this community were therefore not only constructed by Saxons and Swabians for Romanian Germans, but were also reaffirmed and challenged by outside onlookers. Germany – in its guises as the second German Empire, the Weimar Republic, and the Third Reich – took centre stage in the first half of the twentieth century and beyond. Saxons and Swabians were intricately connected to Germany, a place that was at the heart of the Romanian German imaginary. Austria, émigrés in the Americas, and interactions with Romanian society, all explored in later chapters of this book, also shaped Romanian German identities beyond the interwar period.

The interest in so-called *Auslandsdeutsche* – Germans abroad – gained momentum in Germany in the nineteenth century. In the Weimar Republic, following the loss of lands in the East, this interest was injected with a new impetus.[160] *Osteuropaforschung* (the study of eastern Europe) and later *Ostforschung* (the study of the East) documented German societies across east-central Europe often with an anti-Slavic and *völkisch* bent.[161] Yet, interest in all things German extended beyond the far-right milieu. Publications in interwar Germany covered 'Germanness' across the globe, including Germans in Romania. In a special issue of the journal *Deutsche Kultur in der Welt*, titled *Deutschland und der Osten*, one Dr Franze published an exposé on Germanness in Romania.[162] Franze enthused about the foundation myths of Saxons and Swabians, and he was particularly taken by the notion of Saxon superiority. He even contended that German culture in Wallachia and Moldova – in reality a minor presence – had helped to establish the two principalities' regal culture.[163] The city of Iaşi, Franze claimed, was actually of German origin.

[160] See Loránt Tilkovszky, 'Die Weimarer Republik und die Nationalitäten in Südosteuropa, mit besonderer Berücksichtigung der deutschen und ungarischen Minderheiten in Rumänien', in König (ed.), *Siebenbürgen zwischen den beiden Weltkriegen*, pp. 115–27.
[161] For an excellent history of *Ostforschung, Osteuropaforschung*, and other scholarly focus on east-central Europe, see Michael Burleigh, *Germany Turns Eastwards: A Study of* Ostforschung *in the Third Reich* (Cambridge: Cambridge University Press, 1988), esp. pp. 22–39. For a longer history of German interest in 'the East', see Liulevicius, *The German Myth of the East*.
[162] Dr Franze, 'Das Deutschtum in Rumänien', *Deutsche Kultur in der Welt* (Special Issue: *Deutschland und der Osten: Eine Betrachtung der völkischen und wirtschaftlichen Beziehungen der Deutschen mit den Ländern des Ostens*) 6/1 (1920), pp. 41–4.
[163] Ibid., p. 41.

Foreshadowing the commonalities of a Romanian German diaspora, he identified three periods of *Deutschtum* in Romania: the initial arrival of Saxons in the twelfth century; the Reformation period in the sixteenth and seventeenth centuries; and, third, the arrival of Swabians in the Banat and the southern edge of the Carpathians in the eighteenth century. These two groups were treated as separate in provenance, but their stories were woven together into a longer, common Romanian German narrative.[164] Time and again, Franze emphasised the importance of the presence of German culture for the development of Romania and the southern Carpathians.[165]

And then there were the threats: German-language newspapers in Romania, such as the *Bukarester Tageblatt*, stood no chance against the 'enormous capitalist superpower of the great Romanian dailies', Franze continued.[166] Echoing Saxon and Swabian fears, Franze found it 'very difficult indeed to speak of the possibility of a continuation of Germanness in Romania, given these circumstances [following the First World War and the enlargement of the Romanian state]'.[167] Meanwhile, German newspapers extended their coverage of Romanian Germans, giving a voice to Romanian German writers. The *Hamburger Nachrichten* announced 'German Hardship in Romania' to its readers in 1930.[168] The presbytery in Sibiu reported a drying up of funds since Transylvania had become part of Romania.[169] In the same issue, the newspaper surveyed the latest findings on the origins of Transylvanian Saxons.[170] Other papers from Germany followed suit: in April 1930, the *Schwäbischer Merkur* published a report on the origins – the *Urheimat* – of Transylvanian Saxons.[171] Citing the work of Bernhard Capesius, the renowned linguist from Transylvania, both newspapers portrayed Saxons as a German '*Mischvolk* [mixed race]' from all over the German Lands and not just from Moselle-Franconia.[172] Transylvanian Saxons were seen as representatives from the whole of Germany. Germans in Romania were being courted as 'one of us', ordinary yet proud Germans who deserved to

[164] Ibid., pp. 40, 41.   [165] Ibid., pp. 42, 43.   [166] Ibid., p. 44.
[167] Ibid. Original: Es ist außerordentlich schwierig, unter diesen Umständen überhaupt von der Möglichkeit eines Fortbestehens des Deutschtums in Rumänien zu sprechen.
[168] 'Deutsche Not in Rumänien', *Hamburger Nachrichten* 139 (257)/145, 27 March 1930.   [169] Ibid.
[170] 'Die Urheimat der Siebenbürger Sachsen', *Hamburger Nachrichten* 139 (257)/145, 27 March 1930.
[171] 'Die Urheimat der Siebenbürger Sachsen', *Schwäbischer Merkur*, 3 April 1930.
[172] 'Die Urheimat', *Hamburger Nachrichten*, and 'Die Urheimat', *Schwäbischer Merkur*. These articles can also be found in Bernhard Capesius's legacy in the Siebenbürgisches Institut; see Siebenbürgisches Institut, B I 56, 3/2.

be heard. Romanian Germans were also under threat and were suffering, they were told by Germans in Germany proper.

Such publications did not exist in a vacuum. Instead, they formed part of a network between Germany and Romania and Austria that inscribed and affirmed notions of Germanness in Romania. Cross-references in publications in Germany, Romania, and Austria formed a transnational web around Romanian German identity. Ernst Zander, in a press review in *Deutsche Kultur in der Welt* published in Leipzig, cited an article by Transylvanian Saxon linguist and historian Adolf Schullerus on the church and schools in Bessarabia.[173] Schullerus lobbied strongly for the unification of the Protestant Church of Bessarabia and the Protestant Church of Transylvania. The author saw this as a welcome development that might help protect Germanness in Romania.[174] Such comments on the state of Germans in Romania resonated in Germany and, in turn, helped shape the German discourse on Romanian Germans. Pooling resources rather than insisting on regional divisions set the agenda for the future of Romanian Germans. In any case, as the Klagenfurter *Alpenländische Rundschau* reminded its readers in 1936, Transylvanian Saxons and Banat Swabians were simply part of the greater German nation.[175]

Exchanges between writers in Germany, Romania, and Austria inscribed the main themes of Romanian German histories in the twentieth century. Again, it was Viktor Orendi-Hommenau, the Saxon champion of Swabians, who played a crucial role in this. Writing in 1929 in *Heimat und Welt*, the yearbook of the Leipziger Deutsche Kulturpolitische Gesellschaft (Leipzig German Cultural Political Association), Orendi-Hommenau explained the Swabian *Leidensweg* to a German audience. The last two decades of the Austro-Hungarian Empire had been the 'most difficult times in the Banat'.[176] Germans were aware of Romanian German narratives, and Romanian Germans gladly received German writing on themselves. In extensive correspondence between luminaries and writers in Romania and Germany, both before and after 1933, Orendi-Hommenau continued to weave a network of correspondence that reinforced the message: Swabians suffered ordeals, Germans suffered ordeals, and Romanian Germans became a community of fate.[177]

[173] Adolf Schullerus, 'Kirche und Schule in Beßarabien', cited in Ernst Zander, 'Rundschau', *Deutsche Kultur in der Welt* 6/4 (1920), pp. 41–2.
[174] Ibid., p. 42.
[175] 'Volk – Nation – Nationalismus', *Alpenländische Rundschau*, 27 June 1936, p. 4.
[176] Viktor Orendi-Hommenau, 'Aus schwerster Zeit im Banat', *Heimat und Welt: Beiträge zur Kulturpolitik, Auslandskunde und Deutschtumforschung* 11/16 (1929), pp. 35–40.
[177] Gudrun-Liane Ittu, 'Vom Ministerialrat, geschätzten Publizisten und Übersetzer zum mittellosen Bittsteller: Viktor Orendi-Hommenau (1870–1954) im Jahre 1944', *Germanistische Beiträge* 28 (2011), pp. 56–66.

Orendi-Hommenau was not alone, but he was part of the German world represented in Romania. Austrian newspapers dutifully name-checked German artists and writers in their coverage of *Deutschtum* abroad. Newspapers such as the *Wiener Zeitung* and *Grazer Tagblatt* co-ordinated their reporting of German cultural life outside Austria and Germany. After the Lenau Museum in the municipality of Lenauheim in the Banat opened a German poets' hall (Deutsche Dichterhalle), the two papers listed the names of those Romanian German artists in whose honour the Dichterhalle had been designed. Viktor Orendi-Hommenau was among them.[178] In this view, cultural activists, such as Orendi-Hommenau, belonged to a vanguard of defenders of *Deutschtum* in Romania. In an article from 1926 on Germans in Transylvania and the Banat, the Austrian newspaper *Tiroler Anzeiger* explained Romanian German culture in precisely the terms used by Romanian Germans: superiority, defensiveness, and hardship.[179] Berlin, the article explained, was an important hub for Romanian Germans as a way of gaining international recognition.

The dissemination – as well as the broader reception – of intricate details of Germans in Romania was a crucial task for Romanian Germans. Scholars such as Karl Kurt Klein (1897–1971), a prominent Transylvanian Saxon academic, did much for the field of Transylvanian studies. He brought regional histories to the fore, made them accessible to a broader, international audience, and helped to shape a Romanian German community. As the founder of the *Siebenbürgische Vierteljahresschrift*, he set the agenda for Transylvanian studies in Romania and abroad.[180] Klein did not confine his writings to a Romanian German audience and published widely in Austria and Germany, both in the Weimar Republic and in the Third Reich.[181] He reviewed between thirty and forty books in the Transylvanian Saxon *völkisch* journal *Klingsor*, founded by Adolf Meschendörfer and other

---

[178] 'Eine deutsche Dichterhalle im Banat', *Wiener Zeitung*, 13 September 1932, p. 7, and 'Eine deutsche Dichterhalle im Banat', *Grazer Tagblatt*, 15 September 1932, p. 5.

[179] 'Das Siebenbürger Sachsenland', *Tiroler Anzeiger*, 19 May 1926, pp. 7–8.

[180] The *Siebenbürgische Vierteljahresschrift* was founded in 1931 and published until 1941. It was revived in 1971 by the Arbeitskreis für Siebenbürgische Landeskunde and changed its name to *Zeitschrift für Siebenbürgische Landeskunde* in 1978, which is the name it still goes by. For a good overview of Klein's publication record, see Anton Schwob, 'Fünf Universitäten, vier Staaten und drei Sprachen: Karl Kurt Klein als Lehrer und Forscher', in Peter Motzan, Stefan Sienerth and Anton Schwob (eds.), *Karl Kurt Klein: Leben – Werk – Wirkung* (Munich: Verlag Südostdeutsches Kulturwerk, 2001), pp. 9–20.

[181] Sigurd Paul Schleichl, 'Karl Kurt Klein (1897–1971): Aspekte eines vielfältigen germanistischen Lebenswerks', in Motzan, Sienert and Schwob (eds.), *Karl Kurt Klein*, pp. 21–69.

Saxon personalities in 1924.[182] Writing for an increasingly right-wing and *völkisch* readership, Klein set the tone for Romanian German myths.[183] 'They have risen like the phoenix from the ashes', Klein reminisced in 1932 about Transylvanian Saxons through the ages.[184] Saxon history had not been one of 'losses and roll-back'; instead they had stood firm as frontier guards against external threats.[185] His audiences stretched well beyond Romania. In November 1932, Klein spoke to the listenership of *Deutsche Welle* about 'German Men in the *außerdeutscher* South-east'.[186] By 1942, his rhetoric had shifted further towards National Socialist visions of *Deutschtum* in Europe: Klein had now identified 'occidental communities of fate in the south-east of Europe'.[187] In this confluence of ideas, Saxon and Swabian identities did not simply remain separate, but joined up to a Romanian German experience of superiority, threats, and suffering.

Conclusion: Border Changes

Border changes create facts on the ground. For Transylvanian Saxons, Banat Swabians, and other German groups in Romania, new borders meant being part of a polity as a German minority and sharing a common fate for the first time in their history. Living in interwar Romania made the creation of a usable past necessary. Older Saxon and Swabian myths coalesced into a common Romanian German mythology. Against the backdrop of minority rights and German-language education, Saxon history gave Romanian Germans a sense of being in the vanguard of Germanness in a region of religious, cultural, and political diversity and tensions. Their stories formed the material for the themes of superiority and privilege, on the one hand, and being under siege, on the other, in Romanian German identity narratives. But it was the Swabian ingredient of the *Leidensweg* and the rural world that made Romanian German

---

[182] For a very good article on the context of the right-wing shift among Transylvanian Saxons, see Cristian Cercel, 'The Relationship between Religious and National Identity in the Case of Transylvanian Saxons, 1933–1944', *Nationalities Papers* 39/2 (2011), pp. 161–80. Chapter 3 deals with *Klingsor* in more depth.

[183] Peter Motzan, 'Wegbegleiter und Wegbereiter: Karl Kurt Klein und die "siebenbürgische Zeitschrift" *Klingsor* (1924–1939)', in Motzan, Sienert and Schwob (eds.), *Karl Kurt Klein*, p. 164.

[184] Karl Kurt Klein, 'Finis Saxoniae? Nein!', *Siebenbürgisch-Deutsches Tageblatt*, 27 August 1932, in Karl Kurt Klein (ed.), *Saxonica Septemcastrensia: Forschungen, Reden und Aufsätze aus vier Jahrzehnten zur Geschichte der Deutschen in Siebenbürgen* (Marburg: N. G. Elwert Verlag, 1971), pp. 12–14.

[185] Ibid., p. 13.   [186] *Radio-Wien*, 1 November 1932, p. 49.

[187] Karl Kurt Klein, 'Abendländische Schicksalsgemeinschaft im Südostraum', *Südostdeutsche Rundschau* 1/1 (1942), in Klein (ed.), *Saxonia*, pp. 43–53.

identity debates such a potent force both inside Romania and in Germany and Austria.

The Banat's position as a borderland played a decisive role in this, as a quirk of geopolitical history made the visible representation of Swabian hardship and suffering a central theme for Romanian Germans. The Romanian–Yugoslav border ran through the region of Jimbolia/Hatzfeld where Stefan Jäger lived. But, unlike other towns and villages in the Banat that had become Romanian after the First World War, Hatzfeld was initially incorporated into the Kingdom of Serbs, Croats, and Slovenes. Jäger's name and work found, unsurprisingly, no reception in the new and buoyant Romanian German press. After all, he was not part of their world, but a German in the Serbian part of Yugoslavia. All the while, German newspapers from the Romanian–Yugoslav borderlands, such as the *Hatzfelder Zeitung*, based in Jäger's hometown, were more concerned with the rapid erosion of minority rights under the new Yugoslav state.

Žombolj, as it was then called, remained Yugoslav from the Treaty of Trianon in 1920 until January 1924 when a border revision between Romania and the Kingdom of Serbs, Croats, and Slovenes saw a small number of villages swap places across the border. Žombolj became Jimbolia and Romanian, which dragged Jäger and his triptych beyond its local Swabian reception and into the Romanian German orbit. Jäger's small world of Jimbolia now patronised Germans on the Yugoslav side of the border by worrying about Yugoslav German rights from a position of relative privilege in Romania and by covering these issues in local Romanian German newspapers. If their German compatriots stuck in Yugoslavia were worthy of pity, the growing authoritarianism in Romania in the 1930s amplified a sense of besiegement for Romanian Germans, too. As their world collapsed around them by the end of the Second World War, that crucial Swabian foundation narrative of the *Leidensweg* became the linchpin for Romanian German identity. The close proximity of both success and catastrophe would be a crucial theme in Romanian Germans' stories. It was these older narratives from the Saxon and Swabian communities respectively that made it possible for Romanian Germans not only to think of themselves as a group with a common destiny, but also to make sense of their catastrophic experiences in the twentieth century.

Scholarly claims that Romanian German identities are 'artificial', therefore, miss the point.[188] Being Romanian German could coexist with local

---

[188] See, for instance, Annemarie Weber, *Rumäniendeutsche? Diskurse zur Gruppenidentität einer Minderheit (1944–1971)* (Cologne: Böhlau, 2010). Weber follows tradition by claiming that the notion of being 'Romanian German' meant little to nothing to Germans in Romania.

and regional identities. Stefan Jäger was the *Schwabenmaler*, and yet his life and work also resonated more broadly as a Romanian German story. Likewise, Adolf Meschendorfer's poetry was emphatically Saxon while becoming Romanian German in its rural gaze and in its later reception by Romanian Germans other than Saxons. While older identities – regional, religious, and otherwise – persisted after 1918, the sudden creation of the Romanian German community constitutes a classic case of identity formation in modern Europe.[189] It is the seemingly arbitrary nature of this development that is so interesting, since it lays bare the synthetic processes of identity formation itself. By engaging with Romanian Germans' attempts at explaining and narrating their own deep history, this chapter has laid the foundation for the rest of the book, tapping into the voices that allow us to craft knowledge of the community and its formation over the course of the twentieth century and into the twenty-first.

---

[189] A good example of this is a recent study on Germans in Hungary; see Swanson, *Tangible Belonging*.

CHAPTER 2

Transnational Germans

The history of Romanian Germans is often told backwards. By the end of the Cold War, they were leaving Romania for (West) Germany in droves, which seemed like the culmination of an inexorable force pulling them towards their foregone conclusion: Germans from Romania had, to varying degrees, always felt drawn to their 'real' homeland, Germany.[1] Romanian German explanations of their own historical trajectory following the Second World War oscillated between a sense of injustice over the Romanian communist regime's attempts at ostracising them and an insistence that they had always really belonged to Germany.[2] An examination of Romanian German networks and their relationships with Romania, Germany, and the rest of Europe, as well as their global connections, complicates this picture. Their sense of belonging often shifted and was punctuated by events, personal connections, and changing political landscapes. Recent studies on other minorities in Europe have also elucidated that minority identities resist simple, linear explanations,[3] and Romanian Germans are no different in that respect. Multiple networks of loyalties and

---

[1] Examples from 'partisan literature' abound; a good example of a scholarly interpretation reading their history backwards is Annemarie Weber, *Rumäniendeutsche? Diskurse zur Gruppenidentität einer Minderheit (1944–1971)* (Cologne: Böhlau, 2010). Likewise, much of the *Landsmannschaft* literature reinforced the narrative that Germany was the Romanian Germans' true home.

[2] The two opposing views, fleshed out in this chapter, are that of the *Landsmannschaften* and that of writers who were often close to the church, especially the Lutheran Church in Transylvania.

[3] See, for instance, James E. Bjork, *Neither German nor Pole: Catholicism and National Indifference in a Central European Borderland* (Ann Arbor: University of Michigan Press, 2009), Mark Cornwall, 'Loyalty and Treason in Late-Habsburg Croatia: A Violent Political Discourse before the First World War', in Jana Osterkamp and Martin Schulze Wessel (eds.), *Exploring Loyalty* (Göttingen: Vandenhoeck & Ruprecht, 2017), pp. 97–120, Tomasz Kamusella, *Silesia and Central European Nationalisms: The Emergence of National and Ethnic Groups in Prussian Silesia and Austrian Silesia, 1848–1918* (Lafayette, Ind.: Purdue University Press, 2007), John Eicher, *Exiled among Nations: German and Mennonite Mythologies in a Transnational Age* (Cambridge: Cambridge University Press, 2020), and John Swanson, *Tangible Belonging: Negotiating Germanness in Twentieth-Century Germany* (Pittsburgh: University of Pittsburgh Press, 2017).

disloyalties – even indifference[4] – came together in a period of fast-moving politics to play a decisive role in situating Romanian Germans in the twentieth century within a fundamentally transnational picture.

This chapter examines the ways in which Romanian Germans explored multiple possibilities in their search to define a *Heimat*, mainly in the period after 1945, taking us beyond the known narrative of the 'other homeland' in Germany. The question of where they belonged was the most hotly contested issue in the twentieth century, and it turned particularly acute during the Cold War, as the Romanian German community became more fractured and physically separated. Romanian German identity in this period, this chapter argues, was flexible and far more transnationally defined than is often assumed. At its heart were opposing views of 'regionalism', nationalism, and other forms of belonging. Romanian German identity debates operated on different scales in the community, which made identity contestation particularly messy.[5] Romanian Germans debated their place intensely by considering their local roots, their links to the broader German-speaking world, and, to a more limited extent, even their 'overseas' connections. Their own battles over identity and belonging revealed the intricacies and nuances of Romanian German concepts of an 'external homeland'. Their relationships to other places – often, but not always, Germany – were under constant review and discussion.[6] Germany, of course, loomed large in this picture, but it was never the monolithic entity,[7] nor was it the only alternative *Heimat* to make a mark on Romanian German self-understanding.

---

[4] There is a vast literature on 'national indifference', especially for modern east-central European history. See, for instance, Pieter Judson, *Guardians of the Nations: Activists on the Language Frontiers of Imperial Austria* (Cambridge, Mass.: Harvard University Press, 2006), Tahra Zara, *Kidnapped Souls: National Indifference and the Battle for Children in the Bohemian Lands, 1900–1948* (Ithaca, N.Y.: Cornell University Press, 2008), and a recent edited volume with examples from across Europe, Maarten van Ginderachter and Jon Fox (eds.), *National Indifference and the History of Nationalism in Modern Europe* (New York: Routledge, 2019).

[5] For a study on interwar regionalism and conflicting nationalisms, see Florian Kührer-Wielach, *Siebenbürgen ohne Siebenbürger? Zentralstaatliche Integration und politischer Regionalismus nach dem Ersten Weltkrieg* (Munich: De Gruyter, 2014).

[6] Here, I will draw on existing literature on the concept of identity formation: Karl Kaser, *Südosteuropäische Geschichte und Geschichtswissenschaft* (Cologne: Böhlau, 2002), in particular, pp. 95–118, and Rogers Brubaker, *Nationalism Reframed: Nationhood and the National Question in the New Europe* (Cambridge: Cambridge University Press, 1996), pp. 55–76.

[7] Pieter Judson's work, in particular, has resisted a nation-centric analysis of diasporas. See Pieter Judson, 'When Is a Diaspora not a Diaspora? Rethinking Nation-Centered Narratives about Germans in Habsburg East Central Europe', in Krista O'Donnell, Renate Bridenthal and Nancy Reagin (eds.), *The Heimat Abroad: The Boundaries of Germanness* (Ann Arbor: University of Michigan Press, 2005), pp. 219–47.

Affiliation with Germany – be it as a *Kulturnation* (cultural nation), as the Third Reich, the Federal Republic of Germany (FRG), or the German Democratic Republic (GDR) – bolstered Romanian German anxieties in the face of an imminent exodus from their 'actual' homeland, Romania, during the Cold War. By the 1980s, it was becoming apparent that the Romanian German community was dissolving. Large numbers of Saxons and Swabians were leaving Romania for the Federal Republic of Germany and the end of the community was clearly in sight. The German churches in Romania struggled with the rapid changes happening in their communities.[8] The Lutheran Church, in particular, had been at the heart of the Transylvanian Saxon community. And, while its central place had been undermined from the 1920s, the visible disappearance of church members, as they left Romania for Germany in real time, was far more of an existential threat than the power struggles of the 1930s or the Cold War of rival Romanian German groups against the hegemony of the church. If the church pleaded with its community to stay in Romania, the experience of queueing for bread during the economic hardships of late communist Romania won the argument and seemed to finish off long-standing communities. Resistance by the churches – especially the Lutheran Church in Transylvania – to mass emigration lost out to the lure of the imagined new homeland of Germany. Egged on by the *Landsmannschaften* (homeland societies) of both the Transylvanian Saxons and the Banat Swabians in Germany, it seemed an open-and-shut case: what was the point of staying in Romania, where times were desperate? The Germans were at the end of their 'historic mission'.[9] In any case, as the writer Hans Bergel (1925–) mused in 1982, why would anyone want to subject Germans in Romania to the terrible conditions and persecutions of communist Romania by encouraging them to stay, especially since they had an easy way out by escaping to West Germany?[10]

The twentieth century had begun for Romanian Germans with uncertainties and possibilities for the future, and it ended in certainty and migration to Germany. In between, however, was a short century of intense ideas and negotiations that transcended a straightforward choice between two nation-states. Romania was not simply understood by

[8] See, for example, Christoph Klein, *Auf dem andern Wege: Aufsätze zum Schicksal der Siebenbürger Sachsen als Volk und Kirche* (Erlangen: Martin-Luther-Verlag, 1986).
[9] Hans Hartl, 'Am Ende einer historischen Aufgabe', in Oskar Schuster (ed.), *Epoche der Entscheidungen: Die Siebenbürger Sachsen im 20. Jahrhundert* (Cologne: Böhlau, 1984), pp. 370–88.
[10] Hans Bergel, 'Was soll denn noch mit diesen Menschen geschehen dürfen?', in Schuster (ed.), *Epoche der Entscheidungen*, pp. 389–95.

Romanian Germans as a 'nationalising' homeland, but it was – at times at least – a state towards which Germans felt a good degree of loyalty. As far as 'Germany' was concerned, things were not as straightforward as they seemed. There were numerous incarnations of 'external' homelands: the dying Habsburg Empire, the second German Empire, Hungary, Austria, Weimar Germany, the Third Reich, the Federal Republic of Germany, the German Democratic Republic, reunified Germany, and a whole host of other vague associations, from Switzerland to Canada to the United States. These places elicited different responses and fantasies from Germans in Romania, and they often split communities as they tried to find their 'correct' place in twentieth-century Europe. In the end, a glorified image of a historic, 'apolitical', and affluent West Germany emerged as an integral part of Romanian German identity and contributed in the most significant way towards the exodus at the close of the twentieth century.[11] Romanian Germans left for their new home in Germany, seen as superior to their environs in south-east 'Balkan' Europe.

Destinations

Long before the beginning of the twentieth century, Germans around the southern Carpathians had a long-standing and multifarious relationship to a German homeland elsewhere. Emotional ties to Germany were partly rooted in the migratory patterns of Saxons and Swabians from the twelfth and eighteenth centuries respectively, but they were also a product of a 'national awakening' across central and eastern Europe from the late eighteenth century.[12] Although Saxons still drew on an identity of high privilege in the eighteenth century, the reforms by Emperor Josef II in 1784 abolished the centuries-old feudal structures in Transylvania.[13] Many of the special privileges the Saxons had enjoyed since 1224 were gone.[14] For Paul Philippi (1923–2018), an opponent of immigration to Germany, the

---

[11] James Koranyi and Ruth Wittlinger, 'From Diaspora to Diaspora: The Case of Transylvanian Saxons in Romania and Germany', *Nationalism and Ethnic Politics* 17/1 (2011), pp. 96–115.

[12] By Germany, I loosely mean the 'German Lands'; see Rainer Ohliger, 'Vom Vielvölkerstaat zum Nationalstaat: Migration aus und nach Rumänien', in Heinz Fassmann and Rainer Münz (eds.), *Migration in Europa: Historische Entwicklung, aktuelle Trends und politische Reaktionen* (Frankfurt am Main: Campus, 1996), pp. 285–302; see also Paul Philippi, 'Nation und Nationalgefühl der Siebenbürger Sachsen 1791–1991', in Hans Rothe (ed.), *Die Siebenbürger Sachsen in Geschichte und Gegenwart* (Cologne: Böhlau, 1994), pp. 69–87.

[13] Keith Hitchins, *The Romanians, 1774–1886* (Oxford: Oxford University Press, 1996), p. 207.

[14] István Keul, *Early Modern Religious Communities in East-Central Europe: Ethnic Diversity, Denominational Plurality, and Corporative Politics in the Principality of Transylvania (1526–1691)* (Leiden: Brill, 2009), pp. 30–3.

late 1780s and early 1790s ushered in the beginning of modern German history in Transylvania: Josef II's death in 1790 and Mozart's in 1791 marked the political and cultural onset of the modern and final era of Transylvanian Saxons in the region.[15] After that, Germans, most prominently Saxons and Swabians, began negotiating new forms of identity in which references to Germany – in all its forms – played a greatly enhanced role. Association with German culture, from 'over there', became a defining way of confirming German privileges and superiority when faced with the erosion of those rights in the political restructuring of the nineteenth century. This relationship – an imagined and carefully cultivated link to a German homeland elsewhere – framed the history of Romanian Germans in the twentieth century. The new European order after the First World War made possible even stronger links to an imagined Germany, but many identity debates were entrenched in older Saxon and Swabian narratives. A school book for Saxon students in Transylvania claimed in 1844 that Germans are

> forsooth [*fürwahr*] a great, mighty people. To belong to them must be our pride. Back in the old times, the Germans had already been an excellent people: very tall, robust, agile, trained in using weapons, pious, loyal, full of valour ... Even now there is no people that is more educated, more jovial [*gemütlicher*], more God-fearing, more courageous, more efficient [*tüchtiger*], more persevering, and more even-handed towards others than the German people; yes, they beat all the other peoples on earth in many respects. No other can boast [such] heroes, inventors, artists, scholars – in short, excellent men – than the German people.[16]

As part of German nationalism in the German Lands, the 1840s witnessed the eruption of intense discussions around the topic of Saxon identity. The regional identity of Saxons came under pressure from pan-German nationalism, as the extract exemplifies. As a precursor to responses to the rise of National Socialism in the interwar period, Transylvanian Saxons became captivated by the issue of their 'rootedness' (*Verwurzelung*). For some, Germany represented their true *Heimat*, which was a 'utopian place of arrival [and] ... a frame of mind'.[17] By the last few decades of the nineteenth century, two camps had emerged. The contest over *kleinsächsische Verwurzelung* (lesser Saxon rootedness) and the *alldeutscher Geist* (greater German spirit) was battled out in diverse publications and

---

[15] Philippi, 'Nation und Nationalgefühl', pp. 69–70.   [16] Cited ibid., pp. 73, 74.
[17] Elizabeth Boa and Rachel Palfreyman, *Heimat: A German Dream – Regional Loyalties and National Identity in German Culture 1890–1990* (Oxford: Oxford University Press, 2000), p. 195.

public associations and would remain at the heart of identity debates throughout the twentieth century.[18]

Nineteenth-century Transylvanian Saxon literature epitomised this conflict. Some, such as Joseph Halter (1822–86) and Friedrich Wilhelm Schuster (1824–1914), collected and collated Transylvanian German stories as a way of preserving a local Transylvanian identity.[19] The *Kleinsachsen* advocated that Transylvania should still be regarded as a distinct homeland, which would not benefit from a closer association with Germany.[20] Others, however, regarded Transylvanian Saxon cultural heritage as part of the greater German *Kulturnation*. In his collections of German songs in Transylvania, published 1847 and 1851, Johann Friedrich Geltch (1815–51) defined Saxon culture as a quintessential part of the German cultural sphere. Lifting Transylvanian 'folk songs' out of the 'confinement of the province' and placing them at the heart of German nationalism, Geltch and others represented a growing trend to balance out Transylvania's loss of political autonomy by attaching Saxons to the greater German project.[21] Schoolbooks, as the quotation above demonstrates, taught young Germans in Transylvania to feel themselves part of German greatness, while so-called *Nachbarschaften* (neighbourhoods) in local Saxon villages – a local community support network – emphasised the importance of local loyalties and traditions.

The debates between Jakob Rannicher (1823–1975), G. D. Teutsch (1817–93), and Guido Baussnern (1839–1917) about place and belonging after the Austro-Hungarian compromise of 1867 revealed a disunited Saxon understanding of identity pitched somehow between pan-Germanness and local tradition.[22] Their uncertainty about German nation-building arose in response to efforts from the German Lands to reach out to German minorities across east-central Europe.[23] The Allgemeiner Deutscher Schulverein (ADS, the German school association) was set up in 1880 in Berlin and spread across the Austro-Hungarian

---

[18] See Philippi, 'Nation und Nationalgefühl', pp. 80, 81.

[19] Stefan Sienerth, 'Weltoffenheit und Provinzenge: Die siebenbürgisch-deutsche Literatur von ihren Anfängen bis zum Ausgang des 19. Jahrhunderts', in Rothe (ed.), *Die Siebenbürger Sachsen*, pp. 63, 64.

[20] Philippi, 'Nation und Nationalgefühl', p. 81.

[21] Sienerth, 'Weltoffenheit und Provinzenge', pp. 54–8.

[22] See Jonathan Kwan, 'Transylvanian Saxon Politics and Imperial Germany, 1871–1876', *Historical Journal* 61/4 (2018), pp. 991–1015.

[23] Günter Schödl, 'Am Rande des Reiches, am Rande Der Nation: Deutsche im Königreich Ungarn (1867–1914/18)', in Günter Schödl (ed.), Deutsche Geschichte im Osten Europas: Land an der Donau (Berlin: Siedler Verlag, 1995), pp. 349–455.

Empire. Especially in contested regions such as Transylvania and the Banat, the ADS devoted much attention to, and seemed to indicate, a rapprochement between local Germans and the new Prussian-led German Empire. Yet the internal debates among Transylvanian Saxons revealed a complexity that would lie beneath Romanian German identity in the twentieth century:[24] pan-German enthusiasm met regional stoicism in a battle over local and national identity.

The First World War acted as a catalyst for alignment with Germany. Saxons were able to recast themselves as defenders of a German *Kulturnation* against 'eastern' invaders. For this reason, the interwar period marked a new phase of consolidating an imagined link to Germany in a number of ways.[25] Crucially, though, Germany spoke back more force-fully. Saxons and Swabians had established connections to Germany by studying at German universities; scholars exchanged ideas, religious figures interacted with each other, and travellers explored the German Lands. What changed in the interwar period was the vehemence with which the ties between Germans on the margins – in our case Romanian Germans – and Germany were tightened and institutionalised.[26] Transylvania, in particular, was a hotspot for conflicting identities. Transylvanian Hungarian nationalism was at odds with Romanian nationalism, while an increasing nationalist vein among Germans complicated Transylvanian relations further.[27] At the same time, the regionalist tendency of 'Transylvanianism' conflicted with nationalist movements and was viewed suspiciously as a 'Trojan horse' by central government in Bucharest.[28] And, for Romanian Germans, regional patriotism failed to grip the spirit of the

[24] For an excellent article on the impact of the Allgemeiner Deutscher Schulverein on Transylvanian Saxons, see Jonathan Kwan, 'Transylvanian Saxon Politics, Hungarian State Building and the Case of the *Allgemeiner Deutscher Schulverein*', *English Historical Review* 127/526 (2012), pp. 592–624; see also Philippi, 'Nation und Nationalgefühl', pp. 79–80. For similar studies on Bohemia and the Allgemeiner Deutscher Schulverein, see Pieter Judson, 'Nationalizing Rural Landscapes in Cisleithenia, 1880–1914', in Nancy Wingfield (ed.), *Creating the Other: Ethnic Conflict and Nationalism in Habsburg Central Europe* (New York: Berghahn, 2003), pp. 127–48.
[25] See Chapter 3.
[26] See Neil Gregor, Nils Roemer and Mark Roseman (eds.), *German History from the Margins* (Bloomington: Indiana University Press, 2006), in particular, Eric Kurlander, 'Völkisch-Nationalism and Universalism on the Margins of the Reich: A Comparison of Majority and Minority Liberalism in Germany, 1898–1933', pp. 84–103, and Winson Chu, '"*Volksgemeinschaften unter sich*": German Minorities and Regionalism in Poland, 1918–1939', pp. 104–26.
[27] On Hungarian nationalism and self-determination among the Székely in Transylvania, see Nándor Bárdi, 'Utopias in the Shadow of Catastrophe: The Idea of Székely Self-Determination after the Collapse of Austria-Hungary', in Angela Ilic et al. (eds.), *Blick ins Ungewisse: Visionen und Utopien im Donau-Karpaten-Raum 1917 und danach* (Regensburg: Friedrich Pustet, 2019), pp. 73–94.
[28] Kührer-Wielach, *Siebenbürgen ohne Siebenbürger?*, p. 30.

time, especially since Germans in Germany seemed interested and genuinely enchanted by them. Research into Germans in the East became a focal point in Weimar Germany, where defeat and the loss of territories in the East were essential to interwar political culture.[29] *Ostforschung* injected confidence into otherwise disparate German groups across east-central Europe, and Romanian Germans were no exception to this. It paved the way for a much closer bond between the German periphery and the centre.[30]

Two developments changed the nature of the relationship between Romanian Germans and Germany: first, Romanian Germans became integral to the Nazi war effort, as around 75,000 Romanian German men fought in the Waffen-SS from 1940 until the end of the war.[31] Secondly, and more importantly, the Cold War transformed Germany into a concrete place to which increasing numbers of Romanian Germans wanted to emigrate, namely to 'West Germany'. Their alignment with Nazi Germany and its fallout, as well as the subsequent political division within Europe, turned the Federal Republic of Germany into their ultimate goal. Emigration from Romania to the promised 'West' became an obsession for Romanian Germans during the Cold War. Yet emigration did not settle Romanian German identities. In practice, Romanian Germans continued to live as transnational Germans. As this chapter charts, the nation occupied a prominent position for Romanian Germans, but Romanian German lives and habits during the Cold War presented a transnational picture made up of multiple networks of belonging.

K. und K. Nostalgia

'We were like this with Vienna.' Christa König crossed her index and middle fingers to illustrate the close bond Germans in Transylvania had once felt towards the Habsburg centre. Then she continued: 'For us, Vienna was the most beautiful and the best. And we also liked talking

---

[29] For a longer history of German images of the East, see Vejas Liulevicius, *The German Myth of the East, 1800 to the Present* (Oxford: Oxford University Press, 2009).

[30] This will be explored in more detail in Chapter 3. See Michael Burleigh, *Germany Turns Eastwards: A Study of Ostforschung in the Third Reich* (Cambridge: Cambridge University Press, 1988).

[31] This, too, is explored in more detail in Chapter 3. See also Thomas Casagrande, *Die Volksdeutsche SS-Division 'Prinz Eugen': Die Banater Schwaben und die Nationalsozialistischen Kriegsverbrechen* (Frankfurt am Main: Campus, 2003), and Thomas Casagrande et al., 'The "Volksdeutsche": A Case Study from South-Eastern Europe', in Jochen Böhler and Robert Gerwarth (eds.), *The Waffen-SS: A European History* (Oxford: Oxford University Press, 2016), pp. 209–51.

Viennese, we loved it, everything about it. Our High German [*unser Hochdeutsch*] sounds almost Viennese anyway [...] And we were always very impressed by Vienna.'[32] König, an émigré in her early seventies who left Sibiu in the late 1980s, spoke glowingly of Romanian German connections to Vienna and the Habsburg Empire. Sitting in her flat in Lower Bavaria during an interview in the late 2000s, Christa König jumped between stories in Romania and her emigration from Romania to West Germany. Every so often, she spoke about *Wien*.[33] Her indulgence in *K. und K.* nostalgia[34] seemed almost to deny the vexed history of Saxons, Swabians, and *Zipser* within the Austro-Hungarian Empire and the complicated relations with the empire's successor state, Austria. The First Austrian Republic, 1919–34, struggled to compete with the dominance of the Weimar Republic for the attention of the *Auslandsdeutsche*. The Austrofascist state, 1934–8, was far more proactive in taking a leading role in pan-Germanism, but ceased to exist with the Anschluss in 1938.[35] In any case, Saxons and Swabians initially endorsed, with mixed enthusiasm, the new Romanian regime in Transylvania and the Banat after the First World War.[36] After decades of tension between the German outliers in Transylvania and the Banat, on the one hand, and the imperial centre on the other, 1918 was a moment to cut definitively any formal ties with Vienna.[37] Memories of persecution by the Austrian imperial centre ran deep among Germans around the Carpathian Arc. Protestants, such as the Transylvanian Saxons, had felt the heat of the anti-Protestant political culture of Empress Maria Theresa in the second half of the eighteenth century while watching their special privileges dwindle over the coming century.[38] Other groups, such as the *Landler*, suffered the ignominy of

---

[32] Interview with Christa König and Robert König, 14 February 2005, Passau. References to the Habsburg past were made by just under half the respondents, twenty-eight of whom were émigrés. In the main, these references were positive, but also expressed a degree of difference and distance.

[33] This link was also quite tangible in the similarities in architecture and cityscapes throughout the region when compared to Austrian cities; see Harald Heppner, 'Wien als Orientierungsraum städtischer Gestaltung im Karpatenraum', *Transylvanian Review* 14/1 (2005), pp. 69–79.

[34] *K. und K.* is an abbreviation for *kaiserlich und königlich* (imperial and royal) and became a synonym for the Habsburg Empire.

[35] See Julie Thorpe, *Pan-Germanism and the Austrofascist State, 1933–1938* (Manchester: Manchester University Press, 2011), esp. chapter 3.

[36] Harald Roth, *Kleine Geschichte Siebenbürgens* (Cologne: Böhlau, 2012), p. 123.

[37] Ibid., pp. 105–9, and Gerald Volkmer, *Die Siebenbürgische Frage (1878–1900)* (Cologne: Böhlau, 2004), pp. 54–8.

[38] For more detail on the religious intricacy of Transylvania, see Volker Leppin and Ulrich A. Wien (eds.), *Konfessionsbildung und Konfessionskultur in Siebenbürgen in der Frühen Neuzeit* (Stuttgart: Franz Steiner Verlag, 2005).

deportation to Transylvania at the hands of the anti-Protestant Austrian fervour.[39] Many of the Germans who would later constitute the Romanian Germans had already been disconnected from the Austrian centre for decades before the end of the First World War.

Even in the mid-2000s, this history still mattered. Christa König fluctuated between a certain wistfulness towards Habsburg Austria and local defiance towards past imperial rule:

> The only thing they didn't manage to push through [*durchsetzen*] was their Catholicism. They tried to win over hearts and minds by building churches, but that didn't change anything [*es hat keinen Abbruch getan*]. The Transylvanians [*Siebenbürger*] stayed Protestant. But apart from that they [the Transylvanian Saxons] were wholeheartedly pro-Austrian. There were also advantages to that. As soon as the *K&K* [imperial] officers turned up [in Transylvania], they got whichever women they wanted, our women.[40]

The Habsburg Empire had been a major constituent of Saxon and German identity in the region, but it also remained at odds with it.[41] A pre-modern relic, the Habsburg centre had clashed with Saxons over religion and self-governance. In König's story, Austrians fraternised with 'their' women by simply taking them. But Vienna had never stirred the same passions that a *German* homeland would in the twentieth century. Other respondents in oral history interviews mentioned Austria, too, accentuating the tension between competing visions of belonging. Johann Simon, a retiree who had stayed in Sibiu, explained:

> Transylvanian Saxons developed an awareness of all things German [*Deutschbewusstsein*] [...] Here the Transylvanian Saxons felt part of the German *Kulturnation* and not part of the German state [*Staatsnation*]. Oddly enough that changed while Bismarck was in power. As you know, Bismarck defeated Austria. Catholic Austria had exercised great pressure on Protestant Transylvania, not only on the Germans in Transylvania, but also the Hungarians of Transylvania. The whole principality of Transylvania came under immense pressure from Catholics [*katholisierender Druck*]. That is why Transylvanian Saxons felt closer to the Protestant Prussian-dominated

[39] Stefan Steiner, *Reise ohne Wiederkehr: Die Deportation von Protestanten aus Kärnten 1734–1736* (Munich: Oldenbourg, 2007), pp. 16–24.
[40] See ibid. Religious difference from the Habsburg Empire and its Austrian successor state played a big role for Transylvanian Saxons. Of the twenty-six Saxons who spoke about the Habsburg past, twelve highlighted the importance of confessional differences. Although in some cases this point was only made in passing, it nevertheless underlined the real importance of religion for Transylvanian Saxons.
[41] Since all respondents spoke about their images of Germany, those interviewees who did talk about the Habsburg past therefore also juxtaposed images of Germany with those of the Habsburg Empire.

Germany under Bismarck. Even then the affiliation wasn't really political in nature, but it was rather more idealistic and enthusiastic [*schwärmerisch*]. You could say that Richard Wagner was kind of a symbol for an emotionally elevated Germanness [*pathetisches Deutschtumsgefühl*], but one which had nothing to do with the German *state* [emphasis added].[42]

The Habsburg monarchy mattered to Transylvanian Saxons, even to those who had been born after the demise of the former empire, not necessarily as a positive reference point, but as a unconvincing counterpoint to Germany.

But the Cold War saw a rise in 'Kakania nostalgia' – that is nostalgia for Austria-Hungary – among Romanian Germans. How so? Part of the answer lies in the way the Romanian German community *lived* during the Cold War. *K. und K.* nostalgia was everywhere: in the midst of Cold War politics, Romanian Germans would still drink their coffee at the hotel Römischer Kaiser in Sibiu, a site of deep Habsburg nostalgia in the region. Émigrés would read the regular column 'Aus der K. und K. Zeit' ('From Habsburg times') in the *Siebenbürgische Zeitung*, the main émigré newspaper in West Germany. Here, they would learn about eccentric fencing masters and other misfits who struggled to adapt to the new political situation after 1918.[43] Readers were able to reminisce with wry humour about a bygone age when people spoke differently, acted differently, and 'had class'.[44] And yet they also remembered their uneven relationship with the Habsburg Empire. How much money had the city fathers of Hermannstadt given away as dowries to imperial officers far away, a writer lamented in the women's supplement of the *Siebenbürgische Zeitung* in 1964.[45] Yet Habsburg nostalgia saw the rediscovery of Romanian German literature on the imperial past. Erwin Neustädter's forgotten novel *Mohn im Ährenfeld* – written in 1943 in the context of Romanian German *Gleichschaltung* – enjoyed a minor revival in the 1970s.[46] The story follows the fate of a Transylvanian Saxon lieutenant who falls in love with the daughter of a disabled, Habsburg-loyal Hungarian colonel while fighting the Hungarian Soviet Republic of Béla Kun in early 1919. The deeply felt connections to the Habsburg Empire gave way to a confused and politically uncertain world after 1918, which seemed to echo Romanian German history.

[42] Interview with Johann Simon, 23 February 2005, Sibiu. It is perhaps somewhat difficult to quantify the range of the responses to the question of 'Germanness'.
[43] 'Aus der K. und K. Zeit', *Siebenbürgische Zeitung*, 25 March 1960, p. 8.   [44] Ibid.
[45] 'Was sie voneinander halten: Von wahren und angedichteten Eigenschaften der verschiedenen Siebenbürger Sachsen', *Siebenbürgische Zeitung*, 15 March 1964, p. 11.
[46] Erwin Neustädter, *Mohn im Ährenfeld* (Munich: Verlag Hans Meschendörfer, 1974).

But these flashbacks to the Habsburg Empire were only superficial. In reality, Austria had seemingly deserted Romanian Germans, while (West) Germany supported them with financial and political acknowledgement.[47] Concern for modern-day Austrian affairs was primarily bound up with worries about the small yet vocal group of Saxon and Swabian compatriots in Austria. The main émigré newspaper dedicated a regular page to news from the *Landsmannschaft* of Transylvanian Saxons in Austria as well as from their regional branches in Austria's eight *Bundesländer*. From the late 1950s, Romanian German émigrés in Austria generated a more visible presence, which also allowed them to reach out to Romanian Germans across the German border. In 1959, Transylvanian Saxons organised their first *Heimattag* (homeland festival) in Wels, Austria. Saxons in West Germany were invited to join them a year later in August 1960, with the *Siebenbürgische Zeitung* advertising the event (Figure 2.1).

Austrian affairs, though, were part of a patronage network that emanated from Romanian Germans in West Germany. In the first few decades of the Cold War, Romanian Germans living in the Federal Republic of Germany were keen to keep up with Austrian issues. The émigré community in Germany suggested how Austrian politics might deal more fairly with the issue of *Lastenausgleich* (equalisation of burdens).[48] Any nostalgic allure of Habsburg Austria was muted by contemporary Austria's palpable indifference towards the plight of Romanian Germans. In response, Romanian Germans conceived of Austria in ever vaguer terms. Wolfgang Amadeus Mozart, for instance, strikingly held no special place in the imaginary of Romanian Germans during their Cold War odysseys.[49] Austria had moved to the mental periphery of the Romanian German imagination, despite

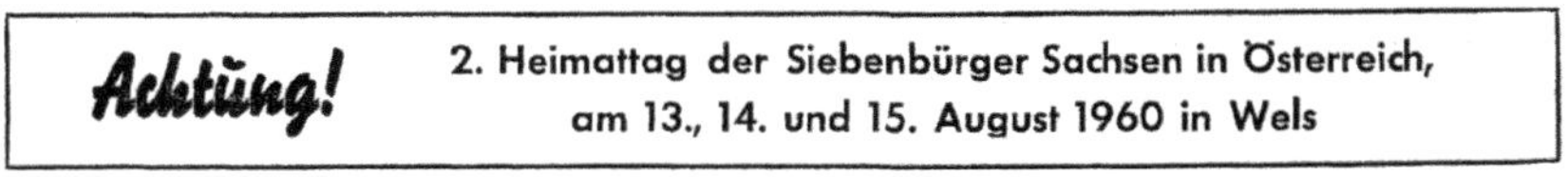

Achtung!   2. Heimattag der Siebenbürger Sachsen in Österreich, am 13., 14. und 15. August 1960 in Wels

Figure 2.1 Advert for the second 'homeland festival' in Wels from the *Siebenbürgische Zeitung*, March 1960.

[47] Ohliger, 'Vom Vielvölkerstaat zum Nationalstaat', pp. 292–3.

[48] For an explanation of the *Lastenausgleich*, see Michael L. Hughes, '"Through No Fault of Our Own": West Germans Remember Their War Losses', *German History* 18/2 (2000), pp. 193–213.

[49] See Philippi, 'Nation und Nationalgefühl', pp. 69–70. Of all the Romanian German respondents, not a single one mentioned Mozart. Philippi's instinct, that world had died in 1791 with Mozart's death, seemed to be confirmed.

their shared common history. In print, Austria's marginalisation became more evident: next to the coverage of émigré politics in Austria, the *Siebenbürgische Zeitung* ran advertisements for the shipping company Hapag Lloyd for emigration to the USA (Figure 2.2). The trans-Atlantic imaginary still exerted a powerful draw on Romanian Germans long after its high point of the late nineteenth and early twentieth centuries.[50] The letters section of the *Siebenbürgische Zeitung* featured correspondence and reports from Romanian German compatriots overseas. The reports were mixed: one anonymous Transylvanian Saxon spoke glowingly of the togetherness among their *Landsleute* (compatriots) in South Africa.[51] Another, however, complained bitterly about the terrible conditions for settlers in northern Paraguay.[52] The anonymous writer warned that 'a European could fall to the level of an Indian' if they settled in the north of that country.[53] The USA, though, continued to hold a special place in the Romanian German imagination. In January 1962, the *Siebenbürgische Zeitung* told of the warm welcome Hermann Oberth (1894–1989), the unconventional Transylvanian Saxon aviation pioneer, received during his visit to Cleveland, Ohio.[54]

Figure 2.2 Advert 'Nach den USA' from *Siebenbürgische Zeitung*, February 1962.

---

[50] On migration to North America, see Tara Zahra, *The Great Departure: Mass Migration from Eastern Europe and the Making of the Free World* (New York: Norton, 2016), and Ulf Brunnbauer, *Globalizing Southeastern Europe: Emigrants, America, and the State since the Late Nineteenth Century* (Lanham, Md.: Lexington Books, 2016).
[51] 'Briefe von nah und fern', *Siebenbürgische Zeitung*, 15 September 1952, p. 3.   [52] Ibid.   [53] Ibid.
[54] Sara D. Schneider, 'Von Unseren Landsleuten in Amerika: Prof. Hermann Oberth bei den Siebenbürger Sachsen', *Siebenbürgische Zeitung*, 15 January 1962, p. 7.

There was a bigger world out there where Germans from Romania and elsewhere in east-central Europe lived and experienced adventures of all kinds. Austria, by contrast, featured only as a problem, where Romanian Germans were unable to get the same levels of support as in West Germany.

For non-émigrés, Austria occasionally still stirred some excitement. When the Austrian chancellor Rudolf Kirchschläger visited Romania in November 1978, the newspaper *Neuer Weg* splashed the event all over its front page for four days running.[55] Some visits by foreign dignitaries deserved more coverage than others, and Austria still occupied a prominent place in the Romanian German world regardless of the political control over the media. Generally, though, Austria's standing among Romanian Germans continued to decline as it lost more and more ground to North America as a possible destination for Romanian Germans and as more and more Germans left Romania. The Habsburg successor transformed mainly into a place of *K.-und-K.* nostalgia.

East German Entanglements

Other places closer to home did more to capture the Romanian German imagination. Dismissed by scholars as a politically impossible place for Germans from Romania, the German Democratic Republic (GDR) in fact played an important role in the construction of Romanian German identities.[56] If Austria was marginalised as a destination in the Romanian German imaginary, the GDR, by contrast, opened up and complicated the Romanian German Cold War world. Romanian Germans were not simply torn between the two ideologically competing states, Romania and the FRG, nor were they bounded by national borders. The presence of the East German state was crucial in making sure of that, and the GDR in fact became a key partner in an intricate pattern of German–German relations between the country and Romania.[57] A reciprocal relationship emerged, in

---

[55] 'Bundespräsident Österreichs, Dr. Rudolf Kirchschläger, in der Hauptstadt eingetroffen', *Neuer Weg* 30/9169, 9 November 1978, pp. 1, 2, 'Im Zeichen gutfreundschaftlicher und gedeihlicher Zusammenarbeit', *Neuer Weg* 30/9170, 10 November 1978, pp. 1, 3, 'Rumänien-Besuch des Bundespräsidenten der Republik Österreich, Dr. Rudolf Kirchschläger', *Neuer Weg* 30/9171, 11 November 1978, pp. 1, 5, and 'Hervorragendes Moment im Ausbau traditioneller Beziehungen in der Freundschaft und Zusammenarbeit', *Neuer Weg* 30/9171, 12 November 1978, pp. 1, 3.

[56] See Ulrich Burger, 'Bundesrepublik oder DDR? Anmerkungen zum Deutschlandbild der Rumäniendeutschen nach 1970', *Transylvanian Review* 12/3 (2003), pp. 63–84.

[57] See, for instance, ibid. and Weber, *Rumäniendeutsche?*, for a more conventional interpretation that the GDR was irrelevant to Romanian Germans. For a revision of this assumption, see James Koranyi, 'Voyages of Socialist Discovery: German–German Exchanges between the GDR and Romania', *Slavonic and East European Review* 92/3 (2014), pp. 479–506.

which a number of institutions and actors created strong networks between the GDR and the German population of Romania. Knowledge of each other – Germans in Romania and German citizens of the GDR – was sketchy to begin with, and the early years of the Cold War formed an exploratory phase between the two countries. The GDR state apparatus was keenly aware of the issues German minorities faced in east-central Europe, and Romania was no exception.[58] For a start, East Germany had to accommodate a large number of German refugees and expellees from the East.[59] By 1950, 25 per cent of the East Germany's population was made up of Germans from east-central Europe.[60] Public debates on expulsions and German victims were constrained by the need to adhere to a pro-Soviet foreign policy 'party line'.[61] From the 1950s, the term *Umsiedler* – expellees from the East in GDR speak – disappeared from the public domain.[62] Yet the issue of Germans from the East was not simply expunged from public memory.[63] Connections to Germans in east-central Europe were simply too strong, and the GDR did in fact develop cultural ties with Romania, and specifically with Romanian Germans, from the 1950s.[64]

The early stages of this connection were circumscribed by greater state involvement and surveillance, and yet these close links between Germans

---

[58] Only a few, such as Stefan Wolff and Karl Cordell, have pointed to some ideological inconsistencies in the GDR's approach towards 'ethnic' Germans in Czechoslovakia. See Stefan Wolff and Karl Cordell, 'Ethnic Germans in Poland and the Czech Republic: A Comparative Evaluation', *Nationalities Papers: The Journal of Nationalism and Ethnicity* 33/2 (2005), pp. 255–76. Examples of recent scholarship that have addressed the German East while neglecting life in the region itself during the Cold War include R. M. Douglas, *Orderly and Humane: The Expulsion of the Germans after the Second World War* (New Haven: Yale University Press, 2012), Andrew Demshuk, *The Lost German East: Forced Migration and the Politics of Memory, 1945–1970* (Cambridge: Cambridge University Press, 2012), Pertti Ahonen, *After the Expulsion: West Germany and Eastern Europe 1945–1990* (Oxford: Oxford University Press, 2003), and Bill Niven (ed.), *Germans as Victims: Remembering the Past in Contemporary Germany* (Basingstoke: Palgrave Macmillan, 2006).

[59] Pertti Ahonen, 'Taming the Expellee Threat in Post-1945 Europe: Lessons from the Two Germanies and Finland', *Contemporary European History* 14/1 (2005), pp. 6–9.

[60] Rainer Schulze, 'The Struggle of Past and Present in Invididual Identities: The Case of German Refugees and Expellees from the East', in David Rock and Stefan Wolff (eds.), *Coming Home to Germany? The Integration of Ethnic Germans from Central and Eastern Europe in the Federal Republic* (New York: Berghahn Books, 2002), p. 38.

[61] See, for instance, Jeffrey Herf, *Divided Memory: The Nazi Past in the Two Germanys* (Cambridge, Mass.: Harvard University Press, 1997), Ahonen, *After the Expulsion*, pp. 200–13, and Ahonen, 'Taming the Expellee Threat', pp. 6–10.

[62] See Philipp Ther, 'Expellee Policy in the Soviet-Occupied Zone and the GDR: 1945–1953', in Rock and Wolff (eds.), *Coming Home to Germany?*, pp. 56–76.

[63] Bill Niven, 'On a Supposed Taboo: Flight and Refugees from the East in GDR Film and Television', *German Life and Letters* 65/2 (2012), pp. 217–36.

[64] See Peter Ulrich Weiß, *Kulturarbeit als diplomatischer Zankapfel: Die kulturellen Auslandsbeziehungen im Dreiecksverhältnis der beiden deutschen Staaten und Rumäniens von 1950 bis 1972* (Munich: R. Oldenbourg Verlag, 2010), pp. 88–106.

from the GDR and Romania played a much bigger role than is generally supposed.[65] Family connections and reciprocal visits, as well as the countries' mutual *Programmarbeit* (cultural programme) ensured a good relationship between the two countries and their German citizens. Romania became a destination for East German backpacking tourists and travellers, especially the mountainous region of Transylvania, where they encountered and befriended local Germans.[66] In the other direction, a small yet noticeable number of Romanian Germans ventured to the GDR: this was the easiest way of exploring 'Germany', since East Germany was far more accessible for Romanian Germans than West Germany.[67] The Cold War world of Romanian Germans was not simply binary between Romania and West Germany; it was part of a transnational Cold War network that included the GDR.

Exchanges with the GDR also had the effect of allowing Romanian Germans to resist, in a small way, the official stance of the Romanian government. Connections, though, were also contingent on the shifting political context throughout the Cold War. Until roughly 1962, the Stasi (the state security in East Germany) and the Securitate (the secret police in Romania) collaborated across borders on information exchange regarding émigrés from Romania and the GDR.[68] Both sides could rally around a common enemy, namely West Germany, caricatured as an appendix to Nazism and the Third Reich.[69]

---

[65] See Koranyi, 'Voyages of Socialist Discovery'.

[66] The most prominent East German 'backpack tourist' to Romania is Chancellor Angela Merkel. According to Romania's former foreign minister and former rector of Babeş-Bolyai University in Cluj-Napoca, Andrei Marga, Merkel visited the two main hotspots for East German tourists: the mountainous Făgăraş region and Mamaia on the Black Sea Coast. I would like to thank Cristian Cercel for pointing this out to me. See Marius Fratila, 'Angela Merkel, în tinereţe, cu rucsacul în spate, în Făgăraş şi la Mamaia', *Gândul*, 17 May 2012, at www.gandul.info/magazin/angela-merkel-in-tinerete-cu-rucsacul-in-spate-in-fagaras-si-la-mamaia-vezi-aici-o-fotografie-de-arhiva-9634903 (accessed 15 Nov. 2017).

[67] For literature on travel and 'escapes' in east-central Europe during communism, see Anne E. Gorsuch and Diane P. Koenker (eds.), *Turizm: The Russian and East European Tourist under Capitalism and Socialism* (Ithaca, N.Y.: Cornell University Press, 2006), especially 'Part II: Socialist Tourism', and Cathleen M. Giustino, Catherine J. Plum and Alexander Vari (eds.), *Socialist Escapes: Breaking Away from Ideology and Everyday Routine in Eastern Europe* (New York: Berghahn, 2013). On Romanian tourism abroad, see Adelina Ştefan, 'Between Limits, Lures and Excitement: Socialist Romanian Holidays Abroad during the 1960s–1980s', in Kathy Burrell and Kathrin Hörschelmann (eds.), *Mobilities in Socialist and Post-Socialist States: Societies on the Move* (London: Palgrave, 2014), pp. 87–104.

[68] Georg Herbstritt has shown in meticulous fashion the development of official East German attitudes and policies vis-à-vis Romania during the Cold War; see Georg Herbstritt, 'Stasi in Siebenbürgen: Eine geheimdienstliche Regionalstudie', *Zeitschrift für Siebenbürgische Landeskunde* 29/2 (2006), p. 188.

[69] 'Bonn bereitet "Wirtschaftssanktionen" vor', *Der Neue Weg*, 23 August 1961, p. 3.

As Romania moved its position under Nicolae Ceauşescu (1965–89) onto politically more neutral ground, the necessity of painting such a polarised picture of Europe began to lose significance. There were a number of reasons for this, including the gradual decline in Soviet–Romanian relations in the 1950s and 1960s as well as Ceauşescu's attempts to normalise relations with the West.[70] Likewise, the new foreign policy direction taken by Ceauşescu's predecessor Gheorghe Gheorghiu-Dej and then by Ceauşescu himself after 1965 turned Romania into a 'hostile fraternal country' for the GDR. The relationship between the two countries – and the position of the Saxons and Swabians within that picture – grew tenser and more complicated. Although the Stasi and Securitate had collaborated at the start of the Cold War, by 1973 both secret security organisations were conducting respective investigations in Romania and GDR independently.[71] Romanian Germans often featured in official documents of the East German Ministry for Security as potential dissidents and separatists.[72]

Romanian Germans developed a paradoxical yet intimate relationship with the GDR. Germans from Romania recognised East Germany as part of the history of the German *Kulturnation*, yet the GDR was also at odds with their image of a historic Germany. Reviewing their relationship with the two Germanys a couple of decades after the fall of the Berlin Wall revealed an odd attitude towards the former GDR. Some respondents rejected the GDR. As one interviewee, Michael Bogdan – who was in his sixties and still in the Banat – explained, going to the GDR would have been a case of 'out of the frying pan and into the fire'.[73] Still, the German Democratic Republic played an important role in shaping an image of Germany.[74] Hermann Frühbeis, a Romanian German who never left the city of Sibiu in southern Transylvania, in fact, asserted that Romanian society had been far less authoritarian than that of the GDR. When asked about the possibility of voicing dissent and discussing political topics,

---

[70] Dennis Deletant, *Communist Terror in Romania: Gheorghiu-Dej and the Police State 1948–1965* (London: Hurst & Company, 1999), pp. 269–88.

[71] See *Dokumente und Materialien der Zusammenarbeit zwischen der Sozialistischen Einheitspartei Deutschlands und der Rumänischen Kommunistischen Partei, 1972 bis 1977* (Berlin: Dietz-Verlag, 1979), p. 187, and Georg Herbstritt, 'Ein feindliches Bruderland: Rumänien im Blick der DDR-Staatssicherheit', *Halbjahresschrift für südosteuropäische Geschichte, Literatur und Politik* 16/1 (2004), pp. 5–13.

[72] Herbstritt, 'Stasi in Siebenbürgen', p. 194.

[73] Interview with Michael Bogdan, 2 August 2005, Sibiu.

[74] Of all the interviewees, only eleven spoke of the GDR in some detail. Of these, nine were in fact non-émigrés. This may well be due to the fact that many émigrés had left before being able to establish any meaningful links with the GDR, such as through teaching exchange programmes.

Frühbeis explained the differences between state socialism in the GDR and
Romania:

> Well, granted, general experiences are always subjective [...] so [these are
> no] more than subjective experiences. Here, everything was far more open
> and easy-going than it was in the GDR. During the entire communist
> period, among family and friends no one spoke highly of the system.
> Everyone thought it was absolute nonsense [*totaler Scheiß*], and that was
> obvious in any and every situation [*zu jeder passenden und unpassenden
> Situation*] ... I can't remember ever feeling any inhibitions during my
> spare time, that is inhibitions to call a spade a spade [*die Dinge beim
> Namen nennen*]. Ceaușescu was a crazy dictator, that's life, and there
> wasn't really anything else we could have said.[75]

Frühbeis's comparison between the GDR and Romania during the Cold
War reveals a long-standing paradox for Romanian Germans. While he
remembered enjoying considerably more freedom in communist
Romania's society when compared to East Germany, it was clear that
both countries were marked by the experience of dictatorship. In the case
of the GDR, this meant an odd and incongruous combination of belonging to the German sphere while being under the control of an authoritarian
system. The combination of a historic Germany and a dictatorial Germany
laid bare the inherent tensions between Cold War politics and Romanian
German images of a German *Kulturnation*. Still, there was something very
German about it, as Frühbeis continued to explain his reasons for visiting
East Germany in 1982:

> Well, I had a number of good friends there [in East Germany], and we
> always ended up having long conversations. We used to stay with friends,
> with so-called GDR citizens [*DDR-Bürger*] whom I had got to know in
> Romania ... So really there were two aspects to this. On the one hand, they
> had all the necessities of life [*das Lebensnotwendigste*], such as foodstuffs,
> health insurance, and all of that, which was an absolute catastrophe in
> Romania. But, on the other hand, there was obviously the heightened
> political pressure. I mean, a teacher would never have been able to work at
> school the way I did ... [it was] far, far more German; not better, not worse,
> but [...] far more precise. All the imprecision [here in Romania] and its
> Balkan tardiness [*balkanische Schlender*] were actually quite beneficial [for
> us] during communism, because no one took anything too seriously, not
> even in politics. That would have been unthinkable [*undenkbar*] in the
> GDR. For example, at my school, we should have attended political educa-
> tion on Mondays at 1 pm, from 1 pm to 3 pm. Come 1.10 pm, there was no

[75] Interview with Hermann Frühbeis, 24 February 2005, Sibiu.

one left ... Everyone just left, and that was a known fact. In the GDR, that would have been absolutely unthinkable.[76]

East Germany's authoritarian state system was also its saving grace. The Romanian system, so it had seemed to Frühbeis, was simply not as good at being authoritarian when compared to its East German counterpart.[77] The GDR represented something German precisely because it was not 'Balkan' in its execution.[78] By contrast, Romanian communism was an unsophisticated and almost benign system characterised by its 'balkanisches Schlendern'.[79] In making these comparisons, Frühbeis stepped into a long tradition of constructing 'Balkan commonality' and 'backwardness', and these ideas were already very prominent again during the Cold War.[80] Articulated in the aftermath of the post-communist world, Romanian communism was reinterpreted as 'backward' while the East German communist state system was, for all its foibles, at least fundamentally German.[81]

What made the GDR German was more than its authoritarian efficiency. Its presence in the Romanian German imaginary transcended both national borders and the 'Iron Curtain'. Oswald Kessler, a philologist from Transylvania, and his friend Willy had both left Romania and continued writing letters to each other in the 1970s and 1980s while living in West Germany. The two letter writers repeatedly pondered the place of Transylvanian Saxons in Europe during the Cold War. Kessler restated

---

[76] See ibid. Such strong differences between the GDR and communist Romania were only rarely articulated. Yet, it is a useful indication of the way in which Germanness and Balkanism have been juxtaposed in Romanian German narratives.

[77] Daniel Ursprung critically challenges the prevalent idea that Romanian communism was different from other forms of communism due to historical continuities in despotism. See Daniel Ursprung, *Herrschaftslegitimation zwischen Tradition und Innovation: Repräsentation und Inszenierung von Herrschaft in der rumänischen Geschichte in der Vormoderne und bei Ceaușescu* (Heidelberg: Studium Transylvanicum, 2007).

[78] There is ample literature on the construction and meaning of the Balkans. While some of it has been revised and critiqued, the pioneering literature on this is still greatly informative, albeit too one-directional. See, for instance, Maria Todorova, *Imagining the Balkans* (Oxford: Oxford University Press, 1997), and Vesna Goldsworthy, *Inventing Ruritania: The Imperialism of the Imagination* (New Haven: Yale University Press, 1998). For revisionist Balkan studies, see, for instance, Wendy Bracewell and Alex Drace-Francis (eds.), *Balkan Departures: Travel Writing from Southeastern Europe* (New York: Berghahn, 2009), and Wendy Bracewell and Alex Drace-Francis (eds.), *Under Eastern Eyes: A Comparative Introduction to East European Travel Writing on Europe* (Budapest: CEU Press, 2008).

[79] Interview Hermann Frühbeis.

[80] See Todorova, *Imagining the Balkans*, pp. 140–1, and Maria Todorova, 'The Balkans: From Discovery to Invention', *Slavic Review* 53/2 (1994), pp. 453–82.

[81] See Todorova, 'The Balkans'. For a good overview of the history of the idea of a backward, other Europe, see Goldsworthy, *Inventing Ruritania*.

time and again that the GDR and Romania belonged to the same favour-
able sphere for Germans in east-central Europe.[82] In socialist Europe, he
asserted, the GDR and Romania were unequivocally the only two countries that allowed Germans to be 'German'.[83] Romanian Germans who had
never left Romania for West Germany reminisced in even more glowing
terms of the former GDR. Visits to the GDR were remembered fondly for
the country's German cultural heritage, and the GDR retained a special
place in the memories of Germans still living in Romania after the Cold
War. Ingrid Aufgang, a teacher in her seventies from southern
Transylvania, remembered her first trip to the GDR in the 1960s. Sitting
in her living room, she indulged her memories of an advanced training
course in Dresden for German teachers from across east-central Europe.
She began by speaking about her experiences of sitting through German
lessons, which had originally been designed for non-native German
speakers.

> There was a person from every [east-central European] country in the
> group, so we had to communicate in German. Many of them weren't very
> fluent [in German], especially when it came to everyday conversations. Of
> course, they knew all about the grammar, and they probably knew some of
> the key texts, you know what it's like when you are learning a foreign
> language. Yet we [the Romanian Germans] had a sort of special status, but
> of course we had to attend [the classes].
> [...] I was in a group on my own with a Yugoslav, a Pole, a Czech,
> a Ukrainian, who was actually from Tbilisi, so from Tiflis [German for
> Tbilisi], a Georgian, she was actually the Russian representative;
> a Hungarian, and she probably spoke the best German, albeit with
> a Hungarian accent. She always said: 'Morning, Ingrid, how are you today
> [*Morgen, Ingrid, wie gäht äss hoite* – spoken with a Hungarian dialect]?' But
> anyhow, somehow she spoke [good] German. So there we were in our little
> group, and the person in charge of these exercises asked me: 'What am I to
> do with you?' So I say: 'That's quite simple: Get me some GDR textbooks.
> I want to see what they teach here, how everything is set out, just to see what
> there is and some of the new literature.' So I sat at the back and read while
> the others did their exercises. And there was also a language lab where we
> took our exams, and they picked me up on my thick 'L',[84] because that's the
> way I pronounce it. I know that. That's because of my [Saxon] dialect . . . If
> I really try hard, I can get rid of it. But why should I? The others had entire

---

[82] Oswald Kessler correspondence with 'Willy', 20 March 1978, IKGS, B 152/3.   [83] Ibid.
[84] This is a characteristic of the Transylvanian Saxon dialect. Similar to Moselle-Franconian and
North Rhine dialects, rather than pronouncing the 'L' at the front of the tongue, Saxons tend to
pronounce it at the back, making it sound 'thick'.

lists [of faults]. They had to listen to tapes and repeat exercises. I had my
books, and I did exactly what I wanted to do.[85]

Ingrid Aufgang was both an insider and an outsider. Her Germanness
set her apart from others, and she placed herself firmly within the German
culture alongside East Germans, yet her pronunciation and dialect were
obvious markers. Her avid interest in GDR textbooks suggested a broader
interest in the GDR.[86] It not only showed that she belonged to Germany,
culturally speaking, regardless of political divisions, but also that the GDR
was very much part of her Germany. Fundamentally, though, the connection she felt to East Germany was more substantial than for the other east-
central Europeans present. Her time in Dresden allowed her to immerse
herself in the cultural nation of Germany, as she fondly pointed out:

> They really put on a show. They showed us around. We had tickets to the
> Zwinger Palace. Whenever we had spare time, we could go and see anything
> we wanted; and that didn't include the official galleries and the official tours,
> which we were rushed through. But we were allowed to see everything
> whenever we wanted to. We also went to see performances with which
> I more or less agreed. We visited the Goethehaus in Weimar.
> [...] That was overwhelming. I really broke down in tears when I was
> there [*dort verrannen einem dann die Tränen*]. Honestly. But the actual
> house, the way it had been done, you've really got to give the GDR credit for
> that; they did a really good job. There were flowers on the windowsill that
> had just been watered. It looked as if he [Goethe] had just gone out, maybe
> into another room. It looked like someone was actually living there. And
> there was also the room he died in, and I must say it was very impressive.[87]

Despite the GDR's position as yet another communist state, the idea of
a German *Heimat* and *Kulturnation* prevailed over an ideological disparity.
The Goethehaus, in the territory of the GDR, was still the Goethehaus; it
was part of the wider cultural capital of 'German heritage' which spoke to
Romanian Germans such as Ingrid Aufgang, who associated themselves
strongly with Germany and Germanness. For them, the political status quo
was an entirely separate issue; historically important literature, architecture, and thought, by contrast, represented unshifting nodal points in
a cultural continuity of what they perceived to be 'Germanness'. Yet
there were always moments of tension: the Goethehaus and the GDR
never fitted together entirely. Aufgang's account of the GDR reflected her

[85] Interview with Ingrid Aufgang, 6 August 2005, Sibiu. This was one of the nine non-émigré
interviews in which the GDR featured quite prominently. Of these, this interview emphasised the
German cultural aspects of the GDR most forcefully.
[86] Ibid.   [87] Ibid.

ambiguity towards East Germany. Throughout her story, she appeared to be deliberating what to make of it. On the one hand, she was thoroughly impressed by the cultural riches of Weimar and Dresden but, on the other hand, she was wary of the GDR: different and politically suspect, it was not necessarily a reliable custodian of 'Germanness'. The GDR, had managed to restore Goethe's house in an exceptional manner, but the interpretation of Schiller's *Fiesco*, which she had gone to see while in Dresden, had been 'utterly unsatisfactory'.[88]

Reflections such as these were grounded in a long-standing relationship between Romanian Germans and the GDR. Particularly from the 1970s onwards, a number of German-language publications in Romania either covered the GDR more extensively or were produced for an East German audience. The daily newspaper *Neuer Weg* ran regular features on the GDR. Romanian Germans who did not visit East Germany could indulge in the exciting travel accounts published in the paper. Hans Frick, for instance, enthused over the rebuilt modern 'metropolis' East Berlin while name-checking historical Berlin on a tour past Humboldt University and the Charité.[89] The Romanian German-language literary journal *Neue Literatur* often published and commented on literature from the GDR.[90] The journal's cultural review section frequently featured exhibitions, publications, and symposia in the GDR. One issue in 1975, for instance, had as its main focus cultural and literary exchanges with the GDR.[91] The journal ran an interview with the East German culture minister, Hans-Joachim Hoffmann, in which the interviewers interrogated the East German representative's views on the 'cultural and spiritual' exchange between the Romanian and East German partners.[92] To be sure, Hoffmann's answers were often wooden and rehearsed, as expected, but the strong presence of the GDR in such a prominent German-language literary journal highlighted the important part East Germany had to play in the cultural life of Romanian Germans.

[88] *IA*: 'I was utterly dissatisfied with the interpretation [*[M]it der Interpretation war ich absolut unzufrieden*]'; see ibid.
[89] Hans Frick, 'Metropole an der Spree: Aufzeichnungen von einer Reise durch die DDR', *Neuer Weg* 30/9167, 7 November 1978, p. 4.
[90] The journal was founded in 1949 as *Banater Schrifttum* and was renamed *Neue Literatur* in 1956. Publication ceased in 1995. It was a Romanian German journal that straddled the Saxon and Swabian communities.
[91] *Neue Literatur* 16 (1975), p. 10. The journal featured the most prominent names of Romanian German literature including Richard Wagner, Wolf Aichelburg, Franz Hodjak, and others.
[92] 'Intensivierung des Informationsaustauschs – Fragen an Hans-Joachim Hoffmann, Kulturminister der DDR', ibid., p. 60.

Such exchanges occurred not only on paper, but also in practice. *Literaturtage* (literary festivals) that celebrated GDR literature were regular occurrences at Romanian universities. The German philology department at 'Lucian Blaga' University in Sibiu/Hermannstadt, for instance, maintained exchanges with German philology departments in the GDR. Throughout the 1970s, it also hosted the so-called 'Days of German Studies from the Democratic Republic of Germany' (*Die Tage der Germanistik der DDR in Rumänien*).[93] This involved public readings by East German visitors, excursions to fortified Saxon churches, and a dinner in the presence of the East German ambassador.[94] According to Gerhard Konnerth, the former dean of the Faculty of Philology and History (1976–84), this organisational link was of utmost importance to the German philology department and was treated accordingly, even though the Ministry for Education curtailed these activities towards the end of the Cold War.[95] Newspapers such as *Neuer Weg* would then give good coverage of these events, cementing the central role the GDR took in the lives of Romanian Germans.[96]

One of the most prominent links to the GDR, however, came in the form of the popular annual travel guide for Romania, *Komm Mit*, published in Bucharest by the publishing house *Neuer Weg*.[97] Serialised between 1970 and 1990, *Komm Mit* was designed to serve a number of purposes. First of all, it functioned as a form of *Heimatkunde* (local history) for Romanian Germans. In a period when emigration was a huge driving force among Romanian Germans, this publication presented the beauties and wonders of their socialist homeland.[98] At the same time, it also provided one of the few forums for Germans to explore their own cultural

---

[93] See Gerhard Konnerth, 'Jubilee Address: Forty Years of Philological Studies in Sibiu', in Eric Gilder, Alexandra Mitrea and Ana-Karina Schneider (eds.), *The English Connection: Forty Years of Studies at 'Lucian Blaga' University of Sibiu* (Bucharest and Sibiu, 2010), pp. 19–29, at http://unesdoc.unesco.org/images/0019/001907/190746e.pdf (accessed 19 Aug. 2016).

[94] Email correspondence with Gerhard Konnerth, 18 August 2013.

[95] Ibid. He also emphasised that the lecturers sent to Romania on exchange were very highly qualified, even more so than their West German counterparts – an important point to note, as this demonstrates further that the GDR played an active and crucial role for Romanian Germans in constructing their German cultural sphere.

[96] 'Literaturtage an der Philologie-Fakultät Sibiu', *Neuer Weg* 30/9162, 1 November 1978, pp. 1, 4.

[97] See *Komm Mit: Reisen, Wandern, Erholung in Rumänien*, Vols. 1–21 (Bucharest: Neuer Weg, 1970–90).

[98] This was also part of a deeply contradictory stance, since the Romanian state both actively encouraged and dissuaded Germans from leaving the country. This schizophrenic position became most pronounced from the late 1970s on after the official agreement on emigration to West Germany in 1977. See Hannelore Baier, 'Ceaușescu und die Aussiedlung der Deutschen aus Rumänien', *Zeitschrift für Siebenbürgische Landeskunde* 35/1 (2012), pp. 27–50.

heritage in Romania. Above all, however, *Komm Mit* played a role in bolstering cultural diplomacy abroad. While the guide was read in West Germany and Austria, its main target audience was in the GDR and Czechoslovakia.[99] The quality of print and paper of the series reveals the extent to which official channels were behind its dissemination.[100] Nicolae Ceauşescu was concerned with rectifying Romania's tarnished image not only in the West (and such a publication went some way to contributing towards this aim) but also among its (former) socialist brother countries, and *Komm Mit* was perfectly placed to do both. It allowed Romanian Germans to write about their interests within the controlled confines of the regime while co-opting them within Romania's campaign to polish its image.

It would be too simple to discount the *Komm Mit* travel guides as mere 'propaganda'. In spite of all the machinations of control behind the scenes, this book series represented a rare possibility for Romanian Germans to write about their homeland for other Germans in the GDR. In turn, it proved a crucial source of information for East Germans, enabling them to explore Romania and Transylvania in particular.[101] The print run was between 20,000 and 30,000 copies a year, and each contained a large number of articles spread over approximately 200 pages. The articles, written mainly by Romanian Germans, focused on the Carpathians, in particular, (often the German areas) and on the Black Sea. Stepping into the tradition of Meschendörfer's celebration of rural Transylvania in his *Siebenbürgische Elegie*, they described rural idylls and guided readers on journeys through both 'Romanian' and 'German' places.[102] They were even allowed to use the German names of some places, something that was better avoided in other German-language publications during communism. *Komm Mit* therefore allowed Romanian Germans to imagine themselves as part of a wider German community by communicating with citizens of the GDR.

Komm Mit was an important outlet for Romanian Germans. With a readership in the GDR in mind, regular contributors such as Erika

[99] According to Rothraut Wittstock, editor-in-chief of the *Allgemeine Deutsche Zeitung für Rumänien* (*ADZ*), the successor to *Neuer Weg*, an unspecified number of the 20,000 to 30,000 copies each year also went to Czechoslovakia: email correspondence with Rothraut Wittstock, 18 October 2012.

[100] I am particularly grateful to Christian Noack for his observations on the quality of print and paper of the series *Komm Mit*.

[101] An East German called 'Karpatenwilli' hosts a fantastic online collection of *Komm Mit* travel guides, which is – in turn – indicative of the role it played in his own motivation to discover Romania in the 1980s: www.karpatenwilli.com/kommmit.htm (accessed 16 Aug. 2013).

[102] See Chapter 1 for Meschendörfer's *Siebenbürgische Elegie*.

Figure 2.3 An advert in the newspaper *Neuer Weg* encouraging Romanian Germans to send the travel guide *Komm Mit '82* to friends and family abroad. Most of the readers abroad lived in the GDR.

Schneider and Gerhard Bonfert gave detailed descriptions of the flora, fauna, and culture of the region, using German terms and expressions that would otherwise have been printed only in Romanian.[103] For these writers, the GDR was their main point of contact (Figure 2.3). To the founding editor of the series, Georg Hromadka, a left-wing Swabian from the Banat, links with the GDR made more sense ideologically than with the 'home-land societies', the so-called *Landsmannschaften*, in West Germany. *Komm Mit* acted as a counterweight to the *Landsmannschaften*'s push for ever more Romanian German emigration from Romania.[104] In this way, it was possible for Romanian Germans – especially those who wanted to stay in Romania – to imagine themselves as belonging to a world that was at once both German and ideologically 'correct'. The connections to GDR readers

---

[103] From the 1970s onwards, place names could appear only in Romanian. *Komm Mit* therefore represented a real and important exception to this. Furthermore, the tradition of writing for a broader German audience continued after 1989 for many of those who did not immigrate to Germany. See, for instance, Erika Schneider, Hansgeorg von Killyen and Eckbert Schneider (eds.), *Naturforscher in Hermannstadt: Vorläufer, Gründer und Förderer des Siebenbürgischen Vereins für Naturwissenschaften* (Sibiu, 2007).

[104] On the *Landsmannschaften*, see Ahonen, *After the Expulsion*.

offered the Romanian German writers of *Komm Mit* a way of safely communicating their Germanness within a socialist ideological framework. Articles such as 'Es blüht "an der Burg"' ('In Bloom by the Castle') and 'Burgen im Repser Land' ('Castles in the Rupea Region'), published in the early 1980s, must also be read as a plea by Romanian Germans to East German readers to view their landscape and community as part of the same ideological and German world.[105]

The Lure of West Germany

In the end, though, it was West Germany that became the unrivalled point of reference for Romanian Germans. By the end of the Cold War, hundreds of thousands of Romanian Germans had left Romania for the Federal Republic of Germany. Yet what seemed like an inexorable drive towards the West had not been a foregone conclusion.

There were a number of pragmatic, contemporary, and historic reasons for West Germany's pre-eminent position in the Romanian German imaginary. For a start, the political division in Europe during the Cold War did not break the link between Germany and Romania, but in fact, strengthened it: with a large number of Romanian Germans now living in the FRG, a strong bridge between the two countries and the 'divided' Romanian German community emerged. The critical mass of Romanian Germans living in Germany – by the 1980s there were more Romanian Germans in Germany than in Romania – created a subcultural network of Cold War correspondence, which strengthened ties between East and West.[106] Regular visits from relatives and friends helped to form an image of Germany that lured Romanian Germans to the West. In combination with letter-writing, such visits gave Romanian Germans an insight into what might be. The *Westpaket* or *Geschenkpaket*[107] – that is, packages and presents made up of food, magazines, and other material – as well as enthralling first-hand stories made the desire to immigrate to West Germany greater. In the other direction, visits to West Germany enchanted Romanian Germans. Their ideas about West Germany were not unique to east-central Europeans, but they had a more tangible link

---

[105] Erika Schneider, 'Es blüht "an der Burg"', *Komm Mit '84: Reisen, Wandern, Erholung in Rumänien* (Bucharest: Neuer Weg, 1984), pp. 145–52, and Juliane Fabritius-Dancu, 'Burgen im Repser Land', *Komm Mit '81: Reisen, Wandern, Erholung in Rumänien* (Bucharest: Neuer Weg, 1981), pp. 129–59.
[106] For an excellent study on the Cold War 'subculture' of correspondence, see Ina Dietzsch, *Grenzen Überschreiben? Deutsch–Deutsche Briefwechsel 1949–1989* (Cologne: Böhlau, 2004).
[107] See Christian Härtel and Petra Karbus (eds.), *Das Westpaket* (Berlin: Christian Links Verlag, 2000).

and a comparatively easy escape route, and so more and more Romanian Germans left for the FRG. And yet this teleological story of migrating 'back' to the Federal Republic of (and later reunified) Germany as their ancestral land of calling was not a settled issue from the outset.

The Cold War produced intense debates about the place and belonging of Romanian Germans within the community itself. Already in the nineteenth century, Transylvanian Saxons disagreed on their countryfolk's 'rootedness': would they remain local patriots or would they become part of a broader German sense of belonging?[108] A century later, a similar division appeared within the Romanian German community between those urging Germans to leave Romania and those in favour of staying there. By the 1960s, the battle over the community's future took shape as a dispute between sections of the Protestant Church and the *Landsmannschaften* (homeland societies) in Germany. *Landsmannschaft* activists, such as Hans Hartl (1899–1980) and Hans Bergel, strongly supported a new beginning in the Federal Republic of Germany. Hartl and others urged their fellows in Romania to abandon their homeland in favour of the new West German state, spurring on a Romanian German exodus. Repetition of these arguments in a number of publications added to a sense of urgency among Romanian Germans.[109] With Saxon and Swabian life in Romania in flux, Romanian Germans around the organisation Hilfskomitee der Siebenbürger Sachsen und evangelischen Banater Schwaben im Diakonischen Werk der EKD e.V. (Hilfskomitee der Siebenbürger Sachsen) tried to counter the dominant narrative of escaping Romania for West Germany.

The prominent theologian and historian Paul Philippi and his brother Hans were the most vocal representatives of Romanian German resistance to emigration pressure. Paul Philippi in particular understood himself as a reluctant émigré living in exile in West Germany after the Second World War.[110] He accused the homeland societies of accelerating the end of the

---

[108] See Chapter 1.

[109] For a good example of the *landsmannschaftliche* discourse, see Schuster (ed.), *Epoche der Entscheidungen*, and in particular, the chapter by Hans Hartl, 'Am Ende einer historischen Aufgabe'; see also Hans Hartl, 'Die Lage der Deutschen in Rumänien', *Südosteuropa Mitteilungen* 4 (1981), pp. 112–25, and Kulturreferat der Landsmannschaft der Siebenbürger Sachsen in Deutschland e.V. (ed.), *Rumänien nach 1945: Die Referate der Tagungen der Arbeitsgemeinschaft siebenbürgischer Jungakademiker (ASJ), 1987–1989* (Munich: Kulturreferat der Landsmannschaft der Siebenbürger Sachsen in Deutschland e.V., 1989). For one of the most famous publications to support the church's stance on emigration, see Andreas Möckel (ed.), *Gerhard Möckel: Fatum oder Datum? Aufsätze und Briefe* (Munich: Südostdeutsche Kulturwerk, 1997), which is a collection of essays and letters of Gerhard Möckel from the 1960s to the 1990s.

[110] He was also one of the few returnees during the Cold War, as he moved back to Romania in the late 1970s, where he became active in politics, academia, and religion. He still resides in Sibiu.

Transylvanian Saxon community in Romania by arguing for *Familienzusammenführung* (bringing families back together) from 1962 on. While the *Landsmannschaften* urged Germans in Romania to emigrate, Philippi emphasised the particularism of Saxons against the call from West Germany. As early as the beginning of the 1950s, Philippi was on collision course with the *Landsmannschaften*. He was deeply concerned that Romanian Germans 'in exile' in West Germany would forget their roots and be merged into a society to which they did not really belong. In 1955, he urged a Romanian German cleric in Munich, one Dr Florian Müller, to encourage Romanian children to participate in a planned summer camp that year.[111] An ecumenical summer school would ensure 'that our young ones won't lose their connection to their homeland and its people'.[112] Paul Philippi understood Transylvanian Saxons as part of the Romanian land-scape: they were *Romanian* German and not simply German. Even within the *Landsmannschaften* there was some initial disagreement on the future of the Saxons. Roland Melzer, for instance, had been an officer for the regional homeland society of Transylvanian Saxons in Rhineland Palatine, but resigned his position in 1953, because he felt that the Landsmannschaft increasingly advocated emigration from Romania.[113] But it was in church circles that resistance against emigration was most visible.

Hans Philippi, Paul Philippi's brother, set up a publication designed to counter the dominant voice of the homeland society newspaper, *Siebenbürgische Zeitung*. By 1953, both Philippi brothers were working on a Sunday supplement to the *Siebenbürgische Zeitung* called *Lichter der Heimat* (later *Licht der Heimat*), which had initially been called *Korrespondenzblatt*.[114] Fellow Saxon and Romanian German émigrés were intrigued by this project, calling the name 'meaningful and linked to the past'.[115] Yet the first fissures were already palpable between the desire to build a bridge back to Romania and the overriding urge by many Romanian German émigrés to start afresh in West Germany. One Raimond Pilder lampooned Hans Philippi's attempt to reanimate an old publication (in name) from the interwar period, since it had been 'rejected by the members of the "church study group"' then and

---

[111] Paul Philippi correspondence with Dr Florian Müller, 5 February 1955, Siebenbürgen Institut, B III 39.
[112] Ibid.   [113] Roland Melzer, 'Vertriebenenarbeit (Bericht)', Siebenbürgen Institut, B I 54, 4/2.
[114] The name *Lichter der Heimat* ('Lights of the Homeland') was a reference to an interwar supplement with the same name in the *Kronstädter Zeitung*. The supplement was published between 1919 and 1940 under the editorship of Georg Alfred Scherg (not to be confused with Georg Scherg, the novelist). See Cornelia Schlarb, *Tradition im Wandel: Die evangelischen-lutherischen Gemeinden in Bessarabien 1814–1940* (Cologne: Böhlau, 2007), p. 157.
[115] Pilder and Philippi correspondence, 20 August 1953, Siebenbürgen Institut, B III.

now.[116] By the time the publication was properly established under the name *Licht der Heimat*, it was fully at odds with the politics of the homeland society's newspaper *Siebenbürgische Zeitung*. 'I want to take this opportunity to tell you that your "*Licht der Heimat*" continues to impress our compatriots with its fine quality, unlike the *Siebenbürgische Zeitung* with its offensive position, presentation, and "jargon"', declared one such 'compatriot', Günther Ott, in a letter to Hans Philippi in 1956.[117] The split went beyond mere preferences in reading material. Instead, it laid bare the most funda-mental debate in modern Romanian German history over whether to stay in or leave Romania.

The Philippi brothers were fighting a losing battle from the 1960s, but this did not dampen their zeal. Paul Philippi was especially vocal in his views and postulated four theses to refute the prevailing thinking on Romanian German, and specifically Transylvanian Saxon, identity in the 1960s. The four theses were written in Saxon, German, English, and French.

1. *Dat mir Sachsen Detschen senj, às gewàss* (Saxon dialect: It is certain that we Saxons are Germans).
2. *Ob man die Siebenbürger Sachsen als 'Deutsche' bezeichnen darf, hängt davon ab, wie man 'deutsch' definiert oder versteht* (It depends on the definition and understanding of the word 'German' whether it is valid to call Transylvanian Saxons Germans).
3. *It leads to mistakes to call Transylvanian Saxons 'Germans'.*
4. *Les Saxons de Transylvanie ne sont pas des Allemands* (Transylvanian Saxons are not Germans).[118]

Philippi's contradictory statements went to the heart of the Romanian German conflict over identity and belonging. Of course Saxons were Germans, Philippi claimed in Saxon dialect, but every statement led further away from that pan-German certainty. The order of Philippi's theses gave credence, in the end, to the regional particularity of Saxons, which distinguished them from Germans. His choice of languages also revealed a sense of cultural hierarchy – from Saxon dialect as regional identity to French as the *lingua franca* of European intellectuals – in which

---

[116] Pilder and Philippi correspondence, 20 August 1953, Siebenbürgen Institut, B III.
[117] Günther Ott correspondence with Paul Philippi, 31 December 1956, Siebenbürgen Institut, B III 39, HiKO.
[118] Paul Philippi, 'Von Deutschtum und Zukunft der Siebenbürger Sachsen: Das Gerücht', in Paul Philippi (ed.), *Land des Segens? Fragen an die Geschichte Siebenbürgens und seiner Sachsen* (Cologne: Böhlau, 2008), p. 352.

Romanian did not feature, even though he was making the argument for staying in Romania. Philippi tried to speak to a constituency both in Germany and in Romania who were not yet convinced that their future lay in the West and in West Germany. The Hilfskomitee stood in clear contrast to the policy of the *Landsmannschaften* which advocated the exact opposite in the name of 'bringing families together again', which he saw as a clandestine way of forcing through emigration.[119] *Landsmannschaft* figures clashed with members of the Hilfskomitee. Hans Bergel and Robert Gassner, a Romanian German émigré vicar (1910–90), fell out over the policy clashes between the Landsmannschaft and the Hilfskomitee.[120] Surprisingly, despite multiple disagreements, *Licht der Heimat* continued to be published as a supplement to the official homeland society's newspaper, *Siebenbürgische Zeitung*, until the 1980s.

Licht der Heimat was enveloped in nostalgia. It was delivered to the doors of Romanian German émigrés, slipped into the *Siebenbürgische Zeitung*, which dwarfed the supplement's size. The absurdity of having both publications delivered together was all too obvious. While the *Siebenbürgische Zeitung* was busily calling for more Romanian Germans to emigrate,[121] its supplement *Licht der Heimat* reminded its readers of the 'bells of their homeland' beckoning them home to Romania.[122] 'We will stay who we are', *Licht der Heimat* admonished its readers in West Germany, while at the same time the political context of oppression in Romania and pressure from West Germany to emigrate closed in on Romanian Germans.[123] Transylvanian Saxons were caught between 'homeland and outland [*Fremde*]': they did not belong to Germany and yet faced 'apartheid' back home in Transylvania, as Paul Philippi noted while commenting on the political situation in Romania.[124] It became abundantly clear, however, that Romanian Germans were abandoning Romania for good. On average, 12,000 Germans a year left during the last decade and a half of the Cold War. Romanian German luminaries on the right of the émigré community wanted to discredit and purge their opponents once and for all. In the late 1970s, Hans Bergel and other leading figures in the Landsmannschaft der Siebenbürger Sachsen were plotting to remove *Licht*

[119] Ibid., p. 351.
[120] Letter Hans Bergel to Robert Gassner, 16 August 1977, and letter Robert Gassner to Hans Bergel, 25 August 1977, Siebenbürgen Institut, B I 51, 2/1.
[121] See, for example, 'Die Landsmannschaft vor neuen Aufgaben', *Siebenbürgische Zeitung* 14/6, 15 April 1964, pp. 1, 2.
[122] 'Die Glocken der Heimat', *Licht der Heimat* 126, April 1964.
[123] 'Bleiben, was wir sind . . . ', *Licht der Heimat* 116, June 1963.
[124] 'Siebenbürger Sachsen zwischen Heimat und Fremde', *Licht der Heimat* 125, March 1964.

der Heimat from the Transylvanian Saxon newspaper. By the autumn of 1981, the *Landsmannschaft* succeeded in ridding their newspaper of *Licht der Heimat*. The debate over the future of Germans in Romania seemed settled in favour of emigration, and yet their existential question returned time and again as '*finis Saxoniae*' loomed large over a shrinking community back in Romania.

The Feedback Effect

As feared by the Philippi brothers, this growing presence of Romanian Germans in West Germany contributed towards emigration in the name of *Familienzusammenführung*. Exchanges between émigrés and non-émigrés were founded on an uneven relationship in which émigrés were usually in a position of strength, and similar dynamics between divided families and friends appeared in other contexts during the Cold War, as German–German relationships between the GDR and the FRG attest.[125] In the Romanian German case, émigrés, who were materially much better off than Germans in Romania, sent their relatives and friends presents of items unattainable for *Sachsen* and *Schwaben* in Romania, and with them they passed on an idea of wealth, safety, and comfort. Germans in Romania developed a dependence on Romanian German émigrés for supplying them with West German goods. Thank-you letters between Romania and Germany, in which Romanian Germans in Romania asked for and thanked their family and friends for goods, not only revealed a material dependence on Romanian German émigrés, but also highlighted a broader paternalistic pattern. Concern for the poor living standards and life in general in Romania was of chief importance to letter writers. Typically, non-émigrés would write about their troubles in Romania, which émigrés would reciprocate by expressing sympathy.[126]

The extensive correspondence between the siblings Martha Mesch (Sighişoara, Romania) and Roland Melzer (Mayen, West Germany) illustrate that very point.[127] Martha Mesch (née Melzer) and Roland Melzer were born in Sighişoara/Schässburg in 1906 and 1911 into a middle-class German household. The family formed part of the town's *Bildungsbürgertum* and served as a central nexus for fostering German

---

[125] Dietzsch, *Grenzen Überschreiben?*
[126] See, for instance, Bernhard Capesius, B I 56, 3/1–6, Roland Melzer, B I 54, 4/1–4, 5/1–3, 6/4–5, 7/6–7, 8/1–4, and Andreas Kloos, B I 115, A-5944, all in Siebenbürgen Institut.
[127] Letter Martha Mesch to Roland Melzer, 10 July 1967, Siebenbürgen Institut, B I 52, 34 and Letter Martha Mesch to Roland Melzer, 4 April 1952, Siebenbürgen Institut, B I 52, 34.

culture and language during the interwar period. Roland Melzer studied in Cluj-Napoca/Klausenburg, Graz, and Leipzig and ended up working in Berlin for the Arbeitswissenschaftliches Institut in the Third Reich as a lawyer from 1940.[128] Despite his entanglement with the Nazi regime, his work was not political in obvious ways. By the end of the war, Melzer managed to dodge any repercussions as his *Persilschein* (clean bill of health) attests.[129] His Romanian citizenship certainly helped him navigate the immediate post-war period without being identified as a 'German' as such. He moved to Mayen in Rhineland-Palatinate in post-war Germany with his second wife, Annette (called Annalie), and lived there until his death in 1988. Throughout the Cold War, postcards, letters, parcels, and visits crossed borders between Melzer, Mesch, and friends elsewhere. Their correspondence quickly established a hierarchical relationship where the Romanian side of the family kept asking for West German goods, and Roland Melzer duly obliged with an abundance of material from the West. Melzer also formed a close friendship with a Romanian German couple who lived in Leipzig in the GDR.[130]

But it was his sister, Martha Mesch, and her family who were locked into an intense web of correspondence with him. As Mesch contemplated emigration, the stories she told about the situation in Romania played a great role in affirming the desire to leave Romania. The correspondence highlighted the inverse relationship between Germany as a mythical home-land and Romania as the central point of reference for their correspond-ence. Martha Mesch was able to describe episodes from her life in some detail, knowing that her brother was capable of understanding the feelings and situations she was describing. In this way, Roland Melzer needed Martha Mesch as a living link back to his former homeland and to his own past. Time and again, he asked his sister for details about the town. Details of buildings gripped him: 'And what was the name of the pharmacy run by the Capesius family, "Zum *Something*"?', Melzer desperately asked his sister about the former townscape of Sighişoara in a letter from 1979.[131] But the relationship between the two siblings was never an equal one. Romania represented the past – Melzer wanted to *know* about the past – and Germany what might be in the future. In between seemingly banal issues of everyday life, Martha Mesch asked Butzi, as she called her brother, for goods and thanked them for their efforts:

---

[128] Siebenbürgen Institut, B I 54, 8, 10.   [129] Ibid., B I 54, 8/1–4.   [130] Ibid., 4/1–4.
[131] Ibid., 8/1–4.

My Dear Butzi!

I'm also writing to you about the fishing rods: of course, you can send a parcel; things rarely go missing like that. Fishing equipment is very much in demand right now and parcels usually arrive in one piece. It's all about fishing at the moment to make cooking and food more interesting.

You would also do us a huge favour if you sent us some pepper. There is none available here at the moment, and it will soon be that time of year when we'll need pepper. You can send pepper in packages of half a kilogram.[132]

Romanian German non-émigrés were also expected to confirm the receipt of goods or letters from the West, reinforcing the imbalanced relationship between émigrés and non-émigrés. Writing in late 1952, Martha Mesch sounded a grateful note in a letter to her brother and sister-in-law:

Dear Butzi and Annelie!

I'm slightly horrified by the fact that it's almost Christmas and I still haven't written to you. I got your letter dated 30 November. Thank you ever so much. I will take care of it [the letter] in the next couple of days.[133]

On other occasions, Martha Mesch's thank-you notes had an apologetic tone to them. In a letter dated 6 February 1974, she regretted her late acknowledgement of the Christmas gifts she and her family had received from Roland Melzer.

My Dear Butzi,

I am sure you are quite angry with me, because I'm replying to you so late. But I simply did not manage to get around to it. I can, however, confirm the receipt of all the parcels on a Christmas card: six parcels full of crossword puzzle books (which you could kindly send more often) and detective stories [*Krimis*])! Thank you very much for all of that!

Roland [her son] was thrilled to bits by it all, especially when he saw the Lego bricks.[134]

The power of crosswords, crime novels, and toys was too great to resist, and émigrés were all too aware of their role in sending presents or bringing things with them when visiting from West Germany.

---

[132] Letter Martha Mesch to Roland Melzer, 4 August 1952, Siebenbürgen Institut, B I 52, 34.

[133] Ibid., 23 December 1952, Siebenbürgen Institut, B I 52, 34.

[134] Ibid., 6 February 1971, Siebenbürgen Institut, B I 52, 34.

Roland Melzer kept meticulous records of the goods he had purchased for his relatives in Romania.[135] A voluminous collection of receipts from local pharmacists, the departmental store Kaufhof, sports shops, and clothes outlets hinted at an embarrassment of riches on which non-émigrés such as Martha Mesch were missing out: a woolly hat from Kaufhof for 39.95 DM; a knife from an ironmonger for 2.50 DM; medicine from Melzer's local *Reichskronen-Apotheke* for 20 DM.[136] On visits to Romania, Saxon and Swabian émigrés brought with them luxury goods such as these as well as information on the world beyond. They were able to tell friends and relatives of their first-hand experiences of the consumerist paradise in the West. Particularly in the 1980s, when a 'culture of shortage' was prevalent in Romania, stories of full shelves in supermarkets acted as a catalyst for emigration.[137] The West German idyll, to which Romanian Germans were drawn, was constantly reinforced by the goods and stories they received from the West.[138] Gift-giving was also read as part of a success story:[139] West Germany was a place of overabundance, affluence, and accomplishment. The extensive correspondence across the Iron Curtain helped Romanian Germans 'mentally map' the differences between Romania and Germany. In turn, the increasing numbers of émigrés from the 1970s intensified this *Rückkoppelungseffekt* – the feedback effect – cementing a picture of West Germany as the desired homeland for Romanian Germans in Romania.[140] German literature also played a crucial role in shaping an image of West Germany as a place for which they longed.[141] Goethe, Lessing, and Kleist acted as positive counterpoints to consumerism: Germany was not only materially affluent but also culturally rich. Romanian Germans often ended up imagining West Germany 'in terms of Goethe and Schiller'.[142]

---

[135] Siebenbürgen Institut, B I 52.   [136] 'Privatkorrespondenz', Siebenbürgen Institut, B I 54, 5/2.

[137] Liviu Chelcea, 'The Culture of Shortage during State Socialism: Consumption Practices in a Romanian Village in the 1980s', *Cultural Studies* 16/1 (2002), pp. 16–43.

[138] Anneli Ute Gabanyi, 'Geschichte der Deutschen in Rumänien', in Bundeszentrale für politische Bildung (ed.), *Aussiedler: Informationen zur politischen Bildung* 267 (Bonn: Bundeszentrale für politische Bildung, 2000), pp. 10–16.

[139] Ina Dietzsch, 'Geschenkpakete – Ein Fundamentales Mißverständnis: Zur Bedeutung des Paketaustausches in Persönlichen Briefwechseln', in Härtel and Karbus (eds.), *Das Westpaket*, pp. 105–7.

[140] Anneli Ute Gabanyi, 'Die Deutschen in Rumänien: Exodus oder Neuanfang?', in Rothe (ed.), *Die Siebenbürger Sachsen*, pp. 89–104.

[141] John J. White, 'A Romanian German in Germany: The Challenge of Ethnic and Ideological Identity in Herta Müller's Literary Work', in Rock and Wolff (ed.), *Coming Home to Germany?*, p. 177.

[142] Interview Hermann Frühbeis.

There were efforts by the dwindling Romanian German community in Romania to resist the pressure of emigration which went beyond church circles. German-language publications in Romania subtly argued for Romanian Germans to remain in Romania. The daily *Neuer Weg* reminded its readers in 1978 that the Germans of the Lugoj in the Banat had endorsed unification with Romania in 1918.[143] *Komm Mit*, that delightful travel guide, celebrated Romanian landscapes.[144] Romanian German newspapers likewise feted Saxon and Swabian places and spaces throughout Romania. The *Karpatenrundschau*, a weekly newspaper published in Braşov, ran a regular series called 'Das schöne alte Bild der Heimat' ('Once upon a Time in Our Homeland'), which took readers on a tour around the beauties of the Romanian German world in Romania (Figure 2.4). Other regular features of the newspaper included 'Zeugen der Zeit' ('Witnesses of History') and 'Taten und Gestalten' ('Events and People'). Public Romanian German figures such as Maja Philippi and Gernot Nussbächer were the main contributors to these vignettes, which celebrated German history in Romania in a politically correct way.[145] Occasionally, the editors gave a subtle but clear riposte to the financial promises offered by the Federal Republic. Under the headline 'His Help Is Tangible', the *Karpatenrundschau*'s editorial from 20 January 1978 talked up Ceauşescu's assistance to the Romanian German community.[146] Such headlines and articles were of course politically controlled. Yet, as they appeared just at the time of the Schmidt–Ceauşescu agreement, which officially regulated Romanian German emigration, it is not difficult to see such headlines and articles as a last attempt to dissuade fellow Romanian Germans from leaving Romania. In any case, life in the West, German-language newspapers in Romania emphasised, was not as good as it seemed. The *Karpatenrundschau* ran an exposé on the terrible treatment of *Gastarbeiter* and other migrants in Germany and elsewhere in western Europe.[147] In an attempt to pour cold water on ideas of affluence in the West, the newspaper also reported that car production in western Europe was in decline.[148] The Rhine was filthy, and it was practically suicide to live

[143] Heinrich Lay, 'An der Schwelle einer neuen Zeit: Die Einstellung der deutschen Bevölkerung des Banats zur Vereinigung von 1918 dargestellt am Beispiel Lugosch (I)', *Neuer Weg* 30/9171, 11 November 1978, p. 3.
[144] *Komm Mit*, 1970–90.
[145] For a collection of drafts and publications of Maja Philippi's work, see Siebenbürgen Institut, B I 75, 4.
[146] 'Seine Hilfe ist konkret', *Karpatenrunschau*, 20 January 1978, pp. 1, 2.
[147] '14 Millionen Emigranten – ein Volk von Verirrten', *Karpatenrundschau* 6/1976, p. 2.
[148] 'Westlicher Autoboom rückläufig', *Karpatenrundschau* 3/1980, p. 2.

Figure 2.4 'Das schöne alte Bild der Heimat', *Karpatenrundschau* (1976).

anywhere close to it, the newspaper's editors claimed, citing the West Germany weekly *Der Spiegel* as their source.[149] The main daily newspaper in German, *Neuer Weg*, chimed in: more and more Americans were committing suicide, it quoted *Newsweek*, in November 1978 just as emigration from Romania was becoming easier.[150]

But these Romanian German voices were fighting a losing battle. Public proclamations of loyalty were drowned out by facts on the ground. 'Our Commitment to Our Homeland', the *Karpatenrundschau* proudly trumpeted in April 1977 by reproducing a telegram, which had been sent by the 'Council of German Workers' ('Rat der Werktätigen deutscher Nationalität') to the Central Committee of the Romanian Communist

---

[149] 'Selbstverschuldeter Selbstmord: Der Rhein so schmutzig wie eh und je', *Karpatenrundschau* 9/1979, p. 2.

[150] 'Immer mehr junge Amerikaner wählen den Freitod', *Neuer Weg* 30/9154, 3 November 1978, p. 2.

Party reiterating their commitment to Romania.[151] In this diffuse picture of multiple voices, more and more Germans emigrated, and more and more émigrés passed on filtered information about success in Germany, which in turn made the remaining Germans in Romania hanker after West Germany. Emigration, in the end, became the ultimate objective.

Afterlives

Yet emigration was not a full stop, and it did not sever ties with the old homeland in Romania. Romania never went away. The connections between émigrés in West Germany and Saxons and Swabians back in Romania were too numerous and too complex for there to have been a clean break.[152] The Romanian German press in Germany tirelessly covered developments 'back home' in Romania. Romanian Germans were constantly on the move, and West Germany was not, despite all the rhetoric around emigration, the final goal: it simply set in motion new trails and routes that mapped out the Romanian German world. Émigrés sent back *Geschenkpakete* to their relatives and friends in Romania. Numerous adverts in the *Siebenbürgische Zeitung* and correspondence across the Iron Curtain attest to a vibrant culture of exchange (Figure 2.5).

Figure 2.5 Advert for sending parcels to Romania, *Siebenbürgische Zeitung* (1961).

---

[151] 'Unser Bekenntnis zur Heimat: Das erweiterte Plenum des Rates der Werktätigen deutscher Nationalität in der Sozialistischen Republik Rumänien', *Karpatenrundschau* 14/1977, p. 1.

[152] Koranyi and Wittlinger, 'From Diaspora to Diaspora'.

Companies that provided assistance with customs clearance targeted Romanian German émigrés as part of a wider web of cross-Iron Curtain exchanges. Numerous recent arrivals from Romania opened up a network of parcels and goods crossing the ideological divide of Europe. Of course, this had an impact on Romanian Germans wishing to leave Romania, as they were inundated with delights from the West. But it equally reflected a deep connection to Romania for émigrés despite their decision to abandon their former homeland.

The *Siebenbürgische Zeitung* was full of advertisements for trips to Romania. An advert (Figure 2.6) from March 1958, for example, was strategically placed directly beneath a long list of recent Romanian German immigrants to West Germany: the migrants may have left, and they were honoured in the paper, but readers were simultaneously reminded of their connections to Romania by the advertised bus trip.[153] The movements of migration, so the *mise-en-page* implied, could go both ways for Romanian Germans. Such adverts featured in almost every issue of the paper. Between March 1958 and May 1961, all but three monthly

Figure 2.6 Advert for bus trips to Romania, *Siebenbürgische Zeitung*, March 1958.

---

[153] 'In die Bundesrepublik eingewandert', *Siebenbürgische Zeitung* 8/3, 25 March 1958, p. 4.

issues ran advertisements for companies offering bus trips to Romania. By
the early 1960s, several competing travel agents regularly displayed their
offerings in the newspaper. The adverts catered for everyone: families could
choose a summer holiday tour with the travel agent Eisenburger in
Stuttgart; the Schwäbischer Reisedienst promised flights to Mamaia for
a fortnight on a Black Sea beach; Reisebüro Capri in Vienna offered trips
by train to Arad, Timișoara, Brașov, and Bucharest. Other companies
explicitly marketed these journeys to visiting relatives: Ost-Süd-Reisen –
Obermüller & Co. in Munich, for instance, suggested a variety of trips, all
under the banner of *Verwandten-Besuchsreisen*, or family visits (Figure 2.7).
Month after month, adverts for travel back to Romania cemented émigré
links back to Romania. Even at the height of emigration in the 1980s,
return travel was very popular with Romanian Germans in Germany. Not
only did adverts and travel reports lure Romanian Germans back 'home',

Figure 2.7 Adverts for tour operators and trips to Romania, *Siebenbürgische Zeitung*
(1961).

but they also created a mental landscape in which Romania could feature prominently in the Romanian German spatial identity: those who did not physically embark on journeys back to Romania could still read in meticulous detail the itineraries of the trips of their fellow émigrés.[154]

Whether they travelled home or followed imaginary itineraries, Romanian German émigrés recreated their former lives in Romania. With the financial assistance of money from the Federal Republic of Germany and states such as North-Rhine Westphalia and Baden-Württemberg, bespoke Romanian German *Siedlungen* (urban developments) were established in places such as Drabenderhöhe (North-Rhine Westphalia) and Bietigheim-Bissingen and Gundelsheim (both Baden-Württemberg). The *Siedlungen* provided one of several contexts in which Romanian Germans could engage in reconstructing their Romanian lives within Germany. Other networks within cities and towns gave Romanian Germans a culinary-cultural infrastructure to navigate around their new West German world. They would meet at Doina, a Romanian restaurant, at the heart of Munich's art scene in the Galeriestraße close to Odeonsplatz, where Transylvanian Saxon brass bands and Transylvanian delicacies eased their arrival in the Federal Republic of Germany (Figure 2.8). Food and music were a crucial part of the world Romanian German émigrés inhabited, and places such as Munich were crammed with Transylvanian and Swabian eateries (Figure 2.9). As they read their monthly émigré paper the *Siebenbürgische Zeitung*, they were introduced to the culinary and cultural delights of the Romanian and Romanian German diaspora in almost every issue. They could listen to the sound of their former homeland, with marching bands performing on a regular basis across West Germany (Figure 2.10). The Landsmannschaft helped co-ordinate performances at prestigious venues all across West Germany. In September 1985, for instance, the *Beethovenhalle* in Bonn hosted a Transylvanian Saxon musical comedy, *Bauernhochzeit in Siebenbürgen*.[155] Emigration may have dictated Romanian German politics, but Romanian Germans still took their old homeland very seriously, and it still formed an integral part of their self-understanding after emigration. As one advert in the *Siebenbürgische Zeitung* made clear in 1951, 'every advert by a Transylvanian company is an advert for Transylvania'.[156] Connected to the 'old country' back in Romania, they would seek out places that were not

---

[154] 'Urlaub- und Verwandtenbesuche nach Siebenbürgen-Rumänien', *Siebenbürgische Zeitung* 32/5, 31 March 1982, p. 6.
[155] Siebenbürgen Institut, B I 54, 8/1–4.
[156] 'Advert', *Siebenbürgische Zeitung* 2/4, 1 April 1952, p. 8.

Ladet Sie ein
zu Ihren Spezialitäten

Ein neues Rumänisches
Restaurant in München

GALERIESTRASSE - ECKE BRUDERSTRASSE
(Gegenüber vom Haus der Kunst)

Siebenbürgische Spezialitäten

Holzfleisch, Flecken oder unsere guten Weine:

Kokeltaler Mädchentraube - Reichesdorfer Mädchentraube - Langenthaler Mädchentraube, Spätlese Karlsburger Traminer Auslese und immer noch den Mönchtaler Cabernet finden Sie in der

Gaststätte Görresgarten

München 13, Görresstr. 1 (100 m v. d. Josephskirche)
Pächter: **F. u. V. Geisberger,** früher Hermannstadt
Ideale Nebenräume für Festlichkeiten, Hochzeiten usw.
Neu: der berühmte Moldauer Weißwein „Grasa" aus Cotnar

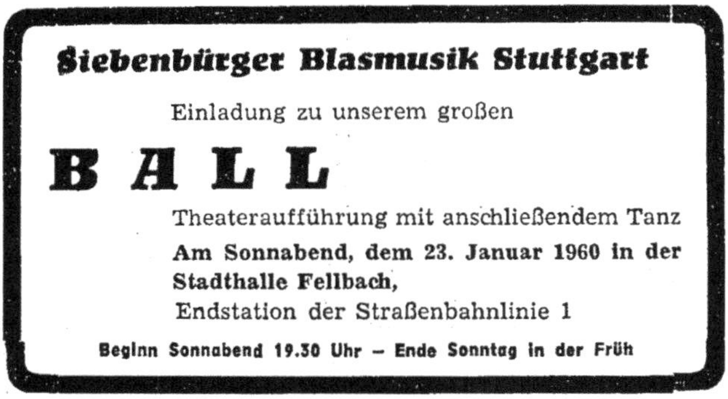

Siebenbürger Blasmusik Stuttgart

Einladung zu unserem großen

BALL

Theateraufführung mit anschließendem Tanz
Am Sonnabend, dem 23. Januar 1960 in der Stadthalle Fellbach,
Endstation der Straßenbahnlinie 1

Beginn Sonnabend 19.30 Uhr — Ende Sonntag in der Früh

Figures 2.8–2.10 Adverts for Romanian and Transylvanian restaurants (1961, 1960) as well as a Transylvanian music ball, *Siebenbürgische Zeitung* (1959).

quintessentially 'West German' but were part of their transnational and shifting identities.

Amid the turbulent back and forth of emigration, correspondence, visits, and diasporic spaces, the debate about staying or emigrating raged on. And still Romanian Germans kept on moving to West Germany. First impressions and memories of Romania were often crucial. Even years after emigrating, some Romanian Germans felt vindicated when reflecting on their decision to leave Romania. They still associated the act of immigrating to Germany with images of freedom and with affluence and culture. Thomas and Gerlinde Schräger, an émigré couple from northern Transylvania who had moved to southern Bavaria, recalled in an interview the moment of realisation after emigrating from Romania what life was like in Germany and how they had a sense of it before they arrived. How had they imagined Germany?

TS: Her parents had emigrated three years earlier, and they knew . . .

GS: In any case, my mother had already visited before she emigrated . . .

TS: She communicated with us quite a bit, and well . . . they really convinced us that we ought to leave . . . and they supported us and helped us realise our wish, the fact that we really wanted to make the move. And that's what we did. And so, three years later, we also managed to emigrate.

GS: Before that, borders were something absolute, something we couldn't over-come. And then suddenly we were *allowed* to travel to Salzburg . . . my goodness! Or I remember going to Italy, our first journey to Italy, through Switzerland, we crossed borders so many times. I was so excited that I felt physically sick. I really felt sick, and so we had to stop off somewhere in the middle of nowhere [*irgendwo raus ins Grüne*] and we just sat down. I could barely cope. The fact that we were allowed to do all of this was unimaginable to us, and it wasn't dangerous, and it wasn't illegal.[157]

The Schrägers' account continued the emotions around the act of emigration including the powerful *Rückkopplungseffekt*.[158] Their story was a powerful reminder of the deep psychological fracture that emigration created. Their lives had been decoupled from their normality in Romania. The acute sense of sickness was an overwhelming response to the disappearance of a border that had determined much of their lives. The freedom they had looked for did not necessarily translate into something positive. Instead, the upheaval was too much to process. Gerlinde Schräger's mother had immigrated to Germany and had repeatedly told them how wonderful it was, which heightened their own urge to follow her

[157] Interview with Gerlinde Schräger and Thomas Schräger, 16 February 2005, Traunstein.
[158] Gabanyi, 'Die Deutschen in Rumänien', pp. 94–7.

and leave Romania. Monumental decisions and intense emotions left the Schrägers in a state of uncontrollable feelings. And yet, as time passed, the Schräger couple themselves turned into new conduits for transferring similar, idealised ideas about Germany back to Romania.[159]

The Schrägers' story also tells us a lot about the mindset with which many Romanian Germans arrived in Germany. For the Schrägers and many other Romanian Germans, Romania represented absolute oppression. In Romania, all they could see were borders; these borders were, of course, very real, but it was the image of the West that made the borders more visible. Their first experience of the freedom they had hoped for led to Gerlinde and Thomas Schräger 'trying to make up for lost time [*Nachholbedarf*]'.[160] Like many other east-central European migrants during the Cold War, the experience of leaving for the West conjured up a number of conflicting emotions, from celebration to feeling physically sick.

Not everything turned out to be as rosy as the Schrägers made out. 'Blending in' with West German society proved to be difficult. The gap between an idealised picture of Germany and German 'reality' soon hit home, especially for the Romanian Germans who emigrated late on in the 1980s and early 1990s. Dieter Schlesak (1934–2019), a Romanian German author and émigré, wrote extensively about the disappointment Romanian Germans suffered after arriving in West Germany.[161] Schlesak had positioned himself against the prevailing view of the Landsmannschaft that advocated emigration from Romania under all circumstances. Schlesak warned against rushing into an irreversible decision, which, he felt, would not be vindicated for many Romanian Germans. And so quite a substantial number of émigré respondents expressed a feeling of not quite fitting in with West German society

---

[159] For a nuanced understanding of travel under Ceauşescu, see Alex Drace-Francis, 'Paradoxes of Occidentalism: On Travel and Travel Writing in Ceauşescu's Romania', in Andrew Hammond (ed.), *The Balkans and the West: Constructing the European Other, 1945–2003* (Aldershot: Ashgate, 2003), pp. 69–80, and Alex Drace-Francis, *The Traditions of Invention: Romanian Ethnic and Social Stereotypes in Historical Context* (Leiden: Brill, 2013), pp. 251–64.

[160] This phenomenon of the so-called *Nachholbedarf* was described by Daphne Berdahl in her study of Kella, a small German town on the German–German border. See Daphne Berdahl, *Where the World Ended: Re-Unification and Identity in the German Borderland* (Berkeley: University of California Press, 1999), in particular, p. 173.

[161] Schlesak, a German author from Transylvania, lived much of his émigré life in Italy. He emigrated in 1969 and wrote a number of books that dealt with the East–West clash and the disappointed illusions Romanian Germans were faced with in West Germany. See, for instance, Dieter Schlesak, *Visa: Ost–West Lektionen* (Frankfurt am Main: S. Fischer, 1970), and Dieter Schlesak, *Vaterlandstage und die Kunst des Verschwindens* (Zürich: Benziger, 1986).

once they had arrived.[162] Even Hans Bergel – a huge advocate for emigration and *Landsmannschaft* activist during the Cold War – recalled his initial feeling towards West Germany, echoing, perhaps unwittingly, some of Dieter Schlesak's observations:

> It felt a bit eerie after being here for a month. The mentality seemed somewhat foreign to me [*Die Mentalität war mir etwas fremd*]. [...] I couldn't talk about like I can today, because I've since been able to work through this. I've even got proof that it felt eerie to me, because I went to Goethestrasse number 49, to the Canadian consulate [...] I wanted to move to Canada. Because I said to myself: this is not my Germany. I didn't leave, because I was in the middle of a divorce, and my wife had the rights to look after the children. They were still underage, but she wouldn't back down. If it hadn't been for that, I'd be in Canada now. I've been to Canada lots of times. I've been at least twenty times since then. I've got friends there. Actually, I feel quite at home in Canada. I feel very good there.[163]

After the accomplishment of the *Landsmannschaften* in pushing the emigration agenda, Bergel revised his position. He did so, perhaps, in order to respond to the criticisms of his actions, but there was more to it: the context of living in a united Germany, where the East–West dichotomy was no longer as important, deprived Bergel of his original rationale for emigration. Germany was no longer a Cold War destination.

Romanian Germans had imagined West Germany not just as a bastion of high culture, but also as a country made up of a cohesive German community. Yet their experiences in Germany map onto their expectations. Many respondents articulated a feeling of alienation in their new homeland. This was particularly the case for Romanian Germans from tightly knit rural communities. The more urban and western way of life they encountered in Germany was quite a shock for many émigrés. The developments in migration and integration in Germany, too, jarred with some Romanian Germans. Robert Türk, a Saxon from a rural community close to Braşov/ Kronstadt who had moved into a retirement home in Gundelsheim in south-western Germany, echoed a feeling of being disappointed by what he encountered after immigrating to Germany in 1990. He conveyed his expectations of Germany by reciting part of a poem.

---

[162] Of all forty-one émigré respondents, nineteen expressed quite explicit negative associations with the reality they encountered following emigration.
[163] Interview with Hans Bergel, 18 February 2005, Munich.

I imagined everything to be perfect here, everything was tickety-boo [*piko-bello*], but I was very disappointed . . . I'm sorry. I'm extremely disappointed with Germany [. . .] Yes, it was a disappointment. Yes. I imagined [it] differently, I had imagined Germany to be different [. . .]

All I can say is this: 'Above all, my child: be loyal and honest. Never let a lie tarnish your lips. From ancient times, the greatest glory among the German people was for you to be loyal and true. You are still young, it is not yet difficult. But boys turn into men. While saplings are still capable of bending, trees are not. Speak the truth, and don't twist and turn, whatever you say, do so plainly and simply. Whatever your vows and promises, they should be your highest duty. Your word is sacred, so do not waste it.'[164]

For Robert Türk, the image of Germany had been based on a nineteenth-century Romantic poem written by the poet and painter Robert Reinick from Gdańsk/Danzig.[165] It encapsulated the idyllic vision of Germany endorsed by many *Sachsen* and *Schwaben*. Türk's emigration from Romania had shattered his vision of Germany. The absence of Germany as he had imagined it evoked a sense of longing for

---

[164] Interview with Robert Türk, 12 August 2005, Gundelsheim. Of the nineteen émigrés who expressed their dissatisfaction with (West) Germany explicitly, Türk's was particularly scathing. That said, other respondents expressed their distaste for contemporary Germany in different ways, but perhaps less no less intensely. One interviewee, Frank Hausenstein, admitted his disappointment with Germany, but did this with humour.

[165] The poem is 'Vor allem eins mein Kind'. The above is a translation of the first part of the original:

Vor allem eins, mein Kind: Sei treu und wahr,
laß nie die Lüge deinen Mund entweih'n!
Von alters her im deutschen Volke war
der höchste Ruhm, getreu und wahr zu sein.

Du bist ein deutsches Kind, so denke dran!
Noch bist du jung, noch ist es nicht so schwer;
aus einem Knaben aber wird ein Mann;
das Bäumchen biegt sich, doch der Baum nicht mehr.

Sprich ja und nein und dreh und deutle nicht;
was du berichtest, sage kurz und schlicht;
was du gelobtest, sei dir höchste Pflicht;
dein Wort sei heilig, drum verschwend es nicht!

Leicht schleicht die Lüge sich ans Herz heran,
zuerst ein Zwerg, ein Riese hintenach;
doch dein Gewissen zeigt den Feind dir an,
und eine Stimme ruft in dir: 'Sei wach!'

Dann wach und kämpf, es ist ein Feind bereit:
die Lüg' in dir, sie drohet dir Gefahr!
Kind, Deutsche kämpfen allezeit!
Du deutsches Kind, sei tapfer, treu und wahr!

a homeland as it ought to have been according to him. Many oral history interviewees described a sense of loss. The psychologist Hans-Joachim Maaz considered *Verlustsyndrom* (loss syndrome), part of a Europe-wide phenomenon after the Cold War, to be widespread among citizens of the former GDR after unification.[166] Romanian German émigrés experienced something similar after emigration from Romania, though the sense of loss was rather more closely connected to their imaginary and idealised homeland of West Germany than to their 'actual' homeland of Romania.[167] While East Germans had lived through the loss of a known environment, the Romanian German case was more poignant due to the physical detachment from Transylvania and the Banat. Nevertheless, the similarities between the two groups are striking, as the vision of the West was broken after reunification and emigration respectively.

The hope of success, both financially and personally, was often the first aspect to be put under pressure after immigrating to Germany. In Romania, West Germany had always represented success. But the reality of living in Germany challenged a naïve view of the Bundesrepublik. Even the more positive accounts of emigration were often tainted with difficult episodes. Gerlinde Schräger remembered what she called 'anticlimaxes' after emigrating from Romania:

> Then there was the quality and the way in which they ran the school [*die Qualität des Hochschulbetriebs*] in [name of city]. I had always imagined it to be super, right? But it was only so-so. And I had also expected to get justice, to have the same opportunities as others, but I didn't, for organisational reasons. I didn't manage to get a job, partly because it was a bad time for being a teacher. I had to work part-time for thirty years, and I only got half a salary [*halbe Norm*].[168]

Gerlinde Schräger went on to qualify her statement by insisting that this did not 'have any impact on everything else [*das hat dem Rest keinen Abbruch getan*]'.[169] Still, her first encounter with capitalism in practice was her inability to find a full-time job. The failure was not only financial in nature, but could also be extended to the failure to 'blend in' or indeed 'catch up' with West German society. For all the positive images of Germany, there seemed to be a negative counterpart. In Gerlinde Schräger's case this did not destroy her enthusiasm for Germany, but it

---

[166] Hans-Joachim Maaz, *Das Gestürzte Volk: Die Unglückliche Einheit* (Berlin: Argon Verlag, 1991), pp. 34–5.
[167] Brubaker, *Nationalism Reframed*, pp. 56–7, 66, 71–5.
[168] Interview Gerlinde Schräger and Thomas Schräger.   [169] Ibid.

muted it slightly. Age played a role in this, too. The Schrägers had been in their late twenties when they emigrated, and the ability to adapt would have been greater for those who emigrated at a younger age than for those who arrived in Germany later in life.

While disappointment loomed large over the émigré community of Romanian Germans, *Sachsen* and *Schwaben* also tried to leave the past behind them. In an attempt to integrate into the new setting in Germany and avoid social stigma, some émigrés relegated their Romanian past to a trivial footnote in their biographies. Gerlinde Schräger revealed that her last visit to Romania had been in 1982:

> And if someone finds that strange [the fact that she has not been back in Romania since 1982], then I always say to them: nobody can take my memories away from me. The bad memories help me to find my way back to reality, to deal with things. And the good ones enrich my life. It would not make much sense [*es wäre müßig*] to go back and search for something that simply isn't there any more. And while we were still working, our holidays were too short, and we didn't have too much money. We needed the time and money for proper recreation. And going back to Romania would never have been proper recreation.[170]

Their ability to compartmentalise their memories in this way helped the Schrägers to challenge their position in Germany as 'us' versus 'them'. In order to avoid being labelled as '*Ausländer im Ausland* [foreigners in a foreign country]', the Schrägers attempted to relegate their Romanian past as best they could to the realms of memory, while reinventing themselves as German *Bundesbürger* ('going back to Romania would never have been proper recreation').[171] Some émigré interviewees, including the Schrägers, had also clearly adopted linguistic codes that marked them out not as Romanian German, but simply as German. They had managed to purge their so-called *Minderheitendeutsch* (minority German language) and adopt new, contemporary German expressions:[172] the

---

[170] Ibid.

[171] Herta Müller, one of the most prominent Romanian German authors of the second half of the twentieth century, has articulated the problems Romanian Germans faced in West Germany quite well. She has also provided one of the few meaningful and critical approaches to Romanian German involvement in National Socialism. See White, 'A Romanian German in Germany', p. 177, and especially Brigid Haines (ed.), *Herta Müller* (Cardiff: University of Wales Press, 1998), and Brigid Haines and Lyn Marven (eds.), *Herta Müller* (Oxford: Oxford University Press, 2013), for a comprehensive edited volume on Herta Müller. Brigid Haines is the pre-eminent expert on Herta Müller; see Brigid Haines (ed.), *Herta Müller and the Currents of European History* (Oxford: Wiley, 2020).

[172] See White, 'A Romanian German in Germany', p. 182.

Schrägers had recast both their biographies and their mannerisms in order to avoid being identified as 'foreigners' or Romanian German on German soil.

And yet, the relationship to Germany, Romania, and the local always remained a vexed issue. Between stories of success, instances of disappointment, and the wish to leave the past in the past, émigrés struggled to express the complexity of their identities. While the *Landsmannschaften* and the church had assumed, during the Cold War, that the issue would be decided by either leaving Romania or staying, the transnational Romanian German world turned out to be a far more intricate affair, reflecting broader experiences of twentieth-century European migration. The Schrägers searched in the most torturous manner to describe their complex feelings towards their old home. Did they miss anything about Romania?:

> *TS:* Well, of course you always feel a bit homesick [*Heimweh hat man natürlich immer*], especially when it comes to places, when you think of where you might like to be and all that. And people always say of course, and you probably recognise that feeling, too: I'd really like to be there and there again … Or do you remember friends, who were still there, who didn't emigrate, well yes, of course there's that, but apart from that …
>
> *GS:* I always say, when people ask me: 'Are you homesick [*Hast du Heimweh?*]?', then I say: 'I sometimes feel sick [*Weh*] … but home?' […] And yes, pain [*Weh*], pain too.
>
> *TS:* And anyway, it's not the case that we'd suddenly say I really want to give up everything here and go back to Romania. That's most definitely not the case.[173]

For decades, emigration had been the yardstick of the Romanian German community. In Germany, Romanian German publications seemed to cover little else. In Romania, in a far more guarded manner, sections of the shrinking Romanian German community tried to battle against the pull of the West. Escaping Romania seemed to be the only goal that counted. Once in Germany, émigrés were caught between reconstructing Romanian German life and rejecting it at the same time, and the Schrägers' account expressed this tension as they searched for the correct way of talking about their memories of Romania.

But not all Romanian Germans left Romania. Nor had all of them planned to remain in Germany. Paul Philippi, who had fought emigration all his life from his 'exile' in Germany, returned to Romania and become a vital figure for the German Democratic Forum. Eginald Schlattner

---

[173] Interview Gerlinde Schräger and Thomas Schräger.

(1933–), a famous novelist and vicar whose work we will encounter later, reinvented himself as the last man standing in the Transylvanian countryside. Instead of preaching to his German countryfolk in the village of Roşia, near Sibiu, Schlattner found himself a new community: his 'brown brothers' (as he called them), the Roma, who now occupied many of the abandoned Saxon villages in the Transylvanian countryside.[174] Others enjoyed the British enthusiasm for Saxon villages in the form of the Mihai Eminescu Trust and sought to reanimate dead villages. Caroline Fernolend, a Romanian German activist for the trust who remained in Romania, discovered her passion for renovating Saxon villages with Prince Charles's money.[175] Together with the trust, she helped to create a topography of facades of former German life in the Transylvanian mountains.

There were many attempts to find a useable and recognisable homeland by Romanian Germans in Romania. For some interviewees who had not left Romania, however, the quest for Germany never really ended. It was the only way to make sense of their increasingly forlorn position as part of a shrinking community in Romania. Elisabeth Schneider from Sibiu still envisaged herself as part of an imagined transnational German community; it allowed her to live in the hope that one day she could also be part of dream despite having opted against it. Those Romanian Germans who had emigrated had lost their ability to dream and imagine a life beyond the present. But for the disintegrating Romanian German community in Romania, the future was still being fought out. In Schneider's Romania after the mass exodus of her fellow Germans, she still admired Germans and spoke badly of Romanians:

> The Romanian is like this: they will go where the wind blows [*Der dreht sich wie das Blatt im Wind*] [*sic*]. When things are OK, they're like this; when things are going badly, then they simply change direction. They are not like us. Germans are sincere people, and that's the way it is. And had we not received any help from Germany after the revolution in 1989, then it would have been difficult. They sent us parcels, duty-free. It was a little embarrassing for us when we went to collect them from the customs office. Not just for us, but for all Germans here. And as I was saying, my daughter had a baby in 1986 and twins in 1990, so they sent us baby clothes, and we used to admire them; it really was like Christmas. I can't even remember all the things that were in these parcels ... delicious chocolates; things we could

[174] Peter Miroschnikoff, 'Zigeuner in Siebenbürgen: "Meine braunen Brüder am Bach" – Interview mit Eginald Schlattner', *Südosteuropa Mitteilungen* 4–5 (2005), pp. 43–9.
[175] See Chapter 5 for more on the Mihai Eminescu Trust.

have barely imagined [*Wir haben solche Sachen gar nicht gekannt*]. We didn't even have any underwear left. We didn't have any bed linen. The only way we ever got those things was by [collecting] tokens. Even tissues and towels and things like that.[176]

For Elizabeth Schneider, the Cold War conundrum had never ended: parcels continued to arrive, and they were still shaping Romanian German images of the West with things barely imaginable to them. She still lived with the dream of western affluence and was still deferential towards Germans in Germany. Germans were magnanimous and sincere; Romanians were callous fellow travellers.[177] This was her way of expressing her allegiance towards what she perceived to be her cultural homeland of Germany, which remained an unfulfilled ideal: and it was precisely this decision that enabled her to sustain her unchanged image of Germans and Germany.

Conclusion: Beyond the Community

After the fall of the Ceaușescu regime in December 1989, more than 200,000 Germans left Romania. This final exodus left behind a rump community with little to sustain it. The Demokratisches Forum der Deutschen in Rumänien (Democratic Forum of Germans in Romania), based in Sibiu, achieved some moderate success in the post-communist period. The German theatre in Timișoara enjoyed a revival. Yet, on the whole, the community in Transylvania and the Banat was left abandoned. Villages emptied almost overnight, leaving behind vicars preaching to empty churches. Whole classrooms were vacated on an almost daily basis between 1990 and 1992. Meanwhile, back in what was becoming reunified Germany, places such as Bietigheim-Bissingen in Baden-Württemberg and Drabenderhöhe in North Rhine-Westphalia swelled in numbers.[178] Schloss Horneck in Gundelsheim was gradually transformed into a library, an archive, and a retirement home for ageing Romanian German émigrés who felt lost in the new Germany. While the large number of Romanian German arrivals went unnoticed among the wider German public, who were busily engrossed in broader discussions about belonging, neo-Nazism, and integration, the identity debates did not abate among the Romanian German community. Even though the

---

[176] Interview with Elizabeth Schneider, 24 February 2005, Sibiu.   [177] Ibid.
[178] See Katrin Ingenhoven, *'Ghetto' oder gelungene Integration? Untersuchung sozialräumlicher Entwicklungsprozesse in der bedeutesten Siedlungskonzentration von Aussiedlern aus Rumänien, der Siebenbürger-Sachsen-Siedlung in Wiehl-Drabenderhöhe* (Munich: LIT Verlag, 2003).

Landsmannschaften had seemingly achieved their aims of mass immigration to Germany, the contest was still far from over.

The question over a Romanian German homeland had defined Romanian German life during the communist era and continued to do so into the new millennium.[179] As this chapter has shown, debates about whether to stay in Romania or leave for Germany or elsewhere revealed an intricate web of identity contestation that operated on different scales within the Romanian German community. Community leaders, represented by the *Landsmannschaften*, insisted on a monochrome view of a community 'back' in Germany, while 'ordinary' Romanian Germans reacted in quite varied ways to the idea and reality of emigration. Meanwhile, the Lutheran Church presented quite a different idea of life under communism, namely one of accommodation for the sake of survival. And, towards the high political, Romanian Germans became caught up in Cold War politics and cultural diplomacy around the issue of emigration and German cultural life in Romania.

In the new millennium, Romanian Germans were to play out a number of disputes over their past.[180] The central question of their position between Romania and Germany remained very much at the centre of it all. In interviews with Romanian German émigrés, the conflict over belonging was still very much a live topic. Two decades after the German exodus, Hans Bergel continued to reassess Saxon culture as unique and separate from Germany:

> In Transylvania, we were able to look back on a rich [*wohlhabend*] history of almost 900 years. I believe we were brought up [*erzogen worden*] to survive. [We needed] sobriety [*Nüchternheit*], practicality [*Sachlichkeit*], and also calmness [*Ruhe*].[181] There was so many things that didn't unnerve us; the Turks came, and that didn't unnerve us. Here in Germany history developed quite differently to our history. What was absent from the history of the Transylvanian Saxons was the element of aggression, which has largely characterised German history. Just look at the many castles in Transylvania. There is only one other European region that is comparable to Transylvania as far as the number of castles is concerned, and that is South Tyrol. It's a comparable area [in terms of size]: there are just as many castles as in Transylvania. But not one, and I'm immensely proud of this as a Transylvanian Saxon, not one was designed as a castle to launch attacks

---

[179] Gerhard Möckel was one of the most outspoken opponents of emigration during the Cold War. His opinions and writings have been documented in great detail. See, for instance, Möckel (ed.), *Gerhard Möckel: Fatum oder Datum.*

[180] Two of these disputes form the core of the two chapters that follow; see Chapters 3 and 4.

[181] Here, we see a further echo of Meschendörfer's *Siebenbürgische Elegie.*

from [*Angriffsburg*]. They were all only [designed as] defensive castles [*Verteidigungsburgen*].[182]

As the Romanian German community began to dissolve, some Transylvanian Saxons started to re-emphasise their local particularity by using history to back up their position. This led some of them to revert to older ideas of Saxon particularism, which placed them at odds with the notion of a strong external German homeland.[183] Yet, as I show in the following chapters, distancing themselves from a broader German sphere was a powerful weapon for retrospectively exculpating Romanian German involvement in National Socialism and the Second World War as something substantially different from German involvement. The real Nazis, many Romanian Germans would insist, were Germans, not Romanian Germans.

---

[182] Interview Hans Bergel. The notion of Transylvanian Saxons acting as a bastion of western civilisation throughout history is a recurrent theme in Romanian German narratives. It is also striking that presence of the Teutonic Knights in Transylvania played no role in Bergel's understanding of Transylvanian history. This was true of all interviewees and most *Heimat* histories. Of all Saxon interviewees, more than a third made a reference to the history of defensive battles against outside forces.

[183] See Chapter 1.

CHAPTER 3

Fascist Divisions in the Romanian German Past

In des Krieges toben Wirren,
und die Front zu uns auch kam,
mussten wir mit wehen Blicken,
Abschied nehmen vom Heimatland.[1]

Romanian Germans were deeply implicated in the rise of National
Socialism and fascism in Europe in the 1920s and 1930s. Their involvement, and its legacy, became one of the most central facets of Romanian
German identity. It largely determined their position within post-war
Romania, challenged their views on Germany, and has dominated identity
debates into the present. Romanian Germans' experiences before, during,
and after the war exemplify a European story: fascism, collaboration,
revenge, deportation, and, finally, tortured disputes about memory. Like
many other European communities and societies, Romanian Germans
primarily understood themselves as victims. They framed their experience
of fascism and the Second World War in line with a broader post-war
European trend that portrayed Europe as a continent of victims: victims of
fascism, victims of expulsions, victims of 'Asiatic communism', victims of
a Hitler clique, victims of bombs, victims of a small number of outsiders who
led the community astray.[2] During the Cold War, Romanian Germans had
to negotiate their memories with two seemingly incompatible public narratives about the Second World War. In Romania, they were in direct conflict
with the antifascist public narrative of the war – particularly early on in the
Communist period – which contributed towards their alienation from

---

[1] This is the first stanza of a poem titled 'Die Vertreibung aus der Heimat' by Maria Müller. She wrote
the poem in private for Hans Philippi, who was the head of the organisation Licht der Heimat. Licht
der Heimat was set up as a rival to the *Landsmannschaften* with its main priority being to discourage
Siebenbürger Sachsen from emigrating; see Maria Müller, 'Die Vertreibung aus der Heimat',
Siebenbürgen Institut, B I 51, 2/2.

[2] See, for instance, Richard Lebow, Wulf Kansteiner and Claudio Fogu (eds.), *The Politics of Memory
in Postwar Europe* (Durham, N.C.: Duke University Press, 2006).

Romanian society. Their gradual migration to West Germany over the course of the Cold War then put them on a collision course with an emerging, and to them bewildering, memory culture that dealt with German perpetrators. Just as Romanian Germans were arriving in West Germany, West German public memory debates were shifting away from victimhood towards self-criticism, which resulted in frequent public quarrels over the past.[3] Alienated from the mainstream public narrative for a second time, Romanian Germans embarked on their own internal memory battles over the topic of National Socialism from the late Cold War period on; this continued to define Romanian German communities both within and outside Germany.

This chapter argues that the National Socialist period was the central formative experience for Romanian Germans. Romanian German identity debates were refracted through the legacy of National Socialism and the Second World War, as were many other memory conflicts in European societies after 1945. To understand the centrality of fascism and National Socialism, this chapter charts the origins of these debates in the interwar period, places them in their respective contexts of Cold War Romania and West Germany, and explores the reverberations of these debates in post-communist Europe. The focus on particular episodes shows that arguments over Romanian German belonging were channelled through debates on National Socialism. The circle around the Romanian German literary magazine *Klingsor* in the 1920s and 1930s rehearsed many of the arguments that were to occupy the Romanian German émigré public in the 1970s and 1980s. If the *Klingsor* writers were part of an interwar European right-wing 'youth' movement, then the same 'old men' of the 1970s and 1980s formed the vanguard in a turbulent revisionist decade over the fascist past.[4] Far from being a parochial debate about a marginal group,

---

[3] Bill Niven, 'Introduction: German Victimhood at the Turn of the Millennium', in Bill Niven (ed.), *Germans as Victims: Remembering the Past in Contemporary Germany* (Basingstoke: Palgrave Macmillan, 2006), p. 3, and Wulf Kansteiner, 'Losing the War – Winning the Memory Battle: The Legacy of Nazism, World War II, and the Holocaust in the Federal Republic of Germany', in Lebow, Kansteiner and Fogu (eds.), *The Politics of Memory in Postwar Europe*, pp. 124–9.

[4] For an excellent study on youth and fascism in Romania and the Iron Guard movement in the interwar period, see Roland Clark, *Holy Legionary Youth: Fascist Activism in Interwar Romania* (Ithaca, N.Y.: Cornell University Press, 2015). See also Rebecca Haynes, 'Saving Greater Romania: The Romanian Legionary Movement and the "New Man"', in Mark Cornwall and John Paul Newman (eds.), *Sacrifice and Rebirth: The Legacy of the Last Habsburg War* (New York: Berghahn, 2016), pp. 174–96. For Sudeten Germans in interwar Czechoslovakia, see Mark Cornwall, *The Devil's Wall: The Nationalist Youth Mission of Heinz Rutha* (Cambridge, Mass.: Harvard University Press, 2012).

Romanian German memory wars reflect a European and transnational process of making sense of European fascism, war, and expulsions.

Fascists and Victims

Throughout the interwar period, the Romanian German community found itself torn between the so-called *bürgerliche Parteien* (mainstream political parties), around locally illustrious figures such as Hans Otto Roth and Adolf Schullerus, and the rising nationalist, fascist movements across Europe.[5] Some, such as the privileged, Protestant Transylvanian Saxons, were more enthusiastic about the rise of fascism compared to others, such as the rural, Catholic Banat Swabians, who were more hesitant in their embrace of National Socialist advances.[6] The breakthrough of the National Socialists in Germany and the political ascendancy of the right under King Carol II of Romania in the 1930s created an environment in which the radicalisation of the Saxons and Swabians could flourish.[7]

The alignment of Romanian Germans with Nazi Germany has been subject to heated debate.[8] From *Selbsthilfe* (self-help) to *Unzufriedenenbewegung* (movement of the malcontent) to the literary *Klingsor* circle founded in 1924, large sections of the Romanian German community were finding purpose in

[5] See Karl M. Reinerth, *Zur politischen Entwicklung der Deutschen in Rumänien 1918–1928: Aus einer siebenbürgisch-sächsischen Sicht* (Thaur: Wort und Welt Verlag, 1993), in particular, pp. 108–296, and Harald Roth, *Kleine Geschichte Siebenbürgens* (Cologne: Böhlau, 2003), pp. 132–4. See also Tudor Georgescu, *The Eugenic Fortress: The Transylvanian Saxon Experiment in Interwar Romania* (Budapest: CEU Press, 2016), in particular, pp. 17–28, 70–7.

[6] See Balázs A. Szelényi, 'From Minority to *Übermensch*: The Social Roots of Ethnic Conflict in the German Diaspora of Hungary, Romania and Slovakia', *Past & Present* 196 (2007), pp. 215–51, and Sacha E. Davis, 'Constructing the *Volksgemeinschaft*: Saxon Particularism and the German Myth of the East, 1919–1933', *German Studies Review* 39/1 (2016), pp. 41–64.

[7] Roth, *Kleine Geschichte Siebenbürgens*, p. 133. See also Thomas Șindilariu, 'Sportpolitische Impulse aus dem "Dritten Reich" und der Strandbadbau in Siebenbürgen 1936–1939', in Mariana Hausleitner and Harald Roth (eds.), *Der Einfluss von Faschismus und Nationalsozialismus auf Minderheiten in Ostmittel- und Südosteuropa* (Munich: IKGS Verlag, 2006), pp. 163–82.

[8] See, for instance, Paul Milata, *Zwischen Hitler, Stalin, und Antonescu: Rumäniendeutsche in der Waffen-SS* (Cologne: Böhlau, 2009), Thomas Casagrande, *Die Volksdeutsche SS-Division 'Prinz Eugen': Die Banater Schwaben und die Nationalsozialistischen Kriegsverbrechen* (Frankfurt am Main: Campus, 2003), Cristian Cercel, 'The Relationship between Religious and National Identity in the Case of Transylvanian Saxons, 1933–1944', *Nationalities Papers* 39/2 (2011), pp. 161–80, Tudor Georgescu, 'Ethnic Minorities and the Eugenic Promise: The Transylvanian Saxon Experiment with National Renewal in Interwar Romania', *European Review of History/ Revue Européenne d'Histoire* 17/6 (2010), pp. 861–80, Johann Böhm, *Die Gleichschaltung der Deutschen in Rumänien und das 'Dritte Reich'* (Frankfurt am Main: Peter Lang, 2003), Konrad Gündisch, *Siebenbürgen und die Siebenbürger Sachsen* (Munich: Langen-Müller, 1998), pp. 185, 191–200, and, crucially, Georgescu, *The Eugenic Fortress*.

far-right thought and movements.[9] By the mid-1930s a majority of Romanian Germans were entangled with Nazi Germany to such an extent that the course of the war determined much of the fate of Romanian Germans at the end of the war. The *Erneuerungsbewegung* (rejuvenation movement) under the leadership of Fritz Fabritius gained much popularity among Transylvanian Saxons,[10] and such political developments and currents were part of wider trends in Europe.[11] In Romanian society more broadly, the political world of the interwar period was torn between bourgeois parties and radical forces on the right. Biopolitics and eugenicist ideas formed the backbone of collective politics among Romanian Germans, other minorities in Romania, and Romanian society.[12] Alexandru Cuza (1857–1947), a leading far-right Romanian politician in the first half of the twentieth century, transformed his movement from abstinence to an antisemitic far-right force.[13] Rival groups on the right further cemented the role of youth in 'renewal'. In the midst of far-right rivalry, the Legion of the Archangel Michael – better known as the Iron Guard – emerged as one of the strongest movements in Romanian society in the 1930s.[14] Under Corneliu Cordreanu until his assassination in 1938 and then Horia Sima until 1941, the far right mixed fascism with Orthodox Christianity to give rise to a potent force in Romanian society.[15] Meanwhile, King Carol II fostered a cult of personality that clashed with the aims of the Iron Guard and ultimately saw the Legion removed from public politics after the king's political coup in 1938, before those same far-right forces forced Carol to abdicate in 1941 in favour of the dictatorship of Marshal Ion Antonescu (1882–1946). In parallel with these developments, the Romanian German community became a *Volksdeutsche Gruppe* (ethnic German group) under the command of Andreas Schmidt (1912–48) and fully in line with the

---

[9] Gündisch, *Siebenbürgen*, pp. 185–90.

[10] Valdis O. Lumans, *Himmler's Auxiliaries: The Volksdeutsche Mittelstelle and the German National Minorities of Europe 1933–1945* (Chapel Hill: University of North Carolina Press, 1993), p. 109.

[11] See, for instance, Samuel Kalman, 'Faisceau Visions of Physical and Moral Transformation and the Cult of Youth in Interwar France', *European History Quarterly* 33/2 (2003), pp. 343–66.

[12] See, for instance, Lucian Butaru, 'Biopolitică identitară în Transilvania interbelică', *Studia Universitatis Cibiniensis: Seria Historica* 5 (2008) pp. 195–209, and Marius Turda, 'The Nation as Object: Race, Blood, and Biopolitics in Interwar Romania', *Slavic Review* 66/3 (2007), pp. 413–41. On Hungarian eugenics towards the Csangos in Moldavia, see R. Chris Davis, *Hungarian Religion, Romanian Blood: A Minority's Struggle for National Belonging, 1920–1945* (Madison: University of Wisconsin Press, 2019), and specifically on Transylvanian Saxons and eugenics see Georgescu, *The Eugenic Fortress*.

[13] See Constantin Bărbulescu, *Physicians, Peasants, and Modern Medicine: Imagining Rurality in Romania, 1860–1910* (Budapest: CEU Press, 2018), pp. 123–45.

[14] Roland Clark, 'From Elite Pamphleteers to Social Movement Protagonists: Antisemitic Activism in 1920s Romania', *Studies on National Movements* 4/1 (2019), pp. 1–35.

[15] See Clark, *Holy Legionary Youth*, pp. 184–215.

Hauptamt Volksdeutsche Mittelstelle (VoMi) and the policies of the Third Reich, ironing out any regional particularities between Saxons and Swabians.[16] The connections between Romanian German radicals and the Volksdeutsche Gruppe, on the one hand, and Romanian fascists, on the other, were vague und uneasy, though Romanian Germans generally welcomed the antisemitic measures put in place after 1938. At the same time, their allegiances belonged mainly to the Third Reich. Following a clandestine '1,000-man action' in 1940, when roughly 1,000 Romanian Germans joined the Waffen-SS, enlistment into German military forces, chiefly the Waffen-SS, continued apace.[17] By the end of the Second World War, approximately 54,000 Germans from Romania had joined the Waffen-SS, and many of those who survived ended up in prisoner-of-war camps in the Balkans and the Soviet Union.[18] The end of the war also marked a huge rupture for the Romanian German community.

It was the 'rejuvenation movement [*Erneuerungsbewegung*]' of the 1920s and 1930s, however, that would frame the Romanian German memory conflict after 1945. Long before Adolf Hitler's NSDAP (Nationalsozialistische Deutsche Arbeiterpartei, known in English as the Nazi Party) seized power in Germany in 1933, Romanian Germans were showing clear signs of alignment with far-right German politics.[19] As early as 1924, contributors to the newly founded literary journal *Klingsor* – a monthly journal published in Braşov, which would become a leading voice for Romanian Germans – called for an 'unconditional nationalism' in an unmistakable appeal for German nationalism against local and liberal patriotic traditions.[20] On occasion, Romanian Germans would espouse openly antisemitic sentiments with the backing of the main editor at *Klingsor*, the literary luminary Heinrich Zillich. Writing in 1925, Erwin Reisner dealt at length with the 'Jewish question', warning his readers that hankering after material success would only harm

---

[16] Ibid., pp. 107–13.

[17] Anthony Komjathy's and Rebecca Stockwell's classic study on German minorities and the Third Reich is still the standard work on the *Gleichschaltung* of Transylvanian Saxons and Banat Swabians; see Anthony Komjathy and Rebecca Stockwell, *German Minorities and the Third Reich: Ethnic Germans of East Central Europe between the Wars* (New York: Holmes & Meier, 1980), pp. 103–24.

[18] Lumans, *Himmler's Auxiliaries*, p. 230, Paul Georgescu, '"Volksdeutsche" in der Waffen-SS', *Südostdeutsche Vierteljahreshefte* 53/2 (2004), pp. 117–23, and Casagrande, *Die Volksdeutsche SS-Division 'Prinz Eugen'*, pp. 207–11; Casagrande's study focuses on Banat Swabians in Yugoslavia, though the overlap between German personnel from Romania and Yugoslavia is obvious in his work.

[19] See, for instance, Olga Schüller, *Für Glaube, Führer, Volk, Vater- oder Mutterland? Die Kämpfe um die deutsche Jugend im rumänischen Banat (1918–1944)* (Berlin: LIT Verlag, 2009), pp. 80–4, 113–24, 141–66. For a slightly polemical, yet useful analysis of the National Socialist enthusiasm among Transylvanian Saxons, see Johann Böhm, *Die Deutschen in Rumänien und das Dritte Reich 1933–1940* (Frankfurt am Main: Peter Lang, 1999).

[20] Karl Hoch, 'Die Grüne Generation', *Klingsor*, 1/2 May 1924, p. 68.

Germans and play into the hands of 'the Jewish beneficiaries'.[21] 'Jews', Reisner continued, 'controlled the earthly part of the Christian world through capital, the press, etc.'[22] It was a fate, he argued, that Germans could challenge only through a 'fundamental, internal change and renunciation of all desires for material successes [*äußere Erfolge*]'.[23] Such evidence belies the claim, as this chapter shows, that Romanian Germans were duped into blindly following National Socialist Germany after the rise of the NSDAP in Germany in 1933.

Older establishment figures were under siege from young Romanian German nationalist enthusiasts. Dr Hans Otto Roth, the prominent interwar politician who advocated Romanian German pluralism rather than nationalism, faced the young generation's ire. He was intellectually 'risible', the editors of *Klingsor* insisted in 1924.[24] Fourteen years later, in 1938, readers of the *Deutsche Tageszeitung* were reminded that their one-time leaders – most prominently Roth – had acted only in their self-interest and with the banks against the interests of *Deutschtum* in Romania.[25] Those same bourgeois 'liberal' politicians were found to be conspirators and collaborators with Jews, the *Deutsche Tageszeitung* claimed during a crucial period when the regime of Octavian Goga (1881–1938) and the Third Reich had put paid to any semblance of political normality.[26] Education was a particularly sore point, and a younger generation eschewed the co-operative approach taken by 'establishment' figures towards the new states of east-central Europe. Contemporaries such as Bernhard Capesius, a moderate writer and linguist, were aware of this and, to some extent, plugged into the discourse.[27] Romanian Germans were frantically discussing youth, education, and rejuvenation, as numerous articles to the teachers' journal *Schule und Leben*, including by Capesius himself, attest.[28] Generational questions and ideas of rejuvenation dictated politics and culture and found particularly fertile ground on the extremes of the political spectrum. The Saxon Alfred Bonfert, for example, led the group Südostdeutsche Wandervögel, a Romanian German umbrella

[21] Erwin Reisner, 'Das auserwählte Volk', *Klingsor*, 2/7 July 1925, p. 262.   [22] Ibid., p. 263.
[23] Ibid.   [24] 'Rundschau: Zum Schulkampf', *Klingsor*, 1/5 August 1924, p. 196.
[25] 'Volksgenosse, hast du schon vergessen?', *Deutsche Tageszeitung*, 4 January 1938, p. 4.
[26] 'Liberale, Volksgemeinschaftler und Juden auf einer Liste!', *Deutsche Tageszeitung*, 4 January 1938, p. 5.
[27] Bernhard Capesius, 'Vollkommenheit und Vollständigkeit: Zur Psychologie des Gegensatzes zwischen Jungen und Alten', *Klingsor*, 7/7 1930, pp. 255–61. See also Bernhard Capesius, *Nachlass*, Siebenbürgen Institut, B I 56, 1/1–8. For a comparison to developments of far-right youth movements in Romania more broadly, see Clark, *Holy Legionary Youth*.
[28] See, for instance, 'Die Jugend und die rumänische Schule', *Schule und Leben: Fachzeitschrift des Siebenbürgisch-Sächsischen Lehrerbundes* 6 (1936), pp. 271–4.

organisation devoted to physical education, who themselves were in close contact with the Jungschwaben, a radical youth movement, with Hans Beller at the helm.[29] German youth movements, above all the Wandervögel, captured the spirit of the time and exerted power over the Romanian German imagination.[30] *Klingsor* covered all aspects of Romanian German youth movements and saw itself as the vanguard of a new pan-German spirit among Saxons and Swabians.[31]

Their earnest attention was gripped by developments in Germany. German concern for so-called *Auslandsdeutsche* (Germans abroad) was met with great enthusiasm by Romanian German nationalists. *Auslandsdeutsche*, the Auslandsinstitut in Stuttgart confirmed to Romanian Germans, were 'carriers of the spirit of German high culture [*Kulturgedankengut*]' and stood 'in opposition to western liberalism'.[32] Such sentiments were not the preserve of National Socialists. Instead, they formed part of a 'conservative revolution', but in reception among Romanian Germans they quickly mutated into something more recognisably racialised and defensive. Yet, even as Romanian Germans drew closer to Germany, a nagging inferiority complex towards so-called *Reichsdeutsche* was plain to see. 'As *Auslandsdeutsche*, we sometimes complain that the Reich shows insufficient interest in us', noted Heinrich Zillich in 1930.[33] *Auslandsdeutsche* shared the same fate as Jews in their sense of unity in the face of defeat, the former German diplomat Gerhard von Mutius boldly claimed in *Klingsor*.[34] That sense of inferiority would dominate Romanian German identity debates for the rest of the century, and the comparison with Jews laid the foundations for historical revisionism after the Second World War. But it was the interwar years that provided the most fruitful ground for pan-German enthusiasm to cover over any Romanian German self-doubts.

Meanwhile, the so-called self-help movements (*Selbsthilfegruppe*) plunged their way into the heart of German communities in Romania in

---

[29] Mariana Hausleitner, *Die Donauschwaben 1868–1948: Ihre Rolle im rumänischen und serbischen Banat* (Stuttgart: Franz Steiner Verlag, 2014), p. 110.

[30] Albert Hermann, 'Die deutsche Jugendbewegung', *Klingsor*, 1/5 August 1924, pp. 189–94.

[31] See, for instance, Karl Hoch, 'Die siebenb.-sächsischen Jungen des 20. Jahrhunderts', *Klingsor*, 2/9 September 1925, pp. 341–8, Karl Hoch, 'Die siebenb.-sächsischen Jungen des 20. Jahrhunderts', *Klingsor*, 2/10 October 1925, pp. 380–8, and Karl Hoch, 'Die siebenb.-sächsischen Jungen des 20. Jahrhunderts', *Klingsor*, 2/11 November 1925, pp. 418–25.

[32] Misch Orend, 'Deutschland und die Auslandsdeutschen', *Klingsor*, 2/7 July 1925, p. 279.

[33] Heinrich Zillich, 'Kritik für die Auslandsdeutschen?', *Klingsor*, 7/8 August 1930, p. 304.

[34] Gerhard von Mutius, 'Auslandsdeutscher und Reichsdeutscher', *Klingsor*, 7/9 September 1930, p. 325.

the 1920s and 1930s. They married the élan of youth movements with concerns over German 'racial hygiene' in the face of supposed 'eastern threats'.[35] Leading Romanian Germans such as Fritz Fabritius advocated *Selbsthilfe* in order to both 'protect' and strengthen Romanian German racial purity and national unity.[36] In 1932, Fabritius founded the umbrella organisation Nationalsozialistische Selbsthilfebewegung der Deutschen.[37] Couched in the language of eugenics, Romanian Germans increasingly conceived of themselves as an organism that had to reconnect with 'species-led and blood-led thinking [*art- und blutgemäßes Denken*], [and] an organic sense of togetherness [*organisches Zusammengehörigkeitsgefühl*]'.[38] Political developments in Germany at the beginning of 1933 emboldened the radicals in the Romanian German community and made German belonging even less inclusive.[39] Heinrich Zillich visited Germany on a number of occasions and reported with growing enthusiasm on the 'revolution' taking place in Germany in 1933.[40] Without ever declaring himself a National Socialist, Zillich, for instance, still managed to reproach the 'Jewish press' in Cernăuți for speaking ill of Germany and Hitler.[41] Against the global conspiracy against Germandom, Zillich wrote glowingly of the rise of National Socialism in Germany as a reassertion of a 'pure and courageous manhood'.[42] The antisemitic actions of the Hitler government, Zillich continued, were not really antisemitic, but merely addressed the Jewish imbalance in state offices and the civil service.[43] On a visit to Nazi

---

[35] For an excellent and succinct overview of the Transylvanian Saxon self-help movement, see Tudor Georgescu, 'Pursuing the Fascist Promise: The Transylvanian Saxon "Self-Help" from Genesis to Empowerment, 1922–1935', in Robert Pyrah and Marius Turda (eds.), *Recontextualising East Central European History: Nation, Culture and Minority Groups* (London: Legenda, 2010), pp. 55–73. See also Hausleitner, *Die Donauschwaben*, pp. 109–31, Georgescu, *The Eugenic Fortress*, pp. 143–4, 165–202, 204–7, and Böhm, *Die Deutschen in Rumanien und das Dritte Reich*, pp. 28–31.

[36] See Fritz Fabritius, 'Selbsthilfe', *Klingsor*, 7/10 October 1930, pp. 412–14, and Georgescu, 'Pursuing the Fascist Promise', p. 57.

[37] See Georgescu, *The Eugenic Fortress*, pp. 51–69, 166–71, and Böhm, *Die Deutschen in Rumänien und das Dritte Reich*, p. 30.

[38] See Fabritius, 'Selbsthilfe', p. 413. For an understanding of how Romanian German eugenicist thought fitted in more broadly with trends in Romania and south-eastern Europe, see Marius Turda, 'Controlling the National Body: Ideas of Racial Purification in Romania, 1918–1944', in Christian Promitzer, Sevasti Trubeta and Marius Turda (eds.), *Health, Hygiene and Eugenics in Southeastern Europe to 1945* (Budapest: CEU Press, 2011), pp. 325–50, and Turda, 'The Nation as Object'.

[39] See also Sacha E. Davis, 'Maintaining a "German" Home in Southeast Europe: Transylvanian Saxon Nationalism and the Metropolitan Model of the Family, 1918–1933', *History of the Family* 14/4 (2009), pp. 386–401.

[40] Heinrich Zillich, 'Deutsche Revolution', *Klingsor* 10/5 May 1933, pp. 165–77.

[41] Heinrich Zillich, 'Rundschau', *Klingsor*, 10/4 April 1933, p. 154.

[42] Zillich, 'Deutsche Revolution', p. 172.   [43] Ibid.

Germany five years later in the autumn of 1938, he almost certainly witnessed *Reichskristallnacht*, yet he made no mention of it in his writings for *Klingsor*.

When the young Romanian German Andreas Schmidt, backed by Berlin, finally headed the Romanian German *Volksgemeinschaft* from 1940, the Romanian German community had been softened up and, in part, enthusiastically welcomed their inclusion into the Greater German *Volksgemeinschaft*.[44] Alignment with National Socialism also revealed a deeper battle over the heart of the community. If religious institutional affiliation had been a constant for Catholic Swabians and Protestant Saxons, National Socialism broke down that certainty. The Lutheran Church in Transylvania came under enormous pressure under the leadership (1931–41) of Bishop Viktor Glondys (1882–1949). As a critic of the efforts to align the church with National Socialist politics, Glondys was eventually forced into early retirement in 1941 at the age of fifty-eight.[45] Attacks against him came from two directions. There was the ongoing feud with the vicar Konrad Möckel (1892–1965), who thought Glondys's opposition to the 'new heathens' of the Nazi activists was weak.[46] Glondys also faced opposition from the far right, both within and outside the Lutheran Church. Wilhelm Staedel (1890–1971), Glondys's successor as bishop of the church in Transylvania from 1941 to 1944, represented the victory of the *völkisch* activists in the Romanian German clerical world.[47] Staedel had himself been part of Bonfert's *Wandervögel* before rising through the ranks of the Lutheran Church. The generational struggle of the 1920s and 1930s thus found its conclusion with Staedel's tenure as bishop in 1941. Although the Lutheran Church had put up a fight, the Romanian state afforded the Romanian German *Volksgruppe* a privileged position in Romania. In the early 1940s, the Romanian German school system was under the control of National Socialists, and many of the *Landsmannschaft* activists in West Germany during the Cold War were products of this system, despite their

[44] Mariana Hausleitner, 'Politische Bestrebungen der Schwaben im serbischen und im rumänischen Banat vor 1945', in Mariana Hausleitner (ed.), *Vom Faschismus zum Stalinismus: Deutsche und andere Minderheiten in Ostmittel- und Südosteuropa 1941–1953* (Munich: IKGS Verlag, 2008), pp. 47–9, and Böhm, *Die Deutschen in Rumänien und das Dritte Reich*, pp. 256–62. For a diplomatic history of Romanian policy towards Nazi Germany leading up to 1940, see Rebecca Haynes, *Romanian Policy towards Germany, 1936–1940* (Basingstoke: Palgrave Macmillan, 2000).
[45] Andreas Möckel, *Umkämpfte Volkskirche: Leben und Wirken des evangelisch-sächsischen Pfarrers Konrad Möckel (1892–1965)* (Cologne: Böhlau, 2011), pp. 133–6.
[46] See ibid.
[47] For a detailed study of the splits within the Lutheran Church, see Ulrich A. Wien, *Kirchenleitung über dem Abgrund: Bischof Friedrich Müller vor den Herausforderungen durch Minderheitenexistenz, Nationalsozialismus und Kommunismus* (Cologne: Böhlau, 1998).

later insistence that National Socialism had passed them by.[48] While there was mutual mistrust between Marshal Antonescu's regime and the Romanian German radicals, a period of 'co-habitation' served both groups well.[49]

Ultimately, the rejuvenation movement won, and the result was more than 50,000 Romanian Germans enthusiastically enlisting into the Waffen-SS.[50] They were integral to the war and to the killing machine of the Third Reich as well as being active participants in the Holocaust in the Balkans. Meanwhile, in northern Transylvania, which had been 'awarded' to Hungary in August 1940, around 160,000 Jews were deported to their deaths in 1944 as part of the Hungarian Holocaust, and Romanian Germans in the region were both active and passive participants.[51] The impact of the Holocaust on Romanian Transylvania – southern and central Transylvania – was far less comprehensive and severe than other regions, such as Bessarabia, Moldova, and Transnistria, where most of the murders took place. That geographical disparity, where Romanian Transylvania was curiously less violent than the Hungarian part and eastern Romania,[52] would also serve as an excuse for Romanian Germans to avoid any critical examination of Romanian German involvement in the Holocaust. After all, as Romanian Germans would argue after 1945, the Holocaust had not really happened in Transylvania where Romanian Germans were, while Romanians had committed crimes in the east and Hungarians in the north.

By 1944, after years of fighting for the Nazi war effort, the Romanian–German alliance collapsed. As the Red Army advanced westwards into Romania, the country's alliance with the Third Reich was on its last legs. Then, on 23 August 1944, General Antonescu was deposed in a coup by bourgeois and democratic forces around the figurehead of King Michael I. That date, 23 August, gained legendary status in post-war narratives in Romania. It struck fear into the memories of Romanian Germans and other 'losers' of the war, and was triumphantly appropriated and celebrated by the Romanian Communist Party as the symbol of victory over fascism. For Romanian Germans, the consequences of this political realignment

[48] See Hans Bergel, cited ibid., p. 183.   [49] Georgescu, *The Eugenic Fortress*, pp. 241–54.
[50] Hannelore Baier, 'Die Deutschen in Rumänien in den Jahren 1945 bis 1948', in Hausleitner (ed.), *Vom Faschismus zum Stalinismus*, p. 173.
[51] Zoltán Tibori Szabó, 'The Holocaust in Transylvania', in Randolph L. Braham and András Kovács (eds.), *The Holocaust in Hungary: Seventy Years Later* (Budapest: CEU Press, 2016), pp. 147–82.
[52] See Jean Ancel, *The History of the Holocaust in Romania* (Lincoln, Neb.: University of Nebraska Press, 2011).

were real and immediate. Particularly in the north and west of the country, Saxons and Swabians were caught between a rock and a hard place. They were put under immense pressure by the retreating German Wehrmacht to evacuate and flee, which resulted in around 100,000 Romanian Germans leaving the Banat and northern Transylvania.[53] Stories of Red Army rape and plunder prompted Saxons and Swabians to leave hastily with the Germans. Those who remained were instantly affected by land distribution measures. German farms and property were either expropriated or repurposed as accommodation for the sizeable Red Army units that were now stationed in Romania. At the beginning of January, following months of rumours, the deportation of Germans to the Soviet Union began. Starting on 6 January 1945, over the next few weeks 75,000–80,000 Germans were deported to the Soviet Union; many ended up in the Donbass region in present-day Ukraine.[54] As recent research has shown, the Romanian government, at this point not yet communist, had been asked by Stalin to send workers to the Soviet Union, and Romanian Germans were the obvious choice.[55]

Other Romanian Germans ended up in one of the two Germanys, unable to return to Romania because they had fought for Nazi Germany. They included those who had been 'evacuated' by the retreating Wehrmacht in 1944, which had temporarily severed their links to the homeland in the Banat and northern Transylvania.[56] Those who returned from the hard labour camps in the USSR came back to a Romania where a new communist state system oversaw land redistribution and the German community were excluded (though later officially reintegrated). In 1948, there were around 344,000 Germans in Romania, and the rupture within the community was palpable.[57] Romanian Germans who experienced the start of the Cold War in West Germany also felt disoriented. Treated both as aliens and as ultimate symbols of German victimhood, Romanian Germans struggled to fit their narratives into a society that played host to increasingly diverse stories of the war, National Socialism, and the Holocaust. It is within this context that Romanian German stories of victimhood flourished.

---

[53] See Baier, 'Die Deutschen in Rumänien', pp. 173, 174.
[54] Georg Weber et al. (eds.), *Die Deportation von Siebenbürger Sachsen in die Sowjetunion 1945–1949: Die Deportation als historisches Geschehen*, Vol. I (Cologne: Böhlau Verlag, 1995), pp. 1–11. See also Pavel Polian, *Against Their Will: The History and Geography of Forced Migrations in the USSR* (Budapest: CEU Press, 2004), pp. 249–60.
[55] See, for instance, Hannelore Baier, *Germanii din România, 1944–1956* (Sibiu: Honterus, 2005).
[56] Hausleitner, *Die Donauschwaben*, p. 356.   [57] Baier, 'Die Deutschen in Rumänien', pp. 176–9.

Post-War Stories

Romanian German stories of the interwar and wartime period often begin with the end of the war:[58] the Soviets came in 1944 and deported them, with the connivance of the Romanians, to the USSR. Memories of the war were being formed while the fighting was still underway. Even before Romania joined the Allied forces, Romanian Germans remembered themselves as victims of German lies. After all, Romanian Germans had expressed loyalty towards both Nazi Germany and Romania right up until 23 August 1944. Adorned with a swastika, the *Südostdeutsche Tageszeitung*, previously known as *Banater Deutsche Zeitung*, was still celebrating the Romanian air force and German ground troops in July 1944 as the world around them gradually collapsed.[59] But it was 23 August 1944 that canonised Romanian Germans as victims of historical fate. Romania ousted Marshal Antonescu and welcomed the Soviets in a deal struck in early 1944.[60] Romanian Germans found themselves immediately isolated and in a precarious situation in Romania. The rapid changes that swept across Romania in 1944 and 1945 allowed Romanian Germans to reinterpret their own standing as defined by isolation, victimhood, and a lack of agency. Their voices, as ideologically bound as they had been, dried up in public.[61] From '*Übermenschen*' they were transformed into deportees,[62] taken suddenly from their homesteads by the advancing Red Army. Meanwhile, Romanians pounced on the opportunity to settle scores and redistribute land to the detriment of the otherwise passive Germans, or so the latter believed.

---

[58] See, for instance, Kultur- und Erwachsenenbildungsverein 'Deutsche Vortragsreihe Reschitza' (ed.), *Das Schreckliche Jahr 1945: Erzählungen von Russlanddeportierten* (Vol. II) (Bucharest: Allgemeine Deutsche Zeitung für Rumänien, 1997), 'Friedrich-Ebert'-Stiftung Rumänien, *Tief in Russland bei Stalino: Erinnerungen und Dokumente zur Deportation in die Sowjetunion 1945* (Bucharest: Allgemeine Deutsche Zeitung für Rumänien), *Russland-Deportierte erinnern sich: Schicksale Volksdeutscher aus Rumänien, 1945–1956* (Bucharest: Verlag der Zeitung Neuer Weg, 1992), and Volker Petri (ed.), *Not und Neuanfang: Die Evangelische Kirche Österreichs und ihre Siebenbürger Sachsen* (Sibiu: Schiller Verlag, 2014). A collection of eyewitness testimonies by Sören Pichotta confirms this pattern; see Sören Pichotta, *Schicksale: Deutsche Zeitzeugen aus Rumänien: Lebensmut trotz Krieg, Deportation und Exodus* (Sibiu: Schiller Verlag, 2013). See also Erich Phleps's work, published and unpublished, on Transylvanian anecdotes, which situated 1944 as a rupture for century-old traditions: Siebenbürgen Institut, B I 72, 2.

[59] See, for instance, 'Zum Tag der rumänischen Luftwaffe', *Südostdeutsche Tageszeitung* 71/164, 21 July 1944.

[60] Sergiu Verona, *Military Occupation and Diplomacy: Soviet Troops in Romania, 1944–1958* (Durham, N.C.: Duke University Press, 1992), pp. 27–9.

[61] The final issue of *Südostdeutsche Tageszeitung* was published on 11 September 1944.

[62] See Szelényi, 'From Minority to *Übermensch*'.

Romanian German victim stories of the Second World War were firmly embedded in older narratives of victimisation. Their experiences at the end of the war could easily be imagined as another episode in the long-standing Swabian *Leidensweg*.[63] The artist Stefan Jäger's depiction of the Swabians' arrival in the Banat (*Einwanderung der Schwaben*) – reproductions of which could be found hanging on the living room walls of many Romanian Germans – had epitomised the essence of this narrative, as contemporary voices from the unveiling in 1910 up to its Nazi appropriation in 1940 make clear.[64] In a sequel to this work four decades after his first triptych, dubbed *Das Tragische Triptychon* (*The Tragic Triptych*), Jäger updated the theme of ordeal for a new Romanian German framework in the modern world with a further uncompleted painting that echoed the themes of the first by depicting the deportation of Germans from the Banat at the end of the war. The three panels were designed to complement the earlier work on the migration of the Swabians to the Banat in an obvious and important way: '*Migration*' ('*Wanderung*', Figure 3.1) was contrasted with '*Flight*' ('*Die Flucht*', Figure 3.2), '*Rest*' ('*Rast*', Figure 3.3) with '*The Arrival of the Colonists*' ('*Der Einzug der Kolonisten*', Figure 3.4), and '*Arrival*' ('*Ankunft*', Figure 3.5) with '*Deportation to Russia*' ('*Die Verschleppung nach Russland*', Figure 3.6).

The original *Einwanderungs* triptych temporarily disappeared at the end of the war from its public display in the offices of the *Deutsche Volksgruppe* in Timişoara, where it had been housed since 1940.[65] It later reappeared in a farmhouse attic before being returned to the Banat Museum, where it remained in storage until a great retrospective of Jäger's work in 1967.[66] At the time of its disappearance, however, Jäger began work on *The Tragic Triptych*, which depicted another foundational Swabian and German moment: the deportation of up to 80,000 Romanian Germans to the Soviet Union in January 1945.[67] The work was privately commissioned by

[63] Márta Fata, 'Migration im Gedächtnis: Auswanderung und Ansiedlung in der Identitätsbildung der Donauschwaben', in Márta Fata (ed.), *Migration im Gedächtnis: Auswanderung und Ansiedlung in der Identitätsbildung der Donauschwaben* (Stuttgart: Franz Steiner, 2013), pp. 7–21.
[64] See Chapter 1, and see also, for instance, Christian Glass, 'Die inszinierte Einwanderung: Stefan Jägers Triptychon "Die Einwanderung der Schwaben in das Banat" und seine Wirkungsgeschichte', in Fata (ed.), *Migration im Gedächtnis*, pp. 55–70.
[65] Glass, 'Die inszenierte Einwanderung', pp. 66–8.   [66] Ibid.
[67] Annemarie Podlipny-Hehn's study of Stefan Jäger makes no mention of the Tragic Triptych, unsurprisingly perhaps considering that she published her book in communist Romania. See Annemarie Podlipny-Hehn, *Stefan Jäger* (Bucharest: Kriterion, 1972). For details on the deportation, see Weber, *Die Deportation von Siebenbürger Sachsen*, Vols. I–III, and Daniel Bayer, *Deportiert und repatriiert: Aufzeichnungen und Erinnerungen 1945–1947* (Munich: Südostdeutsches Kulturwerk, 2000).

Figure 3.1 Stefan Jäger: Part I ('*Wanderung*') of the triptych *Die Einwanderung der Schwaben* (1905)

a local farmer, one Mr Reichel from Grabaț/Grabatz, in 1950 who had been a deportee himself and had only recently returned from a labour camp in the Soviet Union. Reichel paid a deposit made up in part of money and in part of a payment-in-kind of sugar, flour, and other natural products; by 1951, the triptych was as good as finished. A second wave of deportations, however, this time to the Bărăgan, put a halt to the enterprise.[68] Communities in the borderlands of Romania and Yugoslavia fell victim

---

[68] Karl-Hans Gross, *Stefan Jäger, Maler seiner heimatlichen Gefilde: Aus seinem Leben und Werk* (Mannheim: Oswald Hartmann Verlag, 1991), pp. 144–56.

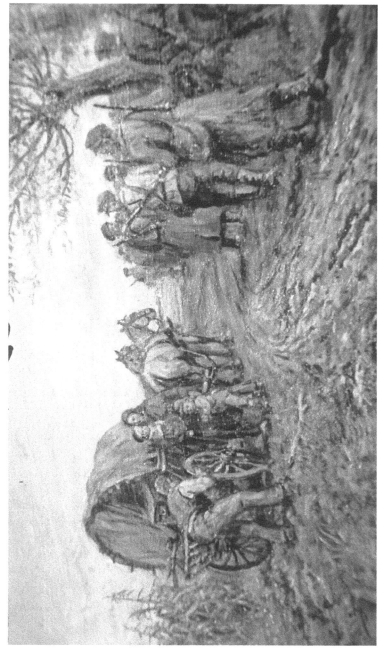

Figure 3.2 Stefan Jäger: Part I ('*Die Flucht*') of the triptych *Das Tragische Triptychon* (1951)

Figure 3.3 Stefan Jäger: Part II (*'Rast'*)

to the general suspicion of being unreliable citizens due to the proximity to the Yugoslav border. Banat Swabians were particularly affected by this, although they were not the explicit target of this wave of deportations.[69] The Bărăgan deportations had a great emotional effect on Jäger. Though physically untouched by the deportations in both 1945 and 1951, he struggled to make sense of the new world which he and other Romanian Germans now inhabited. In correspondence with his confidante, Dr Peter Pink, Jäger explained his decision to abandon the project. Pink encouraged him to complete it, but, ultimately, Jäger painted over the original, leaving behind only preparatory sketches and, later, reproductions based on them.[70]

If the Tragic Triptych emerged out of the dissolution of a community, then its fate illustrates the complex developments in the Romanian German

[69] Smaranda Vultur's work on the deportations has been especially thoughtful. See, for instance, Smaranda Vultur, *Istorie trăită, istorie povestită: deportarea în Bărăgan 1951–1956* (Timişoara: Editura Amarcord, 1997).
[70] Gross, *Stefan Jäger*, pp. 144–50.

Figure 3.4 Stefan Jäger: Part II (*'Der Einzug der Kolonisten'*)

community in the second half of the twentieth century. The events depicted in the triptych became central to Romanian German identity. Jäger's painting – or rather, the sketches that made it popular – captured feelings of victimhood and the end of the community, transcending its immediate subject matter. It spoke to a broader sense of what it meant to be Romanian German. In the left-hand panel, *'Die Flucht'* (*'Flight'*), a German family is stuck in the mud as Soviet soldiers – depicted anachronistically as Russian soldiers from the First World War – pass by menacingly. The sense of dissolution is palpable in the central panel, *'Der Einzug der Kolonisten'* (*'The Arrival of the Colonists'*), where Romanian colonists arrive in the village. A scenario familiar to all Romanian Germans, this image spoke to the fear of loss of land and property in the aftermath of the Second World War, when Romanian newcomers were relocated all over Transylvania, the Banat, and Maramureş as part of land distribution that spanned the late monarchical and early communist periods. Romanian Germans felt these measures keenly, as many of them were farmers and small-holders. This was true for both Banat Swabians and Transylvanian Saxons, and both regions underwent great economic change after the war. Finally, the third panel of the triptych, *'Die Verschleppung nach Russland'* (*'Deportation to Russia'*), depicting Romanian Germans being rounded up in January 1945, encapsulated the negative foundation myth for Romanian Germans after the Second World War. Jäger found inspiration not in the

Figure 3.5 Stefan Jäger: Part III (*'Ankunft'*)

new artistic movements of the twentieth century, but in older depictions of
exile. Representations of Siberian exile were reflected in his work, such as
Aleksander Sochaczewski's paintings of sybiraks – exiles to Siberia – from the
January Uprising in 1863. Sochaczewski's 1894 painting 'Farewell to Europe!'
framed the visual grammar for representing exile and deportation eastwards at
the hands of Russians.[71] Jäger's forgotten Tragic Triptych thus spoke to
a specific Romanian German sense of loss while reflecting broader European
ideas of a creeping 'eastern barbarism' as the Red Army advanced into east-
central Europe.

It is difficult to overstate the impact of the deportation to the Soviet
Union on Romanian Germans. It profoundly altered the make-up of the

[71] Daniel Beer, *The House of the Dead: Siberian Exile under the Tsars* (Harmondsworth: Penguin
Books, 2017), pp. 213, 214.

Figure 3.6 Stefan Jäger: Part III (*'Die Verschleppung nach Russland'*)

community. The German population in Romania was reduced by more than half between 1939 and 1948 – from roughly 786,000 to 343,000 – before increasing back to 400,000 by the mid-1950s. But it was the 75,000–80,000 Germans deported to the Soviet Union – about half of whom had returned by 1949 – that weighed heavily on Romanian German memory. Families were torn apart, and the event set in motion a complicated and distressing process of emigration to West Germany, which culminated with the collapse of communism in 1989–92, in which period up to 200,000 Romanian Germans left the country for good.

Public Memory in Romania

Although Romanian Germans had overcome the ordeal of migrating from Germany to the Banat, the tribulations they faced at the end of the war, encapsulated by Jäger's triptych – flight, Romanian settlers, and deportation – heightened their sense of suffering. The ordeal at the end of the war allowed Romanian Germans to dissolve their connections to Nazism into a long history of continuous suffering.[72] The racialised violence that had

---

[72] Pierre de Trégomain, 'Constructing Authenticity: Commemorative Strategy of the Transylvanian Saxons in West Germany's Early Years', in Mareike König and Rainer Ohliger (eds.), *Enlarging European Memory: Migration Movements in Historical Perspective* (Ostfildern: Jan Thorbecke Verlag, 2006), pp. 106–7.

devastated Europe before 1945 made no appearance in Romanian German memories in the aftermath of the war. On the contrary, as Fred Umbrich, a Romanian German Waffen-SS volunteer, claimed apologetically in his autobiography, unlike their German contemporaries, *they* had always been on good terms with the 'Romanian, Hungarian, Gypsy, Jew'.[73]

Yet how were they to explain the ruins of the Second World War and their own involvement in National Socialism? Romanian Germans in Germany quickly adopted the language of the expellee milieu, portraying themselves as unsuspecting victims of *reichsdeutsch* backhandedness during the war and of Soviet aggression at the end of it.[74] Their involvement in fascism was a naïve act, or so *Landsmannschaft* figures claimed, which was perverted once Germans from the Reich got involved in the 'rejuvenation movement'.[75] But the real catastrophe in the Romanian German story ensued with the political power shift of 23 August 1944. This marked an endpoint for Germans in Romania, and those Germans – approximately half of the pre-war population – who stayed in Romania were left to make sense of the pieces.[76]

If Romanian Germans immersed themselves in a right-wing revanchist climate among expellees in West Germany, Germans in Romania had no such vent. Public memory of the war in Romania was quite different from that in the Federal Republic of Germany. Romanian Germans found themselves entangled in two memory cultures. The end of the Second World War was publicly remembered as a liberation from the German fascists by the Red Army. Although Soviet–Romanian relations deteriorated from the late 1950s, the liberation narrative stayed at the forefront of any public representation of the war.[77] Antifascism, liberation, and victory formed the spine of public Romanian memory, while justice against fascist perpetrators was meted out unevenly in post-war

[73] Friedrich (Fred) Umbrich, *Balkan Nightmare: A Transylvanian Saxon in World War II* (Boulder, Co.: East European Monographs, 2000), p. 21. In this book, Umbrich's commitment to the fascist cause is explained away in stories portraying him as a victim of circumstance.

[74] See de Trégomain, 'Constructing Authenticity', on the language adopted by Heinrich Zillich and others in post-war West Germany. See also Hans Bergel and Hans Myß (eds.), *Wir Siebenbürger* (Innsbruck: Wort und Welt Verlag, 1986), for a collection of essays from more than a century outlining those very themes: duped by the Germans, tortured by the Soviets. Hans Hartl, Ernst Wagner, and Heinrich Zillich's contributions demonstrate this with particular clarity.

[75] Ernst Wagner, 'Siebenbürgen als Teil des Königreichs Rumänien und der Zweite Weltkrieg (1918–1945)', in Bergel and Myß (eds.), *Wir Siebenbürger*, p. 82.

[76] Hans Hartl, 'Am Ende einer historischen Aufgabe', ibid., p. 88.

[77] See Dennis Deletant, *Romania under Communist Rule* (Oxford: Center for Romanian Studies and Civic Academy Foundation, 1999), pp. 68–110, and Maria Bucur, *Heroes and Victims: Remembering War in Twentieth-Century Romania* (Bloomington: Indiana University Press, 2009), pp. 160–2.

Romania[78]. As Maria Bucur's work has demonstrated, the determined focus on individuals and events in Hungarian-controlled territory in northern Transylvania resulted in a skewed memory against Romania's minorities, including the Germans.[79] Aiming their ire at the 'Horthyist–fascist terror' of 1940–4 acted as a conduit for Romanians to recalibrate power relations with Hungarians in and over Transylvania. The Romanian–Hungarian conflict re-emerged with vehemence in the 1980s.[80] And while this memory culture was decidedly anti-Hungarian, it also excluded Germans from public memory.

At the same time, private German memories of the war painted a rather different picture. The majority of Germans in Romania subscribed to a version of the past based on the notion of victimhood and a sudden, unprovoked rupture in 1944.[81] Yet publicly, 23 August 1944 was celebrated as a day of liberation and the foundation of the new communist state.[82] The emphasis on Romanian agency in changing the course of history, by

---

[78] There is a surprising paucity of research on public memory in communist Romania, particularly for the early period. It is taken as read that public memory in Romania was circumscribed by a static antifascist narrative. This overall impression may well be accurate, but there has yet to be a comprehensive study on the construction of such a public memory. Far more attention has been paid to memory in pre- and post-communist Romania. Where work has been done, it has tended to focus either on case studies, with a spotlight on the dissonance with minority memory, or on the nationalist turn in the 1970s/80s during Ceauşescu's regime. The one stand-out exception is Bucur, *Heroes and Victims*, esp. ch. 5. See also Maria Bucur, 'Treznea: Trauma, Nationalism and the Memory of World War II in Romania', *Rethinking History: The Journal of Theory and Practice* 6/1 (2002), pp. 35–55; see also Duncan Light, Ion Nicolae and Bogdan Suditu, 'Toponymy and the Communist City: Street Names in Bucharest, 1948–1965', *GeoJournal* 56/2 (2002), pp. 135–44, and Deletant, *Romania under Communist Rule*, in which Deletant talks implicitly about the construction of an anti-fascist narrative. As an example of literature on Ceauşescu and the silence surrounding the Holocaust, see Adrian Cioflâncă, 'A "Grammar of Exculpation" in Communist Historiography: Distortion of the History of the Holocaust under Ceauşescu', *Romanian Journal of Political Science* 4/2 (2004), pp. 29–46. For an analysis of one particular journal published in communist Romania, *Forschungen zur Volks- und Landeskunde*, see Florian Kührer-Wielach, '"Der gemeinsame Kampf gegen den Faschismus" in der rumäniendeutschen Zeitschrift *Forschungen zur Volks- und Landeskunde*: Ein Diskurs zwischen ideologischer Umziehung, gesellschaftlicher Integration und wirtschaftlicher Wertsteigerung', in Jürgen Lehmann and Gerald Volkmer (eds.), *Rumäniendeutsche Erinnerungskulturen: Formen und Funktionen des Vergangenheitsbezuges in der rumäniendeutschen Historiografie und Literatur* (Regensburg: Verlag Friedrich Pustet, 2016), pp. 153–68.

[79] Bucur, *Heroes and Victims*, p. 156.

[80] See, for instance, Mihai Fătu et al. (eds.), *Teroarea Horthysto-fascista in Nordvestul Romaniei, septembrie 1940–octobrie 1945* (Bucharest: Meridian Books, 1985).

[81] The rupture on 23 August 1944 is a theme that has stayed in place for determining Romanian German memory and history. It has guided historiography and also memory projects as a way of ordering the Romanian German past. See, for instance, Lorenda Buru, Roxana Crăciun and Ioana Stanciu, '"In diesem Augenblick ist alles zusammengebrochen ... ": Zeitliche Zäsuren zwischen 1944–1989 und ihre Auswirkungen auf das Leben der Rumäniendeutschen', in Angelika Herta and Martin Jung (eds.), *Vom Rand ins Zentrum: Die Deutsche Minderheit in Bukarest* (Berlin: Frank & Timme, 2011), pp. 47–65.

[82] Bucur, *Heroes and Victims*, p. 166.

switching sides from an alliance with Germany to an alliance with the
Soviet Union, also played into the hands of a Romanian regime which was
distancing itself from the Soviet Union. The growing rift between the
Soviet Union and Romania after 1955, and especially under Nicolae
Ceaușescu (1918–89) after 1968, thus fitted in neatly with the pre-existing
narrative of liberation. Romanian German mainstream narratives of this
liberation, which simply parroted the state-approved one but in German,
survived for the entire communist period.[83] Minorities were very much
part of the official discourse of building communism. But the nationalist
turn of Romanian communism allowed the memory of the war to focus far
more closely on Romanian heroes, thereby excluding minorities once more
from public commemoration.

   National communism, then, created an obvious tension between the
public narrative of the Second World War and Romanian German experiences and memories of it. Yet in official contexts Romanian Germans toed
the line.[84] The German-language newspapers *Neuer Weg* (1949–92),
Volkszeitung (1957–68), and *Karpatenrundschau* (1968–) reproduced the
party line in every domain.[85] The portrayal of the Second World War
and West Germany echoed the official narrative, denying Romanian
Germans the possibility of introducing non-conformist discourses into
the public domain. The anniversary of 23 August was particularly important
in showcasing the public narrative. Every year, newspapers were adorned
with celebratory articles and images of this foundational date. In 1957, in its
first year of publication, the *Volkszeitung* ran images of liberation
(Figure 3.7) as part of the official memory of the war. It encapsulated the
dilemma Romanian Germans faced in communist Romania as well as the
absurdity of Romania's public memory for Germans: it showed an elated
crowd welcoming the advancing Red Army to a readership that remembered the advance of the Red Army as the beginning of their tribulations.[86]

[83] In the chapter 'From Subservience to the Soviet Union to Autonomy, 1957–1965', Dennis Deletant
   explains the gradual erosion of Romania's dependency towards the USSR and demonstrates
   Gheorghiu-Dej's tactics of breaking ranks with the superpower. See Dennis Deletant, *Communist
   Terror in Romania: Gheorghiu-Dej and the Police State 1948–1965* (London: Hurst & Company,
   1999), pp. 269–88. See also Bucur, *Heroes and Victims*, pp. 160–93.

[84] See Kührer-Wielach, 'Der gemeinsame Kampf gegen den Faschismus'.

[85] *Der Neue Weg*, which was printed in Sibiu, was the first German-language newspaper to re-emerge
   after the Second World War – in 1949. This was also the most widely circulated newspaper among
   Romanian Germans.

[86] Indeed, this was the central theme of the war narrative in east-central Europe during the Cold War.
   See Lebow, Kansteiner and Fogu, *The Politics of Memory*.

Figure 3.7 '23. August – Tag der Befreiung' (23 August – The Day of Liberation),
Volkszeitung (1957).

Often, though, such messages were conveyed in a far more mechanical manner, by simply relaying entire speeches.[87] German-language newspapers differed little in this respect from 'mainstream' Romanian-language publications such as *Scînteia*, the principal daily newspaper of the communist regime. But in Romanian German contexts such stilted reproductions of uninspiring speeches could also be read as a subtle lampoon, laced with irony, of the very dogma on display. Particularly the great dates – 1 May and 23 August – and their accompanying speeches were subject to subtle deadpan humour. When Gheorghe Gheorghiu-Dej praised 23 August as the day of liberation, the translation of his speech alongside 'stage directions' in the text could also be understood by the German readership as

---

[87] See, for instance, 'Zum 15. Tag der Befreiung: Festsitzung der Grossen Nationalversammlung der RVR – Rede des Genossen Gheorghe Gheorghiu-Dej', *Neuer Weg* 11/3211, 23 August 1959, pp. 1–3.

a form of mockery. In his speech on 23 August 1959, Gheorghiu-Dej remembered the Romanian heroes of the 'anti-Hitler' alliance:

> More than 300,000 Romanian soldiers, sergeants, and top-ranking officers received Romanian, Soviet, Czechoslovak, and Hungarian decorations. Their military deeds in the anti-Hitler war added a glorious chapter to the canon of the great tradition of our people fighting for their independence and freedom. (Long-lasting applause.)[88]

It is difficult to conjure up a more ill-fitting description of the end of the war from a Romanian German perspective, especially in the 1950s, when the memory of the deportations was still raw. The stage direction of long-lasting applause – a common feature in reproduced speeches in newspapers – may have been included to augment the state message, but it ended up looking like a bad joke. Even Ceaușescu's controversial break with the Soviet Union over the handling of the Prague Spring in August 1968 did little to make these official public pronouncements look less absurd. In a pointed criticism of Soviet intervention, Ceaușescu used 23 August to argue that the achievements of the war would be undone by invading Czechoslovakia. The defeat of fascism in the Second World War and the establishment of communism had been made possible, Ceaușescu contended, only thanks to those who 'had fought for a better and more worthy life'.[89] Deprived of their own voice in public, Romanian Germans left the officials to do the talking, which often ran for pages and pages, adding to the surreal appearance of these stilted speeches. Once readers had battled through the first three to five pages of predictable text, if they bothered, the content opened up to include more polyphonic perspectives, such as press reports from abroad and short vignettes of local German life, past and present.

Read differently, though, images of liberation also indicated a shift in attitudes towards Romanian Germans: by 1957, Germans had become integrated into an antifascist narrative that had ousted fascism from Romania.[90] Throughout the post-war period, the Romanian government

---

[88] Ibid., pp. 1–2. Other speeches were included over the next two days, which amounted to ten densely printed pages; see *Neuer Weg* 11/3211, 23 August 1959, pp. 1–5, and 11/3212, 25 August 1959, pp. 1–5.

[89] 'Die XI. Ausserordentliche Tagung der Grossen Nationalversammlung: Rede des Genossen Nicolae Ceaușescu', *Neuer Weg* 20/6004, 23 August 1968, pp. 1, 2.

[90] This is reminiscent of the transformation of public memory that took place in East Germany. In that sense, Romanian Germans became part of a much wider, east-central European community of anti-fascist resistance. See, for instance, Mark Allinson, 'Popular Opinion', in Patrick Major and Jonathan Osmond (eds.), *The Workers' and Peasants' State: Communism and Society in East Germany under Ulbricht 1945–1971* (Manchester: Manchester University Press, 2002), pp. 96–111.

undertook concerted efforts to reintegrate the Germans into Romanian society after their initial deportation and expulsion.[91] Romanian Germans were gradually included into the socialist project from the mid-1950s onwards.[92] The reopening of German schools as early as 1948 constituted a first tentative step towards the inclusion of Germans into the socialist order.[93] The circulation of newspapers and other regular periodicals, such as the *Zeitschrift für Siebenbürgische Landeskunde*,[94] helped to normalise relations between Germans and the Romanian state.[95] The partial return in 1956 of farming lands that had been nationalised between 1945 and 1949 signalled to Germans that they had been 'readmitted' to Romanian society, albeit with a very difficult legacy.[96]

By the mid-1950, the last deportees had returned from the Soviet Union, and the state was now concerned with the reintegration of former deportees and their families into society.[97] Since the advent of the Red Army had supposedly removed the fascists from Romania, it seemed contradictory to continue labelling Romanian Germans collectively as fascists. The obvious compromise was to redefine the inclusiveness of fascism by assigning the tag of fascism solely to West Germany.[98] Romanian Germans had done penance and were ostensibly exempt from the fascist legacy, as were the citizens of the GDR.[99] And yet 'readmission' to Romanian society also meant rewriting

[91] Included in the story of deportations are also the Bărăgan deportations in 1951, even though they were not targeted exclusively at Germans. People living within 25 kilometres of the Yugoslav border were at risk of being deported, and this area included a substantial number of Germans. See Vultur, *Istorie trăită*.

[92] See Hannelore Baier, 'Die deutsche Minderheit in Rumänien 1953–1959', in Rudolf Gräf and Gerald Volkmer (eds.), *Zwischen Tauwettersozialismus und Neostalinismus: Deutsche und andere Minderheiten in Ostmittel- und Südosteuropa 1953–1963* (Munich: IKGS, 2011), pp. 107–18.

[93] German schools were shut down in 1944/5. During the following three years, German-speaking students had to attend schools that taught in Romanian, which hampered their academic progress.

[94] The *Zeitschrift für Siebenbürgische Landeskunde* has existed since 1878, but it was officially supported during communism. Similar to articles published in the journal *Forschungen zur Volks- und Landeskunde* during the period, the articles were about *Landeskunde* or applied geography. The journal is still being published today with the difference that it does not have to appear to be apolitical as it did during communism. The articles engage with a range of topics, from contemporary history to pedagogy. See Siebenbürgen-Institut Online at www.siebenbuergen-institut.de/zs/zfsl-haupt.htm for details (accessed 5 Jun. 2016).

[95] Annemarie Weber investigates Romanian German publications in Romania during the Cold War. She traces the dates of Germans to Romanian society later, namely with the advent of Ceaușescu in 1965. See Annemarie Weber, *Rumäniendeutsche? Diskurse zur Gruppenidentität einer Minderheit (1944–1971)* (Cologne: Böhlau, 2010), pp. 249–93.

[96] Deletant, *Communist Terror in Romania*, pp. 235–47.   [97] Baier, 'Die Deutschen in Rumänien'.

[98] Jeffrey Herf makes use of the image of passing guilt across the border; see Jeffrey Herf, *Divided Memory: The Nazi Past in the Two Germanys* (Cambridge, Mass.: Harvard University Press, 1997).

[99] For an excellent overview of historiography in the GDR, including the mental gymnastics of purging the fascist legacy from the country, see Wolfgang Ruge, 'Historiography in the German Democratic Republic: Rereading the History of National Socialism', in Reinhard Alter and

history in a manner that mapped onto the official memory culture. In public, the deportations remained taboo during communism.[100] The official name of the deportations in Romania was the euphemism 'reconstruction work [*Wiederaufbararbeit/reconstrucție*]'. Into this culture of silence, soft criticisms of the past subtly crept into Romanian German discourse in the mid-1970s. Michael Kroner was one of the first – and few – scholars in Romania to quietly advocate a review of the official version of the deportations.[101] But such criticisms were exceptions: Romanian German memories were pushed to the margins of public memory in Romania, leaving the German communities confused, frustrated, and edging further away from Romanian society in search of a sympathetic forum for their stories.

German Public Memory

Public memory in West Germany seemed, on the face of it, far more amenable to Romanian German stories of ordeal than in Romania. Their experience of defeat at the end of the Second World War was remarkably similar to that of their German counterparts in Berlin, Frankfurt, Munich, and Hamburg. Nazi Germany's unconditional surrender in May 1945 was viewed by many in Germany as a defeat and marked a caesura in history.[102] The collapse of the German war effort came with an increase in anti-German repercussions, many of which were seen as arbitrary, premeditated, and unjust.[103] The bombing of

Peter Monteath (eds.), *Rewriting the German Past: History and Identity in the New Germany* (Atlantic Highlands, N.J.: Humanities Press, 1997), pp. 208–21.

[100] Michael Kroner briefly discusses two case studies of the representation of the reprisals against *Sachsen* at the end of the war in Romanian newspapers in 1946. Here, he emphasises the virtual absence of sympathetic accounts of the treatment of Romanian Germans. One article, which was published in the gazette *Poporul*, went as far as to suggest the expulsion (*Ausweisung*) of Transylvanian Saxons from Romania as a means of solving the post-war economic crisis. It portrayed the expulsion of the *Sudetendeutsche* (Sudeten Germans) as an example that should be copied by Romania. Such opinions, even before communism, reveal the strength of feeling in Romanian society about German guilt and punishment through deportations. See Michael Kroner, 'Zwei aufschlussreiche Zeitungsurteile über die Behandlung der Siebenbürger Sachsen im Jahre 1946: Vertreibung, Umsiedlung oder produktive Eingliederung?', *Südostdeutsche Vierteljahreshefte* 53/1 (2004), pp. 31–6, in particular, pp. 32–3. See also Christoph Cornelißen, Roman Holec and Jiří Pešek (eds.), *Diktatur – Krieg – Vertreibung: Erinnerungskulturen in Tschechien, der Slowakei und Deutschland seit 1945* (Essen: Klartext Verlag, 2005).

[101] See Eduard Eisenburger and Michael Kroner (eds.), *Sächsisch-schwäbische Chronik* (Bucharest: Kriterion, 1976); see also Anneli Ute Gabanyi, 'Die Deutschen in Rumänien: Exodus oder Neuanfang?', in Hans Rothe (ed.), *Die Siebenbürger Sachsen in Geschichte und Gegenwart* (Cologne: Böhlau, 1994), p. 91.

[102] Kansteiner, 'Losing the War', pp. 102–7, 111.

[103] Robert G. Moeller, 'The Politics of the Past in the 1950s: Rhetorics of Victimisation in East and West Germany', in Niven (ed.), *Germans as Victims*, pp. 26–42, Herf, *Divided Memory*, pp. 267–74, and Robert G. Moeller, *War Stories: The Search for a Usable Past in the Federal Republic of Germany* (Berkeley: University of California Press, 2003).

Dresden and Hamburg was mirrored in the bombing of Bucharest and the skirmishes in and around Timişoara.[104] The expulsion of Germans from eastern regions such as Eastern Prussia, Pomerania, the Sudetenland, and Silesia was the flip side to the deportations of *Siebenbürger Sachsen* and *Banater Schwaben* to the Soviet Union in 1945.[105] Romanian Germans became *au fait* with the concept of 'victor's justice' (*Siegerjustiz*) and collective guilt (*Kollektivschuld*). Just as *Reichsdeutsche*[106] had 'felt little inclination to see things in perspective',[107] Romanian Germans likewise refused to look beyond the sequence of events in 1944/5 that had led to the disintegration of the Axis powers.

Public memory in the first two decades of post-war Germany was characterised by notions of victimisation and defeat.[108] The broader milieu of expellees and their representative groups – most notably the *Landsmannschaften* and the Bund der Vertriebenen (Federation of Expellees, or BdV) – enhanced this by exerting political pressure on successive FRG governments.[109] They also played a significant role in shaping public memory of the Nazi past by dwelling on German victimhood at the expense of self-reflection.[110] The bombings of German cities, the subsequent occupation of Germany by the Allied forces, and the expulsion of more than 12 million Germans from eastern and south-eastern Europe conjured up an image of innocent Germans caught up in a war that had taken place 'through no fault of

---

[104] The painter Emil Honigberger (1885–1974), for instance, produced artwork that brought numerous memories together for Romanian German consumption, including flight, bombing, and post-war rubble. See Maria König, 'Zwischen Geborgenheit und Moderne: Der Maler Emil Honigberger', *Siebenbürgische Zeitung* 24/14, 15 September 1974, p. 3. For an analysis of Romanian German official memories in the 1950s and 1960s in West Germany, see Cristian Cercel, 'Die Deportation der Rumäniendeutschen in die Sowjetunion und ihre Rolle in den Gedächtnis- und Identitätsdiskursen der in der Bundesrepublik lebenden Siebenbürger Sachsen in den 1950er- und 1960er-Jahren', in Lehmann and Volkmer (ed.), *Rumäniendeutsche Erinnerungskulturen*, pp. 137–52.

[105] Much of this had been confirmed by the West German government's commission in the 1950s of a nationwide documentation of German expellees, refugees, and émigrés from eastern Europe. See Theodor Schieder et al. (eds.), *Das Schicksal der Deutschen in Rumänien: Dokumentation der Vertreibung der Deutschen aus Ost-Mitteleuropa*, Vol. III (Bonn: Bundesministerium für Vertriebene, 1957).

[106] This is a term still used by Germans in Romania to distinguish a person from Germany proper from a *Siebenbürger Sachsen* or a *Banater Schwaben*.

[107] Bill Niven, *Facing the Nazi Past: United Germany and the Legacy of the Third Reich* (London: Routledge, 2002), p. 97.

[108] Kansteiner, 'Losing the War'.

[109] Pertti Ahonen, 'Taming the Expellee Threat in Post-1945 Europe: Lessons from the Two Germanies and Finland', *Contemporary European History* 14/1 (2005), pp. 1–21.

[110] Pertti Ahonen, *After the Expulsion: West Germany and Eastern Europe, 1945–1990* (Oxford: Oxford University Press, 2003), pp. 38, 76.

[their] own'.[111] For many Germans, the memory of the expulsion also provided a basis for Cold War politics. The barbarism of the Russians was evidenced in the wartime and post-war atrocities of the Soviets and their 'accomplices', which mapped onto the political context of the Cold War East–West divide.[112]

Expellee groups flourished in the post-war political climate. Romanian Germans, though fewer in number, drew on victim narratives similar to those of German expellees and refugees from other parts of east-central Europe.[113] There were, however, noticeable differences. The majority of expellees and refugees from Silesia, the Sudetenland, the Baltic region, and elsewhere in east-central Europe had been an integral part of West Germany from the outset. As early as 1945, West German politicians made concerted efforts to incorporate expellees into mainstream West German politics.[114] Consecutive governments in Bonn employed a carrot-and-stick approach by appearing to grant expellee lobbies concessions while ensuring that their demands had little bearing on international politics, and by keeping expellee politicians out of key political positions.[115] Romanian Germans, excluded even from token gestures, were thus constantly playing catch-up with the far more established and organised expellee groups from other parts of east-central Europe. In any case, things were about to change.

It was only a temporary state of affairs that gave expellees and east-central European Germans a prominent position in West German politics and society. The era after the Konrad Adenauer and Kurt Georg Kiesinger governments saw a gradual generational shift in German society. Expellee power, though still very visible, began to wane, and with this battles over Germany's recent past became more common and more ferocious.[116] West German politicians had also grown acutely aware of the danger of becoming internationally isolated by appearing to be too fixated on revisionist *Ostpolitik*.[117] A combination of radicalism and pragmatism saw a reappraisal of the Nazi past in which perpetrators, not victims, took centre stage in public discourse. In this new context, the post-war plight of

[111] Michael L. Hughes, '"Through No Fault of Our Own": West Germans Remember Their War Losses', *German History* 18/2 (2000), p. 201.
[112] Moeller, *War Stories*, pp. 66–9.   [113] See ibid. and Ahonen, 'Taming the Expellee Threat'.
[114] Moeller, *War Stories*.   [115] Ahonen, *After the Expulsion*, p. 80.
[116] Konrad H. Jarausch, 'Critical Memory and Civil Society: The Impact of the 1960s on German Debates about the Past', in Philipp Gassert and Alan E. Steinweis (eds.), *Coping with the Nazi Past: West German Debates on Nazism and Generational Conflict, 1955–1975* (London: Berghahn, 2007), pp. 11–30.
[117] Ahonen, *After the Expulsion*, pp. 199–213.

German victims came into conflict with the new concepts of guilt, responsibility, and *Vergangenheitsbewältigung* (the process of working through the past). The once dominant discourse of victims (*Opferdiskurs*) evolved into a competition with the new discourse of perpetrators (*Täterdiskurs*).[118]

The West German memory landscape, therefore, became far more plural and divided by factional memory cultures. The memory of the Second World War remained a divisive issue, and popular culture reflected these generational and memory disputes. TV series such as *Heimat* (1984), *Tadellöser & Wolff* (1975), and the American mini-series *Holocaust* (1978) highlighted the disparate nature of the memory of the war.[119] The *Historikerstreit* (Historians' Dispute) in the mid-1980s brought to light yet again the deep divisions within West Germany itself on the issue of how to remember and talk about the Nazi past.[120] By the time the *Historikerstreit* had passed into history, reunified Germany was immersed in a surfeit of memory.[121] From Germans as killers[122] to Germans as victims,[123] two seemingly irreconcilable memory cultures were present in the German public sphere for most of the Cold War period (and beyond). It was precisely this shifting and complicated memory that Romanian Germans encountered after emigrating.

A Little Historians' Dispute

Where did Romanian German memories fit in? Their focus on the experience of deportation and loss excluded them from public memory in

---

[118] Mathias Beer, 'Verschlusssache, Raubdruck, Autorisierte Fassung', in Cornelißen, Holec and Pešek (eds.), *Diktatur – Krieg – Vertreibung*, p. 384.

[119] Wulf Kansteiner, 'Television Archives and the Making of Collective Memory: Nazism and World War II in Three Television Blockbusters of German Public Television', in Francis X. Blouin Jr and William G. Rosenberg (eds.), *Archives, Documentation, and Institutions of Social Memory: Essays from the Sawyer Seminar* (Ann Arbor: University of Michigan Press, 2007), pp. 368–78, in particular, pp. 375–6, and Wulf Kansteiner, 'Nazis, Viewers and Statistics: Television History, Television Audience Research and Collective Memory in West Germany', *Journal of Contemporary History* 39/4 (2004), pp. 575–98. It is worth noting that representations of the Second World War, Nazi Germany, and the Holocaust were by no means identical. On the contrary, Germans were exposed to a surfeit of contrasting narratives, from German idylls to Holocaust victims.

[120] Helmut Schmitz, 'The Birth of the Collective from the Spirit of Empathy: From the "Historians' Dispute" to German Suffering', in Niven (ed.), *Germans as Victims*, pp. 93–108.

[121] Ibid.

[122] The prime example here is Daniel J. Goldhagen, *Hitler's Willing Executioners: Ordinary Germans and the Holocaust* (New York: Vintage Books, 1997). For an excellent collection of essays on Goldhagen's book and its impact and reception globally, see Geoff Eley (ed.), *The 'Goldhagen Effect': History, Memory, Nazism – Facing the German Past* (Ann Arbor: University of Michigan Press, 2000), especially Omer Bartov, 'Reception and Perception: Goldhagen's Holocaust and the World', pp. 33–87.

[123] The author Martin Walser famously referred to what he perceived as the predominance of the Holocaust in German history as the *Holocaust-Keule* (the Holocaust cudgel).

Romania. Instead, they left behind fragmented traces of unofficial memory that could only be pieced together decades after the post-war period. Poems, drawings, sketches, and photographs formed part of a private network of memory that found no resonance in the public sphere in Romania.[124] Sketches of the Soviet camps to which Germans were deported in 1945 remained hidden in private collections.[125] Poems were written but never published.[126] Photographs were stowed away and never discussed.[127] The official discourse in Romania ignored and eschewed any conflicting memories of the war and its aftermath, including the deportations of Germans and Romania's wartime alliance with Nazi Germany.[128]

Emigration was meant to liberate Romanian German memories. Instead, the majority of those who left for West Germany, largely from the 1970s on, encountered a bewildering environment in which Germans themselves seemed to be propagating an anti-German message in the public domain. Arriving among a growing interest in German perpetrators and the Holocaust, Romanian Germans found themselves once again on the margins of memory. The final years of the Cold War were especially marked by identity debates in both the Federal Republic of Germany and Romania, and Romanian Germans were caught up in the middle of it all. In both Hungary and Romania, a renewed intensity emerged around the topic of Transylvania.[129] Romanian Germans also had an important stake in this dispute over ownership of the Transylvanian Saxon history of church fortresses (*Kirchenburgen*) and privileges they had acquired (and lost). Caught in the prism of rising nationalist discourses, the Transylvanian disputes reflected a broader European uncertainty in the

---

[124] A collection of such sources from the years 1944 to 1949 (and some from the years afterwards) can be found in the following volume: Günter Czernetzky et al. (eds.), *Lager Lyrik: Gedenkbuch – 70 Jahre seit der Deportation der Deutschen aus Südosteuropa in die Sowejetunion: Gedichte, Fotografien, Zeichnungen, Lieder, Verse, Reime, Sprüche* (Sibiu: Schiller Verlag, 2015).

[125] See, for instance, Hedwig Schwertner, *Zeichnung* (1945), in Czernetzky et al., *Lager Lyrik*, p. 45.

[126] There was an outpouring of poetry during and after the deportations in January 1945. See, for example, Joseph Fuchs, 'Rauhreif blüht im Stacheldraht' (1948), ibid., p. 140. YY ibid

[127] See, for example, 'Zwei Freundinnen im Winter 1947' (1947), ibid., p. 131. YY ibid

[128] See Bucur, *Heroes and Victims*.

[129] This 'Historians' Dispute' was a Romanian–Hungarian bout of antagonism that emerged from the early 1980s. The Hungarian three-volume publication of the history of Transylvania in 1986 set the debate on fire: Béla Köpeczi et al. (eds.), *Erdély Története, Vols. I–III* (Budapest: Akadémiai Kiadó, 1986). See also, for the Romanian position, David Prodan, *Transylvania and Again Transylvania: A Historical Expose* (Bucharest: Romanian Cultural Foundation, 1992); for the Hungarian émigré position, see Elemér Illyés, *National Minorities in Romania: Change in Transylvania* (Boulder, Co.: East European Monographs, 1982). The Romanian publication, Fătu et al. (eds.), *Teroarea Horthysto-fascista*, focused on Transylvania during the Second World War and served up a nationalist and state-endorsed narrative both of the war and of Transylvania as a historic region.

late Cold War. But it was the West German *Historikerstreit*, a far more public and recognisable affair, that captured the Romanian German imagination.[130] Between 1986 and 1989, historians on the right and left of the political spectrum engaged in a very public squabble over the German past. Should the Holocaust be central to German history? Was German memory a captive of a coercive anti-German obsession? Here, too, Romanian Germans were crucially invested in the dispute.

Conservative and right-wing circles in West Germany argued forcefully against the central position of the Holocaust in German history. It stifled national identity, they felt, and burdened the German nation with an immovable stain, as Ernst Nolte contended.[131] The historian Andreas Hillgruber added a further dimension to the debate. His book *Zweierlei Untergang* (*Two Kinds of Ruin*), published in 1986, placed the Holocaust and the expulsion of Germans at the end of the Second World War side by side, granting more attention to the story of German expulsions.[132] German victimhood, set against a self-critical reading of German history, was back and on a full collision course with *Vergangenheitsbewältigung*. Romanian Germans could identify with many of the sentiments expressed by Ernst Nolte, Andreas Hillgruber, Klaus Hildebrand, and others. Self-criticism smacked of the anti-German discourse in Romania from which they had escaped, and the responses by academics such as Jürgen Habermas, Martin Broszat, and Jürgen Kocka were puzzling to a group that had thought of itself mainly as victims of history at the end of their own history. Habermas and others, Hans Bergel claimed, stood accused of politicising a history that the 'level-headed' historian Ernst Nolte seemed to address with calm and consideration.[133] Writing in 1987, Bergel – the editor of the *Siebenbürgische Zeitung* – argued that Nolte had been 'brave' to articulate his opinions in the face of the 'hate-filled reactions' by Habermas and others:[134] 'The *Historikerstreit* – which is more than just that – continues', Bergel concluded in his inimitable style.[135]

---

[130] See James Knowlton and Truett Cates (eds.), *Forever in the Shadow of Hitler? Original Documents of the* Historikerstreit*, the Controversy Concerning the Singularity of the Holocaust* (New York: Prometheus Books, 1993), 'Forum: The *Historikerstreit* Twenty Years On', *German History* 24/4 (2006), pp. 587–607, and Konrad Jarausch, 'Removing the Nazi Stain? The Quarrel of the Historians', *German Studies Review* 11/2 (1988), pp. 285–301.

[131] Ernst Nolte, 'Die Vergangenheit die nicht vergehen will', *Frankfurter Allgemeine Zeitung*, 6 June 1986.

[132] Andreas Hillgruber, *Zweierlei Untergang: Die Zerschlagung des Deutschen Reiches und das Ende des europäischen Judentums* (Berlin: Siedler, 1986).

[133] Hans Bergel, 'Tote erster, Tote zweiter Klasse', *Siebenbürgische Zeitung* 37/16, 15 October 1987, p. 2.

[134] Ibid. [135] Ibid.

Romanian Germans were pioneers of this Historians' Dispute. If the *Landsmannschaften* had dominated politics since the 1940s, they faced a generational and ideological pushback towards the end of the Cold War. In spite of this, the homeland society continued to push the party line of Romanian German victimhood. A seminal collection of Romanian German essays entitled *Wir Siebenbürger: Heimat im Herzen*, edited by Heinrich Zillich and Volkmar Fromm in 1949, made a comeback in 1986 when Walter Myß and Hans Bergel reworked a second edition for Transylvanian Saxons and other Romanian Germans to indulge in unproblematic *Heimat* nostalgia.[136] Myß and Bergel promised to maintain 'the tradition of the first book'.[137] Literary contributions by the good and the great of the Saxon community were interspersed with obvious markers of German victimhood. Frida Franz's contribution on twelve years in captivity in Siberia stood out as a historic document for the twentieth century.[138] Like many other war stories, hers began in 1944 when she was torn from her youthful innocence as Romania changed sides on 23 August 1944. In Ernst Wagner's historical survey of Transylvania in the early twentieth century, the fascist past featured as a result of the terrible economic and political situation in Romania. If anyone was to blame, it was so-called *Reichsdeutsche* who had spoilt Romanian German affairs.[139] Heinrich Zillich, meanwhile, was feted as a Saxon celebrity without any commentary on his Nazi entanglement.

By the mid-1980s, debates among Romanian Germans turned into a veritable *Historikerstreit*. On the fortieth anniversary of the end of the war and the deportation of Germans to the Soviet Union, the *Siebenbürgische Zeitung* ran a series of articles condemning the 'victor's revenge' meted out against Romanian Germans.[140] The newspaper repeatedly highlighted Alfred de Zayas's studies on the expulsion and treatment of Germans in east-central Europe at the end of the war. As an international Anglophone historian, de Zayas played a key role in establishing a strong mandate for the Romanian German narrative of victimhood during the war. Adverts for and articles on his work featured in the newspaper, acting as the legitimising intellectual framework for

---

[136] See Heinrich Zillich and Volkmar Fromm (eds.), *Wir Siebenbürger: Heimat im Herzen* (Salzburg: Akademischer Gemeinschaftsverlag, 1949), and Bergel and Myß (eds.), *Wir Siebenbürger*.

[137] Hans Bergel and Walter Myß, 'Zur Einführung', in Bergel and Myß (eds.), *Wir Siebenbürger*, p. 5.

[138] Frida Franz, 'Zwölf Jahre verschleppt in Sibirien', ibid., pp. 174–81. YY ibid here

[139] Wagner, 'Siebenbürgen als Teil des Königreichs Rumänien', pp. 79–82.

[140] See, for instance, Michael Kroner, 'Die verbrecherische Rache der Sieger', *Siebenbürgische Zeitung* 35/1, 15 January 1985, p. 3.

Romanian German claims to victimhood.[141] This was crucial: Romanian Germans were not merely rehearsing their recent and often traumatic history. Many of the actors involved in the debate on the correct place for remembering Romanian German victims were keen to contextualise Romanian German experiences within the wider German and European framework which de Zayas's work highlighted. 'Expulsion crimes against Germans' read a main feature in the *Siebenbürgische Zeitung* in January 1985. Readers were invited to attend a series of events at Munich's Haus des Deutschen Ostens (House of the German East) to commemorate and revisit the torturous events of German expulsions and deportations at the end of the Second World War.[142] First on the list of speakers was de Zayas himself, who would draw attention to processes that had had 'an enduring effect on German and European history'.[143] Two weeks later, de Zayas featured again in a long exposé on the deportation of Romanian Germans to the Soviet Union in January 1945. For Romanian Germans, the expulsion was still ongoing; for forty years they had been subjected to a 'pressure to leave' as Saxons and Swabians continued to abandon Romania for Germany.[144] There they faced *Aussiedlerfeindlichkeit* (hostility towards German migrants),[145] a point Bavaria's First Minister Franz Josef Strauss was at pains to make in the *Siebenbürgische Zeitung*.[146] Concerns about emigration from Romania were placed next to sources documenting the deportation of Romanian Germans and adorned with poems.[147]

The exuberant restating of the *Landsmannschaften*'s official line on Romanian German memory of the Nazi period emerged in reaction to a group of contenders who were threatening the status quo. With this group bunched around the historian Johann Böhm (1929–) and the pugnacious lawyer Axel Azzola (1937–2007), the debate about the Romanian

---

[141] See 'Blickpunkt: Vertreibungsverbrechen an Deutschen', *Siebenbürgische Zeitung* 35/1, 15 January 1985, p. 2, and 'Die meisten erlitten Schäden für das ganze Leben', *Siebenbürgische Zeitung* 35/1, 15 January 1985, p. 4; see also Alfred de Zayas, *Nemesis at Potsdam. The Anglo-Americans and the Expulsion of the Germans: Background, Execution, Consequences* (London: Routledge, 1977).

[142] 'Blickpunkt', *Siebenbürgische Zeitung*.   [143] Ibid.

[144] Heinrich Plattner and Hans Bergel, 'Es besteht nach wie vor Vertreibungsdruck', *Siebenbürgische Zeitung* 35/2, 31 January 1985, p. 1.

[145] *Aussiedlerfeindlichkeit* is a play on words from the well-known term *Ausländerfeindlichkeit* (hostility towards foreigners).

[146] Plattner and Bergel, 'Es besteht nach wie vor Vertreibungsdruck'.

[147] Michael Kroner, 'Dokumente zur Verschleppung der Rumäniendeutsche in die UdSSR', *Siebenbürgische Zeitung* 35/2, 31 January 1985, p. 3, and Erna Graef-Wagner, 'Die Leiden der Deportation', *Siebenbürgische Zeitung* 35/2, 31 January 1985. See also 'Transport und Empfang der Verschleppten', *Siebenbürgische Zeitung* 35/4, 15 March 1985, p. 3.

German Nazi past became a far more vocal, visible, and confrontational matter in the 1980s. Böhm's publication *Das Nationalsozialistische Deutschland und die Deutsche Volksgruppe in Rumänien 1936–1944 (Nazi Germany and the German Volksgruppe in Romania, 1936–1944)* was the object of particular ire from Romanian German establishment voices.[148] Such defensiveness by the *Landsmannschaften*, Böhm's allies felt, embodied the 'typical Nazi spirit' among 'that generation' of Romanian Germans.[149] The public figures and writers Hans Bergel and Karl Reinhardt epitomised the strong resistance to Romanian German *Vergangenheitsbewältigung*. Bergel's rejection of several articles about the National Socialist past as editor of the *Siebenbürgische Zeitung* in the late 1980s led one Romanian German, Bruno Knopp, to denounce him as 'antidemocratic and antisemitic'.[150] The founding of the Arbeitskreis für Geschichte und Kultur der Deutschen Siedlungsgebiete im Südosten Europas (Workshop for the History and Culture of German-Settled Areas in South-Eastern Europe) in 1988 by the writers and historians Johann Böhm, Dieter Schlesak, William Totok, and others represented a determined challenge to the stranglehold of the *Landsmannschaften* in telling the Saxon and Swabian past. 'Dear compatriots', a call in the newly founded journal *Das Donautal-Magazin* began, '42 years have now passed and we still haven't managed, for various reasons, to turn away from the National Socialist restriction and distortion of our history.'[151] It was imperative for 'Germans from Romania and Hungary' to confront the question of why 'former Nazis in the Federal Republic of Germany were given the financial support to organise themselves politically in order to determine the public spiritual and political position of Germans from south-eastern Europe'.[152] By 1989 these Romanian German memory insurgents were organised, determined, and visible.

With the brief reunification love-in between East and West Germany in the autumn of 1989, debates about the Nazi past seemingly disappeared off the radar in broader German society, at least temporarily. Not so, however, for Romanian Germans: the memory dispute seemed more urgent than ever. On 15 October 1989, just a few weeks before the exuberance of seeing the Wall come down in Berlin, Johann Böhm, Dieter Schlesak, Anton Scherer, and others met in Ingolstadt to discuss Germans in south-eastern

---

[148] Johann Böhm, *Das Nationalsozialistische Deutschland und die Deutsche Volksgruppe in Rumänien 1936–1944* (Frankfurt: Peter Lang, 1985).
[149] Letter Rudolf to Johann Böhm, 2 February 1988, Siebenbürgen Institut, B I 54, 14/5.
[150] Letter Bruno Knopp to Johann Böhm, 27 May 1988, Siebenbürgen Institut, B I 54, 14/4.
[151] *Das Donautal – Magazin*, 15 December 1987, p. 3.   [152] Ibid.

Europe the interwar period.[153] The Arbeitskreis was only just beginning its project of investigating the Nazi past among Romanian Germans, Yugoslav Germans, and other German groups in south-eastern Europe. The memory insurgents worked tirelessly on exposing the 54,000 Romanian Germans who had fought for the Waffen-SS, the more than 22,000 Germans from Yugoslavia who had enlisted in the infamous Prinz-Eugen division of the Waffen-SS, and individuals such Victor Capesius (1907–85), the Romanian German 'Nazi pharmacist' in Dachau and Auschwitz.[154]

At the height of this 'little *Historikerstreit*', the clear lines of who was part of this Romanian German conflict were becoming increasingly fuzzy. What had begun as a largely Transylvanian Saxon affair quickly engulfed young Swabians, too, only to broaden further by making these concerns about Germans in Hungary and Romania and indeed in south-eastern Europe as a whole. Both local and transnational, the memory debates reflected a diverse community, which was difficult to define in scope and membership. The proximity of the Saxon and Swabian homeland societies to other *Landsmannschaften* in the early days of Federal Republic had already blurred the boundaries between individual east-central European German groups. Romanian Germans became intellectual and ideological bedfellows of other, often far more right-wing, homeland societies, such as the Landsmannschaften der Sudetendeutsche, even though their experiences of the end of the war differed considerably. The diverse homeland societies had shared common political platforms from the 1950s on. All twenty-one *Landsmannschaften* were constituent members of the governing body, the Bund der Vertriebenen founded in 1957. Its predecessor, the Bund der Heimatvertriebenen und Entrechteten (League of Expellees and Those Deprived of Rights), founded in 1950, had also levelled out the differences between the disparate German groups to create a more general sense of victimhood and grievance.[155] These interconnections were reinforced in a spatial sense, too, as the numerous *Landsmannschaften* were physically situated close to each other. In Stuttgart, the Landsmannschaft der Siebenbürger Sachsen and the Landsmannschaft der Sudetendeutschen had their offices across the corridor from each other. In Munich, representatives of the various homeland societies

[153] 'Die Weimarer Republik und die deutsche Minderheiten in Rumänien und Jugoslawien', Siebenbürgen Institut, B I 54, 14/5.
[154] See Milata, *Zwischen Hitler, Stalin, und Antonescu*, Dieter Schlesak, *Capesius, der Auschwitzapotheker* (Bonn: Dietz Verlag, 2006), and Lumans, *Himmler's Auxiliaries*, pp. 234–5.
[155] See Hughes, 'Through No Fault of Our Own', and Ahonen, *After the Expulsion*.

would meet and share ideas in the Haus des Deutschen Ostens. Despite the insistence on Saxon and Swabian particularity, in reality east-central European Germans had already created a sphere that had eviscerated many of those distinctions. Even beyond their world of German victims, the Cold War paradigm of a totalitarian eastern Europe did much to support the Romanian German émigré memory culture of victimhood over self-critical introspection.[156]

Those boundaries were loosened further during the little *Historikerstreit*, and some of the participants in this debate defied clear identification. Axel Azzola, with his German-Italian-Jewish background and born in Romania, was neither Saxon nor Swabian and had been involved in issues as diverse as constitutional law and the treatment of Red Army Faction prisoners, for whom he harboured some sympathy. Still, Azzola commanded an audience even in *Landsmannschaft* circles. In a letter to the editor of the *Siebenbürgische Zeitung* in July 1985, he accused Hans Bergel of propagating an 'official doctrine' that whitewashed the Romanian German National Socialist past.[157] Several Saxons responded, including the historian Harald Roth and, of course, Hans Bergel, who rose to the occasion to denounce Azzola's accusations as baseless.[158] Azzola was also annoyed because his critique had not been intended as a letter to the editor, as he explained in private correspondence with Hans Bergel.[159] Bergel responded petulantly in a letter to Azzola with 'braying laughter' to his adversary's arguments.[160] Yet six years later, Axel Azzola had become part of the Romanian German community: such was the transformative effect of the Historians' Dispute. His published work was dutifully listed in the *Siebenbürgische Zeitung* next to that of Hans Bergel, Paul Philippi, and others.[161] When he died in 2007, the *Siebenbürgische Zeitung* published a very generous obituary.[162]

[156] See, for instance, Anna Holian, *Between National Socialism and Soviet Communism: Displaced Persons in Postwar Germany* (Ann Arbor: University of Michigan Press, 2011); in it, Holian charts the way displaced persons in West Germany from the Soviet Union propagated a nationalist anti-communism, which worked well in the West German environment.
[157] Axel Azzola, 'Leserbriefe an die Redaktion: Zu "Die Deutsche Volksgruppe in Rumänien, 1940–1944"', *Siebenbürgische Zeitung* 35/11, 31 July 1985, p. 4.
[158] Harald Roth, 'Lesebriefe an die Redaktion: Zu "Lesebrief von Axel Azzola"', *Siebenbürgische Zeitung* 35/13, 15 August 1985, p. 5, and Hans Bergel, 'Leserbriefe an die Redaktion: Zu "Historische Doktrin, wie sie beispielhaft von Bergel … vertreten wird"', *Siebenbürgische Zeitung* 35/14, 15 September 1985, p. 11.
[159] Letter Axel Azzola to Hans Bergel, 28 August 1985, IKGS, B 7. YY
[160] Letter Hans Bergel to Axel Azzola, 2 September 1985, IKGS B 7. YY
[161] 'Siebenbürgische Bibliographie', *Siebenbürgische Zeitung* 42/1, 20 January 1992, p. 22.
[162] Udo Michael Dieners, 'Axel Azzola: "Das Leben währt siebzig Jahre, … ": Zum Tode des Juristen und Sozialwissenschaftlers Prof. Dr Axel Azzola', *Siebenbürgische Zeitung* 57/19, 5 December 2007, p. 4.

After unification, then, the dynamics of the dispute changed. Johann Böhm, Klaus Popa, and Axel Azzola continued to pursue their determination to uncover the fascist past and highlight its continuities into the present day. The academic journal *Halbjahresschrift für südosteuropäische Geschichte, Literatur und Politik* became the go-to publication for a critical iconoclasm of Romanian German society.[163] Johann Böhm continued to publish mercilessly revelatory studies about the National Socialist entanglement of Germans in Romania and Hungary: Hungarian Germans in the Waffen-SS,[164] Romanian Germans during the Weimar Republic,[165] Romanian Germans in the Third Reich,[166] Hitler's vassals in the German *Volksgruppe* in Romania before and after 1945[167] – nothing and no one was spared. Klaus Popa, William Totok, and later Mariana Hausleitner, Hildrun Glass, and others, meanwhile, facilitated a comprehensive unmasking of the age-old Romanian German explanation of coercion, defence, and victimhood.[168] Resembling a speeded-up version of broader German memory developments over the course of the Cold War, Romanian German victimhood was attacked, perpetrators were sought and found, and, finally, in a strange twist of the memory wars, victimhood once again returned.

New Victim Stories

A special constellation emerged in reunified Germany: the thorny issue of emigration from Romania was definitively settled in favour of emigration. The exposure of the Romanian German Nazi past went mainstream, and

---

[163] First published in 1989 with the publishing house AKG-Verlag, the journal still appears.
[164] Johann Böhm, *Die Ungarndeutschen in der Waffen-SS* (Ippesheim: AGK-Verlag, 1990).
[165] Johann Böhm, *Die Deutschen in Rumänien und die Weimarer Republik* (Ippesheim: AGK-Verlag, 1993).
[166] Böhm, *Die Deutschen in Rumänien und das 'Dritte Reich'*.
[167] Johann Böhm, *Hitlers Vasallen der deutschen Volksgruppe in Rumänien vor und nach 1945* (Frankfurt am Main: Peter Lang, 2006).
[168] See, for instance, Klaus Popa, *Akten um die deutsche Volksgruppe in Rumänien 1937–1945* (Frankfurt am Main: Peter Lang, 2005), Klaus Popa, 'Erfüllung des NS-Ungeists: Bibliografisch-biografische Porträts aus der "Deutschen Volksgruppe Rumänien" 1940–1941 (I)', *Halbjahresschrift für südosteuropäische Geschichte, Literatur und Politik* 17/1 (2005), pp. 67–76, Klaus Popa, 'Erfüllung des NS-Ungeists: Biografisch-bibliografisch Porträts aus der "Deutschen Volksgruppe Rumänien" 1940–1944 (II)', *Halbjahresschrift für südosteuropäische Geschichte, Literatur und Politik* 17/2 (2005), pp. 81–4, Klaus Popa, 'Erfüllung des NS-Ungeists: Bibliografisch-biografische Porträts aus der "Deutschen Volksgruppe Rumänien" 1940–1944 (III)', *Halbjahresschrift für südosteuropäische Geschichte, Literatur und Politik* 18/1 (2006), pp. 86–90, Klaus Popa, 'Erfüllung des NS-Ungeists: Bibliografisch-biografische Porträts aus der "Deutschen Volksgruppe Rumänien" 1940–1944 (V)', *Halbjahresschrift für südosteuropäische Geschichte, Literatur und Politik* 19/1 (2007), pp. 49–59, and Hildrun Glass, *Minderheit zwischen zwei Diktaturen: Zur Geschichte der Juden in Rumänien 1944–1949* (Munich: Oldenbourg, 2002).

the notion of German victimhood resurfaced with gusto throughout German society, albeit in a different guise from its post-war counterpart.[169] The return to narratives of victimhood around the new millennium in German memory politics was hugely significant for reshaping Romanian German narratives. Romanian Germans were able to envelop themselves in a discourse of victimhood once again – this time, however, without edging dangerously close to the revisionist circles that railed against the perceived 'Holocaust cudgel', as Martin Walser put it in 1998. Romanian German narratives of the war were reanimated at a time when eyewitnesses were gradually dying, and a spate of memoir literature emerged in the 1990s and 2000s. Some of these stories used older tropes by beginning their war stories in August 1944, while others attempted to explain their experiences of the war across that temporal divide.[170] But memoir literature, which rehearsed some established ways of talking about National Socialism and the war's end, was only the prelude to bigger moments of Romanian German commemoration.

The sixtieth anniversary in 2005 of the deportation of Saxons and Swabians to the Soviet Union in 1945 was a grand affair. Both in Germany and in Romania, commemorations featured Romanian German victimhood at the end of the war as the dominant story of the entire war. Despite the earlier heated and energetic debates about the Romanian entanglement with Nazism, the Second World War, and the Holocaust, Romanian Germans returned to being victims. The second wave of German victimhood, however, was not openly set in direct competition with Holocaust memory.[171] Romanian German victimhood followed a similar pattern: stories about deportations were not right-wing apologias. Their focus was directed instead towards the trauma at the end of the lifespan of a particular generation that had direct

---

[169] On the re-emergence of German victimhood in the late 1990s and 2000s, see Niven (ed.), *Germans as Victims*.

[170] Erika Feigel-Burghart begins her book on her time in a labour camp in the Soviet Union in August 1944; see Erika Feigel-Burghart, *Mädchenjahre hinter Stacheldraht: Sowjetunion 1945–1949* (Sibiu: Hora Verlag, 2003). Emil Sigmeth follows a similar timeline; see Emil Sigmeth, *In Krieg und Frieden von Cuenca zum Don: Erlebnisse eines Journalisten aus Siebenbürgen* (Munich: Verlag Südostdeutsches Kulturwerk, 1991). A different approach, which accounts for the 'pre-history' to August 1944, can be seen in Bettina Schuller's and Robert Schiff's memoir novels. See Bettina Schuller, *Führerkinder: Eine Jugend in Siebenbürgen* (Sibiu: Schiller Verlag, 2012), which begins with the Olympics in 1936, and Robert Schiff, *Feldpost: Chronik eines ungebauten Hauses* (Munich: Verlag Südostdeutsches Kulturwerk, 1994), which presents a more passive story of National Socialism among Romanian Germans even while acknowledging that politics existed before August 1944.

[171] See Stefan Berger, 'On Taboos, Traumas and Other Myths: Why the Debate about German Victims Is Not a Historians' Controversy', in Niven (ed.), *Germans as Victims*, pp. 210–24.

experience of the war and its ending.[172] And yet politics seeped into the memory of deportations. Representations oscillated between the personal nature of experience and the use of globally recognisable Holocaust imagery. In 2005 and again in 2013 on the sixty-eighth anniversary of the Romanian German deportations to the Soviet Union, commemorations took place in Reșița/Reschitz, Ulm, and Ingolstadt. They were organised jointly by a number of groups, including the German Democratic Forum in Romania, the Romanian Cultural Ministry, and the homeland societies in Germany, as well as local Banat Highland German (*Berglanddeutsche*) associations. The events were advertised on posters and magazine covers with the striking recurring image of a crown of thorns blended into a barbed-wire fence (Figures 3.8 and 3.9). The unmistakable Christian reference conjured up the Banat Swabian

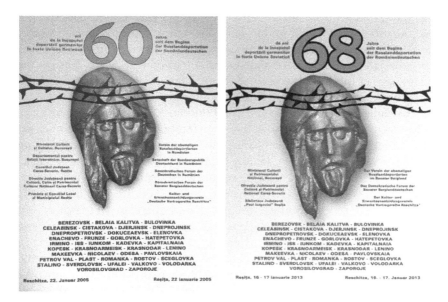

Figures 3.8 and 3.9 Posters announcing commemorative events in Reșița, Ulm, and Ingolstadt in 2005 and 2013 respectively.

---

[172] Jan Assmann's model of communicative and cultural memory, though static in some ways, seems to fit here. See Jan Assmann, 'Collective Memory and Cultural Identity', *New German Critique* 65 (1995), pp. 125–33.

Leidensweg, continuing a tradition that allowed the Swabians' path of ordeal to speak for all Romanian Germans in much the same way that Stefan Jäger's *Tragic Triptych* had done.

At the same time, the image also evoked the presence of the Holocaust in Romanian German memory. Through the prism of global Holocaust memory, the emaciated figure behind barbed wire could function as a striking allusion to iconic depictions of victims of the Holocaust. The resurgence of Romanian German victimhood was clearly informed by the strong presence of Holocaust memory in Germany and Europe more broadly as well as by its entanglement with the memory of communism, though the second wave of German victimhood was less overtly politicised. Ignaz Bernhard Fischer, head of the association of deportees, construed the Romanian German experience as part of a Europe-wide community of victimhood at the hands of the fanatics Hitler and Stalin:[173] Romanian German victimhood in 2005 needed to reference the widespread memory of the Holocaust to make sense of the experiences of deportation. Representations of life for the deportees mimicked Holocaust imagery and had done for quite some time. A sketch by Victor Stürmer, depicting an emaciated camp inmate hanging on a barbed-wire fence, was on the front page of the *Siebenbürgische Zeitung* in January 1985 – at the height of the Romanian German Historians' Dispute – making an implicit reference to Romanian German camp life as a Holocaust experience (Figure 3.10). The image gained a new lease of life when it returned to public visibility on the internet in 2005.[174] Even the Romanian state joined in: a commemorative franking stamp from 2005 featured a train with the dates 1945–2005 as a way of paying tribute to Romanian German deportees (Figure 3.11). All the while Romanian society was steeped in a deeply divisive memory dispute about the Romanian Holocaust in Transnistria.[175] Romania had deported up to 250,000 Romanian and Ukrainian Jews mainly from Moldova, Bukovina, and Transnistria. In all, more than 250,000 Romanian Jews were murdered during 1941 and 1944, the majority of whom were under Romanian authority. Romania's dark Holocaust history had been a taboo subject until the new

---

[173] Ignaz Bernhard Fischer, 'Die Russlanddeportierten', *Echo der Vortragsreihe* 1/181 (2005), pp. 6–9.

[174] 'Vor 40 Jahren Zwangsverschleppung in die Sowjetunion', *Siebenbürgische Zeitung* 35/1, 15 January 1985, p. 1. Viktor Stürmer's depictions have even enjoyed exposure on the German Wikipedia page on the deportation of Romanian Germans to the Soviet Union in the section 'Artistic Representations'.

[175] Roland Clark, 'From Source Collections to Peer-Reviewed Journals: Romanians Write the Holocaust,' *Dapim: Studies on the Holocaust* 31/3 (2017), pp. 307–12.

Figure 3.10 Victor Stürmer's *Blatt 23*, sketch of a Romanian German deportee.

millennium.[176] The train on the stamp was a conciliatory gesture towards

[176] See, for instance, Radu Ioanid, *The Holocaust in Romania: The Destruction of Jews and Gypsies under the Antonescu Regime, 1940–1944* (Chicago: Ivan R. Dee, 2000). Ioanid had been the first heavyweight academic to bring the Romanian Holocaust to the public's attention, and he estimated the figure of Jews murdered (independently of Nazi Germany) in Transnistria at the hands of Romanians between 1941 and 1944 at 380,000. The year 2000 also saw the reissuing of Mihail

Figure 3.11 Commemorative Romanian franking stamp from 2005.

Romanian German victim narratives, but it also implicitly turned the tables on the victim story by stirring up deep anxieties about the large-scale deportation of Jews to Transnistria perpetrated by the Romanian state.[177] Romanian German victimhood was a vent for Romanian Holocaust memory without having to speak openly about the Holocaust.

The tension between victims and perpetrators continued to frame Romanian German memories of the war. Through the Historians'

Sebastian's interwar and wartime diary. He was a Romanian Jewish writer whose testimony made huge waves in Romania with his diary's publication in 2000. See Mihail Sebastian, *Journal, 1935–1944* (Chicago: Ivan R. Dee, 2000). See also Mariana Hausleitner, Brigitte Mihok and Juliane Wetzel (eds.), *Rumänien und der Holocaust: Zu den Massenverbrechen in Transnistrien 1941–1944* (Berlin: Metropol Verlag, 2001).

[177] For the curious celebration of all things German in contemporary Romania, see Cristian Cercel, 'Philo-Germanism without Germans: Memory, Identity, and Otherness in Post-1989 Romania' (PhD diss., University of Durham, 2012). This is discussed in more detail in Chapter 5.

Dispute, the unveiling of the *Landsmannschaft* narrative, and the revival of German victimhood, Romanian German memories remained constrained by a sense of being threatened from the outside. Their experiences of living in communist (and post-communist) Romania and of the memory turns within (West) German society left Romanian Germans suspicious of official and dominant public discourses about the Second World War, fascism, and the Holocaust. Oral history responses reflected this. Interviewees frequently responded by parodying the official representation of the war in communist Romania. The émigré couple Christa and Robert König, whom we encountered earlier in their house in Lower Bavaria, highlighted the obvious mismatch between private and public memories. Over the course of the interview, they explained how ubiquitous the communist narrative was, especially in the education system, by emphasising what they saw as the absurdity of public memory in Romania. Had they discussed the war at all in their family?:

CK: Only within the family. It wasn't possible to do it any other way.
RK: If you read the newspapers, this is how it happened: The fascists ruined us and the . . .
CK: . . . glorious Soviet Army . . .
RK: . . . the glorious Soviet Army liberated us. It was all simply politics.
CK: They taught that in schools, it was everywhere!
INTERVIEWER: What did you make of it?
CK: It was terrible. We thought it was terrible, although that wasn't the only thing that affected us. But still, history had been turned upside down.
RK: They got it completely wrong.
CK: They didn't write anything that was true. Romanian history had it all the wrong way around anyway.
RK: It was all wrong.
CK: We simply put up with everything.[178]

For the Königs, the story of the Second World War existed as a binary in which the Romanian communist narrative was 'simply not true' and 'all wrong'.[179] Their memories of the Second World War were still framed by the mismatch between public and private German memories. This émigré couple, in their late sixties, had had the antagonistic position of their personal memories reaffirmed in contemporary Germany: the *Landsmannschaften* propagated images of Romanian German victimhood against a memory culture that seemed preoccupied with Germans as perpetrators. Christa König did more than just remember the Romanian

---

[178] Interview with Christa König and Robert König, 14 February 2005, Passau.   [179] Ibid.

public narrative as oppressive and overpowering. She contrasted the image of liberation with her own personal experience as a six-year-old giving a voice to German victims.

> And then the collapse happened [*Und dann kam der Zusammenbruch*]. It was all so terrible. We were on our way [to our] house in the mountains, and we were returning just after 23 August 1944. The Romanian army was armed to the teeth, and everywhere – there were placards everywhere. People holding up posters were in their death throes [*die letzten Zuckungen*]. Apparently, they were Hitler-people [*Hitler-Leute*]. There was also a German wearing a helmet with a wooden hatchet plunged into his head. That's where I saw them in their death throes, and it was terrible, because we witnessed all of that. That's what life was like [when the 'Russians' were there], it was horrendous.[180]

The spectre of 23 August was still the central theme, but its meaning had shifted to the opposite end of the spectrum from the official celebratory line. The memory battle against official Romanian doctrine during communism was clearly still a raw experience for the Königs. It was particularly striking, however, that these memories persisted in their new home in Germany. Decades of *Vergangenheitsbewältigung*, of a very public working-through-the-past, had done little to alter the shape of private Romanian German memories. Richard von Weizsäcker's plea in 1985 to complicate the end of the war had, apparently, had little impact on Romanian German stories of the Second World War. That date, 23 August 1944, still governed chronologies of war, suffering, and defeat, but the 'pre-history' of that date remained dislocated from the memory narrative, consigned to the dim and distant past, and obscured behind the dominant story of German victimhood.

Suffering, then, was central to Romanian German identities. It had formed the backbone of foundation stories for Banat Swabians, and it became the central motif for twentieth-century Romanian Germans as they made sense of the past. German suffering thus became a transnational theme: a story for a minority group that moved from Germany and Romania, and to the Soviet Union. The fateful day, 23 August 1944, was one of several 'hot spots' at which the German ordeal came to the fore. An account by Bruno Pilsner, who still lived in the Banat in Arad Nou, followed the same pattern:

> We woke up in the morning and someone told us: the downfall [*Umsturz*] has happened in Bucharest. And that's when the misery [*Elend*] began. It

---

180 Ibid.

was the second or third day, and the German soldiers didn't know what to do. They were then taken as prisoners of war, actually as Romanian prisoners of war. And then the persecution started, in fact it was more than persecution. We weren't even allowed to speak German. All Germans, the intelligent doctors, lawyers, teachers, they were all interned – that had nothing to do with Russia [*sic*] to begin with. I was sixteen at the time. I was an emotional wreck [*Ich war zwischen Himmel und Erde*]. I wasn't old enough to be locked up, but old enough to work. The bridge [leading out of town] was blown up; on a Saturday evening, they blew up the bridge, and so we were sentenced to forced labour [*Fronarbeit*] to rebuild the bridges. We built three bridges in total, and so it carried on until the end of the year. And then we heard that the Germans were being deported. All those who had claimed to be German in the last census had been put on the list. And with a name like 'Pilsner' they of course started looking for my father.[181]

Pilsner was able to place his own story in a wider narrative of the German *Leidensweg*. Success and hardship formed an important part of Romanian German identity, but crucially this portrayal of the end of the war formed a transnational Romanian German understanding of this period.[182] Pilsner, a non-émigré, formulated his memories against the old official discourse of liberation by the Soviets and in line with established *Landsmannschaft* discourses. For those who had stayed in Romania, the fact that they never physically crossed the border into Germany did not stop their memory narratives from moving across borders. Some, such as Bruno Pilsner, were trapped in an insoluble conflict with the past. Others had at least been able to feel a sense of vindication after 1989. Like other non-émigrés, for instance, Elisabeth Schneider highlighted Romanian complicity in deporting the Germans. There were numerous reasons why non-émigrés, in particular, were keen to emphasise Romanian guilt and complicity in the victimisation of Germans. Personal reasons, settling old scores, and 'setting the record straight' were all part of the post-1989 world, where it had become possible for the first time to speak publicly about events and personal experiences during communism and condemn these outright. Elizabeth Schneider claimed that Romanians were forced to eat humble pie by acknowledging the crimes of the deportation of Germans:

---

[181] Interview with Bruno Pilsner, 2 August 2005, Arad Nou.
[182] See, for instance, Wilhelm Weber, *Und über uns der blaue endlose Himmel: Die Deportation in die Baragan-Steppe Rumäniens 1951. Eine Dokumentation* (Munich: Landsmannschaft der Banater Schwaben, 1998), Walther Konschitzky, Peter-Dietmar Leber, and Walter Wolf (eds.), *Deportiert in den Baragan 1951–1956* (Munich: Haus des Deutschen Ostens, 2001), and Vultur, *Istorie trăită*.

It went something like this [after the deportations]: 'Oh, those poor fellows! Great to see they've returned in good health!' And, like I was saying, they [the Romanians] weren't particularly ... pro-German. Then, after the revolution [in 1989] they ran out of ideas of how to get to us. And so then they said: 'Oh! It's so good you are staying here in Romania!' Suddenly, they were all very nice and friendly. People who used to ignore us, and not even so much as look at us, began greeting us again.[183]

Schneider, like many other non-émigrés, was enveloped in a new discourse which required her to tell the new anticommunist 'truth'.[184] The new millennium saw a big effort within the dwindling Romanian German community to uncover Romanian collaboration with Soviet officials in deporting Romanian Germans to the Soviet Union in 1945. Hannelore Baier, an independent scholar and journalist from Sibiu, was a trail-blazer for working through new archival material that shed light on the question of who was culpable for the deportations.[185] Her extensive research revealed a complex picture of denial and guilt. Stalin's command in December 1944 to mobilise Germans in south-eastern Europe for labour had accommodated Romanian claims that the deportations were a Soviet crime, not a Romanian one. Baier's work, though, showed ambiguous Romanian reactions to Soviet demands. There had been some Romanian resistance to the deportations, but also plenty of willing collaboration. Romanian cooperation with Stalin had also allowed Romanian Germans to hide away any reference to Germans as active participants in a fascist war, as Baier also pointed out. The fascist past and its aftermath thus formed the centrepiece of a transnational community in battle with itself, with Romania, and with broader memory cultures in a post-Cold War world. What had started in the 1970s among Romanian Germans in Germany rumbled on for decades and mutated into a multifaceted debate about Romanian Germans in late-modern Europe.

---

[183] Interview with Elizabeth Schneider, 24 February 2005, Sibiu.

[184] This is closely linked to other discourses of 'truth telling' after 1989 and will discussed in more detail in Chapter 4. See, for instance, Timothy Garton Ash, 'The Year of Truth', in Vladimir Tismăneanu (ed.), *The Revolutions of 1989* (London: Routledge, 1999), pp. 108–25.

[185] See, for instance, Hannelore Baier, 'The Deportation of Germans from Romania to Forced Labor in the Soviet Union', *Euxenios* 19–20 (2015), pp. 20–5, Baier, *Germanii din România*, and her edited volume of primary material, Hannelore Baier, *Departe în Rusia, la Stalino: amintiri și documente cu privire la deportarea în Uniunea Sovietică a etnicilor germani din România, 1945–1950* (Brussels: InterGraf, 2003).

Beyond Dispute

There was no great revelation of 'the truth' for Romanian Germans. Despite shifting discourses within the *Landsmannschaften* and efforts by journalists and academics to explain the uncomfortable complexities of Romanian German Nazi allegiances, a culture of denial persisted in Romanian German war stories. Efforts to 'other' National Socialism featured as part of Romanian German narratives. Fascist entanglements continued to occupy a curious external position and could be explained by Romanian German naivety. Hans Bergel, the onetime co-editor of the *Siebenbürgische Zeitung*, Saxon luminary, and historian, still stuck to his guns in 2005 as he explained:

> We didn't quite understand what Hitler wanted. I know all that from conversations with my father and grandfather. I was all ears. I remember it vividly. It all seemed a bit strange to us. What was important to us in our view, in our uninformed view – if I may use that expression – here in Transylvania, was Germany. Germany recovered after the First World War. They created jobs. There was no unemployment. Hitler was of secondary importance in our imagination.[186]

Sachsen and *Schwaben* had been heavily caught up in National Socialism,[187] yet Romanian German memories of the Second World War rested on a particular interpretation of their relationship to Germany and Nazism. The *Gleichschaltung* of educational institutions and the prevalence of youth organisations in Romanian German society during the 1930s and 1940s stood at odds with Bergel's claim of naivety. It was precisely Bergel's generation – he was born in 1927 – that would have been the main target group of a wholesale National Socialist education. But, in Bergel's apologia, Romanian German commitment to National Socialism was a trusting misunderstanding. Secondly, Nazism was *German* and not Romanian German. Nazism was an alien construct, and this seemed to exculpate them from any real involvement.[188] That Bergel, a spokesperson for the

---

[186] Interview with Hans Bergel, 18 February 2005, Munich.

[187] See, for instance, Hausleitner and Roth, *Der Einfluss von Faschismus und Nationalsozialismus auf Minderheiten in Ostmittel- und Südosteuropa* (Munich: IKGS, 2006). YY use verlag or not?

[188] This also applies to the other smaller Romanian German minorities such as the *Bukowinadeutsche* (Germans from the Bukovina), *Dobrudschadeutsche* (Germans from Dobruja), and *Bessarabiendeutsche* (Germans from Bessarabia). These minorities were virtually wiped out by the resettlement policies of the Third Reich, as many of them ended up in the *Warthegau* around Warsaw. They were thus resettled twice: first, from their original homeland and then again during the expulsions of Germans from eastern Europe, in this case Poland, at the end of the Second World War. As a result, these small minorities found themselves dispersed across West and East Germany. See Lumans, *Himmler's Auxiliaries*, for details.

official organs of Romanian German émigrés, took this view should come as no surprise. But it did reinforce the strength and endurance of that position, namely that Romanian Germans were effectively blameless.

Romanian German memories of fascism followed the pattern of 'externalising' involvement by focusing on German culpability.[189] Privately, too, many respondents chose to externalise the overbearingly negative connections associated with Nazism. Racist ideology and the ensuing violence did not really feature as part of their war memory. Connections with Nazi Germany had meant something entirely different to Romanian Germans. Bergel was thus able to continue by making a strong distinction between Germans and Romanian Germans regarding the issue of memory and guilt:

> We didn't talk about fascism publicly, because the state put forward detailed instructions for how one was to talk about the Second World War. But [we did] in private, and I suspect that's the big difference to how things were here in Germany. Privately, we spoke a lot about it. For example, there were those who had fought in the German army and in the Romanian army. Germans were partly in the Romanian army, who were then allied with the Germans. But they were also in the German army. People spoke openly about it in their respective families. You weren't allowed to talk about it publicly. Among friends and acquaintances, perhaps. There [in Romania] . . . I felt that talking was a good thing, especially after I came to Germany where I noticed: Gosh, their fathers never spoke here [*Hier haben die Väter nie gesprochen*]. But there is also something else. Germans here were burdened by their consciousness [*Bewusstsein*], and I'll summarise it with one set phrase: Auschwitz! They [the Romanian Germans] weren't burdened. Because they didn't do Auschwitz there [in Romania] [*Denn dort man hat dort kein Auschwitz gemacht*]. We had a good relationship with Jews . . . right? During the persecution of the Jews under Antonescu's military dictatorship during the war, there were many important Transylvanians – en masse – who hid Jews. Some of them kept up to sixteen people. I know, or rather I knew a number of such Jews. We had a completely different relationship to Jews than the Germans did here. That's why, the older I get, a lot of the German mentality seems so incomprehensible to me. I just don't understand why they treated the Jews like that. I don't understand it.[190]

---

[189] James Mark demonstrates this in his study on remembering communism in east-central Europe by pointing out the memory contests between fascism and communism, particularly in the Baltic states. See James Mark, *The Unfinished Revolution: Making Sense of the Communist Past in Central-Eastern Europe* (New Haven: Yale University Press, 2010), and James Mark, 'What Remains? Anti-Communism, Forensic Archaeology, and the Retelling of the National Past in Lithuania and Romania', *Past & Present* 206 (2010), pp. 276–300.

[190] Interview Hans Bergel.

Antisemitism and the Holocaust, for Bergel, were exclusively *reichsdeutsche* phenomena.[191] The denial of responsibility was emblematic of post-war Romanian German narratives more generally and has remained a central theme to this day: the Germans from Germany did it, not us. It also served to reinforce wider Romanian Holocaust denial. Despite the memory clashes with public Romanian discourses, on this point Romanian Germans readily integrated their own position into mainstream Romanian representations of wartime violence against Jews, which wrote Romanian agency out of the narrative. The Romanian German community could simply ride on the coat-tails of the discussion of the Holocaust, which took place independently in Romania under the auspices of Marshal Antonescu.[192] And, while the Romanian Holocaust began to be tackled by Romanian scholars from the early 2000s, the official narrative in communist Romania – Holocaust denial – was something with which Romanian Germans could readily identify.[193] Bergel thus not only endorsed the view that the Holocaust was exclusively German, but also that it had not really occurred in Romania. *Vergangenheitsbewältigung*, so the argument ran, simply did not apply to the Romanian German past. In part a legacy of the memory politics of the Holocaust in Romania under Gheorghiu-Dej and Ceauşescu regime,[194] Romanian German narratives were sanitised even where violence towards Jews was present. Christine Oberath was born in a city in northern Transylvania in 1920 and emigrated from Romania to West Germany in 1970. While the Holocaust in northern Transylvania was very different from the Holocaust in Romania, as it fell under Hungarian control, Oberath made no distinction and remembered the episode as part of her life in Romania. Her account of violence was unusual for Romanian Germans remembering their experiences during the fascist period. She vividly remembered the Second World War, but the topic of violence towards Jews and Roma appeared in euphemistic terms:

---

[191] For comparative examples, see, e.g., Kristian Gerner, 'Between the Holocaust and Trianon: Historical Culture in Hungary', in Martin L. Davies and Claus-Christian W. Szejnmann (eds.), *How the Holocaust Looks Now: International Perspectives* (Basingstoke: Palgrave Macmillan, 2007), pp. 97–106.
[192] See Cioflâncă, 'A "Grammar of Exculpation"'.
[193] The most detailed studies of this under-researched field are first and foremost Ioanid, *The Holocaust in Romania*, Hausleitner, Mihok, and Wetzel (eds.), *Rumänien und der Holocaust*, and Ancel, *The History of the Holocaust in Romania*.
[194] There was no public engagement with the Romanian entanglement with the Third Reich. See Jean Ancel, 'The German–Romanian Relationship and the Final Solution', *Holocaust and Genocide Studies* 19/2 (2005), pp. 252–75.

> Well, we had heard about Jews. I didn't see anything as far as Gypsies were concerned, but once, while I was working there, I did see something. There is a castle and a hill and on the top of it is a church. And right by the slope is an esplanade. And I remember I was sitting there once and I could see the town square below me. Jews were working there, and they were being goaded [*sie sind angetrieben worden*]. And I was disgusted by that. I found it displeasing that such a thing was happening. But I wasn't the kind of person who could say anything like why are you doing this. But I did see that, and it was displeasing.[195]

Where violence featured as part of the story, it was distant, vague, and agentless. Typical of the detachment from the dark history of the Second World War and fascism, ethnic violence was conceived of as something done by others: maybe Romanians, maybe Germans, but definitely not *Romanian Germans*.[196] For the most part, however, atrocities carried out by Germans during the war simply did not feature that prominently in the oral history interviews.

Rejecting the Romanian public discourse to which Romanian Germans had been exposed during communism meant rejecting 'anti-German' stories about ethnic violence. Hans Bergel thus explained that the memory of the Holocaust – at least in Romania during the Cold War – was tainted by its association with Romanian communism:

> We spoke about it [the Holocaust], but we really weren't informed. Some said: 'Gosh, that's not possible, Germans don't get up to things like that.' This was always led by the fundamental feeling that we, as Germans, had always had a good relationship with Jews. And we were also devoid of any kind of information [regarding the Holocaust]. Whatever the communists wrote, we thought, was a lie. And even when they wrote the truth, we still didn't believe it, because they were communists who always lied. Whether that was right or not, I don't know, but that was the general attitude: 'Well, that's what the communists are saying. That's all a lie.'[197]

Communist 'lies' still loomed large over Romanian German memories, despite the heated debates that dominated the community in the late Cold War and post-communist period. What mattered was not remembering Jewish victims; after all, public engagement with the past in communist Romania, as elsewhere in east-central Europe, was primarily concerned

---

[195] Interview with Christine Oberath, 16 February 2005, Traunstein.
[196] The Swabian author Herta Müller has written about this in meticulous detail. For an excellent analysis of her work and interpretation of Romanian German war memory, see Brigid Haines (ed.), *Herta Müller* (Cardiff: University of Wales Press, 1998), and Brigid Haines and Lyn Marven (eds.), *Herta Müller* (Oxford: Oxford University Press, 2013).
[197] Interview Hans Bergel.

with general victims of fascism.[198] Moreover, particularly in the immediate post-war period, Romanian public memory also focused heavily on 'Nazi barbarism',[199] excluding Germans from the official war memory while limiting the notion of true victimhood to politically useful groups.

The mistrust that the public discourse in Romania had provoked never went away. For some Romanian Germans, the encounter with *Vergangenheitsbewältigung* in (West) Germany engendered consternation. Why were Germans so preoccupied with the Holocaust and their own culpability? Josef and Christa Biblis emigrated from Romania in the mid-1980s and were both from educated middle-class families. Josef Biblis had previously been a teacher in Romania. Over the course of the interview, it became apparent that both interviewees felt that the history of the Second World War had been hijacked by an overbearing narrative of German guilt. Repeating the main position of the *Landsmannschaften* during the Cold War, Josef Biblis felt that public spaces in both Romania – his classroom and the newspapers – and Germany – primarily television – had been usurped by a discourse with which he was unable to identify. Both Josef and Christa Biblis rejected the primacy of the Holocaust as an anti-German conspiracy:

CB: It's impossible even to turn on the TV without, you know, hearing about it all of the time.

JB: These constant reminders, it's sick, it's really sick . . .

CB: Everywhere, all you hear about is the Holocaust; Auschwitz this, Auschwitz that.

JB: That's all they are interested in. But at the same time, I've read things . . . goodness! But you cannot mention these things in public. I might even get locked up for saying things. But then I wonder: is there something we are not being told? Even Helmut Schmidt [the former chancellor of Germany] who was, I think, a quarter Jewish – his grandmother was Jewish, I think – he said that he and his family were not affected in Hamburg! I'm telling you, if even Helmut Schmidt . . . just think about that: Helmut Schmidt! If even Helmut Schmidt, as a Jew himself, a quarter Jew, said such things, then I wonder: maybe things that aren't quite as they seem . . . But you're not allowed to say that.[200]

---

[198] Petru Weber, 'The Public Memory of the Holocaust in Postwar Romania', *Studia Hebraica* 4 (2004), pp. 341–8. In light of the purge of prominent Jewish members of the Communist Party, such as Ana Pauker, the Holocaust was an extremely difficult concept to integrate into public memory.

[199] Ibid., p. 343.   [200] Interview with Christa Biblis and Joseph Biblis, 14 August 2005, Coburg.

For the Biblis couple and others, their memories had been kidnapped by yet another omnipresent anti-German narrative. In echoes of the overbearing doctrine in Romania, Josef Biblis viewed Holocaust memory and *Vergangenheitsbewältigung* as a continuation of memory oppression. Holocaust denial was the ultimate form of resistance against the untruths told by both the Romanian and German states. It was television, in particular, that had apparently been taken over by alleged lobbyists 'obsessed' with German guilt.[201] For Romanian German émigrés, encounters with West German TV were a continuation of the dominance of official discourses in Romania. Viktor Munteanu, who had emigrated in 1990, reacted defensively when asked about his thoughts on the memory of the Holocaust in Germany. Like many other interviewees, rather than expanding on the topic, he dismissed it briefly but firmly. 'I'm not carrying that burden [*Den Schuh ziehe ich mir nicht an*]', he insisted.[202] Munteanu continued: 'Of course you hear about this and that, but, no, I definitely don't buy it!'[203]

A number of personal views remained unshakeable. At the most extreme end, émigrés were able to subscribe to right-wing revisionism, including Holocaust relativism and denial.[204] For Romanian Germans such as Josef and Christa Biblis, the apparent left–liberal consensus on Holocaust memory was simply a continuation of an anti-German rhetoric. A number of émigrés therefore chose to rebuff any negative portrayal of the German past, be it communist propaganda or the concept of *Vergangenheitsbewältigung*. As such the communist public narrative and *Vergangenheitsbewältigung* merged into one. Fundamentally, Romanian German stories stood at odds with narratives that challenged the primacy of Germans as victims, and the Romanian public discourse during communism epitomised this. Reminiscent of post-war West German narratives,[205] Romanian German memories of victimhood persisted into the new millennium,

---

[201] Kansteiner restricted his analysis to viewing statistics of the ZDF (Zweites Deutsches Fernsehen), which is the equivalent to BBC2. Since Germans had access to only three channels until 1984, his study may well be considered to be quite an accurate representation of West German viewing patterns. See Kansteiner, 'Nazis, Viewers and Statistics', pp. 580–1.

[202] Interview with Viktor Munteanu, 15 August 2005, Tübingen.   [203] Ibid.

[204] See Wolfgang Benz, 'Anti-Semitism Today', in Davies and Szejnmann (eds.), *How the Holocaust Looks Now*, pp. 262–3. See also William W. Hagen, *German History in Modern Times: Four Lives of the Nation* (Cambridge: Cambridge University Press, 2012), pp. 366–71, for an overview of the political history of the far right in West Germany.

[205] See, for example, Moeller, *War Stories*.

just as right-wing and conservative stories survived the defeat during the *Historikerstreit*.[206]

Other Romanian Germans were at times more willing to assimilate patterns of remembrance in German society. Even Hans Bergel rethought his own role at the height of the Romanian German dispute over the fascist past:

> I renamed the newspaper, the *Siebenbürgische Zeitung der Landsmannschaft*, I changed it, and the heads of the *Landsmannschaft* couldn't say no to that, because they noticed what a gem I was. I was successful with the masses, because I changed the newspaper. I even managed to change the name of the paper to *Zeitung der Siebenbürgischen Weltföderation* [*Newspaper of the Transylvanian World Federation*]. I founded that, because there are [Saxons] in Canada, the United States, and in Austria. Hence the name 'world federation'. *Landsmannschaft*, what a crap name [*sic*] [*Was für ein scheiß Name*]! 'It's going to incriminate you, politically, are you blind? Can't you see what's going on around you? We don't need this! Let's start a world federation.' That was my idea. You can read up about it. And so, I founded this world federation, changed the newspaper to the Association of the World Federation of Transylvanian Saxons. That was quite comforting for me not to be lumped together with, you know ... I mean these are partly just prejudgements, but unfortunately there were such individuals in the Landsmannschaft. I don't know what it's like nowadays, but these individuals had terrible opinions in my view. I took them on in public, Silesians, Sudeten Germans, but you couldn't talk to these people back then. Then I thought: so what! I'll do what I think is right.[207]

Bergel was acutely aware of the 'dangers' of being associated with revisionist circles. He portrayed himself as a forerunner of a corrected stance towards the National Socialist past, even as his role in the little *Historikerstreit* told a different story. If Bergel had tried to silence dissent in the 1970s through to the 1990s, in retrospect he recast himself as a peace-broker. The dispute over the fascist past had left behind its traces: someone who had originally been a prominent defender of *Vergangenheitsbewältigung* was now telling a very different story twenty years later. For Bergel, the mere name *Die Landsmannschaft* was a political faux-pas. It evoked images of right-wing revisionism and intransigence, which he was keen to avoid. It was the other expellee

---

[206] Karoline von Oppen and Stefan Wolff, 'From the Margins to the Centre? The Discourse on Expellees and Victimhood in Germany', in Niven (ed.), *Germans as Victims*, pp. 194–209.

[207] Interview Hans Bergel.

and émigré groups that were mired in old revisionism, Bergel attempted to explain in an effort to integrate into German society. The Saxons and Swabians were on their way to becoming proper politically correct *Bundesbürger*.

This belated attempt at blending in was not solely about softening the debates about the Nazi past. During the Cold War, migrants from east-central Europe took on two conflicting roles in West Germany.[208] On the one hand, they were seen as irrefutable evidence that living under communist rule was untenable, which is why east Europeans sought political asylum in the West.[209] In that sense, Romanian Germans had a role to play in providing palpable evidence of the crimes of communism, which precluded any critical engagement in the dark fascist past. On the other hand, however, migrants from the East tended to be viewed 'as "aliens", suspicious persons who might have been "infiltrated" by communism',[210] or associated with an aggressive right-wing milieu at odds with (West) German society.

Had the Romanian German Historians' Dispute left behind only rhetoric, double-think, and PR? Twenty years on, a small number of Romanian Germans from an older generation supported the newly found concepts – at least for Romanian Germans – for dealing with the past. While some, such as Hans Bergel, wagged their fingers at German society, because 'their fathers never spoke here',[211] others had reshaped their own narratives since living in Germany. Gerhard Brunner, who arrived in Germany from Timişoara in the mid-1980s, had experienced personal difficulties after arriving in West Germany in the 1980s. He was diagnosed with cancer and, having recovered from the illness successfully, was unable to find a way into the job market for the few remaining years before his retirement. He and his wife became reliant on social benefits and their children's support.

---

[208] Anne von Oswald, Karen Schönwälder and Barbara Sonnenberger, '*Einwanderungsland Deutschland*: A New Look at Its Post-War History', in Rainer Ohliger, Karen Schönwälder and Triadafilos Triadafilopoulos (eds.), *European Encounters: Migrants, Migration, and European Societies since 1945* (London: Ashgate, 2003), pp. 19–37.

[209] A good example of the potent role east Europeans – even non-Germans – played for anti-communism in West Germany, see Anna Holian, 'Anticommunism in the Streets: Refugee Politics in Cold War Germany', *Journal of Contemporary History* 45/1 (2010), pp. 134–61.

[210] Roswitha Breckner, 'Biographical Continuities and Discontinuities in East–West Migration before and after 1989: Two Case Studies of Migration from Romania to West Germany', in Robin Humphrey, Robert Miller and Elena Zdravomyslova (eds.), *Biographical Research in Eastern Europe: Altered Lives and Broken Biographies* (Aldershot: Ashgate Publishing Ltd, 2003), p. 194.

[211] Interview Hans Bergel.

Preoccupied with these personal concerns, the Historians' Dispute might well not have affected him at all. Yet his approach to talking about his understanding of the Nazi past was one of reflection:

> So when I arrived here, I had, how should I put it, certain opinions . . . how can I say this: I was quite patriotic. And then I arrived here and it was different. You hear about this and that [*Man hört so dies und jenes*], well, you know . . . as time goes by, you tend to rethink. I'd say I was pretty patriotic [*national eingestellt*] . . . do you know what I mean? That changed over time, especially when you hear about all these things here [*wenn man hier das so mitbekommt*].[212]

Hidden behind innuendo, Brunner indicated a profound shift in his conception of the implication of Romanian Germans in the Nazi past. In public, reassessments of the Romanian German past were played out on a very public stage and in quite vocal terms. Yet the private views of ordinary Romanian German émigrés have remained shrouded in mystery, negotiating personal memory narratives with shifting public discourses about the past. Here, in Brunner's allusion to his earlier views, he tried to make sense of his changing opinions, as his Romanian German 'patriotism' clashed with the West German zeitgeist of the 1980s. Quietly and unobtrusively, neither 'carrying that burden' nor deliberately eschewing it, Brunner rethought some of his certainties and 'quite patriotic' views.[213]

Reflections

The year 2005 was crucial for revisiting the memory disputes around the fascist past that had plagued Romanian Germans throughout the Cold War and beyond. If the commemorations of the sixtieth anniversary of the deportation of Romanian Germans still felt like a throwback to an earlier period, the public exposure of the Romanian German entanglement with fascism was now inseparable from any portrayal of victimhood. The IKGS (Institut für deutsche Kultur und Geschichte Südosteuropas) in Munich transformed into a publishing machine for studies on fascism in southeastern Europe. Where German victimhood appeared, the other side of the coin was always in view.[214] The flagship journal of the IKGS, the

[212] Interview with Gerhard Brunner, 12 August 2005, Stuttgart.   [213] Ibid.
[214] See, for instance, Joachim Wittstock and Stefan Sienerth (eds.), *'Bitte um baldige Nachricht': Alltag, Politik und Kultur im Spiegel südostdeutscher Korrespondenz des ausgehenden 19. und 20. Jahrhunderts* (Munich: IKGS Verlag, 2003), and Hausleitner and Roth (eds.), *Der Einfluss von Faschismus*.

Südostdeutsche Vierteljahreshefte, was renamed at the end of 2005 fittingly as *Spiegelungen*: reflections. The budding online community of Romanian Germans engaged in heated discussions over the Nazi and communist past.[215] This was not an academic debate, but an attempt to understand their own political identity. No one agreed; instead, they forcefully argued openly about the past. While the few remaining Germans in Romania tried to make sense of the situation they now faced, the émigré community was busily deconstructing long-standing myths. The different interest groups that had sought to either entrench or challenge the post-Second World War myths had splintered further and, in many cases, had come to accept mutual criticism. All the while, new voices were now setting the agenda for remembering fascism and deportation. Herta Müller's *Atemschaukel* made the topic of German victimhood palatable to an international audience in ways that the *Landsmannschaften* never could.[216] This novel, which led in part to her becoming a Nobel laureate in 2009, charted the story of a Romanian German deportee, based loosely on her friend, the novelist Oskar Pastior, without invoking revisionist tropes of Romanian German innocence. Ursula Ackrill, a Romanian German living in the United Kingdom, made a forceful intervention in the question of Romanian German guilt with her disorientating and thoroughly postmodern novel *Zeiden, im Januar*.[217] The fascist past was no longer simply an internal Romanian German dispute, but now belonged to a global culture.

The past impinges on the present at particular moments, and for Romanian Germans these tensions of memory came to the fore at transnational, European junctures. If the post-war period gave the impression of conservative stability throughout Europe, then the 1980s were characterised by radical memory ventures: the Prussian revival in the GDR, the soul-wrenching Vichy trials in France, the *Historikerstreit* in Germany, and the history battle over Transylvania in Romania and Germany.[218] The rapid societal and political changes of the post-communist period also went hand in hand with booming

---

[215] For an interesting current 'insider' discussion, see 'Siebenbürger Sachsen zu Recht im rechten Eck?', *Siebenbürgische Zeitung Online* at www.siebenbuerger.de/ubb/Forum11/HTML/000691.html (accessed 31 May 2016). In 2005, readers of the *Siebenbürgische Zeitung* debated whether or not Transylvanian Saxons were rightly viewed as inherently right-wing. This was not an academic discussion, but rather an attempt to understand their political identity.

[216] Herta Müller, *Atemschaukel* (Munich: Hanser, 2009).

[217] Ursula Ackrill, *Zeiden, im Januar* (Berlin: Verlag Klaus Wagenbach, 2015).

[218] For a collection of essays that – in part at least – study the post-war memory 'consensus', see Lebow, Kansteiner and Fogu (eds.), *The Politics of Memory in Postwar Europe*. For the Vichy memory trials

transnational memory cultures. The first decade of post-communist Europe saw Holocaust memory cemented as *the* most central European *lieu de mémoire*. At the same time, German victimhood made its far-from-triumphant comeback. Despite occasionally upsetting the delicate new relationships between Germany and Czechia, Poland, and other east-central European states, the new German victimhood was, by and large, less threatening and less competitive towards other memory cultures. It had become abundantly clear, however, that European societies were consuming a glut of often contradictory memories. As they moved between East and West, Romania and Germany, Romanian Germans were caught up in this plethora of conflicting memory cultures.

This chapter has demonstrated that the experiences and memories of National Socialism and the Second World War formed an absolutely central part of Romanian German identities. The debates over National Socialism fractured Romanian German identity contests. Conflict over belonging in the interwar period, outlined in this chapter, acted as a rehearsal for the memory debates that followed their alignment with National Socialist Germany. Three significant periods of memory construction and reconstruction – the post-war period, the 1980s, the millennial memory boom – left deep marks on Romanian German memory culture. As this chapter has argued, Romanian German memory conflicts took place in a number of arenas and was not merely a sideshow to (West) German memory culture: in émigré associations, in private remembrance, through 'outsider' voices, in official representations, on a transnational level, and in communist and post-communist Romania. In this web of contestation, émigré associations provided the biggest platform, but their dominant position was always shaky. The certainty with which émigrés had constructed a narrative of grievance and victimhood spoke to both an émigré and a non-émigré constituency: they had been persecuted in Romania and misunderstood by Germans. The Romanian German Historians' Dispute of the late Cold War then plunged the community into a deep identity crisis. The large number of new Romanian German arrivals in the 1980s and early 1990s complicated matters

of the 1980s and 1990s, see Donald Reid, 'Resistance and Its Discontents: Affairs, Archives, Avowals, and the Aubracs', *Journal of Modern History* 77 (2005), pp. 97–137. For the GDR Prussian memory revival, see André Keil, 'The *Preußenrenaissance* Revisited: German–German Entanglements, the Media and the Politics of History in the Late German Democratic Republic', *German History* 34/2 (2016), pp. 258–78.

further. By the 2000s, there were no longer clearly defined camps around the topic of the Romanian German fascist past. Instead, the restatement of Romanian German victimhood around the sixtieth anniversary of deportations masked the multiple divisions of memory that lay beneath these commemorative events. Some rejected Holocaust memory as a conspiracy; others were still fighting their battle against the communist Romanian state; yet others normalised the fascist past in an attempt to finally blend in and be left alone. In any case, whatever each made of the Nazi past, there was a bigger fish to fry: communism.

CHAPTER 4

The Iron Memory Curtain: Romanian Germans and Communism

The whole book is a lie.[1]

Romanian Germans found their experiences of the Cold War deeply puzzling. Unlike many other Germans in east-central Europe, they were not expelled at the end of the Second World War. Instead, they were temporarily deported to the Soviet Union, mainly to the Donbass region, for 'reconstruction work'. The returnees were scattered across Europe. Some ended up in West Germany, others in East Germany. A substantial number, though, were able to return to Romania, where they faced a precarious situation. Caught up between punitive sanctions that saw their land redistributed, on the one hand, and gradual attempts to reintegrate them into Romanian society, on the other, Romanian Germans were never fully confident of their position in communist Romania. Their situation was made more complex by the growing influence of Romanian German émigrés in West Germany. From the émigrés' perspective, Romanian communism represented everything that was opposite to Romanian German identity. And the more vocal they became, the more they began to pit communism against the identity and interests of the Romanian German community. The *Landsmannschaften* committed to the idea of getting Romanian Germans out of Romania, where – so they argued – the political and social climate was hopelessly anti-German. Romanian Germans in Romania were receptive to that narrative, but had to balance it with personal life choices in Romania. Romanian German lives, in other words, became more and more entangled in communist society in Romania, which was increasingly at odds with a mainstream self-construction of Romanian German identity that vocally eschewed any connection to communism. That, in short, was the big dilemma they faced.

[1] Hans Bergel, in response to Schlattner's novel *Rote Handschuhe*, cited in Konrad Klein, 'Zu spät, Herr Schlattner, zu spät', *Siebenbürgische Zeitung* 51/16, 15 October 2001, p. 5.

This chapter traces the origins of Romanian German entanglements with communism. It lays bare the vexed relationship between Romanian Germans and the communist landscape around them. Far from being removed from 'mainstream' society, Romanian Germans were very much enmeshed in Romanian society. While inclusion in and commitment to Romanian society formed one facet of that picture, it was counterposed by moments of intense crisis and oppression. If Romanian German publications and organisations in Romania told a story of attachment to Romania, then show trials, such as the Authors' Trial in Braşov in 1959, revealed the complexities at the heart of Romanian German identities and communism. Such controversies rumbled on and were refracted through the perspectives of the Romanian German émigré community in West Germany and beyond the Cold War period. Romanian German connections with the Romanian communist system – such as joining the Romanian Communist Party – had hugely explosive potential in émigré circles in Germany.

More problematically, the migration of Germans in the 1970s and 1980s as well as the disintegration of communism in east-central Europe in 1989 placed Romanian Germans into contexts where they were confronted with the legacy of communism long before it became a European issue. Escaping Cold War communism, either by emigration or by being in Romania in 1989, also meant actively dealing with the communist past. The Romanian German case of experiencing the Cold War on both sides of the Iron Curtain sheds new light on how societies have been able to deal with the legacy of communism.[2] For Romanian Germans, neither emigration nor 1989 represented a moment of reckoning with communism, as many commentators have claimed for east-central Europe more broadly.[3] Western liberal mythologies of 1989 as a watershed moment of liberation for east-central Europe never mapped on to Romanian German experiences of either communism or, more crucially, life after communism.[4]

---

[2] Anton Sterbling argues that their inclusion in the subculture of the *Landsmannschaften* placed Romanian Germans in a special and problematic position in Germany. See Anton Sterbling, 'Dazugehörende Fremde? Besonderheiten der Integration der Rumäniendeutschen in der Bundesrepublik Deutschland', in Christoph Köck, Aloid Moosmüller and Klaus Roth (eds.), *Zuwanderung und Integration: Kulturwissenschaftliche Zugänge und soziale Praxis* (Münster: Waxmann Verlag, 2004), p. 118.

[3] See, for instance, Timothy Garton Ash, 'The Year of Truth', in Vladimir Tismaneanu (ed.), *The Revolutions of 1989* (London: Routledge, 1989), pp. 108–25, and Robin Okey, *The Demise of Communist East Europe: 1989 in Context* (London: Arnold, 2004), in particular pp. 107–30 and 131–5; see also Tom Gallagher, *Theft of a Nation: Romania since Communism* (London: C. Hurst & Co., 2005), for an account of what went wrong after 1989.

[4] James Mark, Bogdan C. Iacob, Tobias Rupprecht and Ljubica Spaskovska, *1989: A Global History of Eastern Europe* (Cambridge: Cambridge University Press, 2019), pp. 2, 3.

Political crises and personal connections to communism made it difficult to integrate individual narratives into master narratives of liberation after emigration and 1989.[5] Time and again, Romanian Germans, especially émigrés, were engaged in vicious battles over their communist past. The Authors' Trial, the question of emigration, the dominance of right-wing politics, and political disputes in post-communist Romania rendered the legacy of communism a tricky topic that shattered the apparent certainty of Romanian German identity.

If there was one common theme that bound together Romanian German narratives of communism, then it was Romanian German victimhood. As elsewhere in post-communist east-central Europe, Romanian German stories of communism divided people into a large number of victims of communism and a small number of politically opportunistic communists.[6] As this chapter demonstrates, Romanian Germans were able to pioneer first-hand witness accounts of victim stories *avant la lettre* before communism collapsed, namely in émigré circles in West Germany and, to

---

[5] Though there have been attempts to 'root out' former communists by setting up truth commissions, these processes either have been ineffective or have not had the widespread support to 'break with the past'. See, for instance, Jennifer A. Yoder, 'Truth without Reconciliation: An Appraisal of the Enquete Commission on the SED Dictatorship in Germany', *German Politics* 8/3 (1999), pp. 59–80, Csilla Kiss, 'The Misuses of Manipulation: The Failure of Transitional Justice in Post-Communist Hungary', *Europe–Asia Studies* 58/6 (2006), pp. 925–40, Csilla Kiss, 'We Are Not Like Us – Transitional Justice: The (Re)Construction of Post-Communist Memory', in Alice MacLachlan and Ingvild Torsen (eds.), *History and Judgement* (Vienna: IWM Junior Visiting Fellows' Conferences, 2006) at www.iwm.at/index.php?option=com_content&task=view&id=484&Itemid=276 (accessed 10 Apr. 2018), and James Mark, *The Unfinished Revolution: Making Sense of the Communist Past in Central-Eastern Europe* (New Haven: Yale University Press, 2010), pp. 27–61. For oral testimonies from the former GDR, see Barbara Miller, *Narratives of Guilt and Compliance in Unified Germany: Stasi Informers and Their Impact on Society* (London: Routledge, 1999).

[6] It has also been a central theme in right-wing histories of communism in east-central Europe and is reflected in numerous museums across the region. See Nikolai Vukov, 'The "Unmemorable" and the "Unforgettable": "Museumizing" the Socialist Past in Post-1989 Bulgaria', in Oksana Sarkisova and Péter Apor (eds.), *Past for the Eyes: East European Representations of Communism in Cinema and Museums after 1989* (Budapest: CEU Press, 2008), pp. 307–34, James Mark, 'Containing Fascism: History in Post-Communist Baltic Occupation and Genocide Museums', ibid., pp. 335–69, Izabella Main, 'How Is Communism Displayed? Exhibitions and Museums of Communism in Poland', ibid., pp. 371–400, Heiki Ahonen, 'Wie gründet man ein Museum? Zur Entstehungsgeschichte des Museums der Okkupationen in Tallinn', in Volkhard Knigge and Ulrich Mählert (eds.), *Der Kommunismus im Museum: Formen der Auseinandersetzung in Deutschland und Ostmitteleuropa* (Cologne: Böhlau, 2005), pp. 107–16, Mária Schmidt, 'Das Budapester Museum "Haus des Terrors": Museum der modernen Zeitgeschichte und lebendige Gedenkstätte', ibid., pp. 161–9, Ana Blandiana, 'Die Gedenkstätte Memorial Sighet: Ein lebendiges Museum', ibid., pp. 171–80, Duncan Light, 'Gazing on Communism: Heritage Tourism and Post-Communist Identities in Germany, Hungary, and Romania', *Tourism Geographies* 2/2 (2000), pp. 157–76, and Duncan Light, 'An Unwanted Past: Contemporary Tourism and the Heritage of Communism in Romania', *International Journal of Heritage Studies* 6/2 (2000), pp. 145–60.

a limited extent, in Austria and North America. Like other east-central diasporas and exiles during the Cold War, Romanian Germans were able to fashion narratives of victim identity for a post-communist world even before it existed. Unlike other east-central European émigré circles, however, Romanian Germans had an escape route to Germany that was not readily open to other east-central Europeans. The victim stories that emerged were carefully curated by the *Landsmannschaften*. But these narratives were put under pressure and came under particularly intense scrutiny at specific 'memory moments' both during and after the Cold War. Such moments, as this chapter argues, often foreshadowed broader changes in European memory contests over communism. The post-communist period was of special importance for recalibrating Romanian German memory cultures. This chapter teases out those memory convulsions by focusing on two of the most significant Romanian German books of the post-communist period, namely Eginald Schlattner's *Rote Handschuhe* (2001) and Carl Gibson's *Symphonie der Freiheit* (2008). Their broad reception, which went far beyond the Romanian German community, reveals radical shifts in Romanian German memories of communism away from the orthodoxies of the Cold War. The once dominant Romanian German exceptionalism peddled by the *Landsmannschaften* fell apart not with the end of communism but, quite rapidly, in the twenty-first century.

The Schlattner Controversy

On 15 September 1959, Wolf von Aichelburg (1912–94), Hans Bergel, Andreas Birkner (1911–98), Georg Scherg (1917–2003), and Harald Siegmund (1930–2012) were sentenced to a combined total of ninety-five years in prison for conspiracy against the state. They stood accused of producing subversive literature.[7] One of the main pieces of evidence, Bergel's short novella *Fürst und Lautenschläger* (*The Prince and the Lute Player*) from 1957, caught the particular attention of the censors.[8] In a thinly veiled criticism of the communist government, Bergel seemed to draw parallels between the feudal Hungarian lord Gabriel Báthory in the

---

[7] See Michael Kroner, 'Politische Prozesse gegen Deutsche im kommunistischen Rumänien: Versuch einer Bestandaufnahme und eines Überblicks', in Peter Motzan and Stefan Sienerth (eds.), *Worte als Gefahr und Gefährdung: Fünf deutsche Schriftsteller vor Gericht (15. September – Kronstadt/Rumänien), Zusammenhänge und Hintergründe, Selbstzeugnisse und Dokumente* (Munich: Verlag Südostdeutsches Kulturwerk, 1993), pp. 31–49.
[8] Hans Bergel, *Fürst und Lautenschläger* (Bucharest: Jugendverlag, 1957).

early seventeenth century and the contemporaneous communist government of Romania in the 1950s.[9] This novella, combined with other
publications and incriminating oral testimonies, made up the corpus of
evidence that resulted in the draconian sentences for the five Germans. The
'Authors' Trial', as it came to be known, was part of a broader crackdown
during the Gheorghe Gheorghiu-Dej era (1947–65).[10] In the heavy-handed
pre-emptive response against any signs of dissidence following the
Hungarian revolution of 1956, the period 1957 to 1959 marked the end of
a short-lived post-Stalinist thaw in Romania.[11] As punitive as the sentences
were, all five men were released from prison by 1964 following a general
amnesty for political prisoners, and they were officially rehabilitated in
1968.[12]

The trial itself became a crucial moment for the Romanian German
community. The crux of the matter was not the obvious miscarriage of
justice, but the level of German involvement in bringing these five writers
to court.[13] The authors were arrested following a signed confession by
a young student called Eginald Schlattner. Arrested in 1957, he then spent
two years in detention during which he was subjected to various forms of
torture. He stood accused of having failed to report the alleged treasonous
conspiracy of a number of his compatriots.[14] Eventually, he caved in to the
pressure, which resulted not only in the harsh sentences for the five writers,
some of whom he had known personally, but also in further prison
sentences for other individuals, such as Schlattner's own uncle, the art

---

[9] See, for instance, Peter Motzan, 'Risikofaktor Schriftsteller: Ein Beispiel von Repressionen und Rechtswillkür', in Motzan and Sienerth (eds.), *Worte als Gefahr und Gefährdung*, p. 72, and Peter Motzan, 'Die vielen Wege in den Abschied: Die siebenbürgisch-deutsche Literatur in Rumänien (1919–1989): Ein sozialhistorischer Abriss', at www.siebenbuerger-sachsen-bw.de/buch/sachsen/15 .htm (accessed 14 Apr. 2018); see also Kroner, 'Politische Prozesse gegen Deutsche', and for documents and eyewitness testimonies see Sven Pauling, *'Wir werden Sie einkerkern, weil es Sie gibt!': Studie, Zeitzeugenberichte und Securitate-Akten zum Kronstädter Schriftstellerprozess 1959* (Berlin: Frank & Timme, 2012), p. 9.

[10] The trial is known as *Schriftstellerprozess* in German and *Procesul scriitorilor germani* in Romanian. See Kroner, 'Politische Prozesse gegen Deutsche', p. 39.

[11] Motzan, 'Risikofaktor Schriftsteller', p. 53. See also Dennis Deletant, *Communist Terror in Romania: Gheorghui-Dej and the Police State, 1948–1965* (London: Hurst & Company, 1999).

[12] Harald Siegmund, 'Schreiben als Dauerauftrag eines wechselvollen Lebens: Zu Georg Schergs 75. Geburtstag', in Motzan and Sienerth (eds.), *Worte als Gefahr und Gefährdung*, p. 147.

[13] Michaela Nowotnik casts doubts on Schlattner's central role in bringing the five authors to trial; see Michaela Nowotnik, '95 Jahre Haft' – Kronstädter Schriftstellerprozess 1959: Darstellungsformen und Deutungsmuster der Aufarbeitung', *Halbjahresschrift für südosteuropäische Geschichte, Literatur und Politik* 21/1–2 (2012), pp. 173–81.

[14] This was known in Romanian as 'tăinuirea delictului de înaltă trădare [concealing high treason]'; see Oana Corina Moldovean, 'Eginald Schlattner: Raţiunea Turismului Literar la Roşia-Sibiu', *Studii de Ştiinţă şi Cultură* 1/12 (2008), pp. 55–60.

and literary critic Harald Krasser (1905–81).[15] Schlattner's deep level of involvement brought to the fore the intricacy of injustices under communism: he was both an informer and a victim in the story of this trial. And yet this complex duality – which allowed an individual to be both perpetrator and victim of injustice – sat at odds with the ways in which Romanian Germans explained their communist experience.

Romanian German Cold Warriors

For Hans Bergel and others close to the *Landsmannschaft*, the Romanian German relationship to communism had always been clear-cut. In his study of Transylvanian Saxons after thirty years of communism in 1976, Bergel came to the conclusion that communism was undermining Saxon culture specifically.[16] More controversially, many Romanian German émigrés argued that their involvement in fascism and National Socialism, for which they had been initially ostracised in post-war Romania, had happened for all the right reasons. As Kurt Schebesch, the onetime vice-chairman of the Landsmannschaft der Siebenbürger Sachsen, explained in the *Siebenbürgische Zeitung* in January 1977:

> As Transylvanian Saxons, we always knew that our fathers and brothers fought against communism and for Europe back then, and they never let anyone tell us anything different. Do we really want our children and grandchildren to be fighting against Europe and for communism one day?[17]

Ethnicity and ideology were intricately connected in post-war Romanian German narratives. Both the Landsmannschaft der Siebenbürger Sachsen and the Landsmannschaft der Banater Schwaben committed themselves to this view. Walter Myß, founder of the publishing house Wort und Welt in Innsbruck in Austria,[18] sought to rescue Romanian German identity from the 'falsification' of the Romanian communist regime.[19] His *Lexikon der Siebenbürger Sachsen* was going to be published as a '*Volks-Brockhaus*' – a *Volk* encyclopaedia – which could function as an antidote to the ideological

[15] Klein, 'Zu spät, Herr Schlattner, zu spät', p. 5.
[16] Hans Bergel et al., *Die Sachsen in Siebenbürgen nach dreißig Jahren Kommunismus: Eine Studie über die Menschenrechte am Beispiel einer ethnischen Gruppe hinter dem Eisernen Vorhang* (Innsbruck: Wort und Welt Verlag, 1976).
[17] Kurt Schebesch, 'Die vierte Möglichkeit', *Siebenbürgische Zeitung* 27/1, 15 January 1977, p. 5.
[18] The publishing house Wort und Welt Verlag was the main independent German-language publishing house for all things Romanian German.
[19] Walter Myß, 'Ein Nachschlagewerk im Stil des "Volksbrockhaus": Das Lexikon der Siebenbürger Sachsen', *Siebenbürgische Zeitung* 36/8, 31 May 1986, p. 6.

infringements of communism on the Transylvanian Saxon community.[20] Such *Landsmannschaft* discourses were enforced through publications and numerous meetings, talks, symposia, and other events that became rituals of affirming the incompatibility of German ethnicity with communism.[21]

The right-wing discourse of the *Landsmannschaften* offered very little space for dissident voices.[22] Where opposition was voiced, it was often couched in an ideological framework that muted the main arguments. Maja Philippi (1914–93), a Romanian German historian who never moved away from Romania, advocated powerfully in favour of the Romanian communist state's support of the German community in Romania. In the yearbook *Komm Mit* produced by *Neuer Weg*, the main German-language newspaper in Romania, Philippi celebrated the future granted to the Romanian German community by the Romanian communist state after 1948.[23] Romanian Germans, as she pointed out, were able to flourish as part of the cultural and political institutions that had sprung up throughout the country. Her Banat Swabian compatriot, Franz Engelmann, agreed: the nationalities policies of the Romanian state had reinvigorated German culture in Romania and freed the community from the vestiges of Nazism.[24]

Despite all the protestations by the *Landsmannschaften*, the Romanian German entanglement with communism was all too obvious. Romanian Germans had active cultural networks in which they invested much time and effort. A number of Romanian Germans wrote for the state-sanctioned newspapers *Neuer Weg* and *Karpatenrundschau*. Among

[20] Ibid. The Lexicon was eventually published in 1993. See Walter Myß (ed.), *Lexikon der Siebenbürger Sachsen: Geschichte, Kultur, Zivilisation, Wissenschaften, Wirtschaft, Lebensraum Siebenbürgen* (Innsbruck: Wort und Welt, 1993).
[21] See, for instance, the so-called *Sachsentage* at www.sachsentage.de/ (accessed 14 Apr. 2018), the annual *Heimattag* (homeland day) in Dinkelsbühl for Transylvanian Saxons, at www.dinkelsbuehl.de/ISY/index.php?get=203 (accessed 14 Apr. 2018), and the annual *Heimattag* for Banat Swabians in more regional locations, for example in Ulm, at www.dvhh.org/banat/research/ulm-treffen/index.htm (accessed 14 Apr. 2018). The main publishers of literature are the two homeland societies; see *Landsmannschaft der Siebenbürger Sachsen e.V.*, at www.siebenbuerger.de/ (accessed 14 Apr. 2018) and *Landsmannschaft der Banater Schwaben e.V.*, at www.banater-schwaben.de/ (accessed 14 Apr. 2018). Both homeland societies publish their own newspapers, the *Siebenbürgische Zeitung* and *Banater Post* respectively. See www.siebenbuerger.de/ (accessed 14 Apr. 2018) and www.banater-schwaben.de/ (accessed 14 Apr. 2018).
[22] See, for instance, Hans Hartl, 'Die Lage der Deutschen in Rumänien', *Südosteuropa Mitteilungen* 4 (1981), pp. 112–25.
[23] Maja Philippi, 'Seit 800 Jahren: Siebenbürger Sachsen', *Komm Mit '74: Reisen, Wandern, und Erholung in Rumänien* (Bucharest: Neuer Weg, 1974), pp. 132–8.
[24] Franz Engelmann, 'Seit 250 Jahren: Banater Schwaben', *Komm Mit '74*, pp. 139–48.

them were high-profile individuals including the historians Michael
Kroner (later a dissident) and Maja Philippi, the playwright Georg
Scherg, the author Erwin Wittstock (1899–1962), and the linguist Hans
Gehl. Some of these, such as the one-time editor of the *Neuer Weg* Anton
Breitenhofer (1912–89), were explained away in émigré circles as simply
a few bad apples. Breitenhofer had, after all, committed himself to the
Romanian Communist Party as early as 1939. But the sheer number of
contributors to these ideologically 'correct' publications which chimed in
with the Romanian state presented the *Landsmannschaften* in Germany
with a problem. As they were at pains to emphasise the deep conflict
between Romanian communism and the Romanian German community, the widespread collaboration with officially recognised organs of the
state complicated the picture for anticommunist émigrés. This was made
all the more complicated when individuals, such as Erwin Wittstock,
who once had been a stalwart for *völkisch* nationalism, effortlessly turned
into willing collaborators with the new communist regime.

At its zenith in 1964, *Neuer Weg* published 70,000 copies a day. The
newspaper showcased an impressive suite of writers whose coverage ranged
from critiques of adaptations of Johann Nestroy's plays at the German
theatre in Timişoara to entertaining short stories.[25] Letters to the editor
revealed an interactive dialogue, which was, of course, always constricted
by the political boundaries of public discussion, but highlighted that the
public life of Romanian Germans was vibrant within a communist framework. The regular supplement 'For Pioneers and Students' showed how
commonplace it was for Romanian Germans to be part of the Romanian
communist world.[26] And as Cătălin Augustin Stoica's work on
Communist Party membership has demonstrated, membership of the
Romanian Communist Party was higher than in any other east-central
European country by the 1970s.[27] It is true that German-language newspapers ventriloquised pronouncements by Romanian officials, while
Romanian German writers focused on broader journalistic research.[28]

[25] Helga Helter, 'Glanz der Volkskomödie: Zu einer Nestroy-Inszenierung im Temesvarer Deutschen
Staatstheater', *Neuer Weg*, 10 January 1964, p. 3, and Eugen Teodoru, 'Nachts im Kleinbus', *Neuer
Weg*, 10 January 1964, pp. 3, 4.
[26] See, for instance, *Neuer Weg*, 12 January 1964, p. 4.
[27] See Cătălin Augustin Stoica, 'Once upon a Time There Was a Big Party: The Social Bases of the
Romanian Communist Party (Part I)', *East European Politics and Societies* 19/4 (2005), pp. 700–6, and
Cătălin Augustin Stoica, 'Once upon a Time There Was a Big Party: The Social Bases of the Romanian
Communist Party (Part II)', *East European Politics and Societies* 20/3 (August 2006), pp. 451–62.
[28] For a recent study on censorship of German-language publications in Romania in the 1970s and
1980s, see Claudia Spiridon-Şerbu, *Zensur in der rumäniendeutschen Literatur der 1970er und 1980er*

Official statements were simply translated verbatim into German, as was the norm, from Romania's main newspaper of the Central Committee of the Romanian Communist Party *Scînteia*.[29] However, their entanglements with the communist system were all too obvious. How could Romanian Germans *not* have been an integral part of Romanian communism?

And yet Romanian Germans were also on the margins of Romanian society during communism. Despite the efforts by the government of Gheorghe Gheorghiu-Dej to reintegrate Germans into Romanian society after the late 1940s, the rupture from Romania was already very noticeable. Even though Romanian Germans became part of the story of antifascist liberation from the 1950s, there existed a real tension between the official 'rehabilitation' policy and the experiences of the everyday.[30] German antifascist groups and an emphasis on minority representation within the Romanian Communist Party (RCP) may have assuaged some Germans to feel part of the new communist society, but the memory of deportations and the continuation of mutual mistrust between sections of Romanian and German communities made for an uneasy relationship.

Meanwhile, the Federal Republic of Germany and Romania embarked on a path of rapprochement from the 1960s. The early years of Nicolae Ceaușescu's regime, after 1965, were particularly welcomed by governments in western Europe as a new, positive direction. Ceaușescu was someone with whom they could do business, and in the West German case that was understood quite literally. If emigration of Romanian Germans was compensated for informally by the West German government for much of the Cold War, the so-called *Handschlagabkommen* – handshake agreement – between West German chancellor Helmut Schmidt and Nicolae Ceaușescu in 1977 made official a transfer system for Romanian Germans. Depending on qualifications and skills, the West German government would pay around 10,000 DM per Romanian German emigrant.[31] Keen to pay off his national debt, Ceaușescu sold off

---

Jahre (Zurich: LIT Verlag, 2018). Spiridon-Șerbu mentions the two famous trials of Romanian Germans, dealt with later in this chapter, as part of the pre-history to the censorship of the later years. See ibid., pp. 47–50.

[29] See, for instance, Titu Georgescu, '30 Jahre seit dem Prozess der Führer der heldenhaften Arbeiterkämpfer vom Februar 1933', *Neuer Weg*, 5 July 1964, p. 2.

[30] See Gheorghe Zaharia (ed.), *Rezistenta antifascista in partea de nord a Transilvaniei septembrie 1944– octombrie 1944* (Bucharest: Editura Dacia, 1974), the concluding chapter of which emphasises the multicultural makeup of Romanian antifascist resistance.

[31] For an interview with the former chief negotiator for West Germany, Dr Heinz-Günther Hüsch, see Hannelore Baier, Heinz-Günther Hüsch and Ernst Meinhardt, *Kauf von Freiheit* (Sibiu: Honterus Verlag, 2013).

'his' Germans to Germany, while doing the same with Romanian Jews by selling them to Israel. Debates about whether to call this *Menschenhandel* – human trafficking – have been of central importance to Romanian Germans. Scholarship now tends to emphasise the victim's perspective – they were sold – instead of Romanian German agency.[32] A trickle of emigrants turned into steady stream of Germans leaving Romania after 1977: between 10,000 and 15,000 Germans turned their backs on Romania for West Germany annually. Alongside the deteriorating social and political situation in Romania under Nicolae Ceauşescu's national communism and the financial assistance offered by West Germany, the end of the Cold War spurred on German migration from Romania.[33] At the height of this exodus, at the end of communism between 1989 and 1991, a total of nearly 200,000 Germans left Romania, most of whom settled in the Federal Republic of Germany.[34]

The *Landsmannschaften* were unsure how to make sense of Romanian German entanglement during the Cold War other than to throw their weight behind emigration. Although their political power began to wane from the 1970s in the broader German public, the homeland societies continued to shape Romanian German narratives of past and present.[35] Until the 1970s, their first instinct was to flee into established right-wing

---

[32] See Florica Dobre et al. (eds.), *Acţiunea 'Recuperarea': Securitatea şi emigrarea germanilor din România (1962–1989)* (Bucharest: Editura Enciclopedică, 2011). More broadly, this is part of a trend in scholarship to focus secret police encounters through the perspectives of the victims; see Valentina Glajar, Alison Lewis and Corina L. Petrescu (eds.), *Secret Police Files from the Eastern Bloc: Between Surveillance and Life Writing* (Rochester: Camden House, 2016), in particular the chapters Valentina Glajar, '"You'll Never Make a Spy out of Me": The File Story of "Fink Susanne"', pp. 56–83, and Corina L. Petrescu, 'Witness for the Prosecution: Eginald Schlattner in the Files of the Securitate', pp. 84–113. A recent book by Katherine Verdery, an American academic who was both spied on and accused of being a secret police spy while in Romania in the 1970s and 1980s, is an exception: in it, she refuses to portray herself as a passive victim. See Katherine Verdery, *My Life as a Spy: Investigations in a Secret Police File* (Durham, N.C.: Duke University Press, 2018).

[33] Stefan Wolff, 'The Politics of Homeland: Irredentism and Recognition in the Policies of German Federal Governments and Expellee Organizations toward Ethnic German Minorities in Central and Eastern Europe, 1949–1999', in Krista O'Donnell, Renate Bridenthal and Nancy Reagin (eds.), *The Heimat Abroad: Boundaries of Germanness* (Ann Arbor: University of Michigan, 2005), pp. 287–313.

[34] Harald Roth, *Kleine Geschichte Siebenbürgens* (Cologne: Böhlau, 2003), pp. 147–51, and Anton Sterbling, 'Die Aussiedlung der Deutschen aus Rumänien in die Bundesrepublik Deutschland und andere Migrationsvorgänge in und aus Südosteuropa', in Edda Currle and Tanja Wunderlich (eds.), *Deutschland – ein Einwanderungsland? Rückblick, Bilanz und neue Fragen* (Stuttgart: Lucius, 2001), pp. 206–7.

[35] See Pertti Ahonen, 'Taming the Expellee Threat in Post-1945 Europe: Lessons from the Two Germanies and Finland', *Contemporary European History* 14/1 (2005), pp. 1–21, and Pertti Ahonen, *After the Expulsion: West Germany and Eastern Europe 1945–1990* (Oxford: Oxford University Press, 2003), pp. 243–64. In this book, Ahonen offers an impressive study of the development of expellee and émigré organisations during the Cold War period, and yet he understates the continuing importance of the *Landsmannschaften* beyond the 1980s.

stories of the war, in particular stories centred on German victimhood – the deportations – at the end of the war.[36] Since the *Landsmannschaften* attributed victimisation of Germans to communism, and since the Romanians had, at least in part, been seen to have been responsible for the repercussions immediately after the war, the two groups overlapped:[37] being a communist meant being Romanian, and any suggestion that Germans could be part of the communist system was discarded.[38] Debates around emigration were often framed in existentialist terms of 'survival' and 'endurance' in the face of communism.[39] To have complied or even done well in a supposedly anti-German environment was impossible, according to the Landsmannschaft. Any form of complicity with the communist system was thus interpreted as a disloyalty: disloyalty towards their heritage, disloyalty towards their autonomy, and ultimately disloyalty towards their German identity.[40]

The 1959 *Schriftstellerprozess* threw a spanner in the works for the *Landsmannschaften* and émigré circles. After all, a young German had been the main witness in bringing rough communist justice to other Germans. Despite knowledge of the trial, its sentences, and the premature release of the prisoners in the early 1960s, *Landsmannschaft* organs had a simple way of dealing with this episode, at least initially. Schlattner's involvement as a tortured 'traitor' in the trial was so toxic and difficult for the Romanian German community that the *Siebenbürgische Zeitung* simply ignored the issue. Eginald Schlattner received no mention in the newspaper until 1990. Hans Bergel, one of the main defendants during the trial, could look back at a longer history of mentions in the newspaper, but that was partly owing to his career in the homeland society of Transylvanian

[36] See, for example, Ahonen, *After the Expulsion*, and Robert G. Moeller, *War Stories: The Search for a Usable Past in the Federal Republic of Germany* (Berkeley: University of California Press, 2001). For a study on attitudes of expellee groups towards relations with Germany's eastern neighbours in the 2000s, see Steve Wood, 'German Expellee Organisations in the Enlarged EU', *German Politics* 14/4 (2005), pp. 487–97.

[37] See Vasile Morar, 'Dimensiunea etică a relației Sași–Români și Români–Sași', *Studia Hebraica* 4 (2004), pp. 196–9.

[38] A good example of this narrative is Hans Bergel's summary of the impact of thirty years of communism on the Transylvanian Saxon community. See Bergel, *Die Sachsen in Siebenbürgen nach dreißig Jahren Kommunismus.*

[39] See, for instance, Hans Hartl, 'Am Ende einer historischen Aufgabe', in Oskar Schuster (ed.), *Epoche der Entscheidungen: Die Siebenbürger Sachsen im 20. Jahrhundert* (Cologne: Böhlau, 1983), pp. 370–88, and Wilhelm Bruckner, 'Die Landsmannschaft als neue Gemeinschaftsform', ibid., pp. 333–40.

[40] Hans Fink, 'Sachsen als staatstragende Nation', unpublished article, pp. 53–7. Hans Fink was a former editor of the Romanian German newspaper *Neuer Weg* in Romania.

Saxons. Even so, the Authors' Trial did not feature in articles on Hans Bergel until the 1990s.

A comparable trial in 1957 and 1958, the so-called *Schwarze-Kirche-Prozess*, was equally overlooked by Romanian German émigré circles until the very end of the Cold War, although the politics of that particular trial were far more straightforward.[41] The Romanian German vicar Konrad Möckel, along with nineteen other Germans, were condemned to lengthy jail sentences, including four commuted death sentences.[42] Möckel's 25-year prison sentence was first changed to deportation to the Bărăgan and then forced emigration to Germany. The coercive measures of the Securitate were far more obvious and uncomplicated in this trial and its lead-up: Germans had been tortured into confessing to the charges made up by the authorities. The injustice was plain to see, and yet the trial was also ignored by Romanian German émigrés. The first public reception of the trial occurred in 1987 with the posthumous publication of Herbert Roth's personal account of the trial and his time in prison between 1958 and 1964.[43] But this was a rare exception for the period before 1989 and certainly did not apply to the more famous Authors' Trial.

Landsmannschaft politics during the Cold War on how to deal with such trials mirrored the official discourse in Romania. German-language newspapers and publications were completely silent on the *Schriftstellerprozess*. The day after the trial concluded with sentences being handed down, 20 September 1959, *Neuer Weg* kicked off a four-day celebration of the 500th anniversary of the founding of Bucharest without so much as hinting at the drama unfolding in Brașov.[44] Show trials, such as Ana Pauker's in 1953, were often good fodder for communist propaganda in order to consolidate opinion against any enemies of the system.[45] But at a time when relations with the German minority were delicate and the discourse of Romanian Germans as 'Hitlerists' had moved on, there was little to gain from publicising this particular trial. The power of word of mouth was

---

[41] See Corneliu Pintilescu, *Procesul Biserica Neagră: Brașov 1958* (Brașov: Veröffentlichungen von Studium Transylvanicum, 2009).

[42] For a detailed edited book on the trial, its documentation and its aftermath, see Karl-Heinz Brenndörfer and Thomas Șindilariu (eds.), *Der Schwarze-Kirche-Prozess 1957/8: Erlebnisberichte und Dokumentation* (Brașov: Aldus Verlag, 2013).

[43] Herbert Roth, *Kein Jahr war vergeblich: Hinter Stacheldraht und Gittern, 1958–1964* (Munich: Südostdeutsches Kulturwerk, 1987).

[44] See 'Ein halbes Jahrtausend Bukarest', *Neuer Weg*, 20 September 1959, p. 1, 'Galavorstellung zur 500-Jahr Feier', *Neuer Weg*, 20 September 1959, p. 1, and special supplement '500 Jahre Bukarest', *Neuer Weg*, 20 September 1959, p. 2.

[45] See Robert Levy, *Ana Pauker: The Rise and Fall of a Jewish Communist* (Berkeley: University of California Press, 2001).

enough to ensure that Romanian Germans knew exactly what was happening in Brașov. That silence was maintained for the entire communist period. The combination of official communist doctrine in Romania and émigré insistence on the non-collaboration of Romanian Germans with communism created a taboo that was about to be blown wide open.

Communist Trials

The end of the Cold War created a new environment in which the Authors' Trial emerged as a deeply contentious issue among Romanian Germans. The *Siebenbürgische Zeitung* gradually began to engage with the divisive issue of the trial as the Cold War ended. But, initially at least, it struck a sympathetic note towards Eginald Schlattner's impossible choice of collaborating under duress. Writing in 1995, Kurt Franchy, chair of the Hilfskomitee der Siebenbürger Sachsen, regretted the fact that the ARD – one of the two main public television stations in Germany – had allowed Hans Bergel to tarnish Schlattner's name in a documentary portrait of Bergel that was aired as part of the television series called *Nachbarn* in June that same year.[46] Increasingly, though, Romanian Germans – both émigrés and non-émigrés – showed a greater interest in uncovering the injustices of communism meted out against members of the community. The *Schwarze-Kirche-Prozess* in particular attracted the attention of Romanian German scholars and public figures. A relatively uncomplicated trial, where the main victim had been a prominent Romanian German vicar, it was transformed into the ultimate symbol of German victimhood in workshops, conferences, and newspaper coverage.[47]

If the *Schwarze-Kirche-Prozess* became an uncontested symbol of German experiences during communism, then Schlattner's novel *Rote Handschuhe*, published in 2001, challenged an uncritical view of German victimhood. Forty-two years after the *Schriftstellerprozess*, the controversies around Schlattner's publication transformed the Authors' Trial of 1959 into a *lieu de mémoire* of 2001. *Rote Handschuhe* was Schlattner's second book in a trilogy that fictionalised his experiences in interwar, wartime, and

[46] Kurt Franchy, 'Hans Bergel als Grenzgänger in der DDR', *Siebenbürgische Zeitung* 45/10, 30 June 1995, p. 18. See also Michaela Nowotnick, *Die Unentrinnbarkeit der Biographie: Der Roman 'Rote Handschuhe' von Eginald Schlattner als Fallstudie zur rumäniendeutschen Literatur* (Cologne: Böhlau, 2016), p. 236. For an article on Schlattner's life and work, see István Gombocz, '"Sich bewähren, oder bewahren?" Einführung in Leben und Schaffen des siebenbürgischen Autors Eginald Schlattner', *Monatshefte* 106/2 (2014), pp. 270–92.
[47] See Brenndörfer and Șindilariu (eds.), *Der Schwarze-Kirche-Prozess 1957/8*.

post-war Romania.[48] While his first book, *Der Geköpfte Hahn*, was received without controversy, *Rote Handschuhe* triggered an explosive conflict over Romanian German memory and identity. Schlattner's tale of coercion and betrayal, a fictionalised account of the Authors' Trial, attempted to explain the pressures that had led him to confess to the Romanian communist authorities. It was successful in complicating black-and-white accounts of collaboration and coercion.[49] The tone of the novel expressed the deep conflicts that individuals had to negotiate during communism. It certainly communicated some regret by Schlattner himself, while adding the kind of nuance that the *Landsmannschaften* had always denied. Its mixed reception laid bare the fissures within the Romanian German community. His novel highlighted the difficulties for Romanian Germans in remembering a communist system that was not based on a strict division between German ethnicity and ideology.

Romanian German debates over the legacy of communism resonated more broadly among the Romanian and German public.[50] Amid *Ostalgie* and enthusiasm for hunting down communist criminals, the Schlattner controversy brought to the fore the tensions of finding a suitable narrative for post-communist societies. Reactions to his publication in 2001 pushed back against Schlattner's account, which blurred clearly defined roles under communism. Schlattner was perceived as 'cashing in' on the past, trivialising and perverting the course of justice. Schlattner's memory novel stood at odds with a growing voice in Romanian society that demanded condemnation of the communist past. A display about the Authors' Trial at the museum Memorialul Victimelor Comunismului și al Rezistenței (Memorial to the Victims of Communism and the Resistance) in Sighetu Marmației in northern Romania expressed regret that the 'traitor' – that is, Schlattner – was now a celebrated author in German-speaking countries.[51] Founded in 1993, the museum took its mission of uncovering communist

---

[48] Eginald Schlattner, *Der Geköpfte Hahn* (Vienna: Zsolnay Verlag, 1998), Eginald Schlattner, *Rote Handschuhe* (Vienna: Zsolnay Verlag, 2001), and Eginald Schlattner, *Das Klavier im Nebel* (Vienna: Zsonlay Verlag, 2005).

[49] On the complexity of the secret police files, see Petrescu, 'Witness for the Prosecution'.

[50] For an excellent recent book on east-central European memories of communism, see Małgorzata Pakier and Joanna Wawrzyniak (eds.), *Memory and Change in Europe: Eastern Perspectives* (New York: Berghahn, 2016). For a collection of different genres of representation with a good focus on Romania, see Augusta Dimou, Stefan Troebst and Maria Todorova (eds.), *Remembering Communism: Private and Public Recollections of Lived Experience in Southeast Europe* (Budapest: CEU Press, 2014); see also Maria Todorova and Zsuzsa Gille (eds.), *Post-Communist Nostalgia* (New York: Berghahn, 2010).

[51] Jan Koneffke, 'Roman: Hora staccato', *Die Presse*, 2 December 2005, at www.diepresse.com/Artikel .aspx?channel=k&ressortkl&ik=523899 (accessed 2 Feb. 2019).

crimes, remembering the victims of communism, and exposing perpetrators extremely seriously.[52] From this perspective, Schlattner's entanglement with the communist system in the 1950s marked him out as a fraud, shamelessly profiting from his victims' misfortunes.

Schlattner was not the only culprit: especially during and in response to Ion Iliescu's second presidency (2000–4), there were concerted efforts to expose any actions deemed as muddying the past. In particular, Ion Iliescu's claim to victim status after Ceaușescu's regime – based on a political demotion he experienced in 1971 – was galling to sections of the Romanian public.[53] Traian Băsescu, who ran for the 2004 presidential election for the Justice and Truth Alliance against Iliescu's PSD (Partidul Social Democrat, or Social Democratic Party), the successor party to the Communist Party, tried to capitalise on the absence of a clear anticommunist position by tapping into the public mood. Towards the end of the 2004 campaign, Băsescu appealed to the public with his candour by confessing his own involvement in the communist system and the Securitate.[54] Responding to Adrian Năstase – the PSD's candidate – in a televised debate, Băsescu expressed regret that fifteen years after the collapse of communism, Romanians were still entrapped by its legacy. After all, the electorate had the poor choice between two former Communist Party members. Băsescu, sensing the public's need for a strong anticommunist message, won the election. Two years later, Vladimir Tismăneanu and others authored the *Raport Final* (*Final Report*) on the crimes of communism.[55] But already there were the first signs of a change in mood among the Romanian public. Băsescu's unremitting politicking in the name of 'truth-telling' was beginning to show its effects on Romanian society. Schlattner's novel *Rote Handschuhe*, however, had the misfortune of being published in the middle of a frantic

---

[52] Mark, *The Unfinished Revolution*.

[53] See Lavinia Stan, *Transitional Justice in Post-Communist Romania: The Politics of Memory* (Cambridge: Cambridge University Press, 2013), especially pp. 111–35.

[54] Lavinia Stan and Diane Vancea, 'House of Cards: The Presidency from Iliescu to Basescu', in Lavinia Stan and Diane Vancea (eds.), *Post-Communist Romania at Twenty-Five: Linking Past, Present, and Future* (Lanham, Md.: Lexington Books, 2015), pp. 202–4.

[55] Some fascinating contributions to this debate include Vladimir Tismăneau, *Stalinism for All Seasons: A Political History of Romanian Communism* (Berkeley: University of California Press, 2003), and Stan, *Transitional Justice*, as well as Monica Ciobanu, 'Criminalizing the Past and Reconstructing Collective Memory: The Romanian Truth Commission', *Europe–Asia Studies* 61/2 (2011), pp. 315–38. The pinnacle of this memory work was the *Raport Final*, a presidentially commissioned document designed to draw a definitive line under the question of who was to blame for communist crimes. The report itself was deemed to be a political instrument of the then president Traian Băsescu. The full report, in Romanian, can be found at www.presidency.ro/static/ordine/RAPOR T_FINAL_CPADCR.pdf (accessed 15 Nov. 2018). For a critical assessment of the report, see Mark, *The Unfinished Revolution*, pp. 32–46.

search for a simple anticommunist message. His testimony fell on deaf ears in Romania, where there was demand for distinct categories for victims and perpetrators.

But it was Schlattner's book tour in Germany in 2001 that acted like dynamite on a fevered debate about German complicity in Romanian communism.[56] On one particular occasion, in September 2001, Eginald Schlattner introduced his book in a small bookshop called Kirchheim, in Gauting, close to Munich. During the reading of his book, he was confronted by a number of people who challenged his claims about the coercive circumstances of his role as an alleged whistle-blower for the Securitate. Hans Bergel was also in the audience that evening. 'The whole book is lie!', Bergel let Schlattner and the audience know as the evening descended into a heated exchange between the two.[57] The argument that ensued in the weeks and months after this infamous meeting underlined one of the most contested issues among Romanian Germans, namely their role in and relationship to communist Romania.

In the run-up to the publication of *Rote Handschuhe*, the *Siebenbürgische Zeitung* published a series of articles and reviews on Schlattner's book that spilled over into the budding online community of Romanian Germans. One of the discussion threads on the website of the *Siebenbürgische Zeitung* began by asking whether his betrayal was understandable: 'Ist sein Verrat nachvollziehbar?'[58] It was taken as read that Schlattner's involvement in the trial could be interpreted only as an act of betrayal. This was repeated elsewhere in the *Siebenbürgische Zeitung* and other émigré newspapers, most of which were negatively predisposed towards Schlattner's explanation-cum-novel. Writing in the *Siebenbürgische Zeitung*, the journalist Hannes Schuster bemoaned the 'clichés of his fellow Saxon country-men's adaptability and inability to resist in the face of political coercion'.[59] The article condemned not only Schlattner's attempt at 'self-justification' but also his effort at misleading the wider German public into viewing his involvement in communism as understandable. Schlattner, as a 'communist apologist', was blameworthy not simply because of the 'act of betrayal' itself, but because of his

---

[56] See, for instance, Klein, 'Zu spät, Herr Schlattner'.   [57] Ibid.
[58] See discussion thread, 'Eginald Schlattners Roman "Rote Handschuhe"', *Siebenbürgische Zeitung*, 30 April 2001, at www.siebenbuerger.de/ubb/Forum11/HTML/000016.html (accessed 14 Apr. 2018).
[59] Hannes Schuster, 'Zu Eginald Schlattners Roman "Rote Handschuhe"', *Siebenbürgische Zeitung* 51/14, 15 September 2001, p. 8.

attempts to deceive and thereby obfuscate communist crimes and wrongdoings.[60]

Wherever partisan reactions were congratulatory about Schlattner's book, they focused on its literary contribution rather than its content.[61] Reviews by non-Romanian Germans were likewise only ever accepted in Romanian German circles if they agreed with *Landsmannschaft* orthodoxy or if they provided a depoliticised critique of the book, focusing on its aesthetic value.[62] Even seemingly sympathetic receptions of Schlattner's work within the Romanian German sphere tended to assess the book's literary aesthetics, often in positive terms, while eliding the significance of the political themes it treated. Schuster's review of *Rote Handschuhe* in the *Siebenbürgische Zeitung* offered a relatively positive assessment of the book's literary qualities, but ultimately concluded that Schlattner's narrative was nothing more than another 'story of betrayal under the beastly constraints of the communist dictatorship'.[63]

Unlike the post-communist political environment in Romania, which afforded complex stories little space, the situation in Germany was different. Two 'Enquete Commissions' investigating the dictatorship of the SED (Sozialistische Einheitspartei Deutschlands, or Socialist Unity Party of Germany) had punctured widespread frustration in the medium term.[64] Around 180 officials from the former GDR were put on trial after

---

[60] This, too, is a recurring theme of narratives about communism. Émigrés in particular have been inclined to highlight the deceitfulness of communism by pointing to various attempts to cover up its crimes. This in itself is seen as proof of the inherently evil nature of communist systems. For a good analysis on the use of this theme in post-communist museums in the Baltic states, see Mark, 'Containing Fascism', p. 342.

[61] See, for instance, H.-W., 'Lesung Eginald Schlattner auf Schloss Horneck', *Siebenbürgische Zeitung* 53/1, 15 January 2003, p. 6, and Walter Roth, 'Spätes Erstlingswerk', *Siebenbürgische Zeitung Online*, 9 May 2001, at www.siebenbuerger.de/ubb/Forum11/HTML/000016.html (accessed 29 Aug. 2018). See also Oliver Klöck's comment in a discussion thread on Schlattner's book. The commenter assesses the book by claiming that '[u]nfortunately I can only honour Eginald Schlattner's book *Rote Handschuhe* because of its literary quality, not because of its documentary value [Leider kann ich Eginald Schlattners Roman 'Rote Handschuhe' lediglich hinsichtlich seiner literarischen Qualität würdigen, nicht hinsichtlich seines dokumentarischen Wertes]'; see discussion thread 'Eginald Schlattners Roman "Rote Handschuhe"'.

[62] See Walter Mayr, 'Gefrorene Seufzer', *Der Spiegel* 18 (2001), p. 182, and 'Europa in Siebenbürgen – Konversation und Verhör der Kulturen: Eginald Schlattner (*13.9.1933), Dichter in Europa', *KulturLand: Comunicăm & Proiectăm Regional*, 6 October 2004, at www.kulturland.net/2004/10/06/71/ (accessed 29 Aug. 2018).

[63] Schuster, 'Zu Eginald Schlattners Roman'. The original quotation was printed in bold, which accentuated the centrality of the theme of betrayal: 'Es ist die Geschichte eines Verrats unter den Zwängen der kommunistischen Diktatur'.

[64] One from 1992 to 1994 (*Aufarbeitung von Geschichte und Folgen der SED-Diktatur*) and one from 1995 to 1998 (*Überwindung der Folgen der SED-Diktatur im Prozess der deutschen Einheit*); see Yoder, 'Truth without Reconciliation'.

substantial investigations into 50,000 separate cases.[65] The state security files were opened to the public.[66] German society, imperfectly but symbolically, seemed to be dealing with the legacy of the GDR. At the same time, the ironic nostalgia, *Ostalgie*, that enveloped public perceptions of the East German state acted as a vent for post-communist frustrations.[67] And, unlike Romania's, the GDR's legacy was only directly relevant to roughly a quarter of the German population.

These circumstances caused markedly different responses to Schlattner's novel compared to the Romanian German and Romanian reception of his work. Reviews by Germans – not Romanian Germans – were, in general, more sympathetic to the political elements of the book. Paul Gerhard Klussmann's review, for instance, offered a representative assessment of the work, claiming that Schlattner's *Rote Handschuhe* was 'a contemporary historically important and artistically astute novel'.[68] Such critics deemed Schlattner's attempt at *Wiederaufarbeitung* a success, and it was acclaimed for that reason.[69] Yet it was precisely this historical importance that many Romanian Germans rejected out of hand in 2001. Reviews that deviated from the official line were dismissed as naïve, uncritical, or indeed deceptive.[70] Mainstream Romanian German memory still clashed with broader German interpretations of the socialist past.

Romanian German discourses in the new millennium were still embedded in the same Cold War rhetoric that had dominated Romanian German politics and memory. Public figures on the Romanian German émigré scene had long accused deviant and often left-wing Romanian German figures of obfuscating the truth. Authors of an older generation, such as Dieter Schlesak or indeed Schlattner himself, had long been the target of such charges. In a letter by the Romanian German author Wolf von Aichelburg to Hans Bergel in 1975, Aichelburg

[65] Ibid., p. 67.
[66] See, for instance, Sara Jones, 'Conflicting Evidence: Hermann Kant and the Opening of the Stasi Files', *German Life and Letters* 62/2 (2009), pp. 190–205.
[67] Paul Cooke's work on *Ostalgie* is particularly helpful here. See, for instance, Paul Cooke, *Representing East Germany since Unification: From Colonization to Nostalgia* (Oxford: Berg, 2005). For a broader understanding of nostalgia for the communist period, see Todorova and Gille (eds.), *Post-Communist Nostalgia*.
[68] Paul Gerhard Klussmann, 'Verhör und Selbstverhör: Eginald Schlattners Roman *Rote Handschuhe*', *IDF-Publik* 37, 8 December 2004, 6, available at www.ruhr-uni-bochum.de/deutschlandforschung/PDF_Dateien/idfp37.pdf (accessed 15 Nov. 2018).
[69] See, for example, Ursula Pia Jauch, 'Mozart fürs Vieh: Eginald Schlattner erzählt vom Abstieg aus der Beletage', *Neue Züricher Zeitung*, 21 September 2005, p. 37, and Daniela Strigl, 'Liebe eines Sommers, Trauer eines Lebens: Eginald Schlattner über Siebenbürgen und die Ironie der Geschichte', *Der Standard*, Vienna, 4 May 2006, p. 6.
[70] Eginald Schlattner, 'Kaleidoskop einer Freundschaft', *Zugänge* 25 (2000), pp. 58–66.

labelled Schlesak as 'scheming' and a 'communist' simply because he did not uncritically toe the *Landsmannschaften*'s political line.[71] Some years later, in 1988, Bergel branded a younger generation of writers, such as Herta Müller, Richard Wagner, William Totok, and Rolf Bossert as 'intellectually adolescent writers', precisely because of the content of their work.[72] More damningly, they were also called 'fellow travellers'.[73] Von Aichelburg sensed communist plots against Germans everywhere and continued to rail against the 'national spiritual vacuum' in Germany, so much so that he appeared as a candidate for the far-right *Republikaner* in the spring of 1994.[74] 'I am a bit of a *Republikaner*', von Aichelburg admitted to Hans Bergel who had warned von Aichelburg against any association with the party, not for political and moral reasons, but because it would damage his reputation as a writer.[75] What had pushed von Aichelburg over the top and towards the far right, apparently, was Herta Müller's literary success. She received the Kleist-Preis in 1994, which to von Aichelburg was the height of 'a lack of national instinct [*nationale Instinktlosigkeit*]'.[76] Von Aichelburg died just a few months later in August 1994. He ended up just the way the communists had framed him in the Authors' Trial of 1959: a far-right crank on the fringes of society.

Still, the *Landsmannschaften* had successfully lobbied for a strong narrative of denial – that no true German could have collaborated in communism – and feted Romanian German victimhood throughout and beyond the Cold War.[77] Müller, Wagner, and of course Schlattner had become marginalised from the Romanian German community.[78] Unlike their nuanced engagement with the past, many mainstream Romanian German publications still reproduced this 'victim's perspective' with little space for complexity or subtlety in post-communist Europe.[79] Bergel in particular made it his goal

---

[71] Letter Wolf von Aichelburg, 18 November 1975, IKGS, B (o) 5.
[72] Letter Hans Bergel to Wolf von Aichelburg, 15 June 1988, IKGS, B (o) 5.
[73] Letter Bergel to von Aichelburg, 15 June 1988.
[74] Letter Hans Bergel to Wolf von Aichelburg, 27 May 1994, IKGS B 7.
[75] Ibid. and Letter Wolf von Aichelburg to Hans Bergel, 15 June 1994, IKGS B 7.
[76] Letter von Aichelburg to Bergel, 15 June 1994.
[77] See, for example, Hans Bergel, 'Die kulturelle Machtübernahme in Rumänien durch die Kommunisten', in Kulturreferat der Landsmannschaft der Siebenbürger Sachsen in Deutschland e.V. (ed.), *Rumänien nach 1945: Die Referate der Tagungen der Arbeitsgemeinschaft siebenbürgischer Jungakademiker (ASJ), 1987–1989* (Munich: Kulturreferat der Landsmannschaft der Siebenbürger Sachsen in Deutschland e.V., 1989), pp. 53–71, and Michael Kroner, 'Die Deutschen Rumäniens in den Jahren 1944–1947', ibid., pp. 72–84.
[78] See, for example, Brigid Haines, '"Leben wir im Detail": Herta Müller's Micro-Politics of Resistance', in Brigid Haines (ed.), *Herta Müller* (Cardiff: University of Wales Press, 1998), pp. 109–25.
[79] A telling example of this is Motzan and Sienerth (eds.), *Worte als Gefahr und Gefährdung*, and Joachim Wittstock and Stefan Sienert (eds.), *'Bitte um baldige Nachricht': Alltag, Politik und Kultur*

to dismiss Schlattner's claims that his confession back in 1957 had been coerced under torture. Bergel frequently contrasted Schlattner's story with his own experience of being imprisoned by the Securitate. In a poignant interview in 1995, Bergel recounted his experiences of being physically and psychologically abused and tortured without succumbing to pressure to betray a friend:

> The behaviour of the officials varied from brutality, to cynicism, to polite-ness. Once, while I was being interrogated, they broke my nose, knocked out three teeth, and extinguished a cigarette on my bare chest – all because I refused to give incriminatory information against a friend. I still bear the scars, as I didn't receive any medical treatment in my cell; I was so disfigured from the beatings, my fellow inmates did not recognise me. During a different interrogation, however, they offered me chocolate, sweets, and bread. An officer then spoke to me for hours about new German literature. The unpredictability was the system. It unsettled us.[80]

Hans Bergel did not mention Eginald Schlattner by name, but the subtext was clear. Bergel and Schlattner had both experienced similar episodes of torture, but it was Schlattner who had given in. The Authors' Trial, Bergel claimed, had been an integral part both of a specifically anti-German drive in Romania and, more broadly, of the 'regimes of violence of the twentieth century – Lenin's and Stalin's Bolshevism and Hitler's National Socialism'.[81] Those who had failed to resist had also ended up on the wrong side of history, and Eginald Schlattner remained, at least for the time being, a *persona non grata* in mainstream Romanian German circles.[82]

Carl Gibson's Crusade

If the furore surrounding Schlattner's publication *Rote Handschuhe* revealed deep divisions around the legacy of communism, then Carl Gibson's auto-biographical book *Symphonie der Freiheit* (*Symphony of Freedom*), published

---

im Spiegel südostdeutscher Korrespondenz des ausgehenden 19. und 20. Jahrhunderts (Munich: IKGS Verlag, 2003). Both publications focus on the victimisation of Germans in Romania without contextualising this enough within wider issues of complicity and coercion. *Worte als Gefahr und Gefährdung* acts as an homage to the five imprisoned writers, while '*Bitte um baldige Nachricht*' is a collection of correspondence that omits those of Romanian German 'collaborators' during communism. Publications in journals such as *Zeitschrift für Siebenbürgische Landeskunde*, however, demonstrate that these approaches have changed over the past decade.
[80] Hans Bergel cited in '"Das Jahrhundert, an dem ich teilhatte": Hans Bergel im Gespräch mit Dieter Drotleff (1995)', in Pauling, '*Wir werden Sie einkerkern*', p. 104.
[81] Ibid., p. 105.
[82] Renate Windisch-Middendorf, *Der Mann ohne Vaterland: Hans Bergel – Leben und Werk* (Berlin: Frank & Timme, 2010), pp. 37–9.

in 2008, also showed the limits of this identity conflict.[83] In the new millennium, Romanian German memory culture, and indeed Romanian memory cultures more broadly, gradually changed into something rather more 'German': despite the anticommunist politics of Băsescu and others, the communist past became a more complex, intricate affair.

Gibson's book reiterated a Romanian German anticommunist senti-ment as he tried to establish himself as the true face of German opposition during the Ceauşescu period. Gibson, who left Romania for West Germany in 1982, claimed to be 'the most famous human rights activist from Romania in Germany' and gave quite gruelling accounts of his arrest by the Securitate in April 1979.[84] As he was part of a younger generation, Gibson's story differed from that of the Authors' Trial and its legacy, yet he used the same tactics of discrediting anyone who could be accused of deviating from the 'correct' anticommunist narrative. Yet his verbose and long-winded account failed to make a real impact beyond Romanian German circles. Ultimately, his voice was drowned out by Herta Müller's rise to international fame a year later in 2009 when she won the Nobel Prize in Literature after the publication of her novel *Atemschaukel* (origin-ally published in English as *Everything I Own I Carry with Me*).[85] While the book and reactions to its content showed that the Schlattner debates of 2001 had not fully subsided, it also became obvious that the strident claims put forward by Gibson no longer had much traction.

Against the new zeitgeist, Gibson embarked on a mission to discredit Herta Müller, Richard Wagner, and others associated with the Banater Autorengruppe – a Banat literary circle better known as Aktionsgruppe Banat. The Aktionsgruppe Banat was a Banat Swabian literary organisa-tion, which had its roots in the German-language section of a secondary school in the Banat that most of the members had attended.[86] The group was founded in 1972 and disbanded after 'increasing pressure on its former members' over the course of the year 1975.[87] The name Aktionsgruppe was

---

[83] Carl Gibson, *Symphonie der Freiheit: Widerstand gegen die Ceauşescu-Diktatur* (Dettelbach: J. H. Röll, 2008).

[84] Gibson has since claimed that it was his publisher's decision to call him the most famous human rights activist; see 'Carl Gibson: Legitimer Protest gegen Ceauşescu-Diktatur', *Siebenbürgische Zeitung* 59/5, 31 March 2009, p. 5. Georg Herbstritt has cast doubt on that claim; see Georg Herbstritt, 'Rumänische Zeitgeschichte: Vier Arbeiten über Rumänien während der kom-munistischen Diktatur', *Horch und Guck: Zeitschrift zur kritischen Aufarbeitung der SED-Diktatur* 62/4 (2008), pp. 70–2.

[85] Herta Müller, *Atemschaukel* (Munich: Hanser, 2009).

[86] Anton Sterbling, '*Am Anfang war das Gespräch': Reflexionen und Beiträge zur 'Aktionsgruppe Banat' und andere literatur- und kunstbezogene Arbeiten* (Hamburg: Krämer, 2008), pp. 11, 12.

[87] Ibid., p. 18.

retrospectively applied to the Banater Autorengruppe in an article in the *Neue Banater Zeitung*, an émigré newspaper, as an ironic remark about the group's perceived aimless activism.[88] Banat Swabian luminaries such as Richard Wagner (1952–), Rolf Bossert (1952–86), Johann Lippet (1951–), Anton Sterbling (1953–), William Totok (1921–2017), Gerhard Ortinau (1953–), Werner Kremm (1951–), Ernst Wichner (1952–), and Albert Bohn (1955–) made up the group's membership, and they continued to have an impact on Romanian German and Banat Swabian matters even after the dissolution of the group. Others, such as Herta Müller and Werner Söllner (1951–), were associated with the group, despite not having been part of its activities.[89] Its legacy remains contested to this day. Even former members disagree on the importance of the group. Some played up their image as dissidents after immigration to West Germany.[90] Dieter Schlesak, for instance, a writer with political leanings similar to those of the group, repeatedly made the point that they were active during a relative thaw at the beginning of Ceaușescu's regime.[91] Others, such as the former member Anton Sterbling, warned against creating a 'myth' surrounding the group's history.[92]

For Gibson, attacking this circle of Banat authors went beyond differences in interpreting the effectiveness of the group. Gibson claimed that they had acquired the dissident tag precisely because they were regime-friendly.[93] The group did view itself, initially at least, as part of the Romanian socialist state with a duty to criticise the state, not to abandon or dismantle it.[94] But their stance shifted from constructive criticism of the regime, to open criticism of it, to outright opposition to it, and finally to reluctant emigration.[95] The Aktionsgruppe were part of a broader patter of minority dissident groups in east-central Europe during communism. The Hungarian Limes Circle, an informal group of Hungarian intellectuals set

---

[88] Ibid., p. 15.

[89] Diana Schuster, *Die Banater Autorengruppe: Selbstdarstellung und Rezeption in Rumänien und Deutschland* (Konstanz: Hartung-Gorre Verlag, 2004), pp. 40, 41.

[90] Ibid., pp. 110–37.

[91] Dieter Schlesak, 'Wir wurden erpresst', *Die Zeit*, 23 September 2010, at www.zeit.de/2010/39/Oskar-Pastior/seite-2 (accessed 15 Nov. 2018).

[92] Sterbling, 'Am Anfang war das Gespräch', p. 20, and Sarah Langer, *Zwischen Bohème und Dissidenz: Die Aktionsgruppe Banat und ihre Autoren in der rumänischen Diktatur* (Chemnitz: Inistitut für Europäische Studien, 2010), p. 5, at www.tu-chemnitz.de/phil/europastudien/aktivitaeten/aies/ver oeffentlichungen/LangerBA-Arbeit8.pdf (accessed 15 Nov. 2018).

[93] Gibson followed up this idea with a second autobiographical novel; see Carl Gibson, *Allein in der Revolte: Eine Jugend in Banat – Aufzeichnungen eines Andersdenkenden-Selbst erlebte Geschichte und Geschichten aus dem Securitate-Staat* (Dettelbach: J. H. Röll Verlag, 2011).

[94] Schuster, *Die Banater Autorengruppe*, pp. 75, 76.   [95] Ibid., pp. 109, 136, 137, 200.

up by Gusztáv Molnár in the 1980s around the Kriterion publishing house in Bucharest, followed a similar trajectory from cohabitation with the Romanian regime to rejection.[96] Like the Aktionsgruppe, its aim was to create space for meaningful debate. A number of Transylvanian Hungarian *samizdat* publications such as *Ellenpontok* (*Counterpoints*) tried to provide an opportunity for non-conformists to write and influence Western views on communist Romania.[97] Germans in Romania were also looking for space. Sterbling's 'provocative flight', when he tried to cross the border to Yugoslavia as a seventeen-year-old to highlight his criticisms of the political system, was a particularly poignant story that emerged out of the early history of the Aktionsgruppe.[98] Crucially, their criticisms were directed not only at the regime, but also at their own Swabian community. They rejected the nationalist tendencies of their parents' generation and their unwillingness to be introspective and self-critical.[99] This was also a broader pattern among minorities in Romania. The Hungarian community in Romania was undergoing its own generational battle in the 'mini-thaw' that followed Ceauşescu's rise from 1968 to the mid-1970s.[100] Nonplussed by West Germany, critical of Swabian village life, and having attempted to effect change within the Romanian socialist paradigm by considering 'alternative socialisms', this group and its associates were viewed with misgiving by fellow Romanian Germans, especially fellow émigrés in (West) Germany. Left-wingers and dissenters such as Müller were therefore frequently accused of having been communist collaborators and sympathisers as well as subversive to the Romanian German community.[101]

Carl Gibson's line of attack took the same approach. His book was a moment of reckoning with a group of people he viewed as hypocritical and profoundly un-German. Unfortunately for him, it also came too late. His account of the founding of the Sindicatul Liber al Oamenilor Muncii

---

[96] See Ivo Banac et al., 'National Movements, Regionalism, Minorities', in Balázs Apor, Péter Apor and Sándor Horváth (eds.), *The Handbook of Courage: Cultural Opposition and Its Heritage in Eastern Europe* (Budapest: Hungarian Academy of Sciences, 2018), pp. 535–7.

[97] Ibid., p. 535.

[98] See Anton Sterbling, 'Flucht als Provokation? Bruchstücke einer Erinnerung', *Spieglungen* 1/1 (2006), pp. 58–66.

[99] See, for instance, Ernest Wichner, 'Blick zurück auf die Aktionsgruppe Banat', in Ernest Wichner (ed.), *Ein Pronomen ist verhaftet worden: Texte der Aktionsgruppe Banat* (Frankfurt am Main: Suhrkamp, 1992), p. 8.

[100] Nándor Bárdi, 'Generation Groups in the History of Hungarian Minority Elites', *Regio: Minorities, Politics, Society* 8/1 (2005), pp. 109–24.

[101] See ibid. The sense of being watched by fellow Romanian Germans is also echoed in Herta Müller's description of the *Diktatur des Dorfes* or village dictatorship. See Josef Zierden, 'Deutsche Frösche: Zur "Diktatur des Dorfes" bei Herta Müller', *Text + Kritik* 155 (2002), pp. 30–8.

din România (SLOMR) – the Free Trade Union of the Working People of Romania – was designed as a counter to the better-known story of the Aktionsgruppe Banat and its fame. SLOMR, according to Gibson's book, may have attracted as many as 1,200 dissidents, many of whom were German and who – crucially – wanted to escape Romania for West Germany.[102] Gibson was part of an orthodox dissident movement. The founding of SLOMR was announced on Radio Free Europe and enjoyed the backing of Paul Goma, who himself had attempted to found a Romanian Charter 77 movement in 1977. Müller, Gibson claimed by contrast, had 'conformed to the system [*Systemloyalität*]' under Ceauşescu and had reinvented her story only after the fall of the communist regime.[103] Gibson regarded both Müller and her former partner Richard Wagner with deep suspicion, questioning their 'refusal' to emigrate to Germany until 1987, even after Müller had been approached by (and rebuffed) the Securitate in 1982.[104] He further accused them of moving to a country, West Germany, which they 'had not exactly deeply and dearly loved'.[105] Instead, they marketed themselves as 'dissidents, which was a tag to which they had no justified claim'.[106] Gibson intimated parallels between 'unwilling fellow travellers' in the Third Reich and individuals such as Herta Müller whose claim to dissidence, so Gibson contended, rested on that single instance in 1982 of rejecting approaches by the Securitate.[107] Gibson's clear categories of opponents and conformists made no allowance for Müller's critical writing directed at her own community.

Richard Wagner, too, felt the full force of Gibson's wrath. While the writer William Totok was imprisoned without charge for eight months during the clampdown against the Aktionsgruppe Banat in 1975, Richard Wagner, Gerhard Ortinau, and Gerhard Csejka were released after only a week.[108] Gibson construed this as evidence for these left-wing dissidents' entanglement with the regime.[109] Referring to an interview with Richard Wagner by the Romanian German academic Stefan Sienerth in 1997, Gibson cited Wagner's claim, out of context, that '[w]e did not aspire to dissidence, but rather to

---

[102] See 'Carl Gibson: Legitimer Protest'. Gibson's wish to speak for 'genuine' German resisters probably stems from a mention on Radio Free Europe just before his arrest in 1979. See Herbstritt, 'Rumänische Zeitgeschichte'. Charter 77 was a civic movement set up in Czechoslovakia in January 1977; it was critical of the regime and advocated for human rights in the country. Some of its members rose to prominent positions after 1989.

[103] Gibson, *Symphonie der Freiheit*, p. 345.   [104] Ibid., p. 311.   [105] Ibid.   [106] Ibid.   [107] Ibid.

[108] Ibid., p. 361.

[109] William Totok could be considered a 'true believer' in socialism, yet Gibson ignored this fact and instead chose to cite his suffering as evidence of Wagner's and others' collusion with the system.

a form of loyal criticism'.[110] Instead of understanding this in its historical context of the 'mini-thaw' under Ceaușescu, Gibson interpreted Wagner's claim as evidence of Wagner and others abetting Stalinism.[111]

Gibson's powerful charges had little effect on either Müller's standing or that of her fellow writers. Unlike Eginald Schlattner, they emerged unscathed from Gibson's crusade. What had changed? The timing of Herta Müller's international success by winning the Nobel Prize in Literature in 2009 – just at the time of the publication of Gibson's *magnum opus* – almost marginalised Gibson's account. Her work also questioned the search for clear answers to good and bad during the twentieth century, including the communist period, and thus chimed with public discourse in Germany since the late 1990s. The revelation that Müller's friend, the writer Oskar Pastior (1927–2006) – the Romanian German poet to whom she had dedicated her novel *Atemschaukel*, published three years after his death – had worked for the Securitate may have been a personal blow for Müller, but it only confirmed the complexities of the communist system.

In Romania, she received backhanded praise. The Romanian writer Mircea Cărtărescu, for instance, claimed that it was, after all, Ceaușescu's Romania that made her a household name. Without her life experience in communist Romania, she 'would still have been a great poet, but she would not have been Herta Müller'.[112] Müller's eschewal of simple stories of communism was given further credence by the rise of what Cristan Cercel has termed 'philo-Germanism' in Romanian society.[113] But Müller's success and growing visibility in Romania have formed only one aspect to this. Klaus Iohannis's presidency of Romania in late 2014 confirmed the gradual process in which the Romanian German community – both émigrés and non-émigrés – played an integral part in remoulding the image of post-communist Romania.

Back in Germany, by the late 2000s Carl Gibson's reaction to Herta Müller's international fame heralded the end of the hegemony of a straight

---

[110] Original: 'Wir strebten keine Dissidenz an, sondern eine Art loyaler Kritik.' See Stefan Sienerth (ed.), *Dass ich in diesen Raum hinein geboren wurde: Gespräche mit deutschen Schriftstellern aus Südosteuropa* (Munich: Südostdeutsches Kulturwerk, 1997), and Gibson, *Symphonie der Freiheit*, p. 362.

[111] Gibson, *Symphonie der Freiheit*, p. 362.

[112] Quoted in Valentina Glajar, 'The Presence of the Unresolved Recent Past: Herta Müller and the Securitate', in Brigid Haines and Lyn Marven (eds.), *Herta Müller* (Oxford: Oxford University Press, 2013), p. 51.

[113] See Cristian Cercel, 'Philo-Germanism without Germans in Romania after 1989', *East European Politics and Societies* 29/4 (2015), pp. 811–30.

anticommunist message among Romanian Germans, too. Of course there were important differences between the Authors' Trial and Gibson's experiences of communism in Romania. The Authors' Trial had affected Transylvanian Saxons while Gibson was a Swabian. The five authors in question were also of an older generation. But the different legacies and their reception between 2001 and 2008 indicated a telling shift in the meaning of opposition to communism in Germany and within the Romanian German community. Gibson sensed this and became even more defensive. He hardened his views on the circles in which Müller moved. In an apparent repeat of the persecution he had suffered during the Ceauşescu regime, Gibson now claimed that he was being publicly silenced in Germany, since no one seemed to take his claims seriously. 'Only in *Die Presse* in Vienna have I been allowed to speak freely', Gibson bemoaned on his website.[114] The 'liberal' papers *Die Zeit, Frankfurter Allgemeine Zeitung, Frankfurter Rundschau*, and *Der Spiegel* were all complicit in silencing his resistance for a second time. As such, Gibson declared that he had been forced into exile to Austria, 'like Odysseus'.[115] 'Below the line' of an internet article by Herta Müller in *Die Zeit* about the afterlife of the Securitate, Carl Gibson embarked on a bizarre crusade by littering the website with comments filled with baseless accusations about Müller's own involvement in the communist regime in Romania.[116] Time and again, Gibson questioned the 'moral integrity' of Herta Müller and members of the Aktionsgruppe Banat. For Gibson, extending their criticism beyond the obvious target of the Ceauşescu regime to their own Romanian German community still marked them out as *Nestbeschmutzer*.[117]

Yet the reception by the Romanian German community was not at all that supportive of Gibson's work. In stark contrast to the scandal surrounding Schlattner's book in 2001, even the more sympathetic publications, such as the *Banater Post*, failed to endorse fully Gibson's book and its claims. In a front-page review from December 2008, Dieter Michelbach held back from commenting on Gibson's accusations levelled at Müller and others.[118]

---

[114] See Carl Gibson, 'Herta Müller: Hass als Antrieb literarischen Schaffens. Argumente und Fakten – aus Carl Gibsons "Wiener Kommentaren"', *Carl Gibsons Blog für Literatur, Geschichte, Politik und Zeitkritik*, 27 February 2011, at http://carl-gibson.blogspot.com/2011/02/herta-muller-hass-als-antrieb.html (accessed 15 Nov. 2018).

[115] Ibid.   [116] Herta Müller, 'Die Securitate ist noch im Dienst', *Die Zeit* 31, 23 July 2009.

[117] Translated literally, *Nestbeschmutzer* means someone who soils their own nest. See Carl Gibson, 'Fragen an Nobelpreisträgerin Herta Müller', *carlgibsongermany*, 15 February 2011, at http://carlgib songermany.wordpress.com/tag/nestbeschmutzer/ (accessed 15 Nov. 2018).

[118] Dieter Michelbach, 'Symphonie der Freiheit: Dokument des Widerstands gegen die Diktatur', *Banater Post* 52/23–24 (2008), pp. 1, 6–7.

Instead, the reviewer merely described the points made by Gibson in his book. In a veiled criticism, Michelbach called the book 'difficult to categorise'.[119] Even the more local Banat Swabian organisations regarded his book as 'heartfelt' but 'superficial and indeed simple', as the *Tauber-Zeitung* of the local Banat Swabian association in Reutlingen described it.[120] The *Siebenbürgische Zeitung* also covered Gibson's publication, but his work did not have the same impact as the Schlattner controversy. Thus, Elisabeth Packi complained that the book was not an entertaining read, and highlighted that the exaggerated attacks against his contemporaries raised questions about the 'objectivity' of Gibson's account.[121] In an interview with the author, the newspaper went as far as to question the ideological motivation for his crusade against Herta Müller and Richard Wagner.[122] Although Gibson tried to bat away these insinuations by claiming to have led a 'campaign of enlightenment', he cut a rather tragic figure in the interview, one who seemed to be something of a curious attraction to the interviewer rather than a force to be reckoned with.[123] Gibson was still fighting a battle that had in fact ended some time ago. While the Schlattner controversy had still exemplified the clout of simple stories of communism, Gibson's crusade against some of the biggest literary names in recent Romanian German history was met with embarrassed awkwardness.

Romanian German Victims and Heroes

Schlattner and Gibson bookended a period of shifting Romanian German identities, and Romanian German voices expressed deep uncertainties as once stable narratives about the past collapsed. Reflecting on life in the Protestant Church under communism in 2013, German vicars and other clerics struggled to comprehend the communist period, especially since clerics had been the most reluctant to emigrate. If Bishop Friedrich Müller-Langenthal (1884–1969) had been a figure of German Protestant accommodation with the communist regime, for many others communism was all about the harassment of Romanian Germans and their institutions,

---

[119] Ibid., p. 1.
[120] Hans-Peter Kuhnhauser, 'Auf der Suche nach Freiheit', *Tauber-Zeitung*, 22 June 2013, at http://kv-banater-schwaben-reutlingen.de/wir-informieren.html (accessed 15 Nov. 2018).
[121] Elisabeth Packi, 'Widerstand gegen die Ceauşescu Diktatur: Carl Gibson über Menschenrechtsbewegungen gegen den Kommunismus', *Siebenbürgische Zeitung* 59/13, 10 August 2009, p. 10.
[122] 'Carl Gibson: Legitimer Protest'.   [123] Ibid.

including the church.[124] The Securitate, the Romanian secret police, were
very active in Transylvania, as they suspected conspiracies among the
Hungarian and German population, especially within clerical circles.[125]
Hermann Schuller, vicar of the town of Metiş/Martinsdorf in central
Transylvania from 1960 to 1971, remembered a sense of being watched
and pressurised by the Securitate.[126] For others, like the former vicar of
Şeica Mică/Kleinschelken, Otto Reich, most of the problems they experienced during communism were, at heart, the fault of Romanians.[127] Yet
when it came to articulating personal experience, Romanian Germans
often vacillated between depoliticised stories, blame, and narratives of
resistance.[128] Romanian German respondents, more broadly, echoed
these different narratives in their own stories from the communist period.
Remembering his experiences in the post-war and early communist period,
Hans Bergel, the indefatigable *Landsmannschaft* warrior, spoke candidly
about his involvement in anticommunist partisan groups in the late 1940s.
Speaking in 2005, just as the certainties of the past were being picked apart,
Bergel insisted on his story of German victimhood and resistance. In
a riveting interview, Bergel retold his post-war life with a mission to sustain
a strong division between being German and being a communist. In the
context of the Schlattner controversy, these issues still mattered:

> We had no money after 1946. My father was put into prison for reasons we
> never found out. He was simply arrested . . . and locked up without a trial,
> without anything. Then my mother was arrested. She was released after
> seven months. I had to look after my three younger siblings. That was in '46,

---

[124] He was also known as Friedrich Müller der Jüngere (the younger). For details on his central role for
negotiating National Socialism and communism, see Ulrich A. Wien, *Kirchenleitung über dem
Abgrund: Bischof Friedrich Müller vor den Herausforderungen durch Minderheitenexistenz,
Nationalsozialismus und Kommunismus* (Cologne: Böhlau, 1998).

[125] For a comprehensive edited volume on the Securitate in Transylvania that covers a variety of topics
from individual cases to broader methodological issues around Securitate files, see Joachim von
Puttkamer, Stefan Sienerth and Ulrich A. Wien (eds.), *Die Securitate in Siebenbürgen* (Cologne:
Böhlau, 2014).

[126] Hermann Schuller, 'Im Schatten des Nationalsozialismus und aus der Wirklichkeit des
Nationalkommunismus', in Hermann Schuller (ed.), *Aus dem Schweigen der Vergangenheit:
Erfahrungen und Berichte aus der siebenbürgischen Evangelischen Kirche A.B. in der Zeit des
Kommunismus* (Sibiu: Schiller Verlag, 2013), pp. 313–28.

[127] Otto Reich, 'Ihr seid unverbesserliche Faschisten!', in Schuller (ed.), *Aus dem Schweigen der
Vergangenheit*, pp. 329–43. Daniel Ursprung has thoroughly debunked the idea that Romania's
development of communism was the result of specific Romanian traditions. See Daniel Ursprung,
*Herrschaftslegitimation zwischen Tradition und Innovation: Repräsentation und Inszenierung von
Herrschaft in der rumänischen Geschichte in der Vormoderne und bei Ceauşescu* (Heidelberg:
Studium Transylvanicum, 2007); see also Chapter 2.

[128] Schuller (ed.), *Aus dem Schweigen der Vergangenheit*.

'47 [...] It was my indignation over the unjust treatment of my family that forced me into the anticommunist resistance.

[...] I thought to myself: This isn't right! What has my father done? He hasn't done anything! He wasn't politically active. He was a passionate teacher, a pedagogue, and a very good, popular pedagogue; he was full of charm when it came to dealing with people. And this is how – I was approached by some Romanian friends quite early on without really thinking about the consequences in any great depth – I came to join the Romanian resistance. My mother was released after seven months, but not my dad; she had no idea where he was. We didn't even know whether he was in a Romanian prison or whether they had taken him to the Soviet Union, we didn't know anything. He was released in 1947. By that time, I was already heavily involved in the resistance with Romanian groups. As I was quite sporty, I was a messenger for various partisan groups who were hiding in the mountains and the woods. They needed someone so that they could communicate between each other [...] And so I was constantly on the move in the southern Carpathian Mountains, and I knew my way around there anyway from skiing. That wasn't a problem for me. I can honestly say with hindsight that the political dimension – apart from the personal insult of my family's unjust treatment – the political dimension did not interest me too much to begin with. I wasn't mature enough. I had no experience. I wasn't yet able to assess things politically [*Ich konnte noch nicht einordnen*]. I was just really up for a bit of an adventure. It was a real adventure for me to evade all the Soviet military patrols, the police patrols, the Romanian police patrols, to play cat and mouse with them, because they didn't know the area as well as I did. I set up false leads and then hid somewhere ten metres away in a tree trunk, and then wept with laughter when they were running around looking for me in places where I wasn't.[129]

Romanian German stories about life under communism often drew attention to the ideological commitments of communists, yet framed their own anticommunism as apolitical. In Bergel's case, his anticommunism was little more than his adventurous side getting the better of him. But what did he mean by resistance anyway? Bergel explained:

Well there was this, just as there was here during the Nazi period, so-called inner resistance [*innerer Widerstand*] [...] Initially in Romania there was an inner, a spiritual, moral resistance. And then there were people of diverse social groups who weren't happy with the communist, Muscovite [*sic*] system. To begin with, they were politically committed individuals and partly from former extremist right-wing, antisemitic parties, the Iron Guard.

---

[129] Interview with Hans Bergel, 18 February 2005, Munich.

> [. . .] They were armed. Don't ask me how they got their weapons. They
> either stole them from military depots or they had their connections and
> links, and there were many skirmishes with the Romanian secret police,
> with the Securitate, because these groups were quite small. They were
> constantly exchanging shots . . . in the mountains. There were a couple
> thousand of them, they weren't that many. They came mainly from former
> extreme right-wing parties. But they also came from social classes – you have
> to bear in mind the history of the country [Romania] – that were religiously
> dominated. On the whole, Romanians are a religious, Greek Orthodox
> people; even in part the intellectuals in Romania. They rejected commun-
> ism on the grounds of their Christian belief, which meant that these
> partisans were not only former right-wingers, but also a number of peasants.
> There were students, a lot of students, many students, younger people, even
> younger than I was at the time. There were intellectuals, medical doctors,
> teachers, shepherds. Shepherds: Romania was largely a country of shep-
> herds, spread over 800 kilometres of the Carpathian Mountains and forests,
> and they extended across the country. And they had their sheep taken away
> from them by the advancing Red Army in '44, '45, because they had to feed
> their soldiers.[130]

Bergel's story moved anticommunism from a sphere contaminated by the
far right to a popular resistance to injustice. In this way, Bergel placed his
own story alongside the plight of expropriated shepherds:

> These shepherds were left with nothing . . . because they had their sheep
> taken away from them, whether they had 500 sheep or 3,000. And that of
> course forced them into the resistance. They weren't politically active at all.
> The only political activists were the former Iron Guardists, who were – in
> my own personal experience, without wanting to offend anyone, but
> I always found it quite uncomfortable – fanatical ideologues. I felt more
> at home with the shepherds who had a very human, personal, and under-
> standable reason for their behaviour. But then the partisans . . . after years of
> living together in the mountains, during the summer, during the winter
> they finally became a unit, and the ideological aspects of those former right-
> wingers, the Iron Guardists, gradually wore away. I watched this process
> unfold.

If Bergel was an anticommunist, then it was only in the same manner as
a noble, apolitical shepherd. Even the Romanian fascist elements in the
resistance melted away to make way for an international fraternity of
resisters including Germans, Hungarians, and also Romanians. The
other side, however, included only Romanians, as Bergel explained:

---

[130] Ibid.

But to return to my story, I was betrayed in 1947 by someone who was part [of these groups] and who was picked up by the Securitate. [It was alleged] that I was a messenger . . . in other words the guy who made the connections by passing on information. For instance, they needed fake identity cards, because they needed a disguise. If they ever got caught up in a police patrol, they needed to produce some form of identity.

[. . .]

Well, there were people in the cities, they were men and women, it was pretty much mixed; there were Germans, I mean Transylvanian Germans, there were Romanians, there were Hungarians. We were united in our resistance against [communism], and the national aspect didn't make any difference in these circles. The partisan groups were an international, in fact *the* [emphasis added] international fraternity. That's what it was, or at least it was seen as such. The main thing was to be against communism, against the dictatorship.[131]

Principled resistance to communism, according to Bergel, also included retreating German troops:

Then there were also those who had been left behind by the retreating front line [during the war]. They made up a considerable part [of these groups]: German soldiers and officers of German troops who had been overtaken by the Soviet front line, which was of course moving westwards. And, of course, we had to help them flee the country, because they neither spoke Romanian nor did they know the country. And they, too, got fake passports . . . Some of them were decent lads and some of them were disgusting.

The moral equivalence of the Soviet advance and the retreat of National Socialist troops had fed mainstream Romanian German narratives of both regimes, and Hans Bergel still espoused this view in the new millennium. His first adventure of aiding the anticommunist resistance ended with Bergel being arrested on a technicality in Budapest before being sent back to Romania, where he spent a year in prison for a non-political crime. Thanks to this oversight by officials, the Romanian government 'didn't know about my connections to the partisans', Bergel boasted. Being in prison shielded him from the Securitate, who had been searching for him. The Romanians were so disorganised that they could not even track down their own prisoner. It was only when a German – Eginald Schlattner – got involved ten years later that life got really difficult for Hans Bergel.[132]

Bergel's account was fascinating not just because of his inimitable story-telling talent. Even in the mid-2000s, Bergel still drew on established themes in Romanian German memory culture. Hidden away in the

---

[131] Ibid.   [132] Ibid.

mountains, Bergel and others were under siege from non-German forces, and these non-Germans were communists. It was also quite clear that in Bergel's view it had been possible to resist, something Schlattner had utterly failed to do. Resilience in the face of adversity was there at the beginning of communism and also at the end of communism. In her autobiographical account of her experiences in Timişoara in 1989/90, the Swabian art historian and novelist Annemarie Podlipny-Hehn described the situation in Timişoara as 'a state of besiegement [*Es herrschte Belagerungszustand*]',[133] and extended this to the entire history of Romanian Germans. The period since the *Heim-ins-Reich* policy of 1940 was the 'crossroads for the Romanian German population', which reached its highpoint in 1990 when most Romanian Germans left Romania.[134] According to this view, the battle against communism was on a continuum that had started with malaria in the eighteenth century, and then continued during the turmoil of the Second World War right until the end of communism.[135]

But that master narrative no longer held up as strongly as before. The period between the Schlattner controversy and Gibson's failed crusade against Herta Müller and others destabilised all such certainties. Romanian Germans began to recount the political apathy, the banality of communism, and mundane forms of co-operation with the state system. Away from the celebrity limelight that Hans Bergel occupied, Romanian German respondents were neither firebrand anticommunists nor particularly interested in explaining co-operation in much depth. Gerlinde and Thomas Schräger, who had emigrated from Romania in the early 1970s when they were in their late twenties and early thirties, had grown up with the pressure to join the Communist Party. When asked about the social convention of joining the party, the Partidul Comunist Român (PCR), both were eager to downplay the importance of political involvement:

GS: Well, yes, there were always people who had to be in the Communist Party, but people were generally happy if they didn't have to.
GS: Those who wanted to [join the party], busybodies, but that . . .
TS: People didn't actually . . .
GS: . . . take it that seriously, and it wasn't really an honour [. . .]

<hr />

[133] She is renowned not only amongst Banat Swabians but also amongst Transylvanian Saxons. Her autobiographical eyewitness account has thus been accepted into the canon of so-called *Transylvanica*, that is books on Transylvania and the Banat that have been deemed to be of sufficient quality. See Annemarie Podlipny-Hehn, *Wir waren Zeugen: Temeswar 1989/90* (Munich: Verlag Südostdeutsches Kulturwerk, 1991), p. 17.
[134] Ibid., p. 49.   [135] Ibid., pp. 50, 51.

TS: It really wasn't important whether someone was a member or not as far as everyday life was concerned. It was ... nobody asked whether someone was [a member] or not.
GS: The most revolutionary thing we did was to sing during an art exam.[136]

Germans as truly committed communists did not exist in Romanian German narratives. Of all interviewees, only one admitted sympathies with communism. Robert Frank, who had stayed in Romania all his life and still lived Sântana in the Banat noted in passing that he 'had sort of supported Moscow [*Ich habe eher zu Moskau gehalten*]'.[137] But equally, the position Bergel still held – that of the noble German anticommunist – no longer had any traction. The circumstances had changed, and Schlattner, despite the initial hostility to his book, had at least recognised the shifting discourse on communism. Where Carl Gibson failed, namely at following an orthodox narrative of anticommunism, ordinary Romanian Germans were now at least capable of depoliticising their stories and uncoupling them from the demands of the *Landsmannschaften* to tell a strong anticommunist story.

With anticommunism on the retreat in the 2000s, a new openness about Romanian German entanglement with communism seemed an obvious direction. But in fact, the 'old guard' of Romanian German nonconformists also failed to understand the contemporary zeitgeist. Dieter Schlesak, who had always rejected the widespread tenet that anticommunism has been a fundamental aspect of German identity, continued to speak openly about German affiliation with communism during the Cold War.[138] 'We were all socialists', Schlesak had once claimed.[139] But German communism was often presented as a story of idealistic socialism gone wrong. In a portrayal that was typical of an antifascist narrative, their ideals had been 'betrayed' by Ceaușescu.[140] Such views – common for the left-wing revival in the post-communist period – remained largely uncommon, despite the decline of the *Landsmannschaft* narrative.[141] Instead, the

---

[136] Interview with Gerlinde Schräger and Thomas Schräger, 16 February 2005, Traunstein.
[137] Interview with Robert Frank, 23 July 2005, Sîntana.
[138] See, for instance, ibid. and Dieter Schlesak, *Eine Transylvanische Reise: Ost–West-Passagen am Beispiel Rumäniens* (Cologne: Böhlau, 2004).
[139] He was alluding to the Prague Spring. See interview with Dieter Schlesak, 9 February 2005, Gundelsheim. This was an informal interview in the Siebenbürgen Institut in Gundelsheim.
[140] This is a typical antifascist narrative.
[141] On antifascist, left-wing narratives, see, for instance, James Mark, 'Antifascism, the 1956 Revolution and the Politics of the Communist Autobiographies in Hungary 1944–2000', *Europe–Asia Studies* 58/8 (2006), pp. 1209–40.

mainstream of Romanian Germans treated the issue of complicity in
communist Romania with indifference and by making light of the issue.

Thomas and Gerlinde Schräger's account illustrates this point. Their
response was a very common one among Romanian German respondents.
When asked about their own experiences of affiliation with communist
organisations, the Schrägers maintained that politics did not play an
important role for Germans. Party membership and political activism
were merely formal issues in communist Romania, as Gerlinde explained:

> Lots of people had to [join the party] just so they could keep their job. And
> we were both very lucky. And when you reached a certain age, you dropped
> out of the youth organisation, and they could no longer force you [to be
> a member of the party]. The school I was at was quite laid back. You had to
> attend political events, and they all had their separate mottos, but we also
> arranged what to say beforehand: 'You say that, you say that, and you say
> that. You recommend [him], you recommend him, and you recommend
> him.' There was always someone chairing the whole thing, and everyone
> joined in nicely. Then we were allowed to go home and that was that. People
> usually did what they wanted to if it wasn't their turn. But we had to sit and
> join in just to make sure that we didn't cause any problems for the chairs.
> They had to get it over and done with, too.

When pressed on whether they had also joined the Communist Party,
which would not have been atypical, Thomas insisted that it 'did not
happen' to them, because they were Germans. 'You see', he explained, 'if
someone wanted to emigrate, then there was no real point in trying to
persuade him to join the party . . . they left people like that in peace.'[142]

The Schrägers were neither committed anticommunists nor particularly
forthcoming about any entanglement with communism. They, like most
others, were apolitical people. Their involvement in communism was
confined to political tokenism and depoliticised get-togethers. And,
while the Schrägers claimed that 'it wouldn't have been very good'[143] to
refuse an offer to join the Communist Party, they also insisted that 'people
didn't actually take it, [party membership], that seriously'[144] and that 'it
wasn't really important whether someone was a member or not'.[145] They
may have been freed from the *Landsmannschaft* stranglehold of anticommunism, but they seemed unable to articulate their personal commitment and exposure to the communist system.

Non-émigrés treated the question of party membership and politics in
a comparable way, namely as an unimportant and automatic political

---

[142] Interview Gerlinde Schräger and Thomas Schräger.   [143] Ibid.   [144] Ibid.   [145] Ibid.

process. Veronika Scherg, who had never left Sibiu, had only worked for four years in her adult life in communist Romania and had avoided the decision of having to join the party. Scherg claimed that 'only very few Germans' joined the Communist Party and that those who did were included more or less automatically:

> Yes, you were simply included. There was the youth organisation ... and later people were asked to join the party usually through their employers. You could either try to avoid it or not. Some joined a bit earlier, and others refused, but it was never a good idea to refuse. You would then have to reckon with disadvantages when it came to promotions, or something along those lines. I didn't have to go through all of that, as I was only employed for four years in a factory [. . .]
>
> Then there were these reprisals in factories where they forced people to join the party or at least to join in the demonstrations and to carry some banners. I only did that for a short while. That was during Stalin, and there were meetings in the factory and we had to attend them [and shout]: 'Stalin! Stalin!' But that carried on later, too, but I didn't have to do all of that. I was told about it by others.

Political involvement was a banal reality for Romanian Germans during communism, as Veronika Scherg went on to explain:

> Even if you weren't a member, you still had to go to the meetings [. . .] There was the youth organisation and the pioneers, and goodness knows what they were all called. So, yes, people were simply included [*eingebunden*], but only very few were really forced [into it], I would say. But, of course, you had to join in [somehow]. For example, during the demonstrations on the 1st of May you couldn't simply stay at home. Those who were employed had to go along [. . .] You couldn't simply risk your job by not going along.

Even when Romanian Germans joined the Communist Party, life carried on as normal. According to Scherg, this was nothing unusual nor did it result in any recriminations within the Romanian German community:

> It wasn't anything exceptional. People didn't do it, [join the party], out of conviction. People did it in order to keep a job, or because they had more or less been forced to. Only a tiny minority did it with enthusiasm. It's possible that there were some who were really convinced. I don't doubt it, but I know that most people did it because there was nothing else for it but that [*weil ihnen nichts anderes übrig blieb*].
>
> You just simply accepted it [*einfach hingenommen*]. Only a very few were members out of conviction [*Überzeugte*] and usually you didn't have much

to do with them. But in our circle of friends and acquaintances, whether or not someone was or wasn't [a member] was of no interest to us.[146]

Romanian German involvement was often trivialised to the point that it almost became banal and, in turn, inconceivable that Romanian Germans had been committed to the communist state. In that sense, while such non-émigré stories were more forgiving than the hard-line *Landsmannschaften* in Germany, they were ostensibly a similar way of denying Romanian German involvement, *real* involvement, in communism.

It was the small number of Romanian Germans who had returned to Romania who were the ones who were able to complicate the past. Rosalind Horndasch had been caught up in a wave of arrests in the 1950s, and she was convicted of treason and spent six years in prison. She then emigrated to West Germany and married a West German. Horndasch made it clear that she was not close to the Landsmannschaft der Siebenbürger Sachsen and self-identified as 'liberal left'.[147] After 1989, Horndasch moved back to Romania, where she set up a publishing house that dared to publish non-partisan work.[148] It published Axel Azzola's work, who was once a *persona non grata* among Romanian Germans.[149] His political disagreements were made all the more complex due to a lingering antisemitism among Romanian German émigrés in the Cold War. The *Klingsor* circle of the interwar period and the readiness with which Romanian Germans had served in the Waffen-SS found continuities in antisemitic tropes during the Cold War and beyond. Horndasch, however, came out of a different tradition, which she was keen to articulate. She introduced her story by talking about her father, a politician and an MP in the interwar period for a 'bourgeois party [*bürgerliche Partei*]':[150]

... and as such he [her father] along with all the other bourgeois politicians, regardless of which precise political affiliation, was one day picked up in the middle of the night. No one knew why. All they said was: 'You're in for three years, five years, seven years.' No trial, nothing. That's what happened to my father. He suddenly disappeared during the night in Easter 1952 and died a year later in prison. Of course, there was another factor [that led to my arrest] later on. I was studying, but during the last year of my studies I wasn't part of the youth organisation [UTC] [*sic*], and that definitely had

[146] Interview with Veronika Osterer, 24 February 2005, Sibiu.
[147] She briefly joined the Landsmannschaft der Siebenbürger Sachsen after emigrating from Romania, but left the organisation soon after.
[148] See, for instance, Axel Azzola, *Jüdische und andere Geschichten von der Schöpfung bis zur Gegenwart* (Sibiu: Hora, 2005).
[149] See Chapter 3.   [150] Interview with Rosalind Horndasch, 2 August 2005, Sibiu.

something to do with my arrest. Granted, I wasn't some sort of politician, but I was the daughter of [a politician], and that was enough. They simply loved arresting people like that [. . .] And at first they wanted to persuade us [her brother and her] that they would love to let us go, but under the condition that I work for them. That would have been ideal. People knew me round here. My father had been an MP and politician for such a long time. They would have trusted me. All I had to do was to speak to some people and report it afterwards. No one would have dreamt [that I was a spy]. We would have been the ideal candidates, but unfortunately, well unfortunately for *them*, we both declined.
[. . .]
We got tangled up in a trial that involved twenty people. Some people got harsher sentences. We got the most lenient sentences, but it was nonetheless six years.
[. . .]
They declared an amnesty, but we had just finished our sentences. So, we were let out with those who had been sentenced to life in prison.[151]

Her story was also one of betrayal and yet her German background played almost no role. But, for others, their Germanness did mark them out as special. Others returned to Romania after 1989, too. In 1990, the vicar Gerhard Möckel and Dorothea Koch-Möckel relocated back to Sibiu, where they founded the Evangelische Akademie Siebenbürgen, an academic study circle linked to the Protestant Church.[152] Paul Philippi, the famous Romanian German thinker and writer of the twentieth century,[153] also returned to Romania, like a number of individuals in church circles, after years of living in 'involuntary exile' in Germany after 1989. Having worked actively against the *Landsmannschaften* and their goal of encouraging migration to Germany, he still emphasised the importance of being an 'ethnic German' during communism.[154] Philippi spoke glowingly of an unnamed author friend's role in preserving Germanness during communism:

She was in Bucharest and was really a patron saint for authors who wrote in German. She managed to persevere [*durchhalten*] in the most difficult circumstances. One aspect that was really important at the time for Transylvanian Saxons and Banat Swabians was the fact that she published the German names of places, which had actually been made illegal by

[151] Ibid.
[152] Andreas Möckel, *Umkämpfte Volkskirche: Leben und Wirken des evangelisch-sächsischen Pfarrers Konrad Möckel (1892–1965)* (Cologne: Böhlau, 2011), p. xi.
[153] See Chapter 2.
[154] He was one of the brains behind Licht der Heimat, a group that countered the *Landsmannschaften*'s discourse on 'survival through emigration'. See Chapter 2.

Ceauşescu in 1971. Well, it was so obvious to me that Ceauşescu was pursuing nationalist communist politics here, but I admired the fact that such people managed to hold out with such great talent and cleverness. Here, too, in Sibiu they had the Saxon 'culture tsar' [Kulturpapst], Dr Carl Göllner, who was viewed by some very critically, because he had joined the Communist Party. I found out through conversations with him [. . .] – on the street, he didn't dare say these things at home, because of the microphones – that he did things with such cunning, things that were actually not wanted by the communists. I would have liked to be part of this positive resistance that existed here and was possible here in Romania.[155]

Philippi depicted Germanness as an act of resistance against communism even when people were deeply entwined with the state system. If Germans had been party members, such as Carl Göllner, then it was only as part of their 'positive resistance' to communism.[156] As controversial as Schlattner's public attempt at explaining collaboration had been just a few years earlier, stories were beginning to converge around similar themes of complex entanglement and historical context.

It is then perhaps unsurprising that Eginald Schlattner's book *Rote Handschuhe* was received with a far greater degree of enthusiasm among non-émigrés. It was far easier to conceive of Schlattner as a victim of a totalitarian regime that had pressured people into collaborating from the perspective of those who stayed in Romania. German-language newspapers in Romania, too, employed the image of a victimised individual rather than accusing him of having compromised his loyalty towards his ethnicity. In a review for the *Hermannstädter Zeitung*, Jürgen Henkel described Schlattner as 'broken and worn down by persistent pressure [Gebrochen und vom anhaltenden Druck zermürbt]'.[157] Unlike the unequivocal rejection by the partisan Romanian German press in Germany, Henkel's demonstrated a difference in reception between émigrés and non-émigrés. If the *Landsmannschaften* prescribed a largely static discourse on German involvement and complicity in communism, Germans who stayed in Romania were able to avoid partisanship by focusing on the personal tragedy involved in collaboration. Such an

---

[155] Interview with Paul Philippi, 23 February 2005, Sibiu.
[156] For a good discussion on the spectrum of debates about reckoning with the communist past in post-communist Romania, see Cristina Petrescu and Dragoş Petrescu, 'Mastering vs Coming to Terms with the Past: A Critical Analysis of Post-Communist Romanian Historiography', in Sorin Antohi, Balázs Trencsényi and Péter Apor (eds.), *Narratives Unbound: Historical Studies in Post-Communist Eastern Europe* (Budapest: CEU Press, 2007), pp. 352–69.
[157] Jürgen Henkel, 'Prosa gegen das Vergessen', *Hermannstädter Zeitung* 1707, 15 December 2000, p. 3.

approach allowed Germans in Romania to contextualise complicity more easily than Romanian Germans in Germany. Accordingly, German collaboration came to be regarded as a very specific form of conformity. Most Romanian German voices from Romania treated the issue of collaboration either with disinterest or, more commonly, with a sense of exoneration. Suzanne Hehl's story is typical in that respect. Her father was arrested in connection with the wide scale purges of 1958/9. He had been betrayed to the Securitate by a local man who was a Saxon. Similar to accounts by other non-émigrés, Hehl avoided accusing this particular individual of 'selling out':

> My father was swept up [*wurde ausgehoben*] in September 1959 during the famous *Schriftstellerprozess* in Braşov for the same reason ... 'enemy activity' [*feindliche Aktionen*] or 'attempts to create a hostile mood towards the current regime' [*Versuche feindliche Stimmung gegen das aktuelle Regime zu machen*] [*sic*]. So, they searched our house in the countryside [...] and seized my father's assets. They even took his suits from his [wardrobe], and his typewriter and so on, but we were able to buy all that back [...]
>
> Yes, why did they [arrest] my father, what was the trigger? Of course, my father played cards with a small circle of gentlemen and my father must have made some negative comments about the regime [*regimefeindlich*]. But these comments, or these small remarks, weren't the real reason. The government feared a repeat of the Hungarian revolution of 1956 in Romania. They began arresting people left, right, and centre, so the rest of us knew: 'That's what happens if ... ' [...] And these people also arrested villagers, a well-known family, simple people – I had been to the same school as the children at the village school, the comprehensive school; we even went to visit them a few times at their home – their husband was taken away as a witness. And I spoke to him afterwards. I knew that they had taken him. I knew they were preparing the trial [the *Schriftstellerprozess*]. And so, I went to see him and asked him what it was like, because, you know, he had to give handwritten testimony [...] But he wasn't educated. His Romanian wasn't good enough [...] He told me quite honestly that they had threatened him: if he hadn't signed the written testimony, which hadn't been written by him, then he would have lost his job. He worked on a state-owned farm [...] He was a coachman. So he signed it. I never got to see the testimony.
>
> Later, after 1989, it was possible to look at the files, but I didn't do that. It was pointless. But I reckon the Securitate official wrote down what he wanted, I'm sure about that [...] The poor fellow couldn't have known that [...] He simply had to sign the whole thing [...] In the meantime, my father was in Braşov. I was there, too; it wasn't a closed trial. My father was represented by a public lawyer, but I also hired a private lawyer in order to prevent the very worst [...] But it was all fixed from the word go. They had to be sentenced in order to make an example of them for others [...] for the

whole of the region. I was at the trial. They brought the detainees into the courtroom. I remember my father didn't have any shoelaces ... they took them away, well, you know, in case he hanged himself [...] And I'm sure [they took away] his belt, too. I'm not sure what they did though. Well anyway, I was waiting for him in the corridor. His lawyer took me there, because he knew that they'd arrive there. And that's what happened, but they weren't allowed to look left or right. I'm sure he didn't see me. I didn't ask him afterwards [...] I mean, we never ever spoke about his time in prison.

 We never asked him anything ... He told us quite a bit here and there. I learnt a lot, but none of it is solid proof of anything. It just – how should I say – it gives a human aspect to the whole thing. He got five years in prison.[158]

Suzanne Hehl's story of the coercion and betrayal surrounding her father's arrest was softened by her understanding and forgiveness.[159] 'The poor fellow', as she called him, had been put in exactly the same position as Eginald Schlattner when betraying Hans Bergel and others. Like Schlattner, the 'traitor' in Suzanne Hehl's story was a victim of a totalitarian regime. If Schlattner disrupted the comfortable myths by which Romanian German organisations in Germany made sense of communism, then it seemed his story resonated far more with non-émigrés as well as 'non-conformists'. William Totok, a former member of the Aktionsgruppe Banat, wrote a warm review of Schlattner's *Rote Handschuhe* in which he spoke highly about the absence of resentment and accusations in the novel.[160] The absence of judgement was both admirable and beneficial to reconciliation.[161] Suzanne Hehl also approached the past in order to forget and forgive, which was one way of dealing with the communist past in Romania: Adrian Cionflâncă's typology of dealing with the legacy of Romanian communism identified, among many others, the so-called humanist thesis, namely that 'everybody deserves a second chance', as well as the 'Christian thesis', namely the need

---

[158] Interview with Suzanne Hehl, 23 February 2005, Sibiu.

[159] A similar theme emerges in Octavian Gabor's study on Romanian survivors of mass deportations from Bessarabia to Siberia during the Second World War. The six survivor stories featured exclusively Romanian Orthodox Christians who used similar language of forgiveness. See Monk Moise (comp.), *Do Not Avenge Us: Testimonies about the Suffering of the Romanians Deported from Bessarabia to Siberia*, trans. by Octavian Gabor (New York: Reflection Publishing, 2016).

[160] See, for example, William Totok, 'Omul nu se pentru a fi fericit ci pentru a-și face datoria', *Observator Cultural*, at www.observatorcultural.ro/arhivaarticol.phtml?xid=2472 (accessed 15 Oct. 2016).

[161] Ibid.

'to forget because forgetting is equivalent to forgiving'.[162] By the mid-2000s, the fire around anticommunism was being challenged both in Germany where the *Landsmannschaften* had lost their grip and in Romania where an overexcited *Raport Final* had tried to shut down nuanced discussions about the communist past.

Mănuşi Roşii (Red Gloves)

The film *Mănuşi Roşii (Red Gloves)*, directed by the Romanian Radu Grabea and released in 2010, tells the story of a young German called Felix Goldschmidt in the late 1950s, who is imprisoned and coerced by the Romanian secret police into incriminating a number of friends and acquaintances.[163] Goldschmidt, played by Alexandru Mihăescu, is portrayed as a double victim: a victim of the Securitate and hostage to his recurring and deep pangs of guilt. Produced just after the highpoint of Romanian 'New Wave' cinema, Grabea's film did not create as big an impact as other Romanian films in the mid-2000s about the communist past and its memory.[164] Yet the film was remarkable for a number of reasons. It adapted Eginald Schlattner's novel *Rote Handschuhe (Red Gloves)* just nine years after Schlattner's book had been published.[165] Unlike Schlattner's book, however, which had caused such controversy, Grabea's film provoked no comparable response. Instead, it was received, discussed, and critiqued largely on aesthetic grounds, while the plot – the focal point of the Schlattner debate – no longer appeared to be particularly contested. Nine years after the publication of *Rote Handschuhe*, Schlattner's story of betrayal and coercion had apparently been accepted as a plausible account of life during communism in Romania. The ease with which a Romanian-language film incorporated the story of a German caught up in the complexities of betrayal in communist Romania was

---

[162] Adrian Cioflâncă, 'Politics of Oblivion in Postcommunist Romania', *Romanian Journal of Political Sciences* 2 (2002), pp. 91, 92.

[163] *Mănuşi Roşii*, dir. Radu Grabea (2010).

[164] These include *4 luni, 3 săptămâni şi 2 zile (4 Months, 3 Weeks, 2 Days)*, dir. Cristian Mungiu (2007), *A fost sau n-a fost? (12:08 East of Bucharest)*, dir. Corneliu Porumboiu (2006), and *Moartea domnului Lăzărescu (The Death of Mr. Lazarescu)*, dir. Cristi Puiu (2005). Florentina Andreescu has written most widely on aspects of this movement. See, for instance, Florentina C. Andreescu, 'Seeing the Romanian Transition in Cinematic Space', *Space and Culture*, 16/1 (2013), pp. 73–87, and Florentina C. Andreescu, 'The Changing Face of the Other in Romanian Films', *Nationalities Papers: The Journal of Nationalism and Ethnicity* 39/1 (2011), pp. 77–94. For a collection of recent articles on Romanian New Wave cinema, see special issue 'Romania 100: Nation, Identity, Global Challenge', *Journal of European Studies* 48/3–4 (2019), pp. 215–340.

[165] Schlattner, *Rote Handschuhe*. In his book, the protagonist is nameless.

indeed notable. Radu Grabea explained his motivation for making the film at a film festival in Sibiu in June 2010: 'I tried to show the truth in this film. It is much easier simply to accuse the "traitor" Schlattner in this film rather than to analyse the entire system.'[166]

The absence of a reaction to Grabea's film from both Romanian Germans and other sections of Romanian society seemed to indicate that something fundamental had changed. As this chapter has demonstrated, the frenzied search for perpetrators and victims gave way from the mid-2000s to a fatigue surrounding the endless politicking about who was to blame for the communist past. That palpable shift in Romanian German memories of communism was part of a broader pattern of Romanian German trend-setting in dealing with communism. Romanian Germans were able to frame memories of communism long before communism collapsed in 1989, namely as émigrés during the Cold War. The *Landsmannschaften*'s hegemony over Romanian German memories of communism persisted after 1989, but came under increasing pressure in post-communist Europe. By the new millennium, debates in Germany gradually transcended simple divisions of perpetrators and victims, and Romanian German narratives also began challenging the homeland societies' status quo from the margins. Eginald Schlattner's novel and its warm reception outside the Romanian German mainstream was a seismic moment for Romanian German memory cultures, while Carl Gibson's novel *Symphonies of Freedom* highlighted the lack of traction older narratives of noble resistance to communism had in Romanian German circles and beyond. Meanwhile, in Romania, much energy was spent on challenging political problems of the here and now. The corruption practices in contemporary politics were now the main challenge, which made Vladimir Tismăneanu's hunt for communists, like Gibson's angry triumphalism, seem obsolete and outdated. In practice, however, there remained a considerable overlap between anticommunist and anticorruption activism, which was often targeted at the communist successor party, the PSD. And who could be better placed to sort out the scourge of corruption, and with it the hangover of communism, in Romania than a Romanian German? Step forward Klaus Iohannis, mayor of Sibiu and soon to be president of Romania.

[166] Radu Grabea quoted in Ruxandra Stănescu, 'Premiere in Hermannstadt: "Rote Handschuhe" bei internationalem Filmfestival Transylvania in Hermannstadt präsentiert', *Siebenbürgische Zeitung* 60/10, 30 June 2010, p. 3.

CHAPTER 5

European Bridge-Builders: Romanian Germans
after 1989

Transylvanian Saxons are the only people in history to have committed collective suicide, or so Paul Philippi claimed as he witnessed the Romanian German community disintegrating around him in the latter stages of the Cold War. The large-scale migration of Romanian Germans towards the end of the Cold War and in the immediate aftermath of 1989 left entire villages, schools, and communities in Romania depopulated. In just a few weeks in 1990, classrooms would empty bit by bit. Vicars were left behind to sermonise in front of disappearing congregations. A community that had been gradually shrinking as its members left Romania for West Germany was now utterly collapsing. Yet what appeared to be a full stop in Romanian German history – the *de facto* end of the community in the Banat, Transylvania, and elsewhere – turned out to be a transformative moment for Romanian Germans. If the immediate post-communist period was still largely characterised by Cold War identity disputes over place, fascism, and communism, the prospect of an ever-closer European Union put Romanian Germans back into the limelight. As this chapter argues, the Romanian German community underwent a transnational reinvention in mainstream Romanian and German society as a minority that (re)built bridges across Europe. For Romanian politicians intent on showing a 'western face' during EU accession, Romanian heritage served as evidence of Europeanness. In Germany, even before the end of the Cold War, Romanian Germans were able to recast older Saxon and Swabian myths of civilising colonists as a new Romanian German European mission. Meanwhile, their increasing absence in Romania in the new millennium opened up spaces for wild fantasies of reconstructing Saxon and Swabian worlds: Romanian German activists attempted to muscle their way back into Romanian life, while British imaginings of an untouched rural Saxon world gave Romanian Germans a platform in Europe in the twenty-first century.

Emigration and the opening of borders in east-central Europe did not rupture the connection between Germany and Romania, but in fact strengthened channels through which Romanian Germans could reaffirm their sense of superiority in identity representations. Reflective of broader European trends in the post-communist period, Romanian German debates centred on the supposed backward character of east-central Europe and Romania in particular, which vindicated their decision to leave Romania for Germany in the first place. The financial support given to Romanian Germans 'back home' in Romania confirmed the uneven relationship between Romania and Germany that had already existed during the Cold War. As late as 2007, organisations such as the Sozialwerk der Siebenbürger Sachsen considered their support activities as evidence that nothing had really changed in Romania. The run-up to Romania's accession to the EU in 2007 witnessed an explosion of interest by Romanian Germans émigrés for their former homeland. Often complex and nuanced in their reception of, and interaction with, developments in Romania, Romanian Germans fostered a closer relationship with Romania precisely because they had left. As more and more émigrés and émigré organisations forged closer links with their former homeland, they rein-vented themselves as a 'transnational bridge' for a common Europe, no longer torn between categories of East and West.

If Romanian Germans were still considered a minor German sub-culture in Germany at the end of Cold War, both Romanian and German society took greater note of the Romanian German commu-nity in the years after the end of the Cold War. Andreas Kloos (1915–98), former head of the Stephan Ludwig Roth Gymnasium in Mediaş/Mediasch, enjoyed some modest public recognition after retire-ment and emigration. His work on the history of Transylvanian Saxons generated some attention beyond Romanian German circles, but this was limited to private clubs and local associations. On 14 August 1990, at the height of Romanian German migration to Germany, he was invited to speak at the Rotary Club in Sankt Goar, but, like so many other Romanian Germans, he failed to break into the German mainstream.[1] Barely twenty years later, Herta Müller, Richard Wagner, and others were being feted in the German and international media, commanding audiences that the Romanian German celebrities of the Cold War period could never have imagined. Meanwhile, in Romania, the growing absence of Romanian Germans triggered an

[1] Siebenbürgen Institut, B I 115, A-5944.

obsession with them. From a spate of academic studies[2] to the rebirth of German-language schools,[3] Romanians missed 'their' Germans. Their absence in Romania also served well in cultural diplomacy for Romanian officials. A focus on the case of Sibiu/Hermannstadt as the European Capital of Culture in 2007 demonstrates the significant political currency the remains of the Romanian German community provided. The 2007 celebrations of a distinct Romanian German city coincided with Romania's accession to the European Union. The city put on a thoroughly *German* show. A few years later in 2014, Klaus Iohannis, the former mayor of Sibiu, became president of Romania and was hailed as the person capable of solving the long-standing systemic *Romanian* problem of corruption. Romanian Germans had almost disappeared from Romania, yet they were everywhere.

European Saxons and Transnational Swabians

Romanian Germans had long thought of themselves as the centre of Europe. They believed that their contribution to the development of democratic rights in Europe through the *Diploma Andreanum* in 1224, which enshrined Saxon autonomous rights, had been cruelly overlooked in favour of the English charter of rights Magna Carta from 1215. Their lofty self-understanding had certainly allowed them to create distance between themselves and the Germans 'over there' who had been the real Nazis, even though Romanian Germans had been entangled in National Socialism. Romanian Germans played on this transnational ambiguity during the Cold War. As the *Landsmannschaften* began pushing aggressively for emigration from Romania, they also cast themselves as true Europeans. 'Transylvanians Renew Their Commitment to Europe', the *Siebenbürgische Zeitung* announced on its front page in November 1950.[4] Over two days in Munich in October 1950, Transylvanian Saxons and political dignitaries from the Bundesrepublik celebrated 800 years of Germans in Transylvania. They, the Transylvanian Saxons, would never forget their 'occidental mission [*abendländische Sendung*]'. All the while,

---

[2] See, for instance, Smaranda Vultur (ed.), *Germanii din Banat: prin povestirile lor* (Bucharest: Paideia, 2000), and Smaranda Vultur, *Istorie trăită, istorie povestită: deportarea în Bărăgan, 1951–1956* (Timișoara: Amarcord, 1997).

[3] See, for example, the remarkable resurgence of the Samuel Brukenthal Gymnasium, a secondary school in Sibiu.

[4] 'Siebenbürger erneuern ihr Bekenntnis zu Europa', *Siebenbürgische Zeitung* 1/5, 15 November 1950, pp. 1, 2.

the minister of finance of Schleswig-Holstein and former Nazi official, Waldemar Kraft, stressed that Transylvanian Saxons served as a shining example for 'taking things forward in a new Europe'.[5] As the onetime official in charge of land management in the annexed territories of Poland, Kraft's idea of a new Europe exhibited strong continuities with National Socialist ideas of a 'New Europe' but in the guise of conciliatory post-war language. The literary doyen of Saxondom and editor of the Nazi-aligned journal *Klingsor*, Heinrich Zillich, was quoted approvingly in the *Neue Zeitung*, the American-controlled newspaper printed in Munich between 1945 and 1955, celebrating the pioneering role Saxons had played in Transylvania in establishing 'the first democracy in Europe', even before Switzerland.[6] 'We want Europe', Zillich bloviated before continuing:[7]

> Our Europeanness [*Europeäertum*] doesn't end with being self-evidently indigenous [*erschöpft sich nicht mit dem selbstverständlichen Eingeborensein*], it impels us to plan and act. Not every German in Germany [*Binnendeutscher*] feels this restlessness, but all Germans from the East do. Whatever we suffered and built came out of the East.[8]

In unmistakably German nationalist language, Zillich shifted a Romanian German sense of superiority – smashed to smithereens as the Second World War concluded – towards suffering and, finally, a claim to Europeanness. This was not in itself novel. *Mitteleuropäer* such as Joseph Partsch and Friedrich Naumann had already argued, from different political positions, for German leadership in uniting the larger central European region.[9] Zillich's plea was to place a minority – Germans from Romania and other Germans from the East, removed from 'mainstream' Germans – at the heart of a new vision for Europe.

Europeanness masked revanchist tendencies of laying claim to places beyond the Iron Curtain. In this spirit, the *Landsmannschaften* and other representative bodies of expellees were true 'representatives of a bygone European unity before the Iron Curtain severed east-central Europe from its motherland'.[10] Romanian Germans were rethinking themselves as

---

[5] Ibid.
[6] 'Eine der eindruckvollsten Kundgebungen', *Siebenbürgische Zeitung* 1/5, 15 November 1950, p. 2.
[7] Ibid.
[8] 'Das Abendland ist unser Volksgesetz: Heinrich Zillichs Festansprache auf der 800-Jahrfeier in München', *Siebenbürgische Zeitung* 1/5, 15 November 1950, p. 3.
[9] See Joseph Partsch, *Mitteleuropa: Die Länder und Völker von den Westalpen und dem Balkan bis an den Kanal und das Kurische Haff* (Gotha: Justus Perthes, 1904), and Friedrich Naumann, *Mitteleuropa* (Berlin: G. Reimer, 1916).
[10] 'Repräsentanten europäischer Einheit', *Siebenbürgische Zeitung* 3/8, 20 August 1952, pp. 1, 2.

pioneers of a new Europe that, superficially at least, transcended the nationalism of the pre-1945 period. But much of this discourse was still couched in the same rhetoric of superiority and exceptionalism of the ideological prism of the Cold War. The *Siebenbürgische Zeitung* demanded, in January 1952, that

> [a] new spirit is needed to rebuild Europe. That is true, too, of those Germans who lost their old homeland in 1945. Neither defeatism or desperation, nor a simple rekindling of old and violently tattered politics of yesteryear. Yet again, as so often in the past centuries, the German people with all its members is duty-bound, in spite of all, in spite of the failures by itself and others in the recent past, to make pioneering progress on its historic mission.[11]

The 'historic mission' presented to Romanian Germans had always been about building a Europe as *Kulturträger*, and in the period after the Second World War nationalism and superiority could take on the mantle of 'transnational European politics'. By the 1970s, Romanian Germans were convinced they had a special role as a bridge facilitating peace and understanding across the Iron Curtain. In 1971, the Landsmannschaft of Transylvanian Saxons declared that *Landsmannschaften* across the globe, from Germany to Austria to the USA and Canada, had a special duty of bridging East and West (*Brückenschlag*).[12] Time and again, Romanian German émigré officials emphasised how Saxons and Swabians enabled the *Brückenschlag* between the old and the new homeland, between East and West. At the annual *Heimattag* in Dinkelsbühl in 1967, Erhard Plesch, chairman of the Landsmannschaft der Siebenbürger Sachsen, placed the Romanian German community at the heart of cross-Iron Curtain diplomacy.[13] West German politicians endorsed their role as transnational bridge-builders. Kai-Uwe von Hasselt, then president of the Bundestag and former minister for displaced persons, refugees and war victims (1966–9), addressed representatives of the Landsmannschaft der Siebenbürger Sachsen on the occasion of the *Heimattag* in 1970, reminding them of their cultural mission:

---

[11] A. H., 'Übernationale Europapolitik als Aufgabe', *Siebenbürgische Zeitung* 3/1, 20 January 1952, pp. 1, 6.

[12] Landsmannschaft der Siebenbürger Sachsen (ed.), *Ein Weg zur Verständigung: Die Landsmannschaft der Siebenbürger Sachsen im Dienste einer deutschen Politik der Verständigung mit den Völkern des Ostens* (Munich: Verlag Hans Meschendörfer, 1971), p. 11.

[13] 'Ausschnitte aus offiziellen Erklärungen und Ansprachen des Bundesvorsitzenden der Landsmannschaft der Siebenbürger Sachsen in Deutschland, Erhard Plesch (Aufgrund von Beschlüssen der führenden Gremien der Landsmannschaft, Verbandstag und Bundesvorstand)', ibid., p. 17.

As one of the small ethnic groups, Transylvanian Saxons have always fulfilled a significant cultural mission in the south-eastern region of Europe. In future, you will also make a contribution by utilising your experiences as a mediator in bridging East and West [*Brückenschlag*] for all nations of Europe.[14]

Romanian Germans remained convinced of their 'historic mission' and special role in Europe, and sympathetic voices from outside the community only served to reinforce this self-construction. In the context of the 1970s, statements about bridge-building were also part of a new *Ostpolitik* in German politics. Beyond that, though, Romanian German transnational commitment also masked a difficult past of fascist and communist entanglement and served well during the Cold War as debates raged over Romanian Germans in the twentieth century. By the time communism collapsed, Romanian Germans had a pre-packaged narrative to construct themselves as an essential conduit for European dialogue and reconciliation.

Europe's New Centre

Europe needs a new centre, Hans Bergel announced on the eve of the biggest enlargement of the European Union to date. Writing in 2004, just before the 1st of May of the same year, Bergel expressed a common disappointment with the West.[15] After nearly four decades of living in the West, Bergel's mental map of Europe seemed to be in flux due to the rapidly shifting politics of the post-communist period. The Iron Curtain had propelled Romanian Germans into a special mediating role between East and West, yet the disappearance of the political division of Europe now seemed to threaten their privileged position. All the effort in encouraging emigration from Romania to the new promised land of West Germany seemed futile now that 75 million east-central Europeans could join the club without the same kind of bridge-building that Saxons and Swabians had claimed as their own.

If the Cold War had been all about escaping eastern Europe, then European enlargement encompassing Romania, Bulgaria, and other former communist countries between 2004 and 2007 undermined the life

---

[14] Kai-Uwe von Hasselt, 'Bundespräsident Kai-Uwe von Hasselt in einem Telegramm an den Bundesvorsitzenden der Siebenbürger Sachsen in Deutschland', ibid., p. 44.

[15] Hans Bergel, 'Europa braucht eine neue Mitte', *Südostdeutsche Vierteljahresblätter* 2 (2004), pp. 115–16. For a broader sense of Bergel's mental map of the region, see Raluca Rădulescu, *Das literarische Werk Hans Bergels* (Berlin: Frank und Timme, 2015), especially pp. 39–106.

stories of Romanian German émigrés. The shifting centre of new Europe, where East and West were no longer as stable as before, shook the very foundations of the émigré biographies. Many Romanian Germans continued to think in Cold War terms in order to justify their own act of emigration. Romania under communism was often compared to contemporary Romania both in oral history testimonies and in Romanian German writing on contemporary Romania. For Christine Oberath, who had emigrated in the 1970, the strict division into East and West was crucial for upholding a coherent narrative of her own life. Why had she decided to emigrate in the first place? She replied:

> The reasons? Well, not only was the economic situation tough, you can't really imagine what it was like. The war had been over for a long time. And still, we had to queue for bread, milk, eggs, butter. We only got meat about three or four times a year, and then it usually consisted of gristle and bones. That's what we used to get and if we complained: 'There's no meat on that.' [The response was] 'Well, then just leave it here.' We didn't have any washing-up liquid for months on end. We didn't have sewing needles for months on end. We didn't have the bare essentials for months on end [. . .] And I've already mentioned it: Ceaușescu wanted to push ahead with the Romanisation process and put children through state education. Just the thought of putting my children through a state-run educational institution, or a state school or boarding school [. . .] I would not have been able to cope with that.[16]

Oberath and her husband may have emigrated, but her daughter had stayed in Romania after all. The parents visited their daughter and her family back in Romania during the Cold War. Visiting Romania confirmed her decision to leave. 'Everything seemed so dirty and neglected',[17] Oberath insisted. Impressions on return visits and reports from Romania remained constant, even as Romania came closer to joining the European Union. Shortage, neglect, and a lack of consideration for the German minority continued to frame depictions of Romania. If anything, the Europeanisation process in the 1990s and 2000s confirmed some of the negative connotations Romanian Germans associated with Cold War Romania. In their view, EU enlargement highlighted that Romania's nature was fundamentally incompatible with that of the EU. While the 1990s and early 2000s allowed Romanian Germans to focus more introspectively on their situation in Germany,[18] once the prospect of EU and

---

[16] Interview with Christine Oberath, 16 February 2005, Traunstein.   [17] Ibid.
[18] A good example of this is the lexicon of Transylvanian Saxons published in 1993. See Walter Myß (ed.), *Lexikon der Siebenbürger Sachsen: Geschichte, Kultur, Zivilisation, Wissenschaften, Wirtschaft, Lebensraum Siebenbürgen* (Innsbruck: Wort und Welt Verlag, 1993).

NATO membership became real and immediate issues, their focus turned towards the contemporary situation in Romania.[19]

Decades of introspection and a lack of interest in developments in post-communist Romania had left Romanian Germans émigrés using a vocabulary embedded in Cold War ideas about an East–West division in Europe. Reports and commentaries on the state of Romania in the millennium reflected a static view of their former homeland. Writing for the *Siebenbürgische Zeitung* in 2007, the year Romania joined the EU, Peter Pastior revived the memory of the Cold War dependency Romanian Germans in Romania had felt towards Germany.[20] 'The Hardship of Our Fellow Countrymen Continues' ran the title of the article in which Pastior detailed the suffering his fellow Romanian Germans were still enduring in contemporary Romania. Pastior reprinted a handwritten letter from an eighty-year-old Saxon woman, Martha Reiner. Written as an appeal for donations to the Sozialwerk for Transylvanian Saxons, the letter was reprinted alongside the article and served as an emotive reminder of the power dynamics in the relationship between émigrés and non-émigrés (Figure 5.1).[21] Cold War bowing letters had never disappeared.

Pastior explained the importance of this letter in no uncertain terms: 'Despite Romania's accession to the European Union at the beginning of this year [2007]', he contended, things had not changed for the better for Romanian Germans.[22] Frustration at the situation in Romania spilled over into online forums. 'Shame, shame on Romania!', cried an on-line thread on the website of the *Siebenbürgische Zeitung* in response to a rumour that German umlauts were no longer permitted in Romanian passports.[23] Even as European integration was happening around them, shortage, neglect, and a lack of consideration for Germans still defined their self-image in Romania.

EU expansion to Romania and Bulgaria disoriented Romanian Germans who struggled to locate Europe's shifting centre. Robert König,

---

[19] A good assessment of this can be made when tracing the topics covered in Romanian German émigré press. Until the early 2000s, many articles focused primarily on Romanian German traditions and history. But from 2002, after the height of the Schlattner controversy, there was a marked increase in articles dealing with contemporary political issues such as Romania's EU accession. See, for instance, Simone Fleischer, 'EU-Betritt Rumäniens schon 2007?', *Siebenbürgische Zeitung* 56/13, 10 August 2006, p. 5.

[20] See Peter Pastior, 'Die Not der Landsleute in Siebenbürgen halt an', *Siebenbürgische Zeitung* 57/17, 31 October 2007, p. 4.

[21] Ibid.   [22] Ibid.

[23] 'Pfui und Schande für Rumänien!!!', *Siebenbürgische Zeitung Online*, 8 December 2005, at www.siebenbuerger.de/ubb/Forum11/HTML/000655.html (accessed 1 Jul. 2018).

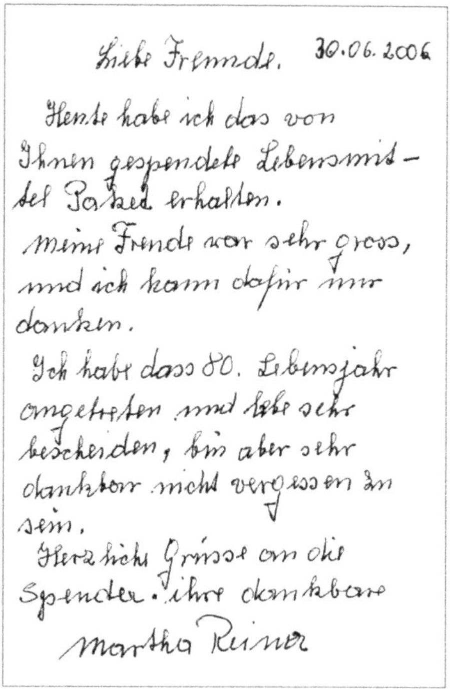

Liebe Freunde. 30.06.2006

Heute habe ich das von
Ihnen gespendete Lebensmit-
tel Paket erhalten.
Meine Freude war sehr gross,
und ich kann dafür nur
danken.
Ich habe dass 80. Lebensjahr
angetreten und lebe sehr
bescheiden, bin aber sehr
dankbar nicht vergessen zu
sein.
Herzliche Grüsse an die
Spender. Ihre dankbare
Martha Reiner

Figure 5.1 Letter from Martha Reiner.

an émigré from Mediaş in Transylvania, who had moved to Lower Bavaria in the 1980s, dismissed the political enlargement of the EU in the new millennium as absurd and dangerous:

> The whole eastern bloc [*Ostblock*] wants to join the EU. They know they are going to get money, but what's in it for us? Just dirt, that's all! It was the biggest nonsense to let those ten states [in 2004] into the EU all at once. Yes, one state, two states, in five, six years another two or three, but not ten at once! Absolute rubbish! But the Germans are so stupid, they are world champions in paying!
>
> And in twenty, thirty years' time, Turkey is meant to join the EU. Then, in fifty years, the whole of Europe will be Muslim. That will be the end of Europe [. . .] It's the Ottoman Empire all over again. Do they want that again? The entire eastern bloc is made up of Asiatic people [*Asiaten*] and Muslims. We've got nothing in common with them. They've got their

beliefs, and we have ours. They are going to join the EU! That's the biggest
load of rubbish I've heard! Turkey to join the EU ... it's going to be
a catastrophe![24]

But Romanian German reception of European enlargement in 2007 was
far more diverse than arrogant scepticism. 'Europe Is Growing Together',
the *Siebenbürgische Zeitung* announced in its first issue in January 2007.[25]
Torn between optimism and scepticism, the Landsmannschaft der
Siebenbürger Sachsen was unsure how to classify the political developments of 2007.[26] Romania's accession to the EU brought with it more
rights for Romanian Germans, which was also seen as beneficial.
Romanian Germans were also delighted that Oliver Hoischen, in the
Frankfurter Allgemeine Zeitung, sounded suspicious as far as Romania's
and Bulgaria's political credentials were concerned, but also drew attention
to the German minority and its success stories in the region.[27] Romanian
Germans revelled in that image: they were an island of Europeanness in
a country that had yet to 'catch up' with Europe. If there was a new centre
of Europe since 1989, then it was in Transylvania and the Banat around the
German cultural centres of Sibiu and Timişoara.

Romanian Germans acted as a European bridge between East and West
and marked them out as special. Hans Bergel used an argument from
history to explain their central role in recentring Europe:

> And you mustn't forget this: there is a Transylvanian Saxon constitution;
> a democratic, republican constitution, which is only nine years younger
> than the Golden Bull of the English. It is one of the oldest European,
> republican constitutions. I'm telling you this for the following reason: the
> republican understanding of life [*Lebensverständnis*] of the Saxons – today
> we'd call it democratic – is far more integral to the Saxons' mentality, far
> more so than for the Germans. For example, they never let the aristocracy
> gain strength in Transylvania. We also didn't have serfdom.
> [...]
> That's something that has always really impressed me. That early repub-
> lican idea is part of the constitution; in Latin, it's *Unus sit populus*: 'The
> people be as one.' Right? That's such a great thing!
> [...]
> Where else could one find a democratic constitution from the early 1200s,
> the thirteenth century, other than with the English and the Transylvanian
> Saxons? Nowhere else! Those were the oldest republican constitutions [...]

[24] Interview Christa König and Robert König, 14 February 2005, Passau.
[25] Siegbert Bruss, 'Europa wächst zusammen', *Siebenbürgische Zeitung* 57/1, 15 January 2007, pp. 1, 4.
[26] Ibid.
[27] Oliver Hoischen, 'Hier spricht man deutsch', *Frankfurter Allgemeine Zeitung*, 1 January 2007.

I have always noticed that comparison with the English. A lot of that always makes me think: gosh! We [the Transylvanian Saxons] are just like the English. Not the genius or greatness of the English [. . .] but the democratic understanding of the English.[28]

But Bergel did not simply discount Romanians as being outside the European community. They were part of Europe, but reinforced the cultural hierarchies that Romanian Germans had constructed over the last century. Bergel continued:

As a child, I was always fascinated by the difference [*das Andersartige*] of Romanians. They were a bit different from us, I told myself as a twelve-year-old. I always had dealings [with Romanians], that wasn't a problem; we used to live with and next to each other. My neighbour was Romanian, and he was as old as I was [. . .] That's why I had contact [with Romanians] from a very early age, with the Romanian way of living [*Lebensweise*] and the Romanian way of life [*Lebensform*], as well as their intellectual life [*intellektuelle Lebensformen*] [. . .] I was simply interested in that difference, the nuance within European culture. The Romanian way of communicating is different in tone; it's far more unexacting [*das Leichte*], as well as more playful [*das Verspielte*], and less precise [*das Wenig-Gründliche*].[29]

Bergel's inclusion of Romanians in the European palimpsest of people and culture was subject to caveats and condescension. It built on deeply embedded North–South and East–West stereotypes that had served well to explain Romanian communism and Romanian German commitment to National Socialism. Romanian Germans still insisted on a civilisational difference from Romanians, but with a new tone of European patronage. Romanians, or so Bergel claimed, were European, but in a childish and unsophisticated way. For other Romanian Germans, even that was a step too far, and EU enlargement crystallised their older attitudes towards Romania and Romanian society. Where enthusiasm for Romania's accession was kindled, it only ever really extended to those parts of Romania deemed 'European' enough, and that meant the Romanian German world of Transylvania and the Banat.[30] Romanian German debates therefore positioned Transylvania firmly at the cultural centre of Europe, a claim that was repeated and affirmed elsewhere in seminars, workshops, newspapers, miscellaneous publications, and oral history interviews.[31] Embedded in a long tradition of marking out Transylvania as

---

[28] Interview with Hans Bergel, 18 February 2005, Munich.   [29] Ibid.

[30] See Dietmar Müller, 'Die Siebenbürgische Frage: Neue Fragestellungen – alte Antworten', *Zeitschrift für Siebenbürgische Landeskunde* 27/1 (2004), pp. 125–32.

[31] See, for instance, Siegbert Bruss, 'Politik gestalten: Tradition und Aktualität', *Siebenbürgische Zeitung* 58/2, 28 January 2008, p. 4.

different from its neighbouring regions, Saxons had long referred to it as an 'eastern Switzerland'. The Transylvanian Saxon vicar George Friedrich Teutsch had been one of the first to articulate this confederal idea of Transylvania.[32] This was also echoed beyond German circles. The Hungarian politician Oszkár Jászi (1875–1957) had envisaged a Danubian Confederation in the aftermath of the First World War, which placed the idea of an 'eastern Switzerland' at the heart of this concept.[33] For Romanian Germans, the idea of Transylvanian and Banat exceptionalism continued to hold much traction in the twenty-first century. Exhibitions in Germany in the 1990s and 2000s entrenched the view of the Banat and Transylvania as a centre of European culture. In conjunction with the Banat Swabian *Heimattag* in 1992, several cities in Germany hosted exhibitions of art by artists from the Banat. In Würzburg, a large exhibition of '200 Years of European Art in the Banat' placed Banat culture at the very heart of a European story.[34] The Romanian German exodus and the breakdown of the Cold War division seemed to propel Romanian Germans into the centre of a new Europe.

But this did not work for Romania as a whole. Under the spotlight of European enlargement, the question of where Romania was located – politically and metaphorically – reflected a deeper conflict in Romanian German identities and belonging. Surprisingly, the two main German-language newspapers in Romania, the *Hermannstädter Zeitung* and the *Allgemeine Deutsche Zeitung (ADZ)*, did not devote a great deal of space to European affairs in the run-up to Romania's accession in 2007. Where opinions were voiced, they addressed the chasm between the expectations set by the EU for Romania and what was often interpreted as the failing reality of being part of the Union. Unlike émigrés who had been forced to rethink and revisit their narratives of emigration, non-émigrés largely dismissed the EU as merely a stage for high political machinations.[35] There was some Euroscepticism, too, among Romanian Germans.[36] As was common in broader Eurosceptic views, the

---

[32] See Balázs A. Szelényi, 'From Minority to *Übermensch*: The Social Roots of Ethnic Conflict in the German Diaspora of Hungary, Romania and Slovakia', *Past & Present* 196 (2007), p. 229.

[33] György Litván, *A Twentieth-Century Prophet: Oszkár Jászi* (Budapest: CEU Press, 2006), pp. 137–9. On the right-wing roots of the idea of federalism, see Holly Case, 'The Strange Case of Federative Ideas in East-Central Europe', *Journal of Modern History* 85/4 (2013), pp. 833–66.

[34] 'Banater Kulturarbeit im letzten Jahrzehnt', in Landsmannschaft der Banater Schwaben (ed.), *Neue Heimat in Deutschland: 50 Jahre Wirken für die Gemeinschaft* (Munich: Landsmannschaft der Banater Schwaben, 2000), p. 114.

[35] See, for example, Beatrice Ungar, 'Auf Schnupperkurs im Hemicycle: Mitglieder und Mitarbeitende des DFDR zu Gast in Straßburg', *Hermannstädter Zeitung*, 5 October 2007, p. 4.

[36] Olaf Leiße, Utta-Kristin Leiße and Alexander Richter, *Beitrittsbarometer Rumänien: Grundprobleme des Landes und Einstellung Rumänischer Jugendlicher auf dem Weg in Europäische Union* (Wiesbaden: Deutscher Universitäts-Verlag, 2004), pp. 7–19, 96, 97.

EU was frequently portrayed by Romanian German non-émigrés as an institution that was endangering 'traditional' ways of life.[37] EU enlargement also threatened to level out what non-émigrés insisted were differences between Romanians and Germans.[38] But while Romanian Germans in Romania struggled to show much enthusiasm for the European Union, they were at least clear about the EU's role as an arbiter on issues such as minority rights.[39] Demands by the EU for greater protection of minority rights were welcomed by Romanian Germans and also confirmed views of Romanian 'backwardness' and unreliability.[40]

Others, though, such as the Romanian German scholar Anneli Ute Gabanyi, sounded a more cautiously optimistic note about Romania joining the European Union.[41] She attributed the *Europa-Müdigkeit* (weariness of Europe) that was palpable among Romanian Germans in Romania to a feeling of disappointment following high expectations of changes after 1989.[42] If the EU had a shortcoming, it was a failure to communicate properly (*Kommunikationsdefizit*).[43] In the period preceding Romania joining the EU, Gabanyi expressed some concern over Romania's readiness but warned against postponing accession.[44] A punitive stance towards Romania would

[37] See Ronald H. Linden and Lisa M. Pohlman, 'Now You See It, Now You Don't: Anti-EU Politics in Central and Southeast Europe', *Journal of European Integration* 25/4 (2003), pp. 311–34, and Andreas Priberksy, Karin Liebhart and Sandór Kurtán, 'A Temple for the Nation: Symbolic Space of Central European Conservatism', *Cultural Studies* 16/6 (2002), pp. 797–808.
[38] See Valentina Glajar, *The German Legacy in East-Central Europe as Recorded in Recent German-Language Literature* (Rochester, N.Y.: Camden House, 2004), pp. 115, 116.
[39] Wolfgang Fuchs, 'The Party Is Over: Europäische Sommerschule: Ethnische Minderheiten in der EU', *Hermannstädter Zeitung*, 29 June 2007, p. 4. See also Guido Schwellnus, 'The Adoption of Nondiscrimination and Minority Protection Rules in Romania, Hungary, and Poland', in Frank Schimmelpfennig and Ulrich Sedelmeier (eds.), *The Europeanisation of Central and Eastern Europe* (Ithaca, N.Y.: Cornell University Press, 2005), pp. 51–70.
[40] This was explored by Dieter Bricke in the 1990s in his analysis of the options for minorities in east-central Europe in light of EU expansion. See Dieter W. Bricke, *Minderheiten im östlichen Mitteleuropa: Deutsche und europäische Optionen* (Baden-Baden: Nomos, 1995), pp. 108–19.
[41] See, for instance, Anneli Ute Gabanyi, 'Rumänien – Anatomie einer Dauerkrise', in Jürgen Elvert and Michael Salewski (eds.), *Der Umbruch im Osten* (Stuttgart: Franz Steiner Verlag, 1993), pp. 135–48, and Anneli Ute Gabanyi, 'Rumänien in (welchem) Europa heute?', in Anton Sterbling (ed.), *Migrationsprozesse, Probleme von Abwanderungsregionen Identitätsfragen* (Hamburg: Krämer Verlag, 2006), pp. 89–110.
[42] Anneli Ute Gabanyi, 'Gefährdet Populismus die Demokratie in Rumänien?', *Siebenbürgische Zeitung* 58/7, 22 April 2008, p. 4.
[43] Ibid.
[44] See Anneli Ute Gabanyi, *Rumänien vor dem EU-Beitritt* (Berlin: Stiftung Wissenschaft und Politik, 2005), as well as Anneli Ute Gabanyi, 'Rumänien und Bulgarien: EU-Beitritt mit Auflagen', *SWP-Aktuell* 27 (2006), at www.swp-berlin.org/common/get_document.php?asset_id=3031 (accessed 16 Sep. 2018), in which Gabanyi deconstructs the EU's leverage over Romania and Bulgaria. See also Anneli Ute Gabanyi, 'Rumäniens Beitritt zur EU: 2007 oder 2008?', *Südosteuropa-Mitteilungen: Vierteljahresschrift der Südosteuropa-Gesellschaft e.V.* 46/1 (2006), pp. 4–17.

be counterproductive, Gabanyi argued, and this was cited in the German media.[45] Her proactive stance towards Romania's accession was met by some Romanian Germans with scepticism.[46] But her commentary on Romania's fulfilment of the Acquis Communautaire gave Romanian Germans a seemingly objective measurement against which their often negative opinions of the country could be tested. Romania, it turned out, was a country riddled with corruption, lacking in good governance, and with serious shortcomings towards its minorities.[47] The Copenhagen Criteria and the Acquis Communautaire, both of which set out clear checklists for newcomers to the European Union, demonstrated these points.[48] For central and east European states to become truly European, they had to meet the targets set by the West, which played to Romanian German mental maps of Europe.[49] Any encouraging developments in Romania were always interpreted as a response to western pressure, not always unreasonably so, with the West telling the East how to act and how to become more western.[50] In this sense, Romanian German images of east-central Europe, and Romania in particular, were confirmed in the process of EU expansion. Academic work and official documentation often repeated long-held Romanian German stereotypes of a lingering 'backwardness' in Romania.[51] Accordingly, Michael Kroner, a leading academic voice for the Romanian German community, has asserted that there has been a direct link between injustices of the past, such as the treatment of minorities during the post-war period, and the contemporary state of affairs in Romania.[52]

It was the language used by sections of Romanian politics and society, however, that played a crucial role in sanctioning Romanian German

[45] See, for instance, Michael Schmidt, 'Bulgarian und Rumänien droht die gelb-rote Karte', *Tagesspiegel*, 26 October 2005.
[46] At a Romanian German colloquium, she was referred to as 'Gabanescu' due to her perceived pro-Romanian stance. See also Siegbert Bruss, 'Rumänienexpertin wechselt nach Berlin', *Siebenbürgische Zeitung* 51/3, 20 February 2001, p. 4.
[47] Such normative views are also reflected in academic studies on the enlargement process, such as David Phinnemore (ed.), *The EU and Romania: Accession and Beyond* (London: Federal Trust for Education and Research, 2006).
[48] See, for example, Horst Günther Krenzler, *Preparing for the Acquis Communautaire* (Florence: European University Institute, 1998). The transcript of the Copenhagen Criteria can be viewed at 'Conclusions of the Presidency', *European Council in Copenhagen*, 21–2 June 1993, at http://ue.eu.int/ueDocs/cms_Data/docs/pressdata/en/ec/72921.pdf (accessed 10 Dec. 2018).
[49] See, for instance, Schwellnus, 'The Adoption of Nondiscrimination and Minority Protection Rules'.
[50] See, for instance, Bernd Fabritius, 'EU-Beitritt Rumäniens: Rechtliche Auswirkungen', *Siebenbürgische Zeitung* 57/1, 15 January 2007, p. 2.
[51] See, for instance, Michael Kroner, 'Im Spannungsfeld zwischen ethnischer Identität und Globalisierung', *Siebenbürgische Zeitung* 58/14, 20 September 2007, p. 7.
[52] Ibid.

views on Romania's position in Europe. Romanian Germans often referred back to a powerful idea within Romanian society of a demi-orientalist position within Europe. Out of a sense of insecurity, a vein in Romanian society continued to emphasise that they existed in an 'in-between' region.[53] Both self-denigrating and sceptical of 'the West', the long tradition of Romanian thinkers who articulated Romania's demi-orientalist position bolstered Romanian German ideas of Romania's persistent 'Balkan' and 'backward' nature.[54] Critical Romanian voices within Romanian society corroborated long-standing Romanian German doubts about Romania's Europeanness.[55] When the chief negotiator for Romania during the accession process, Vasile Puşcaş, conceded on several occasions that deeply embedded problems within the Romanian political system persisted, Romanian German émigrés leaped on these admissions with glee.[56] Having Puşcaş admit to problems was one thing, but in the Romanian German view it was even better since it was a Romanian doing so, laying bare the endemic problems of Romanian society which Romanian Germans had always tried to escape.[57] Failure to meet the terms set for accession was traced meticulously in both the Romanian and the Romanian German press, and this was interpreted as Romania's innate 'un-European' nature.[58] And anyway, so the argument went,

---

[53] Milica Bakic-Hayden's work on former Yugoslavia helps us here. She speaks of 'nesting orientalisms' as a discourse for passing on the label of 'Balkan' to the next neighbour. What matters here is that there is a self-understanding of 'Balkanism', or orientalism more broadly, as a discourse for the broader region. See Milica Bakić-Hayden, 'Nesting Orientalisms: The Case of Former Yugoslavia', *Slavic Review* 54/4 (1995), pp. 917–31.

[54] See, for instance, Neagu Djuvara, *Între Orient şi Occident: ţările române la începutul epocii moderne* (Bucharest: Humanitas, 2002), and Cristina Petrescu and Dragoş Petrescu, 'Mastering vs Coming to Terms with the Past: A Critical Analysis of Post-Communist Romanian Historiography', in Sorin Antohi, Balázs Trencsényi and Péter Apor (eds.), *Narratives Unbound: Historical Studies in Post-Communist Eastern Europe* (Budapest: CEU Press, 2007), pp. 338–9. For a classic work on Romanian national identity and debates around Romania's position vis-á-vis East and West, see Katherine Verdery, *National Ideology under Socialism: Identity and Cultural Politics in Ceauşescu's Romania* (Berkeley: University of California Press, 1991), especially pp. 46–54.

[55] See Viktor D. Bojkov, 'Neither Here, nor There: Romania and Bulgaria in Current European Politics', *Communist and Post-Communist Studies* 37/4 (2004), pp. 509–22. Here, Bojkov argues that the late accession of Romania and Bulgaria has left them in a political wilderness, because they were not treated in the same way as other accession countries. They have thus been marked out as different.

[56] See Vasile Puşcaş, 'EU Accession Negotiations: The Case of Romania', *Transylvanian Review* 16/1 (2007), pp. 34–46, in particular p. 45.

[57] See Dan Cărămidariu, 'Auf steinigen Pfaden in die EU’, in *Deutsches Jahrbuch für Rumänien 2005* (Bucharest: ADZ Verlag, 2005), pp. 59–69.

[58] See, for example, 'Premier Călin Popescu Tăriceanu will nächste Woche zurücktreten: Vorgezogene Wahlen und Verfassungsreferendum vorbereiten', *Allgemeine Deutsche Zeitung*, 15 July 2005, p. 3.

Romanians did not want to join a 'western club', as Romanian 'anti-Europeans' or 'traditionalists' made clear.[59]

Commentary from outside Romania still had the most powerful effect on Romanian Germans' views on European integration. Findings by the European Court of Human Rights of a relatively high number of human rights violations in Romania added force to the argument that Romania had never really belonged to Europe while excluding from this criticism the very elements of its state – Germans and perhaps Hungarians – that were islands of Europeanness.[60] Germans more broadly maintained a negative view of Romania since the collapse of communism,[61] which, in turn, gave credence to Romanian Germans' negative view of Romania and the contemporaneous political and economic situation in Romania. The condemnatory tone of official assessments and popular opinion gave Romanian Germans a channel for highlighting past injustices towards Romanian Germans and their loss of property.[62] Echoing the general tenor of EU progress reports, Romanian Germans saw the Romanian state as a failing and failed state – as it had always been, in their eyes. Right up until accession was imminent in 2006, Romanian German émigré publications maintained that Romania was not quite ready and might yet miss out on accession. Using reports and evaluations by the EU, émigrés could claim that

> [n]onetheless, the chances for EU accession are not very good: a ramshackle [*marode*] economy, a bureaucracy that lacks transparency, and legal uncertainty are all barriers for the aim of EU membership. Approximately one-third of the Romanian population lives below the poverty line. The EU are pouring in money in order to support the country's preparations and efforts to fulfil the criteria for accession. But the process is going ahead very sluggishly; very often EU money simply trickles away into various channels.[63]

---

[59] Martin Brusis, 'Zwischen europäischer und nationaler Identität: Zum Diskurs über die Osterweiterung der EU', in Ansgar Klein et al. (eds.), *Europäische Öffentlichkeit – Bürgergesellschaft – Demokratie* (Opladen: Leske + Budrich, 2003), p. 262.

[60] See, for instance, 'European Court of Human Rights: Violation by Article and by Country 2006', at www.echr.coe.int/NR/rdonlyres/449186A0-1EEB-4247-B2EF-16DE8F465D30/0/Table2006ENG .pdf (accessed 26 May 2018), p. 2.

[61] See Kathrin Kissau, 'Ceauşescu, Dracula und Waisenhäuser? Einblicke in das Image Rumäniens in Deutschland', *Südosteuropa Mitteilungen* 48/4 (2006), pp. 44–55.

[62] See ibid. Reactions by Romanian Germans to these rulings have been well documented in online discussions. See, for example, 'Restitution/Europ. Gerichtshof f. Menschenrechte', at www .siebenbuerger.de/ubb/Forum10/HTML/000206.html, and 'Restitution/Europäischer Gerichtshof für Menschenrechte', at www.siebenbuerger.de/forum/integration/55-restitution-europaeischer-gerichtshof/ (both accessed 26 May 2018).

[63] Elena Drozdik, 'Bundeskanzler Schröder empfing Rumäniens Ministerpräsidenten Năstase', *Banater Berglanddeutsche: Mitteilungsblatt des Heimatverbandes Banater Berglanddeutsche e.V.* 19/110, May/June 2003, p. 13.

Elena Drozdik's assessment of Romania was withering. 'The Romanian government only takes appropriate steps when outside pressure is exerted', she continued in her communiqué to her Banat Swabian readership of the *Banater Berglanddeutsche* in 2003.[64] The EU accession process had only ever been a façade, covering over the inherent problems of the Romanian state and society. The proof of the pudding was in the official documentation of Romania's 'progress', which laid bare the soul of Romania for everyone in Europe to see.[65]

European Opportunities

Multilingual street signs began to appear across Romania in the 2000s.[66] Romania had committed itself, thanks to European integration, to introduce bi- or trilingual street signs in places where at least 20 per cent of the population spoke a minority language. Despite the worries, frustration, and resentment around Romania's accession to the European Union, a new world of possibilities opened up for Romanian Germans. If émigré commitment to strengthening schools, cultural forums, retirement homes, and museums formed one side of that story, pressure groups devoted to property restitution represented the darker elements of these growing links.[67]

As Siegbert Bruss and others within the *Landsmannschaften* reminded their fellow Romanian Germans, EU accession also came with more rights. Émigrés now lived in the hope of 'reclaiming' their lost homeland and property. Accession opened up the prospects of either regaining or buying back former Saxon and Swabian property expropriated under the communists.[68] A number of Romanian German organisations sprang up with objectives ranging from preserving and rebuilding Romanian German

---

[64] 'Kurznachrichten aus Rumänien', *Banater Berglanddeutsche: Mitteilungsblatt des Heimatverbandes Banater Berglanddeutsche e.V.* 19/110, May/June 2003, p. 13.

[65] See, for instance, 'Romania 2005 Comprehensive Monitoring Report', *European Commission*, Brussels, 25 October 2005, pp. 1–102, at http://ec.europa.eu/enlargement/archives/pdf/key_docu ments/2005/sec1354_cmr_master_ro_college_en.pdf (accessed 26 May 2018). See also Klaus W. Grewlich, 'Rumänien auf dem Weg nach Europa: Wirtschafts- und Finanzpolitische Perspektiven des EU-Beitritts', *Internationale Politik* 61/7 (2006), pp. 92–6.

[66] R.S., 'Dreisprachige Ortstafels', *Siebenbürgische Zeitung* 58/9, 15 June 2008, p. 1.

[67] Good examples of such institutions and organisations include the Ev. Honterus-Gemeinde, which is a Protestant organisation concerned with raising money for the maintenance of the Black Church in Brașov/Kronstadt. See *Ev. Honterus-Gemeinde*, at www.honterusgemeinde.ro (accessed 29 May 2018), and the *'Samuel von Brukenthal'-Stiftung*, at www.brukenthal.org/de/ (accessed 29 May 2018).

[68] Gheorghita Geana, 'Nichtorganische Entwicklung, Eigentumsform und die moralische Krise in Rumänien nach 1989', in Anneli Ute Gabanyi and Anton Sterbling (eds.), *Sozialstruktureller*

culture in Transylvania and the Banat to helping Romanian German émigrés recover property. One of the first organisations to was Arche Noah (Noah's Ark), set up in Sibiu in the summer of 1994 by Maria Luise Roth-Höppner.[69] Arche Noah encouraged the return of Transylvanian Saxons to Romania, with ineffective results. But its efforts to reclaim confiscated property and ease inheritance laws were potentially very explosive and a sign of the political clout Romanian Germans could exercise in the new post-communist European world. In May 2007, the organisation ResRo: Restitution und Menschenrechte in Rumänien e.V. (ResRo) put Romanian German property back on the table in the midst of a pan-European interest in Romania and its German culture. ResRo's mission was to redress historic injustices at the hands of the communist state in Romania.[70] In a petition written in both Romanian and German – and addressed to the European Parliament, the vice-president of the European Commission Günter Verheugen, the president of the European Court of Human Rights Jean-Paul Costa, the prime minister of Romania Călin Popescu-Tăriceanu, and others – ResRo demanded among other things the return of German property.[71] German property and heritage in Romania were right back at the centre of European politics.

All these restitution demands turned out to be unsuccessful. But the political agenda behind this petition left politicians in Romania and Germany feeling twitchy. The expellee revanchism of the Cold War period was, apparently, back, as similar movements among *Sudetendeutsche* and others revealed.[72] The enlargement of the EU in 2007 offered a final reckoning with a state that had dispossessed Romanian Germans and then sold them to Germany. On their website, ResRo featured a section

---

Wandel, soziale Probleme und soziale Sicherung in Südosteuropa (Munich: Südosteuropa-Gesellschaft, 2000), pp. 191–204.

[69] See Johann Lauer, 'Siebenbürger Sachsen – morgen', *Siebenbürger Sachsen – Gestern, Heute, Morgen: Von einer festen Burg zu einem offenen Club*, at www.siebenbuergersachsen.de/geschichte/index.htm (accessed 29 Jun. 2019), and *Arche Noah*, at www.sibiweb.de/arche (accessed 4 Jun. 2018).

[70] Katherine Verdery's classic study of the multicultural village Aurel Vlaicu (previously known as Binținți) detailed the tensions of property ownership and redistribution, though her focus was mainly on Romanian peasants despite a strong German presence. See Katherine Verdery, *Transylvanian Villagers: Three Centuries of Political, Economic, and Ethnic Change* (Berkeley: University of California Press, 1983).

[71] The full petition can be viewed in German at 'Petition', *ResRo*, at www.resro.eu/attachments/dok umente/petition_070424.pdf, or in Romanian at 'Petiție', *ResRo*, at www.resro.eu/attachments/do kumente/petitie_070424.pdf (both accessed 10 Dec. 2018).

[72] For an excellent historical explanation of the revanchist tensions between *Sudetendeutsche*, Czechs, and others from 1945 until the mid-2000s, see Christoph Cornelißen, Roman Holec and Jiří Pešek (eds.), *Diktatur – Krieg – Vertreibung: Erinnerungskulturen in Tschechien, der Slowakei und Deutschland seit 1945* (Essen: Klartext Verlag, 2005).

titled 'Successful Cases', which was removed because, 'at the moment, we have no reports of successful cases'.[73] Instead, ResRo published a double CD with twenty cases of historic injustices against ResRo members evidencing a 'betrayal of European values'.[74] As ResRo and other fund-raising organisations failed in their attempts, resentment at the status quo increased. The failure of a dozen Banat Swabians to reclaim their former farmlands was seen as a particularly pernicious court ruling.[75] The next step, the European Court of Justice, also failed to deliver the verdict many Romanian Germans had been hoping for. If Romanian Germans were meant to be bridge-builders, Werner Philippi wondered at the *Heimattag* of Transylvanian Saxons in Dinkelsbühl in June 2011, what kind of bridges were they building when the Romanian state refused restitution claims by frequently changing the laws on restitution to counter Romanian German demands?[76]

Anger at Romanian institutions had gradually reached its peak and began to wane. The moment for reckoning with the past had come and gone in the mid- to late 2000s. Romanian German demands for compensation and restitution were only one facet of a deeper confrontation with communism. While Romanian Germans were poring over the detail of their confiscated lands from the 1940s and 1950s, Romanian society more broadly faced very public attempts to condemn the communist past as a whole. When President Băsescu took office in 2004, he had vowed to face down the dark history of communism and its continuities into the present.[77] Two years later, in 2006 with the clock ticking on Romania's accession to the European Union, the political scientist Vladimir Tismăneanu penned the *Raport Final* (*Final Report*), which indicted a number of high-profile individuals, living and dead, for their criminal responsibility for the communist past.[78] The report triggered a series of fierce reactions and counter-reactions, but ultimately the intensity of the row died down.[79] The report had failed to bring the matter to a close in much the same way that Romanian Germans had been unable to undo the

---

[73] See *ResRo*, at www.resro.eu/f04.html (accessed 29 May 2015).

[74] *Die Restitutionsfalle: Fallbeispiele systematisch verhinderter Immobilienrückgabe in Rumänien*, CD (2015).

[75] Waltraut Eberle, 'Eigentumsrückgabe verweigert', *Siebenbürgische Zeitung* 58/12, 31 July 2008, p. 2.

[76] Werner Philippi, 'Brückenbau zu Menschen', *Siebenbürgische Zeitung* 61/11, 15 July 2011, p. 23.

[77] See Chapter 4.

[78] For a reflective book on the issue by Vladimir Tismăneanu himself, see Vladimir Tismăneanu and Marius Stan, *Romania Confronts Its Communist Past: Democracy, Memory, and Moral Justice* (Cambridge: Cambridge University Press, 2018).

[79] Ibid., pp. 112–29.

injustices of expropriation from the 1940s and 1950s. In the new European framework, though, the absence of a clear resolution of these issues seemed to matter less and less.

European Capitals

Bistriţa burnt on 11 June 2008. The Protestant parish church in the northern Transylvanian town lit up at 7.40 pm. The church spire and part of the nave were gutted by the fire. Just six months after new copper plates had been installed in the main spire and a month after the four turrets had been equipped with similar plates, the Saxon heritage of Bistritz lay in ruins.[80] For Horst Göbbel, the destruction of the church was the symbolic end of the Saxon community. What emigration from the Cold War had started was completed by the fire, namely the dissolution of the Romanian German community.

But all was not lost. Donation networks had woven the rump Romanian German community and its splendid heritage into a well-functioning safety net. Immediate calls for support from abroad were met with international solidarity, especially from émigrés invested in preserving the architecture they had left behind. The fire marked a crossroads of 'destruction and regeneration' for the German community in Romania.[81] Bishop Christoph Klein of the Lutheran Church in Romania appealed nationwide for support and solidarity.[82] The Romanian German *Leidensweg* continued in the twenty-first century, but this time the community was truly 'transnational [*grenzüberschreitend*]', a point the chairman of homeland society of Transylvanian Saxons in German, Bernd Fabritius, emphasised.[83] The catastrophe in Bistriţa did much to parade the international credentials of Romanian Germans. In solidarity with the local community, British artist Michael Sandle produced an ink drawing of the church on fire, which was reproduced in Romanian German newspapers.[84] Money was the decisive factor in rebuilding the church out of the ashes.

---

[80] See Alin Cordoş, 'Flăcările care au distrus turnul Bisericii Evanghelice au aşezat o perdea de linişte peste zgomotul campaniei electorale', *Mesagerul de Bistriţa-Năsăud*, 12 June 2008, at www .mesagerul.ro/index.php?id=id:00000042148 (accessed 17 Aug. 2018), and Horst Göbbel, 'Brand der Stadtpfarrkirche in Bistritz', *Siebenbürgische Zeitung Online*, 12 June 2008, at www .siebenbuerger.de/zeitung/artikel/rumaenien/7843-brand-der-stadtpfarrkirche-in-bistritz.html (accessed 17 Aug. 2018).

[81] Siegbert Bruss, 'Brandkatastrophe in Bistritz: Zerstörung und Wiederaufbau', *Siebenbürgische Zeitung* 58/10, 30 June 2008, pp. 1, 4.

[82] *Landeskirchliche Information* 19/12, 20 June 2008, pp. 1–8.

[83] Bruss, 'Brandkatastrophe in Bistritz', p. 4.   [84] See ibid.

Fundraising was orchestrated between Romania and Germany where the Heimat- und Ortsgemeinschaft Bistritz-Nösen (Home and Local Community) and the Siebenbürgisch-Sächsischer Kulturrat (Cultural Council) steered the main efforts with internet appeals, pamphlets, and circulars.[85] In January 2013 and 3.5 million euros later, the church in Bistritz unveiled its new spire as a confident incarnation of a 'sense of responsibility towards the homeland' and a new, poised Romanian German self-image.[86]

The rebuilding of German Bistritz was not an isolated case. At the turn of the new millennium, with fewer and fewer Germans around, German heritage became Romania's hot currency. Sibiu/Hermannstadt took centre stage when it became European capital of culture in 2007, along with its partner city, Luxembourg. Designated by the European Parliament in 2004, the joint project emphasised their common heritage and the bridge-building that such an East–West application would entail. The linguistic similarities between some Transylvanian Saxon dialects and Luxembourgish were showcased as the link that joined the two cities and regions together.[87]

Romanian German journalists and commentators were at pains to point out the 'unimagined energies' released by the European Capital of Culture.[88] Siegbert Bruss of the *Siebenbürgische Zeitung* stressed that the Transylvanian Saxon cultural contribution to Sibiu 2007 deserved a special mention as 'particularly impressive'.[89] Romanian Germans could now 'carry their heritage into the future with confidence', the headline in the *Siebenbürgische Zeitung* proclaimed as a first impression in the autumn of 2007.[90] The *Hermannstädter Zeitung*, one of the main German-language newspapers in Romania, launched a Sibiu 2007 campaign in 2006 in the lead-up to Romania's accession to the EU and Sibiu's elevation to European Capital of Culture.[91] The time was just

---

[85] See 'Brandgeschädigte Bistritzer Kirche benötigt Ihre Spende', *Siebenbürgische Zeitung* 58/11, 15 July 2008, p. 19.

[86] Holger Wermke, 'Verantwortung für Heimat gewachsen', *Siebenbürgische Zeitung* 63/1, 20 January 2013, pp. 1, 5.

[87] Although there is no single dialect of Saxon, it is still often referred to as Saxon, *Sächsisch*, as if there were one dialect. Luxembourgish has played a big role in the Transylvanian Saxon imaginary and long pre-dated the post-communist period; see, for instance, Karl Kurt Klein (ed.), *Luxemburg und Siebenbürgen* (Cologne: Böhlau, 1966).

[88] Siegbert Bruss, 'Hermannstadt setzt ungeahnte Energien frei', *Siebenbürgische Zeitung* 57/14, 20 September 2007, pp. 1, 9.

[89] Ibid.

[90] Ruxandra Stănescu, 'Das Erbe selbstbewusst in die Zukunft tragen', *Siebenbürgische Zeitung* 57/15, 30 September 2007, p. 1.

[91] Annina Braumann, *Kulturtourismus – Möglichkeiten der Imagemodifizierung am Beispiel der europäischen Kulturhauptstadt 2007: Sibiu/Hermannstadt* (Norderstedt: GRIN Verlag, 2007), pp. 14–16.

right to show off a German 'best of' in Sibiu and the region. Romanian Germans understood very well the opportunity Sibiu 2007 presented to them. They exhibited their community and heritage as a truly European and transnational bridge between East and West.

The European Parliament reciprocated by celebrating Sibiu's German heritage and community as a cornerstone of the theme of 'reaching beyond borders'.[92] 'Ethnic diversity' was key to the decision to award both cities the title of European Capital of Culture. EU commissioner Ján Figel played to the gallery in a speech in Sibiu in September 2007 by claiming that 'as the first East–West partners [. . .] Sibiu and Luxembourg have the honour of and responsibility for setting the standard'.[93] Romanian Germans gladly followed the standards set in the West, which went to the heart of their European *Selbstverständnis*. 'Transylvanian Saxons are a role model for the most enlightened nations', Otfried Kotzian began a speech in the Haus der Heimat in Nuremberg on 25 January 2007.[94] That Sibiu had to fulfil particular criteria and present an acceptable bid to the 'Selection Panel for the European Capital of Culture (ECOC) 2007' was a boon for Romanian Germans intent on emphasising their long-held views of cultural superiority.[95] It was clear that the success of the bid for European Capital of Culture was largely down to the Transylvanian Saxon heritage of the city, especially since Klaus Iohannis had been mayor of Sibiu since 2000. Romanian Germans were very much in control of the German narrative of Sibiu.

Saxon organisations and institutions such as the Demokratisches Forum der Deutschen in Rumänien, the Samuel von Brukenthal Museum and Gymnasium were central pillars for Sibiu 2007 and its image. Romanian Germans were quick to draw attention to the rich German history while distancing themselves from the Romanian, non-German sphere in Transylvania and Romania.[96] Sibiu was rebranded in a way that talked up its western credentials. Casa Rosie (the Red House) – a sixteenth-century

[92] 'Luxembourg and Sibiu: 2007 European Capitals of Culture', *European Parliament – Culture*, 25 January 2007.
[93] Beatrice Ungar, 'Ehre und Verantwortung: Hohe Gäste in der Kulturhauptstadt', *Hermannstädter Zeitung* 2047, 7 September 2007, p. 4.
[94] Horst Göbbel, 'Europäische zivilisatorische Leistung', *Siebenbürgische Zeitung* 57/3, 20 February 2007, p. 18.
[95] 'Report on the Nominations from Luxembourg and Romania for the European Capital of Culture 2007', *Selection Panel for the European Capital of Culture (ECOC) 2007*, at https://web.archive.org/web/20080904005053/http://ec.europa.eu/culture/pdf/doc670_en.pdf.
[96] See Martin Ohnweiler, 'Hermannstadt bereitet sich für 2007 bereits vor: Gespräch mit Marius Constantin, Projektkoordinator für die Veranstaltungen in der europäischen Kulturhauptstadt', *Deutsches Jahrbuch für Rumänien 2005* (Bucharest: ADZ Verlag, 2005), pp. 70–5.

building used as a hotel in central Sibiu – was renamed in the presence of members of the Luxembourgish royal family 'Casa Luxembourg'.[97] In the eyes of Romanian Germans, Sibiu was special, and Sibiu 2007 finally gave the recognition to the Europeanness they had pursued for the entire twentieth century. In the post-communist context, the coverage of Sibiu 2007 outshone all other debates over European integration.[98]

Romanian Germans, particularly visiting émigrés, basked in the limelight of European recognition. The phenomenon of so-called *Sommersachsen* – seasonal returnees in the summer – had already created a steady flow of Romanian Germans travelling back and forth between Germany and Romania. Sibiu 2007 multiplied the numbers of émigrés reaching back out to their former homeland. *Heimat- und Ortsgemeinden* and *Kreisgruppen* (local associations) in Germany organised tours for émigrés to visit Hermannstadt and indulge in *Heimat* nostalgia before returning to Germany. Adverts in the *Siebenbürgische Zeitung* and *Banater Post* revealed a dynamic German tourism attached to the phenomenon of Sibiu 2007.[99] Publications about Sibiu's illustrious German past, always with the imprint of the Sibiu 2007 logo, flourished in Germany and Romania.[100] To visitors in 2007, Sibiu, or at least the city centre, presented itself as beautiful, clean, and orderly. In contrast to previous years, there were no stray dogs, very few construction sites, and a plethora of signs in German, English, French, and Italian.[101] The Romanian Germans who visited Sibiu in the summer of 2007 immersed themselves in a picture-perfect city. As many Romanian German émigrés searched for an authentic experience of being back in Hermannstadt, they were also locked into

---

[97] See Pit Péporté et al., *Inventing Luxembourg: Representations of the Past, Space and Language from the Nineteenth to Twenty-First Century* (Leiden: Brill, 2010), pp. 311–12. Conversely, Sibiu gave Luxembourg the opportunity to present itself as a much greater European entity. A map of the Luxembourgish language today, which was part of an exhibition on Luxembourgish, highlighted Transylvania as part of a greater Luxembourgish sphere.

[98] Dragoş Dragoman, 'National Identity and Europeanization in Post-Communist Romania. The Meaning of Citizenship in Sibiu: European Capital of Culture 2007', *Communist and Post-Communist Studies* 41/1 (2008), pp. 69, 71–4.

[99] See, for instance, 'Reise nach Siebenbürgen 2007', *Siebenbürgische Zeitung* 57/3, 20 February 2007, p. 18, and 'Kultur- und Erlebnisreise: Siebenbürgen – Moldauklöster', *Siebenbürgische Zeitung* 57/5, 15 March 2007, p. 24.

[100] See, for instance, Ana Vasiu and Daniel Bălţat, *Sibiu/Hermannstadt entdecken* (Sibiu: Honterus, 2007), and Erika Schneider, Hansgeorg von Killyen and Eckbert Schneider (eds.), *Naturforscher in Hermannstadt: Vorläufer, Gründer und Förderer des Siebenbürgischen Vereins für Naturwissenschaften* (Sibiu: Honterus Verlag, 2007).

[101] See, for example, the commentary on Sibiu's new look in 'Hermannstadt putzt sich heraus', *Transylvania Travel* 8 (2004), at www.transylvaniatravel.net/newsletter/news8_2004.html (accessed 13 Jun. 2018).

a highly commercialised world of organised trips, excursions, and events.[102] They dined at tourist hotspots such as the Crama Sibiul Vechi, an established restaurant in the city centre, and basked in the sun on the veranda of Casa Luxembourg. From the 1st to the 8th of August 2007, visitors to Sibiu were invited to the *Siebenbürgisch-sächsische Kulturwoche*, a week of cultural Transylvanian Saxon festivities. Here, they could watch topical films, explore the Saxon villages and beautiful surroundings of Sibiu, and watch vernacular Saxon plays. As a highlight – and depending on which side they felt more sympathy for – they could either listen to Eginald Schlattner read from his work on the Thursday or hear Hans Bergel introduce his work on the Sunday, followed by a screening of the film *Die Russen Kommen* (*The Russians Are Coming*).[103] Romanian German visitors from Germany transformed into amused tourists who, at the same time, were aware of the importance of this moment of glory for the homeland they had left behind.

Sibiu was still thoroughly German, or so it seemed. The mayor of Sibiu, Klaus Johannis – who adjusted his name to a more Romanian spelling, Iohannis – became the central figure of Sibiu 2007. His presence and his speeches wooed a European public into believing the fairytale of medieval Hermannstadt. Romanian German émigrés were enthralled by his arrival on the political scene. Here was a potential saviour of Romania's German heritage who was on a mission to revitalise German culture in Romania and bring Romanian Germans – the large number of émigrés and the few who had stayed behind – closer together again.[104] His Saxon background had deeply shaped him and his career, Iohannis explained to a leading question from Friedrich Roth in the *Siebenbürgische Zeitung* in September 2007.[105] Sibiu 2007 allowed Iohannis, who was often reluctant to indulge in too much philo-Germanism, to dabble in a bit of German medieval nostalgia. In a speech given just before the launch of Sibiu 2007, Iohannis repeated the by now familiar trope of Saxons under siege but with a twist for a twenty-first century audience. He explained:

---

[102] The list of venues indicates this and also highlights how almost all of the focus was directed at central Sibiu. For details, see 'Infrastructure', *Sibiu 2007*, at https://web.archive.org/web/2007041 1082434/http://www.sibiu2007.ro/en2/infrastructura.htm (accessed 2 Jun. 2019). For details on organised tours to Sibiu from Germany, see, for instance, *Transylvania Travel*, at www .transylvaniatravel.net/reisen/staedteurlaub/reise309.html (accessed 24 Sep. 2018).

[103] The programme of the *Siebenbürgisch-sächsische Kulturwoche* was printed in the *Siebenbürgische Zeitung* for émigrés. See 'Siebenbürgisch-sächsische Kulturwoche in Hermannstadt', *Siebenbürgische Zeitung* 57/12, 31 July 2007, p. 5.

[104] See, for example, Friedrich Roth, 'Der Stadt zu europäischem Ansehen verholfen: Bürgermeister Klaus Johannis zur aktuellen Entwicklung Hermannstadts', *Siebenbürgische Zeitung* 57/15, 30 September 2007, p. 2.

[105] Ibid. and http://sibiu2007.giftmusic.de/sibiu2007.html.

For hundreds of years the fortified town of Sibiu/Hermannstadt lay in the path of medieval invasions, conflicts, and wars.

That is why in those troubled centuries the town first greeted the strangers who arrived here with cold defensive walls and closed gates. A legend says that eight centuries ago the founders of the town drew the outer limits of the settlement with two swords.

These weapons can be seen now only on the town's historic coat of arms. The swords of the Middle Ages fell into oblivion long time ago, and the town opened its gates to the world and became home to people of many cultures, speaking different languages, and practising different forms of religious life. Sibiu/Hermannstadt with its different ethnic communities developed a unique multicultural life.

The people of Sibiu are warm and hospitable. They welcome visitors with open arms, whether they come on business or as tourists looking for the rich experience at the contact with our cultural heritage, or in search of fun, sports, or nature [*sic*].[106]

Leonard Orban, the European commissioner responsible for multilingualism in Europe, echoed Iohannis's remarks. Speaking at 'Lucian Blaga' University in Sibiu on 1 June 2007, Orban enthused that 'Sibiu is one of the places where cultural interchange has given rise to an impressively polyglot environment.'[107] Sibiu really was the ideal European.

Sibiu 2007 was a multicultural place under the leadership of one of the last remaining Saxons. As the former head of the Samuel von Brukenthal Gymnasium, Iohannis had gained public prominence, and it was his German background that gave him much authority in the political realm of post-communist Romania. If a German could not sort out the political chaos and widespread corruption, then who could? He became mayor of Sibiu in 2000 as a member of the Demokratisches Forum der Deutschen in Rumänien (Democratic Forum of Germans in Romania, DFDR), which he also led as party chairman from 2002 to 2013. His support base went well beyond the dwindling and ageing German population of Sibiu. He enjoyed the support of 70 to 90 per cent of his fellow citizens of Sibiu. What followed was a failed candidacy for the prime minister of Romania in 2009, his switch from the DFDR to the PNL (Partidul Naţional Liberal, the National Liberal Party) in 2013, and, finally, his successful candidacy for the presidency of Romania one year later in 2014, when he also became leader of the PNL. Iohannis ran on an anticorruption and pro-western ticket, and his success, certainly due to his political talent, was also drawn

[106] Klaus Iohannis, 'Welcome of the Sibiu Mayor Klaus Johannis', 15 October 2006.
[107] Leonard Orban, 'The European Union and New Member States' Contribution to Its Future', Speech/07/351, *European Commission Press Release*.

from the widespread view in Romania that a German could get things done.

Romanians transformed the disappearing Romanian German community and its legacy into an asset for Romania's political future, as Cristian Cercel has demonstrated in his work on philo-Germanism in Romania.[108] If their presence had been a problem throughout the twentieth century, their absence in the twenty-first century was an added bonus. As much as Romanian Germans émigrés felt vindicated by the recognition that Sibiu 2007 received, they had little control over any of it. Decisions taken at the highest levels set the tone for the year-long event. The Office of Cultural and National Patrimony (OPCN) gave an overly disproportionate level of financial support to sites in Sibiu that boasted a Saxon heritage.[109] The overall public relations campaign was a carefully co-ordinated German–Romanian enterprise,[110] involving the Romanian government and a German PR company. As part of the PR campaign, the Romanian Ministry of Culture and Arts commissioned a promotional video for Sibiu 2007, which was then broadcast on a number of channels including National Geographic.[111] An internationally known PR company, Scholz & Friends Group, took charge of the video; it was directed by Bogdan Albu and edited by Andrei Nica.[112] Sibiu 2007, as the video demonstrated, became very much a German affair.

The video ran for two minutes and eighteen seconds, long enough to 'westernise' Romania and emphasise the quintessential Europeanness of Sibiu 2007. Only a couple of fleeting images of Romanian heritage flashed onto the screen.[113] The main protagonist of the video, a young woman

[108] See Cristian Cercel, 'Philo-Germanism without Germans in Romania after 1989', *East European Politics and Societies and Cultures* 29/4 (2015), pp. 811–30, and Cristian Cercel, *Romania and the Quest for European Identity: Philo-Germanism without Germans* (London: Routledge, 2018).
[109] This is discussed in more detail in a study on the built environment of Brașov/Kronstadt since the mass emigration by Germans in the 1980s and 1990s. See Joseph J. Gallagher and Philip N. J. Tucker, 'Aussiedler Migration and Its Impact on Brașov's Ethnic German Population and Built Environment', *GeoJournal* 50/2 & 3 (2000), pp. 305–9. See also Alina Hughes, 'Will There Be Conflict? Identity and Values Tensions in Transylvania's Saxon Villages', *Europolis* 4 (2008), pp. 309–28.
[110] That is, German and Romanian co-operation.
[111] Braumann, *Kulturtourismus*, pp. 15, 16, and email correspondence with Andrei Nica, post-producer of the promotional video *Sibiu 2007*, 28 June 2008.
[112] Email correspondence with Andrei Nica. See also Braumann, *Kulturtourismus*, pp. 15, 16, *Sendal*, at www.sendal.ro/ (accessed 2 Jul. 2018), and *Scholz & Friends Group*, at www.s-f.com/ (accessed 13 Jun. 2018).
[113] See *Sibiu 2007 – Promotional Video*, dir. Andrei Nica (2007), at www.youtube.com/watch?v=otJHWO8WC-E (accessed 22 Jul. 2021).

wearing a hoodie, wanders through a series of scenes, taking in the flair of Sibiu. Flashing images of non-Orthodox Christian and humanist images intersperse her journey through the highlights of the city's history. Leonardo da Vinci's 'Vitruvian Man' makes a brief appearance. She peers into a side room to glimpse at medieval-looking Romanian ironmongers, perhaps as a reminder of the slavery that existed in this metier until the mid-nineteenth century. The founding date of Sibiu, 1191, appears repeatedly on the screen, a date which is linked only to the early German settlers (Figure 5.2). Towards the end of the short film, our guide through the dark corridors of the past opens up a set of doors to reveal Sibiu today: a beautiful medieval town in a modern world.

If the *Kirchenburgen* had once been the ultimate symbol of a German presence in the region under siege, German architecture now represented a European spirit of togetherness and progress. Church fortresses embodied a vanishing culture and community that everyone – Romanians, Germans, Romanian Germans, Europeans – seemed to miss. Tourist and travel companies were all too aware of the power of Saxon church fortresses for luring visitors to Romania. German heritage was useful for selling Romania as a destination, but occasionally the pitch was slightly misjudged. An advert in the *Siebenbürgische Zeitung* from 2007 for the Romanian tour company *Rumänien Tourismus* joked: 'Our church spires are the only ones still

Figure 5.2 Still from promotional video for Sibiu 2007 displaying the year 1191.

DIE EINZIGEN, DIE BEI UNS NOCH STRAMM STEHEN
– UNSERE KIRCHTÜRME –
SEHENSWERT: URLAUBSLAND RUMÄNIEN
RoMania
WWW.RUMAENIEN-TOURISMUS.DE

Figure 5.3 Advert for Rumänien Tourismus, a company that promoted Romania as
a tourist destination, especially in the German-speaking world.

standing to attention' (Figure 5.3).[114] Romanian Germans could never quite escape their Nazi past.

But Sibiu 2007 meant more than just a great Romanian German show. It was intended to mean something to all Romanians. In this way, the collaborative efforts of Klaus Iohannis, mayor of Sibiu, the Romanian Ministry of Culture and Arts, the County Council of Sibiu and the NGO Asociația Sibiu Capitală Europeană 2007 (Association of the European Capital of Culture Sibiu 2007) for producing the events surrounding Sibiu 2007 also came to represent a great Romanian summer. President Traian Băsescu and the European Commission were both strongly supportive and emotionally attached to Sibiu 2007, which aimed to 'raise the international profile of the city [and] change [its] image'.[115] Important cultural institutions in the city such as the ethnographic Astra Museum (Complexul National Muzeal Astra) featured alongside the main German attractions.[116] Sibiu 2007 was a perfect combination of German heritage and the Romanian present, as the official history of Sibiu 2007 explained:

> Known in German as Hermannstadt, Sibiu has always been the centre of Romania's German minority since medieval times. Even today, it contains Romania's largest German community, and, due to initiatives by the local government, the Germanic feel of the area has been maintained. Sibiu also has a significant Hungarian minority, remnants of Transylvania's past as part of the Hungarian Empire and, later, Austria-Hungary. Despite this, Sibiu is also distinctly Romanian (95 per cent of the population are ethnic Romanians) and manages to fuse these three cultures, as well as smaller minorities of Roma, Slovaks and Ukrainians, into a city that is as wonderful as it is vibrant.

[114] Sorana Scholters, 'Weg mit den Klischees! Imagekampagne präsentiert das neue Urlaubsland Rumänien', *Siebenbürgische Zeitung* 57/4, 15 March 2007, p. 2.
[115] Braumann, *Kulturtourismus*, p. 15.
[116] See *Complexul National Muzeal Astra*, at www.muzeulastra.ro/ (accessed 17 Aug. 2018).

According to legend, the lost children of Hamelin emerged from the 'Almasch' (Varghis) cave into Transylvania – somewhere close to Sibiu. This is the 'Romantic' explanation for what was for many centuries a strange phenomenon: the presence of blond-haired, blue-eyed, German-speakers following ancient customs, yet isolated from Germany by hundreds of miles.[117]

Beyond the hype of Sibiu 2007, though, a sense of an ending still hung over their former homeland. After the rapid emigration of Germans from Romania, many churches and church fortresses began to fall into disrepair.[118] And the people seemed to be dying, too. By the early 2000s, Romanian German newspapers ran obituaries over eight to ten pages.[119] Elsewhere, articles gave evidence of the derelict state of their former towns and villages. Ioana Vlasiu, an art historian, regretted the parlous state of Saxon villages. In her review of Peter Jacobi's book of photographs of Transylvania's dilapidated Saxon fortresses, she drew parallels between the decaying Saxon architecture and Brâncuşi's modernist sculpture. Fundamentally, though, Vlasiu felt, while digesting the visual material from Jacobi's book, as if she was being led through the British Museum's collection of Egyptian sarcophaguses.[120] Romanian German communities were quickly becoming curious relics of a bygone era, it seemed. If the fire in the church in Bistriţa generated an international flurry of interest in the region, then the demise of other, smaller German towns and villages was left unseen by the international public eye.

Multicultural Imaginings

In fact, the German past in Romania did catch the international gaze. Out of the remains of a Cold War book-smuggling network emerged the Mihai Eminescu Trust, an organisation devoted to the restoration of Saxon villages in Transylvania that had fallen into disrepair or been abandoned.[121] Jessica

---

[117] Taken from *Sibiu 2007*, at www.sibiu2007.ro/en3/sibiu.htm (accessed 12 Sep. 2017). The provenance of this passage is unclear. It appears on several websites including *Beyond the Forest*, a holiday website that promotes the efforts of the *Mihai Eminescu Trust*. See 'Saxon Transylvania "Siebenbürgen"', *Beyond the Forest*, at www.beyondtheforest.com/Romania/SX5.html (accessed 19 Jun. 2019).

[118] See, for example, Ioana Vlasiu, '" … denn es will Abend werden": Peter Jacobis siebenbürgische Wallfahrt / Vom Verfall bedrohte Kirchen fotografiert', *Siebenbürgische Zeitung* 57/12, 31 July 2007, p. 4, and Hans Kremer, 'Verlorene Heimat wiedergesehen', *Siebenbürgische Zeitung* 53/14, 15 September 2003, p. 21.

[119] See, for instance, 'Obituaries', *Siebenbürgische Zeitung* 53/14, 15 September 2003, pp. 23–32.

[120] Vlasiu, ' … denn es will Abend werden'.

[121] The trust is named after Mihai Eminescu (1850–89), who is considered one of the great national poets of Romania. He is also a controversial figure, not least for his latent antisemitism.

Douglas-Home, the founder of the trust, had moved in dissident and book-smuggling circles in the 1980s. Among them were Charles Douglas-Home, her husband and foreign editor of *The Times* from 1978 until his death in 1985, the historians Noel Malcolm and Harold James, and the philosopher Roger Scruton.[122] But it was Jessica Douglas-Home who fell in love with remote Saxon villages after the collapse of communism. Travelling around Transylvania in the summer of 1993, Douglas-Home felt that 'a spell had been cast' on her travel companions and herself.[123] Having been deprived of her calling to help dissidents across the Iron Curtain, Douglas-Home understood her interest in abandoned Saxon villages as part of her obligation to preserve a truly European culture.[124]

Jessica Douglas-Home's Anglo-Saxon fantasy was part of a longer tradition of a British gaze on German culture in Transylvania. Charles Boner, a pioneering self-made ethnographer of Transylvania, had made the region known to a British audience through his travels in 1863 and subsequent book, *Transylvania; Its Products and Its People*, in 1865.[125] This was the tradition that Douglas-Home and others followed. William Blacker, a cousin of the British parliamentarian and peer Zac Goldsmith, absconded to Transylvanian Saxon villages in the early 1990s and accidentally married two Romani woman.[126] German culture and heritage meant something to the new British observers. Once the Mihai Eminescu Trust got going, it began transforming the landscape of Transylvania. Local surveyors on the ground, including the very politically engaged Romanian German Caroline Fernolend from Viscri in Transylvania, selected individual villages as 'cases' for a panel in the UK to consider. The panel consisted of Jessica Douglas-Home, the architect Jeremy Amos, Prince Charles, and others. More remote and dilapidated villages attracted a particular interest. Villages such as Mălâncrav/Malmkroog, Viscri/Deutsch-Weißkirch, and Florești – a village with little significance to the

[122] For a broader history of book-smuggling and *tamizdat* and *samizdat* publications, see Fredericke Kind-Kovács, *Written Here, Published There: How Underground Crossed the Iron Curtain* (Budapest: CEU Press, 2014), and Alfred A. Reisch, *Hot Books in the Cold War: The West's CIA-Funded Secret Book Distribution Program Behind the Iron Curtain* (Budapest: CEU Press, 2013).
[123] Jessica Douglas-Home, 'The Origins of the Trust', *Mihai Eminescu Trust*, at www .mihaieminescutrust.org/about-us#origins (accessed 18 Jun. 2019).
[124] She explains her intellectual transition from book-smuggling to village conservation in her autobiography. See Jessica Douglas-Home, *Once Upon Another Time* (Norwich: Michael Russell Publishers, 2000).
[125] See Charles Boner, *Transylvania; Its Products and Its People* (London: Longmans, Green, Reader, and Dyer, 1865).
[126] William Blacker, *Along the Enchanted Way: A Romanian Story* (London: John Murray, 2009).

Romanian German community – benefited immensely from the new international attention. In Mălâncrav, the Mihai Eminescu Trust restored both the fortified castle and the Apafi Manor House, which stood as a symbol of the serfdom the local Saxon population had endured until the nineteenth century under the Apafi family.[127] In Florești, the trust rebuilt the local Lutheran church, but without much purpose since there was no one there left to use it. Viscri, though, became the true flagship project for the trust. They transformed the village into a pristine copy of an early modern Transylvanian Saxon village in which local Roma were retrained in basket weaving and similar skills. The German cultural heritage became a showcase for successful sustainable tourism.

Meanwhile, Caroline Fernolend, Jessica Douglas-Home, and others continued to travel around Europe to raise awareness of their project. Douglas-Home enthused about the Saxon villages as 'a visual record of rural Europe with all its ancient richness and beauty intact'.[128] In fact, the villages were 'a microcosm of pre-industrial England'.[129] Fernolend toured Europe to explain the incredible work this British enterprise had undertaken. In a public lecture in Düsseldorf in September 2011, she reflected on 'twelve years of effort for a sustainable development of village life'.[130] The impact of the trust was significant and seemed to breathe new life into the dwindling Romanian German communities in Romania. The success also fulfilled two crucial functions beyond restoration and sustainable tourism: British luminaries could indulge their rural fantasies while Romanian Germans were placed at the centre of European debates on sustainability. Even more, they now moved in royal circles. On a tour around Sibiu and its surroundings, a group of Romanian German visitors from Germany caught up with Fernolend, a '*confidante* [*Intima*] of Prince Charles', as the author of the corresponding article was keen to stress.[131]

Preserving and reconstructing the shards of the past became one of the central ways to express Romanian German belonging in the twenty-first century. The Mihai Eminescu Trust emerged as one of the main conduits for Romanian German identity. When the 'Wusch' – a narrow-gauge railway that had connected Sibiu and Agnita in southern Transylvania

---

[127] As it was one of the few Saxon villages in Transylvania, the local population did not enjoy the same rights as other Transylvanian Saxons.
[128] Douglas-Home, 'Origins of the Trust'.
[129] 'Old Frau Fernolend's House', *Mihai Eminescu Trust*, at www.mihaieminescutrust.org/viscri (accessed 19 Jun. 2019).
[130] 'Vortrag Caroline Fernolend', *Siebenbürgische Zeitung* 61/14, 15 September 2011, p. 5.
[131] Kurt Thomas Ziegler, 'Huetplatztreffen mit nachfolgender Rundreise', *Siebenbürgische Zeitung* 68/12, 25 July 2018, p. 11.

from 1898 until its closure in 2001 – captured the imagination of local activists from the 2000s onwards, it was the Mihai Eminescu Trust that supported efforts to reopen the line. The Asociația Prietenii Mocăniței (Friends of the Narrow-Gauge Railway) worked tirelessly with the trust to save the railway line and work towards a reopening of it, albeit with limited success.[132]

Projects such as the 'Wusch' were part of a larger development among Romanian Germans and Romanians in the post-communist period. Immediately after the mass exodus of Romanian Germans at the end of the communist period, the Banat Swabian *Landsmannschaft* scrambled to salvage Swabian *Volkskultur* left behind in Romania. Tools, furniture, household items, and other objects were 'repatriated' to Germany.[133] Transylvania also attracted the attention of conservation efforts. The Saxonia Stiftung (Saxonia Trust) had been set up in Brașov as early as 1992 with the help of émigré money from the Sozialwerk der Siebenbürger Sachsen in Munich to maintain the dwindling German community in Transylvania somehow.[134] Pro Patrimonio, the national trust of Romania, was established a few years later in 2000. It seemed as if everyone in Romania in the new millennium was fleeing into the past. Therefore, Romania's prospect of acceding to the EU was largely accepted as a positive process by Romanian Germans, since it opened up possibilities for preserving forgotten Romanian German centres such as Biertan/Birthälm in central Transylvania.[135] The upkeep of fortified Saxon churches was met with approval from émigré associations that otherwise might have taken a dim view of welcoming Romania into the European Union.[136] For Romanian German émigrés, their exodus from Romania generated feelings of regret at having abandoned their home-land as well as a sense of opportunity for participating afresh in the social and cultural life in Transylvania and the Banat. A spate of projects emerged attempting to bring émigrés closer to their former

---

[132] Its website reveals a great deal about their nostalgia for a German past. See 'Sibiu-Agnita Railway', at www.sibiuagnitarailway.com/index.php (accessed 18 Jun. 2019). See also Ortwin Bonfert, 'Hoffen auf die "Wusch" und Revitalisierung des Harbachtales', *Siebenbürgische Zeitung* 65/8, 20 May 2015, p. 4.

[133] 'Banater Kulturarbeit im letzten Jahrzehnt', p. 113.

[134] See its website *Fundatia Saxonia*, at https://fundatia.saxonia.ro/home/ (accessed 20 Jun. 2019).

[135] See Alexandra Muresan, 'The Fortified Church of Biertan (Transylvania)', in Myra Shackley (ed.), *Visitor Management: Case Studies from World Heritage Sites* (Burlington, Mass.: Butterworth-Heinemann, 1998), pp. 26–45. In this essay, the author illustrates the importance of European (and UNESCO) funds for the maintenance of the fortified church in Biertan/Birthälm in central Transylvania.

[136] See ibid.

homeland.[137] If *Sachsen* and *Schwaben* had initially concentrated on *Zerfall* (decay), thereby emphasising a severing of links with their former homeland, Romanian German organisations shifted their focus in the new millennium towards *Erhaltung* (preservation).[138]

Romanian German efforts alone could not have been enough to propel their heritage into a central concern within Romania. Of course, the Mihai Eminescu Trust was crucial in supporting Romanian German endeavours to revitalise a world they had left behind. But the trust's efforts concerned mainly the rural world of central and southern Transylvania. For the multicultural centres of the Banat, renewed Romanian German interest in Romania coincided neatly with developments within Romania that sought to highlight its colourful and diverse past and present.

The city of Timișoara and the region of the Banat more broadly was transformed in the post-communist period into a symbol of Romania's multiculturalism. Yet this development did not emerge from nowhere. Already towards the end of the Cold War, as the number of German émigrés from the Banat to Germany grew steadily, a sense of loss for a supposedly harmonious past appeared in Romanian German literature. Banat Swabian émigrés in particular reinvented their former homeland as a multicultural and cosmopolitan region. Disappointed by their experiences in West Germany, the émigrés embarked upon a wholesale reimagining of the past. Publications with small print runs, such as local histories and fiction written by Banat Swabians, began emphasising the diversity of the region.[139] The first fractures in Romanian German identities emanated from an emerging Banat regional identity in the late Cold War period. Depictions of a multicultural past filtered through to non-émigrés and, crucially, to Romanians, too. In a joint Romanian and German local history of the town of Arad Nou and its German school, published in 2001, the authors regaled their readers with tales of 'the hustle and bustle [*buntes Treiben*]' and the 'growing exchange in economic and cultural terms

---

[137] For examples of such recent attempts at building bridges between Germany and Romania, see, for instance, Hans-Gerald Binder, 'Bindungen zu Siebenbürgen gefestigt', *Siebenbürgische Zeitung* 57/15, 30 September 2007, p. 5.

[138] The most important actors here were the *Heimatortsgemeinschaften* (hometown communities) or *Hog* for short.

[139] See, for instance, Georg Hromadka, *Kleine Chronik des Banater Berglands* (Munich: Südostdeutsches Kulturwerk, 1998), Stefan Heinz-Kehrer, *Lehrerwahl in Traunhofen – Erzählung* (Munich, 1998), Otto Greffner and Mario Stoica, *275 de ani de învățământ în limba germană în Aradul Nou – 275 Jahre deutschsprachige Schule in Neuarad* (Arad, 2001), and Annemarie Podlipny-Hehn, *Wir waren Zeugen: Temeswar 1989/90* (Munich: Verlag Südostdeutsches Kulturwerk, 1991).

between the populations' of the past.[140] They quoted at length the local Swabian historian Anton Valentin (1898–1967), who had celebrated the 'colourful picture' of the ethnic diversity at the local markets around Arad Nou in the early twentieth century.[141] 'The Romanian, the Serbian, the Hungarian, and the Bulgarian [languages]' created a sense of diversity, Valentin continued, which 'reflected the colourful mishmash of peoples [*das bunte Völkergemisch*] of the old monarchy. They lived in peaceful coexistence and traded their produce in their own language.'[142] For the authors of the local history, this proved that the population of Arad Nou had lived 'in complete harmony and friendship'.[143] Habsburg nostalgia served as a powerful antidote to Romanian Germanness.

For the city of Timişoara, accentuating its multicultural history was an even simpler task. Under the 'western gaze', travel guides to the city in English and German in the new millennium reproduced narratives of diversity. Timişoara proudly proclaimed itself to be 'Romania's most cosmopolitan city' and the 'El Dorado of multiculturalism', and its image fitted in with a broader trend in Romanian politics and society to present the country as a positive and perhaps even 'western' place.[144] Timişoara was also proudly central European. Unlike Sibiu, where German heritage was the sole carrier of its twenty-first century revival, Timişoara's German heritage played an important and co-operative role in combination with the Hungarian, Romanian, and Serbian communities. Events such as *Timişoara, Open Art City* placed the German National Theatre as one of the more prominent and decidedly central European institutions at the heart of the city's cultural life. The long-standing mayor of Timişoara, Gheorghe Ciuhandu, was at pains to emphasise the city's diverse landscape: 'Timişoara has many identities [*Timişoara are mulţi identităţi*]', he announced in 2009.[145] Tourists in the 2000s were invited

[140] Greffner and Stoica, *275 de ani de învăţământ în limba germană în Aradul Nou*, p. 145.
[141] Anton Valentin (1898–1967) was a local historian from the Banat who was also the editor of the *Banater Monatshefte*, a journal dedicated to all things Swabian; he published local histories both under his own name and through the journal. See Hans Diplich, 'Anton Valentin und die *Banater Monatshefte*', in Georg Wildmann (ed.), *Donauschwaben – Entwicklung und Erbe des donauschwäbischen Volksstammes: Festschrift für Josef Volkmar Senz zum 70. Geburtstag* (Munich, 1982), pp. 221–9. See also Greffner and Stoica, *275 de ani de învăţământ în limba germană în Aradul Nou*, p. 146.
[142] Greffner and Stoica, *275 de ani de învăţământ în limba germană în Aradul Nou*, p. 147.
[143] Ibid.
[144] Aziliz Gouez, 'Introduction', *European Works*, p. 7, at https://institutdelors.eu/wp-content/uploads/2018/01/european_works_-_internet_version.pdf (accessed 29 Jun. 2019).
[145] Gheorghe Ciuhandu, 'Cuvânt de bun venit', *Timişoara, Open Art City* (promotional material in author's possession), p. 3.

by the tourist board to visit 'Little Vienna', linking the city more to its German and Austrian connections than to the rest of Romania. Promotional material for tourism featured the city's secessionist architecture at the top of the list of things to see, and only then was the city advertised as the site of the revolution in December 1989. As part of its charm offensive to welcome visitors to Timișoara, the tourist board – Infocentrul Touristic Timișoara – in 2009 produced travel guides, pamphlets, and even a CD in Romanian, English, and German, walking viewers through the city's highlights.[146] German sites, such as the Adam-Müller-Guttenbrunn-Haus and the Banat Village Museum with its strong focus on Swabian peasants, formed the backbone of a 'must-see' inventory in Timișoara.[147] Only then did the heritage of the once sizeable Serbian and Jewish communities make an appearance in PR material, while the Roma received no attention at all.[148] New economic connections to northern Italy, forged in the post-communist period, and a growing Italian community in Timișoara further emphasised the city's European credentials. The old Habsburg Lands found themselves reunited, casting Timișoara as the trendy and cosmopolitan city of 'Trevisoara', a portmanteau name combining Timișoara and Treviso.[149]

Regions with German heritage served well the demands within Romania to prove how European it was. Institutions such as the Economic Development Agency in Timiş county advertised the region and its German influence in the 2000s as 'Romania's "Gateway to Europe"'.[150] Romanian Germans' self-understanding of acting as a bridge between the two Europes of East and West came full circle to fulfil the needs of Romanians to appear quintessentially western and European. If these multicultural imaginings by Romanians and Romanian Germans seemed to overlap, there were still subtle and important differences between their ideas of multiculturalism: for Romanian German émigrés, the German cultural heritage in Romania compensated for narratives of abandonment; for Romanian German non-émigrés it helped articulate their continuing differences with Romanians; and for Romanians, German heritage allowed them to show Romania's 'western face'.[151]

---

[146] *Timișoara: 360° Virtual Tour*, CD (Timișoara: Banat Media, 2009).   [147] Ibid.

[148] For a more detailed examination of Timișoara as a multicultural city, see James Koranyi, 'Reinventing the Banat: Cosmopolitanism as a German Cultural Export', *German Politics and Society* 29/3 (2011), pp. 97–114.

[149] Gouez, 'Introduction', p. 6.

[150] See Vasile Docea, *Relații româno-germane timpurii* (Cluj-Napoca: Presa Universitară Clujeană, 2000).

[151] See Cercel, *Romania and the Quest for European Identity*.

European Voices

Didi Danquart's film *Offset* from 2006 tells the tragi-comic love story of a German engineer, Stefan, and a Romanian secretary, Brânduşa, played by Alexandra Maria Lara.[152] As preparations for their Bucharest wedding get underway, Stefan's family arrive from Germany and meet Brânduşa's father. Over an awkward dinner at the father's flat, the parents of the bride and groom try to hold a conversation but ultimately fail to do so. The language barrier and seemingly irreconcilable cultural differences turn the evening into a disaster. At one point, Brânduşa's father explains enthusiastically that Mihai Eminescu is Romania's great national poet, and in reaction a family friend of Stefan's family raises concerns about Romania's economic and political readiness for joining the EU.

Romanian Germans found themselves similarly caught between two contradictory debates as they reinvented themselves as European bridge-builders. Their emphasis on their culture and heritage in Romania as the new centre of Europe came up against their insistence on questioning how economically and politically ready Romania was. More confusingly, political developments after 1989 and much of the rhetoric coming from the EU seemed irreconcilable with some voices within the Romanian German community that were sceptical of EU enlargement. The EU appeared to be pulling in precisely the opposite direction to Romanian German history: eastward expansion rather than westward flight.

At times, this mismatch in narratives was plain to see. While the European Union was celebrating fifty years of being 'Together Since 1957' in 2007, Romanian Germans were still dealing with the sixtieth anniversary of the deportations of Romanian Germans to the Soviet Union.[153] Clashes such as these were real obstacles for Romanian German enthusiasm towards the EU's political direction. At the *Heimattag der Siebenbürger Sachsen* (Homeland Day of Transylvanian Saxons) in 2005, the commissioner for the Federal Republic of Germany

---

[152] *Offset*, dir. Didi Danquart (2006). Alexandra Lara Maria was born into a Romanian family in Romania, but grew up in Germany: a Romanian German of a different kind.

[153] The contrasts between these two histories are illustrated in two images commemorating both events within the space of two years of each other. The first is that of a smiling child in front of a birthday cake celebrating fifty years of European integration. See 'Together since 1957', at http://europa.eu /abc/symbols/9-may/gallery/2007/index_en.htm (accessed 24 Jun. 2016). The second image is that of a deportee behind barbed wire commemorating sixty years since the deportations of Germans from Romania to the Soviet Union. See '60 ani de la începutul deportării germanilor în fosta Uniune Sovietică / 60 Jahre seit dem Beginn der Russlanddeportation der Rumäniendeutschen' (Reşiţa, 2005), at www.jahrmarkt-banat.de/Russland2013.html (accessed 29 Jun. 2019).

for Issues concerning German Resettlers and National Minorities (Beauftragter der Bundesregierung für Aussiedlerfragen und nationale Minderheiten), Hans-Peter Kemper, highlighted the obvious difficulties Romanian Germans faced when trying to make sense of two contrasting histories.[154] Romanian Germans, Kemper acknowledged, have been confronted with the conundrum of living up to the motto of the *Heimattag* 2005, namely 'Overcoming lows, building bridges [*Tiefen überstehen, Brücken bauen*]'. Their aim of becoming European bridge-builders was a particularly challenging and arduous task in light of 'flight, expulsion, emigration, and integration', which had still not been adequately addressed in the twenty-first century.[155]

Though Europeanisation opened up a useful conduit through which to communicate victim stories, Romanian Germans remade their role in Europe by the mid-2000s as an independent channel from the EU to tell a pan-European history. As this chapter has argued, Romanian Germans benefited from the attention they received from various quarters in Europe: well beyond Romania and Germany, the Romanian German world attracted the fantasies of British money, trying to rebuild an Anglo-Saxon arcadia in the twenty-first century. Meanwhile, Romanian politicians understood the cultural and political value of the Romanian German heritage, and Germans liked the new conciliatory, European tone this German minority had adopted. Romanian Germans sensed, perhaps correctly, that they were more believable as Europeans than were memory activists in the Baltics, Poland, or Hungary who, keen to highlight the dark history of communism, were often unfairly derided as proto-fascists.[156] As Volker Eduard Dürr, chairman of the Landsmannschaft der Siebenbürger Sachsen, reminded them, Germans from Romania had a special responsibility as 'a living link [*ein lebendiges Bindeglied*] between the two continents [eastern and western Europe] [*sic*]'.[157] In their efforts to place stories of flight and deportation and of dispossession under the communists at the heart of a new European identity, Romanian Germans came to regard themselves once again as true Europeans who were able to navigate a number of disparate histories

---

[154] Hans-Peter Kemper, 'Mitbauen am geeinten Europa', *Siebenbürgische Zeitung* 55/8, 31 May 2005, pp. 3, 4.

[155] Ibid., p. 3.

[156] For a substantial overview of this, see James Mark, *The Unfinished Revolution: Making Sense of the Communist Past in Central-Eastern Europe* (New Haven: Yale University Press, 2010). See also Chapter 4.

[157] Siegfried Bruss, 'Heimattag des Brückenbaus', *Siebenbürgische Zeitung* 55/8, 31 May 2005, p. 1.

of twentieth-century Europe. If, as once claimed by Peter Graf von Kielmannsegg, 'Europe is hardly a memory community',[158] then Romanian German activists and politicians, animated by their new historic mission to be bridge-builders, took up the challenge to build that community.

---

[158] See Klaus Schönhoven, *Europa als Erinnerungsgemeinschaft* (Bonn: Friedrich-Ebert-Stiftung, 2007), p. 9; see also Peter Becker and Olaf Leiße, *Die Zukunft Europas: Der Konvent zur Zukunft der Europäischen Union* (Opladen: Leske + Budrich, 2004), p. 31.

The Perpetual Exodus

Mer waellen bleiwen, wat mir sen.

(We want to remain who we are.) Romanian German motto

When asked by a reporter in 2003 how long he had been living in Romania, Eginald Schlattner responded '850 years'.[1] Personal biography, for Schlattner, was interwoven with the long and complex history of 850 years of Germans in Transylvania. The past has always mattered to Romanian Germans, and both Saxons and Swabians have sensed strong continuities in their history as the world changed around them. Epitomised in the Transylvanian Saxon motto, emblazoned on buildings, repeated in songs, poems, speeches and newspapers, 'Mer waellen bleiwen, wat mir sen [We want to remain who we are]', Germans in Romania have long insisted that nothing has changed.[2] It was others around them who had disrupted history and shifted position as it suited them: Romanians had been political 'turncoats' and Germans – that is, Germans from Germany, not Romanian Germans – had been unreliable and never really understood Romanian Germans.

Yet the history of Romanian German identity in modern Europe, charted in this book, is characterised by a remarkable mixture of stories, voices, and developments. Throughout their history, Romanian Germans continually grappled with the question of who they were and where they belonged. Forged out of the shards of empire, they constantly renegotiated their place in Europe. They were early enthusiasts of the enlarged Romanian state after 1918, German nationalists, defenders of the Nazi war effort and Nazis themselves, victims of post-war repercussions, and

---

[1] *Hermannstädter Zeitung*, 31 January 2003.

[2] In German orthography it is 'Wir wollen bleiben, was wir sind'. The motto is originally the title of a poem by the Transylvanian Saxon Otto Piringer (1874–1950) and appears frequently in Romanian German sources, most notably inscribed on the façade of Casa Luxembourg in Sibiu.

good or bad citizens of communist Romania and of West Germany, as well as European bridge-builders. Their internecine battles of the interwar period over belonging continued into the Cold War period, when Romanian German disagreement over emigration from Romania stirred up passions for decades to come. They fell out with each other over their Nazi past and their role in communist Romania. And, even after all that, they were still unsure how to understand their position in a new post-1989 world.

Romanian Germans were in a constant process of becoming and were not fixed in their identity. For all their insistence on remaining who they were, the only real constant in their modern history was how much they changed. And, while Romanian Germans experienced major transformations throughout the twentieth century and into the twenty-first, they were also agents of that change. Uncovering their histories reveals a European story that puts pressure on assumptions around minority groups, identity formation, and modern European memory. Romanian Germans decentre European and German history by directing attention towards east-central Europe and expanding networks across boundaries such as the Cold War East–West division. Simultaneously defined by and defying the states they inhabited (primarily, but not only, Romania and Germany), Romanian Germans were at the centre of many of the crucial European events of the twentieth century. This is of course also true of other groups, but their peculiar (although not necessarily unique) position as a minority group reveals a transnational perspective on many central themes in modern European history. And, if their existence for much of the twentieth and twenty-first centuries has been transnational, then our perspective of what makes a minority shifts, too.

As this book has shown, Romanian German identity was surprisingly adaptable to new circumstances. The Romanian German performativity of everyday ethnicity throughout the twentieth century into the twenty-first and the perpetual reframing of three central themes in Romanian German narratives – superiority, besiegement, and ordeal – have broader implications for understanding European minorities. The fixedness that comes with minority labels remains a challenge to studies of minority groups.[3] Romanian German battles over belonging and identity may have

---

[3] For multiple perspectives on minorities in Silesia, see Tomasz Kamusella et al. (eds.), *Creating Nationality in Central Europe, 1880–1950: Modernity, Violence and (Be) Longing in Upper Silesia* (Abingdon: Routledge, 2016); on Franco-Algerian minorities, see Claire Eldridge, *From Empire to Exile: History and Memory within the Pied-Noir and Harki Communities, 1962–2012* (Manchester: Manchester University Press, 2016).

happened in specific contexts, but parts of the story charted in this book are also applicable to other minorities in Europe.[4] Brubaker's 'ethnopolitical entrepreneurs' loom large in minority studies, but, as shown in this book, the performative 'Germanness' that characterised much of Romanian German belonging was not only the domain of the entrepreneurs, but also of those who performed it. Beyond introducing new entrepreneurs and components to Brubaker's triadic nexus where identity is shaped, *Migrating Memories* has thus shifted the emphasis towards the performativity of identity. Agency in shaping identity was never only the domain of entrepreneurs – the *Landsmannschaften*, the editors of influential journals and newspapers, the church – but it was reliant on 'ordinary' Romanian Germans reciprocating, rejecting, or revising features of Romanian German identity.

Ethnopolitical entrepreneurs thus played an essential role in all of this, but – as this book has shown – identity debates often became decentred from those same entrepreneurs who struggled to maintain their grip on Romanian German identity, which gathered momentum beyond their control. There was little distinction between ethnopolitical entrepreneurs and 'ordinary' Romanian Germans, as this book has argued, in the reframing of Romanian German identity after 1918. That dynamic is partly revealed through the essential diversity of the sources voiced in this book. There have been plenty of 'elite voices' in the story from relatively privileged Romanian German personalities such as Hans Bergel, Heinrich Zillich, and Eginald Schlattner. Yet a substantial number of the voices in this story come from all sections of the community: ego documents, 'fugitive sources',[5] self-published memoirs and literature, a canon of 'Transylvanica' and 'Banatia', and articles, as well as oral testimonies from Romanian Germans who did not occupy the centre stage of Romanian German history. External sources, too, played a vital part in understanding Romanian German identities: German newspapers, documents relating to EU dignitaries, adverts, and Romanian representations of Germans as well as European agencies. Together they reveal the palimpsest

[4] This book thus resonates with recent work on German minorities, but also enhances minority and German minority studies: see, for instance, Peter Polak-Springer, *Recovered Territory: A German–Polish Conflict over Land and Culture, 1919–1989* (New York: Berghahn, 2015), and Gaëlle Fisher, *Resettlers and Survivors: Bukovina and the Politics of Belonging in West Germany and Israel, 1945–1989* (New York: Berghahn, 2020).
[5] I am borrowing the expression 'fugitive sources' from Kristin Ghodsee to describe source material that never ended up in archives in a systematic way.

of identities that were repeatedly shifted and reconstituted in modern Europe.

Those ordinary Romanian German voices have made it necessary to consider the different scales on which Romanian Germans operate: from high politics, to political activists, to outsiders, to artists, to lone voices, to private memories. Seen from multiple perspectives, this book has drawn attention to the tensions and the plurality of voices that complicate the national labels often attached to minorities to present a transnational community operating on different scales. Particularly around the thorny issue of emigration during the Cold War, real divisions emerged between self-confident *Landsmannschaft* activists and ordinary Romanian Germans who felt uncertain in their new assumed role as West Germans. Equally, as Chapter 3 argued, the *Landsmannschaften* and, more obviously, state actors in Romania and (West) Germany found it difficult to control the legacy of National Socialism and the Second World War. Romanian German memories were firmly embedded in private manifestations, while resistance to a victim-centric view of Romanian Germans took hold on the fringes of the homeland societies and in German society more broadly.

Romanian German identities were especially impactful when their surroundings took note of them. The three central themes that Romanian Germans remoulded for particular circumstances found an echo in the societies and political environments they inhabited. Their sense of besiegement mapped onto an ideological imaginary in interwar Germany and Romania. Coverage of the plight of Germans abroad fed a German interwar myth of encirclement, while the Romanian Germans' *Leidensweg* seemed to echo a broader sense of defeat after the First World War. Even locally anchored artefacts, such as Stefan Jäger's depiction of the arrival of Swabians in the Banat, were co-opted into a National Socialist worldview. After the Second World War, Romanian Germans were increasingly locked into the political world of Cold War West Germany. But Romanian Germans failed to excite a West German public to the extent that the *Landsmannschaften* had hoped for, while Romanian German divisions cast the *Landsmannschaften* as a threat to Germans in Romania who refused to leave for the West. Romanian Germans were, however, at their most influential when cast in the role of colonisers equipped with civilisational superiority. Whether it was as members of a 'greater' German world in interwar period or as Cold War warriors, their claim to superiority rarely abated.

Conversely, it was in the period after 1989, when the Romanian German community in Romania almost disappeared, that Romanian Germans reinvented themselves as a civilisational vanguard in a new Europe to a big European reception. As European bridge-builders, Romanian Germans were able to position themselves as colonists once again with a civilisational mission in east-central Europe. Their great success at generating international attention, explained in Chapter 5, thus confirmed that their twentieth-century struggles had been worthwhile, while reinforcing their long-held sense of superiority. It is perhaps no coincidence, and certainly worthy of further exploration, that European interest in Romanian German heritage coincided with a resurgence of the idea of Europe as a fortress, especially at moments of change: EU enlargement between 2004 and 2014, the financial crisis of 2008, the migrant crisis of 2015. The picturesque Transylvanian Saxon church fortresses symbolised a narrow, white Europe that was in need of protection from outsiders. At a time of deep insecurity in European societies, their heritage was easy to elevate to a valuable part of a common European history. Romanian Germans, in their twenty-first century role as civilising colonists under siege after a century of suffering, seemed to have finally found their place in modern Europe.

Romanian German identities always existed in webs of contestation. Their sense of belonging in Europe after 1918 was most pronounced and debated at moments of uncertainty and in reflections on those moments. Their identities spanned a broad spectrum after 1918, which is emblematised by two well-known figures in the popular imagination: Johnny Weissmuller (1904–84), athlete and Hollywood actor most famous for playing Tarzan, and Peter Maffay (1949–), German pop star, music producer, and activist. On the face of it, the two have little in common. Johnny Weissmuller, born János Weißmüller into a Banat Swabian family in the Austro-Hungarian Empire in 1904, left for the USA with his family in the 1900s and became an American celebrity. Back in interwar Romania, when his face became identified with the Hollywood blockbuster *Tarzan the Ape Man* (1932), Weissmuller was elevated by Romanian Germans to their canon of famous Germans from Romania alongside the eccentric inventor Hermann Oberth, the Protestant reformer Johannes Honterus, and, later, author Oskar Pastior. For Romanian Germans, he thus took his place among the 'colourful mixture of figureheads' in their long, proud history, or so Georg Aescht, a Transylvanian writer, claimed in 2007.[6] On the occasion of Weissmuller's hundredth birthday in 2004, the Donauschwäbisches Zentralmuseum in Ulm put on an exhibition

---

[6] Georg Aescht, 'Schon Wiedersehen ist viel', *Siebenbürgische Zeitung* 57/15, 30 September 2007, p. 8.

commemorating their 'lost son'.[7] Weissmuller, citizen of the world and Hollywood superstar, never acknowledged his Romanian German celebrity status and remained aloof towards his Banat Swabian heritage until his death in 1984.

Conversely, Peter Maffay, born in Braşov in 1949, immersed himself in Romanian German affairs. His family left Romania in 1963 when he was nearly fourteen years old, but his stellar music career did not dislodge him from his Romanian German heritage. On the contrary, Maffay became more and more involved in the émigré world, especially from the 1990s on. He joined forces with the Mihai Eminescu Trust in attempting to preserve German heritage in Transylvania while supporting various charities and antiracist initiatives, and his appearance at the *Heimattag der Siebenbürger Sachsen* became a regular feature in the new millennium. One of Maffay's biggest hits from 1980, a cover version of 'Über Sieben Brücken Musst Du Gehen' ('Seven Bridges Must Be Crossed'), originally written by the GDR band Karat, epitomised that hybrid identity. Peaking at number four, it stayed in the West German charts for twenty weeks and has remained a radio favourite ever since. In Maffay's hands, *sieben Brücken* clearly evoked *Siebenbürgen*, the German name for Transylvania. With Maffay being (West) German, Romanian German, European, and an antiracist activist at the same time, the song's bridge metaphor also played into a key emerging idea about Romanian Germans, namely that they were European bridge-builders. While Weissmuller's international persona seemed to buck the trend of a growing exclusionary German nationalism among Romanian Germans in the interwar period, Peter Maffay became one of the faces of a modern Romanian German identity of the late twentieth and early twenty-first centuries.

Weissmuller and Maffay might be celebrities, but they are in many ways emblematic of the spectrum of Romanian German identity. In between Weissmuller's lack of Romanian German identity and Maffay's leadership as the 'new Romanian German', there were a lot of possibilities. From enthusiastic Nazis, to negotiators of a peculiar position in communist Romania, to advocates of the dissolution of their communities in Romania, Romanian Germans experienced significant twentieth-century European conflicts of identity. Their adaptive identity crystallised at key moments, and they could mobilise events and people 'on the outside' to

---

[7] The Donauschwäbisches Zentralmuseum is the main museum of Danube Swabians, encompassing Banat Swabians, in Germany. They produced a catalogue for the exhibition: Donauschwäbisches Zentralmuseum (ed.), *Johnny Weissmüller: Ausstellung zum 100. Geburtstag* (Ulm: Donauschwäbisches Zentralmuseum, 2004).

construct themselves. Weissmuller may have ignored his Romanian German heritage, but, whether he liked it or not, he was co-opted as a Romanian German by voices in the Romanian German community. His construction as a Romanian German by others echoed the interwar German fantasies about hardy Transylvanian Saxons and Axel Azzola's elevation to an honorary Romanian German at the end of the twentieth century.[8] Maffay, meanwhile, co-opted as a pop star by German society, continued to construct himself as a stalwart Romanian German. Though they did so in opposite directions, both were able to shift between different layers of identity, from Banat Swabian migrant to American Tarzan, and from superstar *Schlagersänger* to local *Siebenbürger*. They were never only – nor even primarily – Romanian German, but wherever their paths took them, even posthumously in Weissmuller's case, they were enmeshed in Romanian German debates about identity.

Even in the nineteenth century, when Banat Swabians and Transylvanian Saxons had, superficially at least, little in common apart from being subjects of the Habsburg Empire and after 1867 of the Austro-Hungarian Empire, Romanian German commonalities were being forged. Frantic discussions about the rootedness of Transylvanian Saxons – either as local Saxons or 'greater' Germans – and the cult of the Banat Swabian *Leidensweg*, along with a growing sense of *reichsdeutsch* superiority, laid the foundations for a century of becoming Romanian German. There was no 'full stop' to the Romanian German community. Even the migration of the late 1980s and early 1990s resulted in a dynamic identity that oscillated between affirmation, denial, escape, and return. Romanian German identity in modern Europe was never an 'end product' but was constantly in a state of flux and a perpetual exodus.

In the end, this story is not just a history of a Romanian German exodus. All too often minorities, especially those in east-central Europe, are treated separately from broader European histories that we tell. Yet a focus on Romanian Germans enlarges an understanding of European history decentred from the main arenas and actors of the twentieth and twenty-first centuries. Romanian German history did not happen in a single place: it was multipolar and stretched, to some extent at least, even beyond Europe to the Americas. And Romanian German identity debates often took surprising directions: Hans Otto Roth and Heinrich Zillich, from different vantage points, pulled the generational debate over far-right ideology in the 1930s towards Romania. Paul Philippi spent the best part

[8] See Chapters 1 and 3.

of the Cold War trying to flee back eastwards. Caroline Fernolend was trying to rebuild a medieval past in Transylvania as European integration happened around her. Intertwined with nationalism, National Socialism, communism, modern European memory, twentieth-century celebrity culture, migration, and European integration, Romanian Germans – though ostensibly a minority on the margins – are, in important ways, at the centre of those modern European themes. Enriched by their perspective, the narrative of European history is able to move in directions that defy expectations and assumptions around the rise and fall of fascism, the gradual demise of communism, and the westward movement of history.

Romanian Germans also tell a relatively unusual story after 1945 because they did not experience mass expulsion (like most other Germans from east-central Europe) nor did they mainly stay put on the eastern side of the Cold War division (like most other east-central Europeans). Although they were always looking for certainty in the past, Romanian Germans were torn between different forces, settings, and places in modern Europe. Debates among Romanian Germans about belonging in the 1920s and 1930s not only occurred in Romania, but were also embedded in a European network of ideological and generational conflict. Their experiences of the Cold War were not defined by confinement, but by a dynamic interaction across the East–West boundary. After 1989, despite the fact that most Romanian Germans had left Romania, their long-standing desire to be taken seriously as Europeans was, partially at least, fulfilled. The perpetual exodus of Romanian Germans defines an experiential drama of European history and minority communities. Their memories migrated and changed with them on their journeys through modern European history. The actors may be little known, but their voices are an integral part of the European moment.

Bibliography

Primary Sources

Archives

Hermannstädter Zeitung Archiv, Sibiu

*Institut für deutsche Kultur und Geschichte Südosteuropas
(IKGS), Munich*

65/16 (Correspondence Hans Bergel with Paul Philippi, Dr. Zillich, Andreas
  Birkner, Oskar Pastior, Paul Schuster, Dieter Schlesak, Johann Kochner,
  Wolfgang Bonfert, Bruckner – Bonfert, Harry Binder)
B (0) /5 (Correspondence Wolf von Aichelburg, Johannes Zulter, 1981–5,
  1986) 55 (Berwanger, Dieter Schlesak)
B 7 (Wolf von Aichelburg, Hans Bergel)
B 152/3 (Oswald Kessler)

Landsmannschaft der Banater Schwaben e.V., Munich

Landsmannschaft der Banater Schwaben e.V., Stuttgart

Landsmannschaft der Siebenbürger Sachsen e.V., Munich

Siebenbürgen Institut / Gundelsheim

B I 11 (HiKo) 39
B I 51, 2/1 (Hans Bergel etc. . . .)
B I 51, 2/2
B I 51, 2/3 (Newsletters)
B I 52, 3
B I 52, 4
B I 52, 34
B I 54 (Roland Melzer), 1/6 (Correspondence)

B I 54, 4/1, 2, 3, 4 (Correspondence, packages, *Landsmannschaft*, Martha Mesch, Hans Roth)

B I 54, 5/1–3

B I 54, 6/4–5 (Correspondence Roland Melzer, Martha Mesch, Gerhard Donant)

B I 54, 6 (Correspondence Martha Mesch)

B I 54, 7/6–7 (Correspondence Martha Mesch, Gärtner)

B I 54, 8/1–4 (Correspondence with HiKo, *Landsmannschaften*, and BdV)

B I 54, 10/3

B I 54, 14/4–5 (Correspondence Alfred Graef)

B I 54, 15 (Correspondence Alfred Graef)

B I 56 (Bernhard Capesius), 1/1–8

B I 56, 3/2 (Correspondence)

B I 56, 3/2, 2/1, 2 (Correspondence, family letters)

B I 56, 3/1–6

B I 72, 2 (Erich Phleps)

B I 75, 1–4 (Maja Philippi)

B I 115 (Andreas Kloos), A-5944

B III 2 (Landsmannschaft der Siebenbürger Sachsen in Deutschland), 48/15

B III 2/49/17

B III 3

B III 39 (HiKo, *Siebenbürger Sachsen, Banater Schwaben*) [18], [19] (1952–7, 1955–7, Mo-Rei, correspondence), 40/20–22 (1951–7)

B III 39, 41/23–25 (1951–7)

B III 39, 42/26, 27

Newspapers and Periodicals

Allgemeine Deutsche Zeitung
Alpenländische Rundschau
Banater Deutsche Zeitung
Banater Post
Deutsche Kultur in der Welt
Deutsche Tageszeitung
Deutsches Jahrbuch für Rumänien
Das Donautal – Magazin
Frankfurter Allgemeine Zeitung
Gândul
Grazer Tagblatt
Hamburger Nachrichten
Hermannstädter Zeitung
Karpatenrundschau
Klingsor
Landeskirchliche Information

Licht der Heimat
Neue Literatur (Banater Schrifttum)
Neue Züricher Zeitung
Neuer Weg
Radio Wien
Schwäbischer Merkur
Siebenbürgische Vierteljahresschrift
Siebenbürgische Zeitung
Der Spiegel
Der Standard
Südostdeutsche Tageszeitung
Tagesspiegel
Tiroler Anzeiger
Unterkärntner Nachrichten
Volkszeitung
Wiener Zeitung
Die Zeit

Published Works

Ackrill, Ursula, *Zeiden, im Januar* (Berlin: Verlag Klaus Wagenbach, 2015)
Astfalk, Sabine-Else (ed.), *Josef Nischbach: Ein Leben für Glaube und Volkstum* (Stuttgart: Landsmannschaft der Banater Schwaben Landesverband Baden-Württemberg, 2000)
'Ausschnitte aus offiziellen Erklärungen und Ansprachen des Bundesvorsitzenden der Landsmannschaft der Siebenbürger Sachsen in Deutschland, Erhard Plesch (Aufgrund von Beschlüssen der führenden Gremien der Landsmannschaft, Verbandstag und Bundesvorstand)', in Landsmannschaft der Siebenbürger Sachsen (ed.), *Ein Weg zur Verständigung*, p. 17
Azzola, Axel, *Jüdische und andere Geschichten von der Schöpfung bis zur Gegenwart* (Sibiu: Hora, 2005)
Baier, Hannelore (ed.), *Departe în Rusia, la Stalino: amintiri și documente cu privire la deportarea în Uniunea Sovietică a etnicilor germani din România, 1945–1950* (Brussels: InterGraf, 2003)
'Banater Kulturarbeit im letzten Jahrzehnt', in Landsmannschaft der Banater Schwaben (ed.), *Neue Heimat in Deutschland: 50 Jahre Wirken für die Gemeinschaft* (Munich: Landsmannschaft der Banater Schwaben, 2000), pp. 113–27
Bayer, Daniel, *Deportiert und repatriiert: Aufzeichnungen und Erinnerungen 1945–1947* (Munich: Südostdeutsches Kulturwerk, 2000)
Bergel, Hans, 'Europa braucht eine neue Mitte', *Südostdeutsche Vierteljahresblätter* 2 (2004), pp. 115–16
Fürst und Lautenschläger (Bucharest: Jugendverlag, 1957)

'Die kulturelle Machtübernahme in Rumänien durch die Kommunisten', in Kulturreferat der Landsmannschaft der Siebenbürger Sachsen in Deutschland e.V. (ed.), *Rumänien nach 1945*, pp. 53–71

'Vorgänge letzter Entkolonialisierung – Aus dem Spannungsfeld des Südostens entlassen: die Deutschen', in Hans Bergel (ed.), *Erkundungen und Erfahrungen: Notizen eines Neugierigen* (Munich: Südostdeutsches Kulturwerk, 1995), pp. 93–102

'"Was soll denn noch mit diesen Menschen geschehen dürfen?', in Schuster (ed.), *Epoche der Entscheidungen*, pp. 389–95

Bergel, Hans and Walter Myß (eds.), *Wir Siebenbürger* (Innsbruck: Wort und Welt Verlag, 1986)

'Zur Einführung', in Bergel and Myß (eds.), *Wir Siebenbürger*, p. 5

Bergel, Hans et al., *Die Sachsen in Siebenbürgen nach dreißig Jahren Kommunismus: Eine Studie über die Menschenrechte am Beispiel einer ethnischen Gruppe hinter dem Eisernen Vorhang* (Innsbruck: Wort und Welt Verlag, 1976)

Blacker, William, *Along the Enchanted Way: A Romanian Story* (London: John Murray, 2009)

Böhm, Johann, *Die Deutschen in Rumänien und das Dritte Reich 1933–1940* (Frankfurt am Main: Peter Lang, 1999)

Die Deutschen in Rumänien und die Weimarer Republik (Ippesheim: AGK-Verlag, 1993)

Die Gleichschaltung der Deutschen in Rumänien und das 'Dritte Reich' (Frankfurt am Main: Peter Lang, 2003)

Hitlers Vasallen der deutschen Volksgruppe in Rumänien vor und nach 1945 (Frankfurt am Main: Peter Lang, 2006)

Das Nationalsozialistische Deutschland und die Deutsche Volksgruppe in Rumänien 1936–1944 (Frankfurt: Peter Lang, 1985)

Die Ungarndeutschen in der Waffen-SS (Ippesheim: AGK-Verlag, 1990)

Boner, Charles, *Transylvania; Its Products and Its People* (London: Longmans, Green, Reader, and Dyer, 1865)

Bottesch, Martin, *Landler-Büchlein* (Sibiu: Honterus, 2007)

Bruckner, Wilhelm, 'Die Landsmannschaft als neue Gemeinschaftsform', in Schuster (ed.), *Epoche der Entscheidungen*, pp. 333–40

Capesius, Bernhard, *Im alten Land* (Hermannstadt: Krafft & Drotleff, 1923)

Czernetzky, Günter et al. (eds.), *Lager Lyrik: Gedenkbuch – 70 Jahre seit der Deportation der Deutschen aus Südosteuropa in die Sowejetunion: Gedichte, Fotografien, Zeichnungen, Lieder, Verse, Reime, Sprüche* (Sibiu: Schiller Verlag, 2015)

Dokumente und Materialien der Zusammenarbeit zwischen der Sozialistischen Einheitspartei Deutschlands und der Rumänischen Kommunistischen Partei, 1972 bis 1977 (Berlin: Dietz-Verlag, 1979)

Donauschwäbisches Zentralmuseum (ed.), *Johnny Weissmüller: Ausstellung zum 100. Geburtstag* (Ulm: Donauschwäbisches Zentralmuseum, 2004)

Douglas-Home, Jessica, *Once Upon Another Time* (Norwich: Michael Russell Publishers, 2000)

Eisenburger, Eduard and Michael Kroner (eds.), *Sächsisch-schwäbische Chronik* (Bucharest: Kriterion, 1976)

Engel, Walter and Walter Tonţa (eds.), *Die Banater Schwaben nach dem Ersten Weltkrieg: Kulturelle Kontinuität und neuer Aufbruch* (Stuttgart: Landsmannschaft der Banater Schwaben, 2015)

Engelmann, Franz, 'Seit 250 Jahren: Banater Schwaben', in *Komm Mit '74*, pp. 139–48

Fabritius-Dancu, Juliane, 'Burgen im Repser Land', in *Komm Mit '81*, pp. 129–59

Fătu, Mihai, Mircea Muşat, Ion Ardeleanu and Vasile Arimial (eds.), *Teroarea Horthysto-fascista in Nordvestul Romaniei, septembrie 1940–octobrie 1945* (Bucharest: Meridian Books, 1985)

Feigel-Burghart, Erika, *Mädchenjahre hinter Stacheldraht: Sowjetunion 1945–1949* (Sibiu: Hora Verlag, 2003)

Fischer, Ignaz Bernhard, 'Die Russlanddeportierten', *Echo der Vortragsreihe* 1/181 (2005), pp. 6–9

Fisher-Galaţi, Stefan, *Twentieth Century Rumania* (New York: Columbia University Press, 1970)

Franz, Frida, 'Zwölf Jahre verschleppt in Sibirien', in Bergel and Myß (eds), *Wir Siebenbürger*, pp. 174–81

'Friedrich-Ebert'-Stiftung Rumänien, *Tief in Russland bei Stalino: Erinnerungen und Dokumente zur Deportation in die Sowjetunion 1945* (Bucharest: Allgemeine Deutsche Zeitung für Rumänien)

Fuchs, Joseph, 'Rauhreif blüht im Stacheldraht' (1948), in Czernetzky et al. (eds.), *Lager Lyrik*, p. 140

'Geistige Grundlagen der neuen Erziehung, dargestellt aus der nationalsozialistischen Idee', in Dr Heinz Brandsch (ed.), *Schule und Leben: Fachzeitschrift des Siebenbürgisch-Sächsischen Lehrerbundes* 6 (1934–5), pp. 266–71

Gibson, Carl, *Allein in der Revolte: Eine Jugend in Banat – Aufzeichnungen eines Andersdenkenden-Selbst erlebte Geschichte und Geschichten aus dem Securitate-Staat* (Dettelbach: J. H. Röll Verlag, 2011)

  Symphonie der Freiheit: Widerstand gegen die Ceauşescu-Diktatur (Dettelbach: J. H. Röll, 2008)

Giurescu, Constantin C., *Transylvania in the History of Romania: An Official Outline* (London: Garnstone Press Ltd, 1969)

Göllner, Carl, *Am Rande der Geschichte* (Bucharest: Kriterion, 1973)

Graef-Wagner, Erna, 'Die Leiden der Deportation', *Siebenbürgische Zeitung* 35/2, 31 January 1985, p. 3

Greffner, Otto and Mario Stoica, *275 de ani de învăţământ în limba germană în Aradul Nou – 275 Jahre deutschsprachige Schule in Neuarad* (Arad, 2001)

Gross, Karl-Heinz, *Stefan Jäger, Maler seiner heimatlichen Gefilde: Aus seinem Leben und Werk* (Sersheim: Hartmann, 1991)

Hartl, Hans, 'Am Ende einer historischen Aufgabe', in Bergel and Myß (eds.), *Wir Siebenbürger*, pp. 85–107

  'Am Ende einer historischen Aufgabe', in Schuster (ed.), *Epoche der Entscheidungen*, pp. 370–88

'Die Lage der Deutschen in Rumänien', *Südosteuropa Mitteilungen* 4 (1981), pp. 112–25

von Hasselt, Kai-Uwe, 'Bundespräsident Kai-Uwe von Hasselt in einem Telegramm an den Bundesvorsitzenden der Siebenbürger Sachsen in Deutschland', in Landsmannschaft der Siebenbürger Sachsen (ed.), *Ein Weg zur Verständigung*, p. 44

Heinz-Kehrer, Stefan, *Lehrerwahl in Traunhofen – Erzählung* (Munich, 1998)

Hillgruber, Andreas, *Zweierlei Untergang: Die Zerschlagung des Deutschen Reiches und das Ende des europäischen Judentums* (Berlin: Siedler, 1986)

Hromadka, Georg, *Kleine Chronik des Banater Berglands* (Munich: Südostdeutsches Kulturwerk, 1993)

Iorga, Nicolae, *A History of Roumania: Land, People, Civilisation* (London: T. Fisher Unwin Ltd, 1925)

Illyés, Elemér, *National Minorities in Romania: Change in Transylvania* (Boulder, Co.: East European Monographs, 1982)

Klein, Christoph, *Auf dem andern Wege: Aufsätze zum Schicksal der Siebenbürger Sachsen als Volk und Kirche* (Erlangen: Martin-Luther-Verlag, 1986)

Klein, Karl Kurt, 'Abendländische Schicksalsgemeinschaft im Südostraum', *Südostdeutsche Rundschau* 1/1 (1942), in Klein (ed.), *Saxonica Septemcastrensia*, pp. 43–53

'Finis Saxoniae? Nein!', *Siebenbürgisch-Deutsches Tageblatt*, 27 August 1932, in Klein (ed.), *Saxonica Septemcastrensia:*, pp. 12–14

(ed.), *Luxemburg und Siebenbürgen* (Cologne: Böhlau, 1966)

(ed.), *Saxonica Septemcastrensia: Forschungen, Reden und Aufsätze aus vier Jahrzehnten zur Geschichte der Deutschen in Siebenbürgen* (Marburg: N. G. Elwert Verlag, 1971)

Klusch, Horst, *Zur Ansiedlung der Siebenbürger Sachsen* (Bucharest: Kriterion, 2001)

Knowlton, James and Truett Cates (eds.), *Forever in the Shadow of Hitler? Original Documents of the* Historikerstreit*, the Controversy Concerning the Singularity of the Holocaust* (New York: Prometheus Books, 1993)

Komm Mit: Reisen, Wandern, Erholung in Rumänien (Bucharest: Neuer Weg, 1970)

Komm Mit: Reisen, Wandern, Erholung in Rumänien (Bucharest: Neuer Weg, 1971)

Komm Mit '72: Reisen, Wandern, Erholung in Rumänien (Bucharest: Neuer Weg, 1972)

Komm Mit '73: Reisen, Wandern, Erholung in Rumänien (Bucharest: Neuer Weg, 1973)

Komm Mit '74: Reisen, Wandern, Erholung in Rumänien (Bucharest: Neuer Weg, 1974)

Komm Mit '75: Reisen, Wandern, Erholung in Rumänien (Bucharest: Neuer Weg, 1975)

Komm Mit '76: Reisen, Wandern, Erholung in Rumänien (Bucharest: Neuer Weg, 1976)

Komm Mit '77: Reisen, Wandern, Erholung in Rumänien (Bucharest: Neuer Weg, 1977)

Komm Mit '78: Reisen, Wandern, Erholung in Rumänien (Bucharest: Neuer Weg, 1978)

Komm Mit '79: Reisen, Wandern, Erholung in Rumänien (Bucharest: Neuer Weg, 1979)

Komm Mit '80: Reisen, Wandern, Erholung in Rumänien (Bucharest: Neuer Weg, 1980)

Komm Mit '81: Reisen, Wandern, Erholung in Rumänien (Bucharest: Neuer Weg, 1981)

Komm Mit '82: Reisen, Wandern, Erholung in Rumänien (Bucharest: Neuer Weg, 1982)

Komm Mit '83: Reisen, Wandern, Erholung in Rumänien (Bucharest: Neuer Weg, 1983)

Komm Mit '84: Reisen, Wandern, Erholung in Rumänien (Bucharest: Neuer Weg, 1984)

Komm Mit '85: Reisen, Wandern, Erholung in Rumänien (Bucharest: Neuer Weg, 1985)

Komm Mit '86: Reisen, Wandern, Erholung in Rumänien (Bucharest: Neuer Weg, 1986)

Komm Mit '87: Reisen, Wandern, Erholung in Rumänien (Bucharest: Neuer Weg, 1987)

Komm Mit '88: Reisen, Wandern, Erholung in Rumänien (Bucharest: Neuer Weg, 1988)

Komm Mit '89: Reisen, Wandern, Erholung in Rumänien (Bucharest: Neuer Weg, 1989)

Komm Mit '90: Reisen, Wandern, Erholung in Rumänien (Bucharest: Neuer Weg, 1990)

Konschitzky, Walther, Peter-Dietmar Leber and Walter Wolf (eds.), *Deportiert in den Baragan 1951–1956* (Munich: Haus des Deutschen Ostens, 2001)

Köpeczi, Béla, László Makkai, András Mócsy and Zoltán Szász (eds.), *Erdély Története, Vols. I–III* (Budapest: Akadémiai Kiadó, 1986)

Krier, Peter (ed.), *Hommage an Stefan Jäger* (Ingolstadt: Hilfswerk der Banater Schwaben, 2012)

Kroner, Michael, *Die Deutschen Rumäniens im 20. Jahrhundert: Siebenbürgen, Banat, Sathmar, Bukowina, Bessarabien, Dobrudscha, Altrumänien* (Vienna: Österreichische Landsmannschaft, 2004)

   'Die Deutschen Rumäniens in den Jahren 1944–1947', in Kulturreferat der Landsmannschaft der Siebenbürger Sachsen in Deutschland e.V. (ed.), *Rumänien nach 1945*, pp. 72–84

Kultur- und Erwachsenenbildungsverein 'Deutsche Vortragsreihe Reschitza' (ed.), *Das Schreckliche Jahr 1945: Erzählungen von Russlanddeportierten* (Vol. II) (Bucharest: Allgemeine Deutsche Zeitung für Rumänien, 1997)

Kulturreferat der Landsmannschaft der Siebenbürger Sachsen in Deutschland e. V. (ed.), *Rumänien nach 1945: Die Referate der Tagungen der*

Arbeitsgemeinschaft siebenbürgischer Jungakademiker (ASJ), 1987–1989 (Munich: Kulturreferat der Landsmannschaft der Siebenbürger Sachsen in Deutschland e.V., 1989)

Landsmannschaft der Banater Schwaben e.V. (ed.), *Stefan Jäger: Maler seiner Banater Heimat* (Munich: Landsmannschaft der Banater Schwaben e.V., 1992)

Landsmannschaft der Siebenbürger Sachsen (ed.), *Ein Weg zur Verständigung: Die Landsmannschaft der Siebenbürger Sachsen im Dienste einer deutschen Politik der Verständigung mit den Völkern des Ostens* (Munich: Verlag Hans Meschendörfer, 1971)

'Mediascher Anschlußerklärung des erweiterten sächsischen Zentralausschusses', in Ernst Wagner (ed.), *Quellen zur Geschichte der Siebenbürger Sachsen, 1191–1975* (Cologne: Böhlau, 1981), pp. 266–8

Meschendörfer, Adolf, *Siebenbürgische Elegie* (00000: 0000000000, 1927)
Die Stadt im Osten (Sibiu: Krafft & Drotleff, 1931)

Möckel, Andreas (ed.), *Gerhard Möckel: Fatum oder Datum? Aufsätze und Briefe* (Munich: Südostdeutsches Kulturwerk, 1997)
Umkämpfte Volkskirche: Leben und Wirken des evangelisch-sächsischen Pfarrers Konrad Möckel (1892–1965) (Cologne: Böhlau, 2011)

Möckel, Gerhard, 'Fatum oder Datum?', in Möckel (ed.), *Gerhard Möckel: Fatum oder Datum?*, pp. 23–39

Motzan, Peter and Stefan Sienerth (eds.), *Worte als Gefahr und Gefährdung: Fünf deutsche Schriftsteller vor Gericht (15. September – Kronstadt/Rumänien), Zusammenhänge und Hintergründe, Selbstzeugnisse und Dokumente* (Munich: Verlag Südostdeutsches Kulturwerk, 1993)

Müller, Herta, *Atemschaukel* (Munich: Hanser, 2009)
, *Herztier* (Munich: Carl Hanser Verlag, 2007)

Myß, Walter (ed.), *Lexikon der Siebenbürger Sachsen: Geschichte, Kultur, Zivilisation, Wissenschaften, Wirtschaft, Lebensraum Siebenbürgen* (Innsbruck: Wort und Welt, 1993)

Naumann, Friedrich, *Mitteleuropa* (Berlin: G. Reimer, 1915)

Neustädter, Erwin, *Mohn im Ährenfeld* (Munich: Verlag Hans Meschendörfer, 1974)

Orendi-Hommenau, Viktor, 'Aus schwerster Zeit im Banat', *Heimat und Welt: Beiträge zur Kulturpolitik, Auslandskunde und Deutschtumforschung* 11/16 (1929), pp. 35–40

Partsch, Joseph, *Central Europe* (London: William Heinemann, 1903)
Mitteleuropa: Die Länder und Völker von den Westalpen und dem Balkan bis an den Kanal und das Kurische Haff (Gotha: Justus Perthes, 1904)

Pascu, Ştefan, *The Making of the Romanian Unitary National State* (Bucharest: Editura Academiei Republicii Socialiste România, 1989)

Pauling, Sven, *'Wir werden Sie einkerkern, weil es Sie gibt!': Studie, Zeitzeugenberichte und Securitate-Akten zum Kronstädter Schriftstellerprozess 1959* (Berlin: Frank & Timme, 2012)

Petri, Volker (ed.), *Not und Neuanfang: Die Evangelische Kirche Österreichs und ihre Siebenbürger Sachsen* (Sibiu: Schiller Verlag, 2014)

Philippi, Maja, 'Seit 800 Jahren: Siebenbürger Sachsen', *Komm Mit '74*, pp. 132–8

Philippi, Paul, 'Nation und Nationalgefühl der Siebenbürger Sachsen 1791–1991', in Rothe (ed.), *Die Siebenbürger Sachsen*, pp. 69–87

    'Von Deutschtum und Zukunft der Siebenbürger Sachsen: Das Gerücht', in Paul Philippi (ed.), *Land des Segens? Fragen an die Geschichte Siebenbürgens und seiner Sachsen* (Cologne: Böhlau, 2008), pp. 350–75

Pichotta, Sören, *Schicksale: Deutsche Zeitzeugen aus Rumänien: Lebensmut trotz Krieg, Deportation und Exodus* (Sibiu: Schiller Verlag, 2013)

Podlipny-Hehn, Annemarie, *Stefan Jäger* (Bucharest: Kriterion, 1972)

    Wir waren Zeugen: Temeswar 1989/90 (Munich: Verlag Südostdeutsches Kulturwerk, 1991)

Prodan, David, *Translyvania and Again Transylvania: A Historical Expose* (Bucharest: Romanian Cultural Foundation, 1992)

Puşcaş, Vasile, 'EU Accession Negotiations: The Case of Romania', *Transylvanian Review* 16/1 (2007), pp. 34–46

Reich, Otto, 'Ihr seid unverbesserliche Faschisten!', in Schuller (ed.), *Aus dem Schweigen der Vergangenheit*, pp. 329–43

Reimisch, Fritz Heinz, *Deutsche Männer in Siebenbürgen: Aus der Kampf- und Leidenszeit der Siebenbürger Sachsen (Deutsche in Aller Welt)* (Leipzig: Koehler & Amelang, 1925)

'Report on the Nominations from Luxembourg and Romania for the European Capital of Culture 2007', *Selection Panel for the European Capital of Culture (ECOC) 2007*, at https://web.archive.org/web/20080904005053/http://ec.europa.eu/culture/pdf/doc670_en.pdf

Rieß, Josef (ed.), *Deutsches Volkwerden im Banat: Reden und Aufsätze Dr Kaspar Muth's* (Timişoara: Ideal, 1935)

Roth, Herbert, *Kein Jahr war vergeblich: Hinter Stacheldraht und Gittern, 1958–1964* (Munich: Südostdeutsches Kulturwerk, 1987)

Rothe, Hans (ed.), *Die Siebenbürger Sachsen in Geschichte und Gegenwart* (Cologne: Böhlau, 1994)

Russland-Deportierte erinnern sich: Schicksale Volksdeutscher aus Rumänien, 1945–1956 (Bucharest: Verlag der Zeitung Neuer Weg, 1992)

Schieder, Theodor et al. (eds.), *Das Schicksal der Deutschen in Rumänien: Dokumentation der Vertreibung der Deutschen aus Ost-Mitteleuropa*, Vol. III (Bonn: Bundesministerium für Vertriebene, 1957)

Schielke-Brenner, Alida, 'Unsre Heimat', in Landsmannschaft der Dobrudscha- und Bulgariendeutschen e.V. (ed.), *Heimatbuch der Dobrudscha-Deutschen, 1840–1940* (Heilbronn: Heilbronner Stimme, 1986), p. 30

Schiff, Robert, *Feldpost: Chronik eines ungebauten Hauses* (Munich: Verlag Südostdeutsches Kulturwerk, 1994)

Schlattner, Eginald, *Der Geköpfte Hahn* (Vienna: Zsolnay Verlag, 1998)

    'Kaleidoskop einer Freundschaft', *Zugänge* 25 (2000), pp. 58–66

    Das Klavier im Nebel (Vienna: Zsolnay Verlag, 2005)

Rote Handschuhe (Vienna: Zsolnay Verlag, 2001)

Schlesak, Dieter, *Capesius, der Auschwitzapotheker* (Bonn: Dietz Verlag, 2006)

　　Eine Transylvanische Reise: Ost–West-Passagen am Beispiel Rumäniens (Cologne: Böhlau, 2004)

　　Vaterlandstage und die Kunst des Verschwindens (Zürich: Benziger, 1986)

　　Visa: Ost–West Lektionen (Frankfurt am Main: S. Fischer, 1970)

　　'Wir wurden erpresst', *Die Zeit*, 23 September 2010, at www.zeit.de/2010/39/ Oskar-Pastior/seite-2

Schneider, Erika, 'Es blüht "an der Burg"', in *Komm Mit '84*, pp. 145–52

Schneider, Erika, Hansgeorg von Killyen and Eckbert Schneider (eds.), *Naturforscher in Hermannstadt: Vorläufer, Gründer und Förderer des Siebenbürgischen Vereins für Naturwissenschaften* (Sibiu: Honterus Verlag, 2007)

Schuller, Bettina, *Führerkinder: Eine Jugend in Siebenbürgen* (Sibiu: Schiller Verlag, 2012)

Schuller, Hermann (ed.), *Aus dem Schweigen der Vergangenheit: Erfahrungen und Berichte aus der siebenbürgischen Evangelischen Kirche A.B. in der Zeit des Kommunismus* (Sibiu: Schiller Verlag, 2013)

　　'Im Schatten des Nationalsozialismus und aus der Wirklichkeit des Nationalkommunismus', in Schuller (ed.), *Aus dem Schweigen der Vergangenheit*, pp. 313–28

Schuster, Oskar (ed.), *Epoche der Entscheidungen: Die Siebenbürger Sachsen im 20. Jahrhundert* (Cologne: Böhlau, 1984)

Der Schwarze-Kirche-Prozess 1957/8: Erlebnisberichte und Dokumentation (Braşov: Aldus Verlag, 2013)

Sebastian, Mihail, *Journal, 1935–1944* (Chicago: Ivan R. Dee, 2000)

Seton-Watson, R. W., *A History of the Roumanians from Roman Times to the Completion of Unity* (London: Cambridge University Press, 1934)

　　Roumania and the Great War (London: Constable and Company Ltd, 1915)

Siegmund, Harald, 'Schreiben als Dauerauftrag eines wechselvollen Lebens: Zu Georg Schergs 75. Geburtstag', in Motzan and Sienerth (eds.), *Worte als Gefahr und Gefährdung*, pp. 143–8

Sienerth, Stefan (ed.), *Dass ich in diesen Raum hinein geboren wurde: Gespräche mit deutschen Schriftstellern aus Südosteuropa* (Munich: Südostdeutsches Kulturwerk, 1997)

Sigmeth, Emil, *In Krieg und Frieden von Cuenca zum Don: Erlebnisse eines Journalisten aus Siebenbürgen* (Munich: Verlag Südostdeutsches Kulturwerk, 1991)

Sterbling, Anton, 'Flucht als Provokation? Bruchstücke einer Erinnerung', *Spieglungen* 1/1 (2006), pp. 58–66

Umbrich, Friedrich (Fred), *Balkan Nightmare: A Transylvanian Saxon in World War II* (Boulder, Co.: East European Monographs, 2000)

Valentin, Anton, *Die Banater Schwaben: Kurzgefasste Geschichte einer Südöstdeutschen Volksgruppe mit einem Volkskundlichen Anhang* (Munich:

Veröffentlichung des Kulturreferates der Landsmannschaft der Banater Schwaben, 1959)

Vasiu, Ana and Daniel Bălţat, *Sibiu/Hermannstadt entdecken* (Sibiu: Honterus, 2007)

Wagner, Ernst, 'Siebenbürgen als Teil des Königreichs Rumänien und der Zweite Weltkrieg (1918–1945)', in Bergel and Myß (eds.), *Wir Siebenbürger*, pp. 77–84

Weber, Wilhelm, *Und über uns der blaue endlose Himmel: Die Deportation in die Baragan-Steppe Rumäniens 1951. Eine Dokumentation* (Munich: Landsmannschaft der Banater Schwaben, 1998)

Wichner, Ernest, 'Blick zurück auf die Aktionsgruppe Banat', in Ernest Wichner (ed.), *Ein Pronomen ist verhaftet worden: Texte der Aktionsgruppe Banat* (Frankfurt am Main: Suhrkamp, 1992), pp. 7–11

Wittstock, Joachim, '"Lasst uns durchhalten!" Eine Stimme aus der Russland-Deportation', in Wittstock and Sienerth (eds.), *'Bitte um baldige Nachricht'*, pp. 60–3

Wittstock, Joachim and Stefan Sienerth (eds.), *'Bitte um baldige Nachricht': Alltag, Politik und Kultur im Spiegel südostdeutscher Korrespondenz des ausgehenden 19. und 20. Jahrhunderts* (Munich: IKGS Verlag, 2003)

Zaharia, Gheorghe (ed.), *Rezistenta antifascista in partea de nord a Transilvaniei septembrie 1944–octombrie 1944* (Bucharest: Editura Dacia, 1974)

Zickeli, Gustav, *Bistritz zwischen 1880 und 1950: Erinnerungen* (Munich: Verlag Südostdeutsches Kulturwerk, 1989)

Zillich, Heinrich, 'Achthundert Jahre', in Bergel and Myß (eds.), *Wir Siebenbürger*, pp. 60–76

Zillich, Heinrich and Volkmar Fromm (eds.), *Wir Siebenbürger: Heimat im Herzen* (Salzburg: Akademischer Gemeinschaftsverlag, 1949

Self-Published Works

Fink, Hans, 'Sachsen als staatstragende Nation', unpublished article

Orendi-Hommenau, Viktor, *Deutsche Dichter aus dem Banat: Literarische Skizze* (Timişoara: self-published, 1921)

    Gestern und Heute: Eine kleine Statistik (Timişoara: self-published, 1928)

Oral History Interviews

Aufgang, Ingrid, 6 August 2005, Sibiu

Bergel, Hans, 18 February 2005, Munich

Biblis, Christa and Joseph Biblis, 14 August 2005, Coburg

Bogdan, Michael, 2 August 2005, Sibiu

Brunner, Gerhard, 12 August 2005, Stuttgart

Frank, Robert, 23 July 2005, Sîntana

Frühbeis, Hermann, 24 February 2005, Sibiu

Hehl, Suzanne, 23 February 2005, Sibiu

Horndasch, Rosalind, 2 August 2005, Sibiu

König, Christa and Robert König, 14 February 2005, Passau

Munteanu, Viktor, 15 August 2005, Tübingen
Oberath, Christine, 16 February 2005, Traunstein
Osterer, Veronika, 24 February 2005, Sibiu
Philippi, Paul, 23 February 2005, Sibiu
Pilsner, Bruno, 2 August 2005, Arad Nou
Schlesak, Dieter, 9 February 2005, Gundelsheim
Schneider, Elizabeth, 24 February 2005, Sibiu
Schräger, Gerlinde and Thomas Schräger, 16 February 2005, Traunstein
Simon, Johann, 23 February 2005, Sibiu
Türk, Robert, 12 August 2005, Gundelsheim

Audio-Visual Sources

'60 ani de la începutul deportării germanilor în fosta Uniune Sovietică – 60 Jahre seit dem Beginn der Russlanddeportation der Rumäniendeutschen', poster and stamped invitation (Reşiţa, 2005), at www.jahrmarkt-banat.de/ Russland2013.html (accessed 29 Jun. 2019)
Danquart, Didi (dir.), *Offset* (2006)
Grabea, Radu (dir.), *Mănuşi Roşii* (2010)
Mungiu, Cristian (dir.), *4 luni, 3 săptămâni şi 2 zile (4 Months, 3 Weeks, 2 Days)* (2007)
Nica, Andrei (dir.), 'Sibiu 2007 – Promotional Video' (2007), at https://www .youtube.com/watch?v=otJHWO8WC-E
Porumboiu, Corneliu (dir.), *A fost sau n-a fost? (12:08 East of Bucharest)* (2006)
Puiu, Cristi (dir.), *Moartea domnului Lăzărescu (The Death of Mr. Lazarescu)* (2005)
Die Restitutionsfalle: Fallbeispiele systematisch verhinderter Immobilienrückgabe in Rumänien, CD (2015)
Schwertner, Hedwig, *Zeichnung* (1945), in Czernetzky et al. (eds.), *Lager Lyrik*, p. 45
Timişoara: 360° Virtual Tour, CD (Timişoara: Banat Media, 2009)
'Zwei Freundinnen im Winter 1947' (Photograph, 1947), in Czernetzky et al. (eds.), *Lager Lyrik*, p. 131

Other Sources

Baier, Hannelore, Heinz-Günther Hüsch and Ernst Meinhardt, *Kauf von Freiheit* (Sibiu: Honterus Verlag, 2013)
Ciuhandu, Gheorghe, 'Cuvânt de bun venit', *Timişoara Open Art City* (promotional material in author's possession)
'Conclusions of the Presidency', *European Council in Copenhagen*, 21–2 June 1993, at http://ue.eu.int/ueDocs/cms_Data/docs/pressdata/en/ec/72921.pdf
'Carl Gibson: Legitimer Protest gegen Ceauşescu-Diktatur', *Siebenbürgische Zeitung* 59/5, 31 March 2009, p. 5

Cordoş, Alin, 'Flăcările care au distrus turnul Bisericii Evanghelice au aşezat o perdea de linişte peste zgomotul campaniei electorale', Mesagerul de Bistriţa-Năsăud, 12 June 2008, at www.mesagerul.ro/index.php? id=id:00000042148

Douglas-Home, Jessica, 'The Origins of the Trust', *Mihai Eminescu Trust*, at www.mihaieminescutrust.org/about-us#origins

'Eginald Schlattners Roman "Rote Handschuhe"', *Siebenbürgische Zeitung*, 30 April 2001, at www.siebenbuerger.de/ubb/Forum11/HTML/000016 .html

'Europa in Siebenbürgen – Konversation und Verhör der Kulturen: Eginald Schlattner (*13.9.1933), Dichter in Europa', *KulturLand: Comunicăm & Proiectăm Regional*, 6 October 2004, at www.kulturland.net/2004/10/06/ 71/

'European Court of Human Rights: Violation by Article and by Country 2006', at www.echr.coe.int/NR/rdonlyres/449186A0-1EEB-4247-B2EF-16 DE8F465D30/0/Table2006ENG.pdf

Gibson, Carl, 'Fragen an Nobelpreisträgerin Herta Müller', *carlgibsongermany*, 15 February 2011, at http://carlgibsongermany.wordpress.com/tag/ nestbeschmutzer/

'Herta Müller: Hass als Antrieb literarischen Schaffens. Argumente und Fakten – aus Carl Gibsons "Wiener Kommentaren"', Carl Gibsons Blog für Literatur, Geschichte, Politik und Zeitkritik, 27 February 2011, at http://carl-gibson.blogspot.com/2011/02/herta-muller-hass-als-antrieb .html

Gouez, Aziliz, 'Introduction', *European Works*, at https://institutdelors.eu/wp-content/uploads/2018/01/european_works_-_internet_version.pdf

'*Heimattag der Banater Schwaben*', at www.dvhh.org/banat/research/ulm-treffen/index.htm

'*Heimattag der Siebenbürger Sachsen*', at www.dinkelsbuehl.de/ISY/index.php? get=203

'Hermannstadt putzt sich heraus', *Transylvania Travel* 8 (2004), at www .transylvaniatravel.net/newsletter/news8_2004.html

'Infrastructure', *Sibiu 2007*, at https://web.archive.org/web/20070411082434/h ttp://www.sibiu2007.ro/en2/infrastructura.htm

Iohannis, Klaus, 'Welcome of the Sibiu Mayor Klaus Johannis', 15 October 2006

'"Das Jahrhundert, an dem ich teilhatte": Hans Bergel im Gespräch mit Dieter Drotleff (1995)', in Pauling, *'Wir werden Sie einkerkern, weil es Sie gibt!'*, pp. 103–16

Koneffke, Jan, 'Roman: Hora staccato', *Die Presse*, 2 December 2005, at www .diepresse.com/Artikel.aspx?channel=k&ressortkl&ik=523899

Kuhnhauser, Hans-Peter, 'Auf der Suche nach Freiheit', *Tauber-Zeitung*, 22 June 2013, at http://kv-banater-schwaben-reutlingen.de/wir-informieren.html

Lauer, Johann, 'Siebenbürger Sachsen – morgen', *Siebenbürger Sachsen – Gestern, Heute, Morgen: Von einer festen Burg zu einem offenen Club*, at www.siebenbuergersachsen.de/geschichte/index.htm

'Luxembourg and Sibiu: 2007 European Capitals of Culture', *European Parliament – Culture*, 25 January 2007

Miroschnikoff, Peter, 'Zigeuner in Siebenbürgen: "Meine braunen Brüder am Bach" – Interview mit Eginald Schlattner', *Südosteuropa Mitteilungen* 4–5 (2005), pp. 43–9

'Old Frau Fernolend's House', *Mihai Eminescu Trust*, at www.mihaieminescutrust.org/viscri

Orban, Leonard, 'The European Union and New Member States' Contribution to Its Future', Speech/07/351, *European Commission Press Release*

'Petition', *ResRo*, at www.resro.eu/attachments/dokumente/petition_070424.pdf

'Petiţie', *ResRo*, at www.resro.eu/attachments/dokumente/petitie_070424.pdf

'Pfui und Schande für Rumänien!!!', *Siebenbürgische Zeitung Online*, 8 December 2005, at www.siebenbuerger.de/ubb/Forum11/HTML/000655.html

Raport Final at www.presidency.ro/static/ordine/RAPORT_FINAL_CPADCR.pdf

'Restitution/Europ. Gerichtshof f. Menschenrechte', at www.siebenbuerger.de/ubb/Forum10/HTML/000206.html

'Restitution/Europäischer Gerichtshof für Menschenrechte', at www.siebenbuerger.de/forum/integration/55-restitution-europaeischer-gerichtshof/

'Romania 2005 Comprehensive Monitoring Report', *European Commission*, Brussels, 25 October 2005, pp. 1–102, at http://ec.europa.eu/enlargement/archives/pdf/key_documents/2005/sec1354_cmr_master_ro_college_en.pdf

Roth, Walter, 'Spätes Erstlingswerk', *Siebenbürgische Zeitung Online*, 9 May 2001, at www.siebenbuerger.de/ubb/Forum11/HTML/000016.html

'Saxon Transylvania "Siebenbürgen"', *Beyond the Forest*, at www.beyondtheforest.com/Romania/SX5.html

'Siebenbürger Sachsen zu Recht im rechten Eck?', *Siebenbürgische Zeitung Online* at www.siebenbuerger.de/ubb/Forum11/HTML/000691.html

'STEFAN JÄGER, Der Schwabenmaler (1877–1962)', *Mitteilungen der Landsmannschaft der Donauschwaben in Oberösterreich* 39/1 (2006), p. 23, at www.donauschwaben.at/verbaende/oberoesterreich/download/Mitteilungen%02006–01.pdf

'Together since 1957', at http://europa.eu/abc/symbols/9-may/gallery/2007/index_en.htm

Totok, William, 'Omul nu se pentru a fi fericit ci pentru a-şi face datoria', *Observator Cultural*, at www.observatorcultural.ro/arhivaarticol.phtml?xid=2472

Secondary Sources

Aarons, Victoria, *Third-Generation Holocaust Representation: Trauma, History, and Memory* (Evanston, Ill.: Northwestern University Press, 2017)

Abelhauser, Werner, Wolfgang von Hippel, Jeffrey Allan Johnson and Raymond G. Stokes, *German Industry and Global Enterprise. BASF: The History of a Company* (Cambridge: Cambridge University Press, 2004)

Agnew, Vijay, *Diaspora, Memory, and Identity: A Search for Home* (Toronto: University of Toronto Press, 2006)

Ahonen, Heiki, 'Wie gründet man ein Museum? Zur Entstehungsgeschichte des Museums der Okkupationen in Tallinn', in Knigge and Mählert (eds.), *Der Kommunismus im Museum*, pp. 107–16

Ahonen, Pertti, *After the Expulsion: West Germany and Eastern Europe 1945–1990* (Oxford: Oxford University Press, 2003)

'Taming the Expellee Threat in Post-1945 Europe: Lessons from the Two Germanies and Finland', *Contemporary European History* 14/1 (2005), pp. 1–21

Aldenhoff-Hübinger, Rita, Catherine Gousseff and Thomas Serrier (eds.), *Europa vertikal: Zur Ost-West-Gliederung im 19. und 20. Jahrhundert* (Göttingen: Wallenstein, 2016)

Allinson, Mark 'Popular Opinion', in Patrick Major and Jonathan Osmond (eds.), *The Workers' and Peasants' State: Communism and Society in East Germany under Ulbricht 1945–1971* (Manchester: Manchester University Press, 2002), pp. 96–111

Ancel, Jean, 'The German–Romanian Relationship and the Final Solution', *Holocaust and Genocide Studies* 19/2 (2005), pp. 252–75

The History of the Holocaust in Romania (Lincoln, Neb.: University of Nebraska Press, 2011)

Anderl, Corina, 'Siebenbürger Sachsen, Banater Schwaben und Landler als Deutsche in Rumänien: Zur Ambivalenz der kulturellen Funktion von Ethnizität in multiethnischen Regionen', in Wilfried Heller et al. (eds.), *Ethnizität in der Transformation: Zur Situation nationaler Minderheiten in Rumänien* (Vienna: LIT Verlag, 2006), pp. 42–55

Andreescu, Florentina C., 'The Changing Face of the Other in Romanian Films', *Nationalities Papers: The Journal of Nationalism and Ethnicity* 39/1 (2011), pp. 77–94

'Seeing the Romanian Transition in Cinematic Space', *Space and Culture* 16/1 (2013), pp. 73–87

Andriescu, Monica, 'Identity Politics under National Communist Rule: The Rhetoric Manifestations of Nicolae Ceauşescu's Nationality Policy in 1970s Romania', *Studia Politica: The Romanian Political Science Review* 9/1 (2009), pp. 105–17

Antohi, Sorin, *Civitas Imaginalis: istorie şi utopie în cultura română* (Iaşi: Polirom, 1999)

Ash, Timothy Garton, 'The Year of Truth', in Vladimir Tismăneanu (ed.), *The Revolutions of 1989* (London: Routledge, 1999), pp. 108–25

Ashplant, T. G., Graham Dawson and Michael Roper (eds.), *The Politics of War Memory and Commemoration* (London: Routledge, 2000)

Assmann, Jan, 'Collective Memory and Cultural Identity', *New German Critique* 65 (1995), pp. 125–33

Baier, Hannelore, 'Arbeitslager für die deutsche Bevölkerung im Innern Rumäniens nach 1945', *Südostdeutsche Vierteljahreshefte* 54/4 (2005), pp. 379–87

'Ceauşescu und die Aussiedlung der Deutschen aus Rumänien', *Zeitschrift für Siebenbürgische Landeskunde* 35/1 (2012), pp. 27–50

'The Deportation of Germans from Romania to Forced Labor in the Soviet Union', *Euxenios* 19–20 (2015), pp. 20–5

'Die deutsche Minderheit in Rumänien 1953–1959', in Rudolf Gräf and Gerald Volkmer (eds.), *Zwischen Tauwettersozialismus und Neostalinismus: Deutsche und andere Minderheiten in Ostmittel- und Südosteuropa 1953–1963* (Munich: IKGS, 2011), pp. 107–18

'Die Deutschen in Rumänien in den Jahren 1945 bis 1948', in Hausleitner (ed.), *Vom Faschismus zum Stalinismus*, pp. 173–80

Germanii din România, 1944–1956 (Sibiu: Honterus, 2005)

Bakić-Hayden, Milica, 'Nesting Orientalisms: The Case of Former Yugoslavia', *Slavic Review* 54/4 (1995), pp. 917–31

Banac, Ivo, Stefano Bottoni, Andrei Cuşco and Alexander Vezenkov, 'National Movements, Regionalism, Minorities', in Balázs Apor, Péter Apor and Sándor Horváth (eds.), *The Handbook of Courage: Cultural Opposition and Its Heritage in Eastern Europe* (Budapest: Hungarian Academy of Sciences, 2018), pp. 523–50

Bărbulescu, Constantin, *Physicians, Peasants, and Modern Medicine: Imagining Rurality in Romania, 1860–1910* (Budapest: CEU Press, 2018)

Bárdi, Nándor, 'Generation Groups in the History of Hungarian Minority Elites', *Regio: Minorities, Politics, Society* 8/1 (2005), pp. 109–24

'Utopias in the Shadow of Catastrophe: The Idea of Székely Self-Determination after the Collapse of Austria-Hungary', in Angela Ilic, Florian Kührer-Wielach, Irena Samide and Tanja Zigon (eds.), *Blick ins Ungewisse: Visionen und Utopien im Donau-Karpaten-Raum 1917 und danach* (Regensburg: Friedrich Pustet, 2019), pp. 73–94

Barta, János, '"Pflüg" mir den Boden, wackre Schwabenfaust": Die deutsche Einwanderung nach Ungarn im 18. Jahrhundert und ihre Bedeutung für Staat und Gesellschaft', in Fata (ed.), *Migration im Gedächtnis*, pp. 23–37

Bartov, Omer, 'Reception and Perception: Goldhagen's Holocaust and the World', in Eley (ed.), *The 'Goldhagen Effect'*, pp. 33–87

Baumgärtner, Wilhelm Andreas, *Der Vergessene Weg: Wie die Sachsen nach Siebenbürgen kamen* (Bonn: Schiller Verlag, 2010)

Eine Welt im Aufbruch: Die Siebenbürger Sachsen im Spätmittelalter (Sibiu: Schiller Verlag, 2008)

Becker, Peter and Olaf Leiße, *Die Zukunft Europas: Der Konvent zur Zukunft der Europäischen Union* (Opladen: Leske + Budrich, 2004)

Beer, Daniel, *The House of the Dead: Siberian Exile under the Tsars* (Harmondsworth: Penguin Books, 2017)

Beer, Mathias (ed.), *Krieg und Zwangsmigration in Südosteuropa 1940–1950: Pläne, Umsetzung, Folgen* (Munich: Franz Steiner Verlag, 2019)

'Verschlusssache, Raubdruck, Autorisierte Fassung', in Cornelißen, Holec and Pešek (eds.), *Diktatur – Krieg – Vertreibung*, pp. 369–401

Beer, Mathias, Dietrich Beyrau and Cornelia Rauh (eds.), *Deutschsein als Grenzerfahrung: Minderheitenpolitik in Europa zwischen 1914 und 1950* (Essen: Klartext, 2009)

Beer, Mathias and Dittmar Dahlmann (eds.), *Migration nach Ost- und Südosteuropa vom 18. bis zum Beginn des 19. Jahrhunderts: Ursachen, Formen, Verlauf, Ergebnis* (Munich: Franz Steiner Verlag, 1999)

Beer, Mathias, Sorin Radu and Florian Kührer-Wielach (eds.), *Germanii din România: migraţie şi patrimoniu cultural după 1945* (Bucharest: Editura Academiei Româna, 2020)

Benz, Wolfgang, 'Anti-Semitism Today', in Davies and Szejnmann (eds.), *How the Holocaust Looks Now*, pp. 261–71

Berdahl, Daphne, *Where the World Ended: Re-Unification and Identity in the German Borderland* (Berkeley: University of California Press, 1999)

Berger, Stefan, 'On Taboos, Traumas and Other Myths: Why the Debate about German Victims Is Not a Historians' Controversy', in Niven (ed.), *Germans as Victims*, pp. 210–24

Betea, Lavinia, Cristina Diac, Florin-Răzvan Mihai and Ilarion Ţiu (eds.), *Lungul drum spre nicăieri: Germanii din România deportaţi în URSS* (Bucharest: Cetatea de Scaun, 2012)

Billig, Michael, *Banal Nationalism* (London: Sage, 1995)

Binder, Gustav, 'Die Reformation in Siebenbürgen', *Siebenbürgische Semesterblätter* 1/1 (1987), pp. 37–55

Bjork, James E., *Neither German nor Pole: Catholicism and National Indifference in a Central European Borderland* (Ann Arbor: University of Michigan Press, 2009)

Blandiana, Ana, 'Die Gedenkstätte Memorial Sighet: Ein lebendiges Museum', in Knigge and Mählert (eds.), *Der Kommunismus im Museum*, pp. 171–80

Blustein, Jeffrey, *The Moral Demands of Memory* (Cambridge: Cambridge University Press, 2008)

Boa, Elizabeth and Rachel Palfreyman, *Heimat: A German Dream – Regional Loyalties and National Identity in German Culture 1890–1990* (Oxford: Oxford University Press, 2000)

Boia, Lucian, *History and Myth in the Romanian Consciousness* (Budapest: CEU Press, 2001)

Istorie şi mit în conştiinţa românească (Bucharest: Humanitas, 1997)

Romania: Borderland of Europe (London: Reaktion Books, 2001)

Bojkov, Viktor D., 'Neither Here, nor There: Romania and Bulgaria in Current European Politics', *Communist and Post-Communist Studies* 37/4 (2004), pp. 509–22

Bolovan, Ioan, Diana Covaci, Daniela Deteșan, Marius Eppel and Elena Crinela Holom, *Legislația ecleziastică și laică privind familia românească din Transilvania în a doua jumătate a secolului al XIX-lea* (Cluj-Napoca: Academia Română, Centrul de Studii Transilvane, 2009)

Bolovan, Ioan, Crinela Elena Holom and Marius Eppel, 'Ethnicity and Politics: Censuses in the Austro-Hungarian Empire (Case Study: Transylvania, 1869–1910)', *Romanian Journal of Population Studies* 10/2 (2016), pp. 137–52

Bracewell, Wendy and Alex Drace-Francis (eds.), *Balkan Departures: Travel Writing from Southeastern Europe* (New York: Berghahn, 2009)

(eds.), *Under Eastern Eyes: A Comparative Introduction to East European Travel Writing on Europe* (Budapest: CEU Press, 2008)

Braumann, Annina, *Kulturtourismus – Möglichkeiten der Imagemodifizierung am Beispiel der europäischen Kulturhauptstadt 2007: Sibiu/Hermannstadt* (Norderstedt: GRIN Verlag, 2007)

Breckner, Roswitha, 'Biographical Continuities and Discontinuities in East–West Migration before and after 1989: Two Case Studies of Migration from Romania to West Germany', in Robin Humphrey, Robert Miller and Elena Zdravomyslova (eds.), *Biographical Research in Eastern Europe: Altered Lives and Broken Biographies* (Aldershot: Ashgate Publishing Ltd, 2003), pp. 191–209

Breuer, Lars and Anna Delius, '1989 in European Vernacular Memory', *East European Politics and Societies and Cultures* 31/1 (2017), pp. 456–78

Bricke, Dieter W., *Minderheiten im östlichen Mitteleuropa: Deutsche und europäische Optionen* (Baden-Baden: Nomos, 1995)

Brubaker, Rogers, 'Ethnicity without Groups', *Journal of European Sociology* 43/2 (2002), pp. 163–89

Ethnicity without Groups (Cambridge, Mass.: Harvard University Press, 2004)

Grounds for Difference (Cambridge, Mass.: Harvard University Press, 2015)

Nationalism Reframed: Nationhood and the National Question in the New Europe (Cambridge: Cambridge University Press, 1996)

Brubaker, Rogers, Margit Feischmidt, Jon Fox and Liana Grancea, *Nationalist Politics and Everyday Ethnicity in a Transylvanian Town* (Princeton: Princeton University Press, 2006)

Brunnbauer, Ulf, *Globalizing Southeastern Europe: Emigrants, America, and the State since the Late Nineteenth Century* (Lanham, Md.: Lexington Books, 2016)

Brusis, Martin, 'Zwischen europäischer und nationaler Identität: Zum Diskurs über die Osterweiterung der EU', in Ansgar Klein, Ruud Koopmans, Hans-Jörg Trenz, Christian Lahusen and Dieter Rucht (eds.), *Europäische Öffentlichkeit – Bürgergesellschaft – Demokratie* (Opladen: Leske + Budrich, 2003), pp. 255–73

Bucur, Maria, *Heroes and Victims: Remembering War in Twentieth-Century Romania* (Bloomington: Indiana University Press, 2009)

'Treznea: Trauma, Nationalism and the Memory of World War II in Romania', *Rethinking History: The Journal of Theory and Practice* 6/1 (2002), pp. 35–55

Bucur, Maria and Nancy Wingfield (eds.), *Staging the Past: The Politics of Commemoration in Habsburg Central Europe, 1848 to the Present* (West Lafayette, Ind.: Purdue University Press, 2001)

Burger, Ulrich, 'Bundesrepublik oder DDR? Anmerkungen zum Deutschlandbild der Rumäniendeutschen nach 1970', *Transylvanian Review* 12/3 (2003), pp. 63–84

Burleigh, Michael, *Germany Turns Eastwards: A Study of* Ostforschung *in the Third Reich* (Cambridge: Cambridge University Press, 1988)

Buru, Lorenda, Roxana Crăciun and Ioana Stanciu, '"In diesem Augenblick ist alles zusammengebrochen . . . ": Zeitliche Zäsuren zwischen 1944–1989 und ihre Auswirkungen auf das Leben der Rumäniendeutschen', in Angelika Herta and Martin Jung (eds.), *Vom Rand ins Zentrum: Die Deutsche Minderheit in Bukarest* (Berlin: Frank & Timme, 2011), pp. 47–65

Butaru, Lucian, 'Biopolitică identitară în Transilvania interbelică', *Studia Universitatis Cibiniensis: Seria Historica* 5 (2008) pp. 195–209

Casagrande, Thomas, *Die Volksdeutsche SS-Division 'Prinz Eugen': Die Banater Schwaben und die Nationalsozialistischen Kriegsverbrechen* (Frankfurt am Main: Campus, 2003)

Casagrande, Thomas, Michal Schvarc, Norbert Spannenberger and Otmar Traşcă, 'The "Volksdeutsche": A Case Study from South-Eastern Europe', in Jochen Böhler and Robert Gerwarth (eds.), *The Waffen-SS: A European History* (Oxford: Oxford University Press, 2016), pp. 209–51

Case, Holly, *Between States: The Transylvanian Question and the European Idea during World War II* (Stanford: Stanford University Press, 2009)

'The Strange Case of Federative Ideas in East-Central Europe', *Journal of Modern History* 85/4 (2013), pp. 833–66

Cercel, Cristian, 'Die Deportation der Rumäniendeutschen in die Sowjetunion und ihre Rolle in den Gedächtnis- und Identitätsdiskursen der in der Bundesrepublik lebenden Siebenbürger Sachsen in den 1950er- und 1960er-Jahren', in Lehmann and Volkmer (eds.), *Rumäniendeutsche Erinnerungskulturen*, pp. 137–52

'Philo-Germanism without Germans: Memory, Identity, and Otherness in Post-1989 Romania' (PhD diss., University of Durham, 2012)

'Philo-Germanism without Germans in Romania after 1989', *East European Politics and Societies* 29/4 (2015), pp. 811–30

'Postwar (West) German–Romanian Relations: Expanding Brubaker's Analytical Triad', *Nationalism and Ethnic Politics* 23/3 (2017), pp. 297–317

'The Relationship between Religious and National Identity in the Case of Transylvanian Saxons, 1933–1944', *Nationalities Papers* 39/2 (2011), pp. 161–80

Romania and the Quest for European Identity: Philo-Germanism without Germans (London: Routledge, 2018)

Chelcea, Liviu, 'The Culture of Shortage during State Socialism: Consumption Practices in a Romanian Village in the 1980s', *Cultural Studies* 16/1 (2002), pp. 16–43

Chu, Winson, *The German Minority in Interwar Poland* (Cambridge: Cambridge University Press, 2013)

'"*Volksgemeinschaften unter sich*": German Minorities and Regionalism in Poland, 1918–1939', in Gregor, Roemer and Roseman (eds.), *German History from the Margins*, pp. 104–26

Ciobanu, Monica, 'Criminalizing the Past and Reconstructing Collective Memory: The Romanian Truth Commission', *Europe–Asia Studies* 61/2 (2011), pp. 315–38

Repression, Resistance and Collaboration in Stalinist Romania 1944–1964: Post-Communist Remembering (London: Routledge, 2020)

Cioflâncă, Adrian, 'A "Grammar of Exculpation" in Communist Historiography: Distortion of the History of the Holocaust under Ceaușescu', *Romanian Journal of Political Science* 4/2 (2004), pp. 29–46

'Politics of Oblivion in Postcommunist Romania', *Romanian Journal of Political Sciences* 2 (2002), pp. 85–93

Clark, Roland, 'From Elite Pamphleteers to Social Movement Protagonists: Antisemitic Activism in 1920s Romania', *Studies on National Movements* 4/1 (2019), pp. 1–35

'From Source Collections to Peer-Reviewed Journals: Romanians Write the Holocaust', *Dapim: Studies on the Holocaust* 31/3 (2017), pp. 307–12

Holy Legionary Youth: Fascist Activism in Interwar Romania (Ithaca, N.Y.: Cornell University Press, 2015)

Clavin, Patricia, *Defining Transnationalism* (Cambridge: Cambridge University Press, 2005)

Coldewey, Gaby et al. (eds.), *Zwischen Pruth und Jordan: Lebenserinnerungen Czernowitzer Juden* (Cologne: Böhlau, 2003)

Confino, Alon, 'Collective Memory and Cultural History: Problems of Method', *American Historical Review* 102/5 (1997), pp. 1386–1403

Connerton, Paul, *How Societies Remember* (Cambridge: Cambridge University Press, 1989)

Conrad, Sebastian, *Globalisation and the Nation in Imperial Germany* (Cambridge: Cambridge University Press, 2010)

Cooke, Paul, *Representing East Germany since Unification: From Colonization to Nostalgia* (Oxford: Berg, 2005)

Cornelißen, Christoph, Roman Holec and Jiří Pešek (eds.), *Diktatur – Krieg – Vertreibung: Erinnerungskulturen in Tschechien, der Slowakei und Deutschland seit 1945* (Essen: Klartext Verlag, 2005)

Cornwall, Mark, *The Devil's Wall: The Nationalist Youth Mission of Heinz Rutha* (Cambridge, Mass.: Harvard University Press, 2012)

'Loyalty and Treason in Late-Habsburg Croatia: A Violent Political Discourse before the First World War', in Jana Osterkamp and Martin Schulze Wessel (eds.), *Exploring Loyalty* (Göttingen: Vandenhoeck & Ruprecht, 2017), pp. 97–120

Danneberg, Stéphanie, 'Die politischen Beziehungen zwischen Sachsen und Rumänen Siebenbürgens in den Jahren 1900–1914', in Vasile Ciobanu and Sorin Radu (eds.), *Partide politice și minorități naționale din România în secolul XX, Vol. II* (Sibiu: Editura Universității 'Lucian Blaga', 2007), pp. 277–94

Wirtschaftsnationalismus lokal Interaktion und Abgrenzung zwischen rumänischen und sächsischen Gewerbeorganisationen in den siebenbürgischen Zentren Hermannstadt und Kronstadt, 1868–1914 (Göttingen: Vandenhoeck & Ruprecht, 2018)

Davies, Martin L. and Claus-Christian W. Szejnmann (eds.), *How the Holocaust Looks Now: International Perspectives* (Basingstoke: Palgrave Macmillan, 2007)

Davis, John R. et al. (eds.), *Transnational Network: German Migrants in the British Empire, 1670–1914* (Leiden: Brill, 2013)

Davis, R. Chris, *Hungarian Religion, Romanian Blood: A Minority's Struggle for National Belonging, 1920–1945* (Madison: University of Wisconsin Press, 2019)

Davis, Sacha E., 'Constructing the *Volksgemeinschaft*: Saxon Particularism and the German Myth of the East, 1919–1933', *German Studies Review* 39/1 (2016), pp. 41–64

'Maintaining a "German" Home in Southeast Europe: Transylvanian Saxon Nationalism and the Metropolitan Model of the Family, 1918–1933', *History of the Family* 14/4 (2009), pp. 386–401

'Reflecting on the Diaspora: The Transylvanian Saxon Self-Image and the Saxons Abroad', *Siebenbürgische Landeskunde* 35/2 (2012), pp. 150–70

Deletant, Dennis, *Communist Terror in Romania: Gheorghiu-Dej and the Police State 1948–1965* (London: Hurst & Company, 1999)

Romania under Communist Rule (Oxford: Center for Romanian Studies and Civic Academy Foundation, 1999)

Delouis, Anne, 'Die Delegation der Banater Schwaben bei der Pariser Friedenskonferenz: Hintergrund und Bedeutung eines unbeachteten Memorandums von 1919', *Revue des études sud-est européennes/Journal of South-East European Studies* 53/1–4 (2015), pp. 279–326

Demshuk, Andrew, *The Lost German East: Forced Migration and the Politics of Memory, 1945–1970* (Cambridge: Cambridge University Press, 2012)

Dietzsch, Ina, 'Geschenkpakete – Ein Fundamentales Mißverständnis: Zur Bedeutung des Paketaustausches in Persönlichen Briefwechseln', in Christian Härtel and Petra Karbus (eds.), *Das Westpaket* (Berlin: Christian Links Verlag, 2000), pp. 105–17

Grenzen Überschreiben? Deutsch–Deutsche Briefwechsel 1949–1989 (Cologne: Böhlau, 2004)

Dimou, Augusta, Stefan Troebst and Maria Todorova (eds.), *Remembering Communism: Private and Public Recollections of Lived Experience in Southeast Europe* (Budapest: CEU Press, 2014)

Diplich, Hans, 'Anton Valentin und die *Banater Monatshefte*', in Georg Wildmann (ed.), *Donauschwaben – Entwicklung und Erbe des donauschwäbischen Volksstammes: Festschrift für Josef Volkmar Senz zum 70. Geburtstag* (Munich, 1982), pp. 221–9

Djuvara, Neagu, *Între Orient și Occident: țările române la începutul epocii moderne* (Bucharest: Humanitas, 2002)

Dobre, Florica, Luminița Banu, Florian Banu and Laura Stancu (eds.), *Acțiunea 'Recuperarea': Securitatea și emigrarea germanilor din România (1962–1989)* (Bucharest: Editura Enciclopedică, 2011)

Docea, Vasile, *Relații româno-germane timpurii* (Cluj-Napoca: Presa Universitară Clujeană, 2000)

Douglas, R. M., *Orderly and Humane: The Expulsion of the Germans after the Second World War* (New Haven: Yale University Press, 2012)

Drace-Francis, Alex, 'Paradoxes of Occidentalism: On Travel and Travel Writing in Ceaușescu's Romania', in Andrew Hammond (ed.), *The Balkans and the West: Constructing the European Other, 1945–2003* (Aldershot: Ashgate, 2003), pp. 69–80

The Traditions of Invention: Romanian Ethnic and Social Stereotypes in Historical Context (Leiden: Brill, 2013)

Dragoman, Dragoș, 'National Identity and Europeanization in Post-Communist Romania. The Meaning of Citizenship in Sibiu: European Capital of Culture 2007', *Communist and Post-Communist Studies* 41/1 (2008), pp. 63–78

Duchesne, Sophie, 'Who's Afraid of Banal Nationalism', *Nations and Nationalism* 24/4 (2018), pp. 841–56

Dutceac Segesten, Anamaria, *Myth, Identity and Conflict: A Comparative Analysis of Romanian and Serbian Textbooks* (Lanham, Md.: Lexington Books, 2011)

Egry, Gábor, 'Ein anderer Ausgleich: Einiges zur Vorgeschichte des Sachsentages 1890', *Zeitschrift für Siebenbürgische Landeskunde* 29/1 (2006), pp. 51–61

'Endangered by Alienation? Raising a Minority Elite between Nationalising Higher Education Systems: The New Generation of Hungarians in Interwar Romania', in Florian Bieber and Harald Heppner (eds.), *Universities and Elite Formation in Central, Eastern and South Eastern Europe* (Vienna: LIT Verlag, 2015), pp. 39–59

'Unholy Alliances? Language Exams, Loyalty, and Identification in Interwar Romania', *Slavic Review* 76/4 (2017), pp. 959–82

Eicher, John, *Exiled among Nations: German and Mennonite Mythologies in a Transnational Age* (Cambridge: Cambridge University Press, 2020)

Eldridge, Claire, *From Empire to Exile: History and Memory within the Pied-Noir and Harki Communities, 1962–2012* (Manchester: Manchester University Press, 2016)

Eley, Geoff (ed.), *The 'Goldhagen Effect': History, Memory, Nazism – Facing the German Past* (Ann Arbor: University of Michigan Press, 2000)

Engel, Pál, *The Realm of St Stephen: A History of Medieval Hungary, 895–1526* (London: I. B. Tauris, 2005)

Etkind, Alexander, Rory Finnin, Uilleam Blacker, Julie Fedor, Simon Lewis, Maria Mälksoo and Matilda Mroz, *Remembering Katyn* (Cambridge: Polity, 2012)

Evans, Robert John Weston, *Austria, Hungary, and the Habsburgs: Central Europe c. 1683–1867* (Oxford: Oxford University Press, 2006)

Fassin, Didier and Richard Rechtman, *The Empire of Trauma: An Inquiry into the Condition of Victimhood* (Princeton: Princeton University Press, 2009)

Fata, Márta, 'Die Ansiedlungsgeschichte im Gedächtnis: Wie sie Peter Treffil aus Triebswetter/Banat erzählt', in Kriegleder, Seidler and Tancer (eds.), *Deutsche Sprache und Kultur im Banat*, pp. 197–211

'Einwanderung und Ansiedlung der Deutschen (1686–1790)', in Schödl (ed.), *Deutsche Geschichte im Osten Europas*, pp. 89–197

'Migration im Gedächtnis: Auswanderung und Ansiedlung in der Identitätsbildung der Donauschwaben', in Fata (ed.), *Migration im Gedächtnis*, pp. 7–21

(ed.), *Migration im Gedächtnis: Auswanderung und Ansiedlung in der Identitätsbildung der Donauschwaben* (Stuttgart: Franz Steiner, 2013)

Migration im kameralistischen Staat Josephs II: Theorie und Praxis der Ansiedlungspolitik in Ungarn, Siebenbürgen, Galizien und der Bukowina von 1768 bis 1790 (Münster: Aschendorff, 2014)

Fischer, Lisa, *Eden hinter den Wäldern. Samuel von Brukenthal: Politiker, Sammler, Freimaurer in Hermannstadt/Sibiu* (Cologne: Böhlau, 2007)

Fisher, Gaëlle, *Resettlers and Survivors: Bukovina and the Politics of Belonging in West Germany and Israel, 1945–1989* (New York: Berghahn, 2020)

Fisher, Kate, *Birth Control, Sex and Marriage in Britain, 1918–1960* (Oxford: Oxford University Press, 2006)

'Forum: The *Historikerstreit* Twenty Years On', *German History* 24/4 (2006), pp. 587–607

Fox, Jon E., 'From National Inclusion to Economic Exclusion: Transylvanian Hungarian Ethnic Return Migration to Hungary', in Tsuda Takeyuki (ed.), *Diasporic Homecomings: Ethnic Return Migration in Comparative Perspective* (Stanford: Stanford University Press, 2009), pp. 186–207

Fox, Jon E. and Maarten van Ginderachter, 'Introduction: Everyday Nationalism's Evidence Problem', *Nations and Nationalism* 24/3 (2018), pp. 546–52

Frank, Arne, *Das wehrhafte Sachsenland: Kirchenburgen im südlichen Siebenbürgen* (Potsdam: Deutsches Kulturforum Östliches Europa, 2007)

Frank, Matthew, *Making Minorities History: Population Transfer in Twentieth-Century Europe* (Oxford: Oxford University Press, 2017)

Freund, Alexander, *Aufbrüche nach dem Zusammenbruch: Die deutsche Nordamerika-Auswanderung nach dem Zweiten Weltkrieg* (Göttingen: Vandenhoeck & Ruprecht, 2004)

Fromm, Waldemar, '"Anders rinnt hier die Zeit". Erinnerung und kollektives Gedächtnis in Adolf Meschendörfers *Siebenbürgische Elegie*: Mit Hinweisen zur Rezeption nach 1945', in Lehmann and Volkmer (eds.), *Rumäniendeutsche Erinnerungskulturen*, pp. 47–62

Frühmesser, Thomas, *Hans Otto Roth: Biographie eines rumäniendeutschen Politikers (1890–1953)* (Cologne: Böhlau, 2013)

Gabanyi, Anneli Ute, 'Die Deutschen in Rumänien: Exodus oder Neuanfang?', in Rothe (ed.), *Die Siebenbürger Sachsen*, pp. 89–104

'Geschichte der Deutschen in Rumänien', in Bundeszentrale für politische Bildung (ed.), *Aussiedler: Informationen zur politischen Bildung* 267 (Bonn: Bundeszentrale für politische Bildung, 2000), pp. 10–16

'Rumänien – Anatomie einer Dauerkrise', in Jürgen Elvert and Michael Salewski (eds.), *Der Umbruch im Osten* (Stuttgart: Franz Steiner Verlag, 1993), pp. 135–48

'Rumänien in (welchem) Europa heute?', in Anton Sterbling (ed.), *Migrationsprozesse: Probleme von Abwanderungsregionen Identitätsfragen* (Hamburg: Krämer Verlag, 2006), pp. 89–110

'Rumänien und Bulgarien: EU-Beitritt mit Auflagen', *SWP-Aktuell* 27 (2006) at www.swp-berlin.org/common/get_document.php?asset_id=3031

Rumänien vor dem EU-Beitritt (Berlin: Stiftung Wissenschaft und Politik, 2005)

'Rumäniens Beitritt zur EU: 2007 oder 2008?', *Südosteuropa-Mitteilungen: Vierteljahresschrift der Südosteuropa-Gesellschaft e.V.* 46/1 (2006), pp. 4–17

Gallagher, Joseph J. and Philip N. J. Tucker, 'Aussiedler Migration and Its Impact on Braşov's Ethnic German Population and Built Environment', *GeoJournal* 50/2 & 3 (2000), pp. 305–9

Gallagher, Tom, *Theft of a Nation: Romania since Communism* (London: C. Hurst & Co., 2005)

Geana, Gheorghita, 'Nichtorganische Entwicklung, Eigentumsform und die moralische Krise in Rumänien nach 1989', in Anneli Ute Gabanyi and Anton Sterbling (eds.), *Sozialstruktureller Wandel, soziale Probleme und soziale Sicherung in Südosteuropa* (Munich: Südosteuropa-Gesellschaft, 2000), pp. 191–204

Georgescu, Paul, '"Volksdeutsche" in der Waffen-SS', *Südostdeutsche Vierteljahreshefte* 53/2 (2004), pp. 117–23

Georgescu, Tudor, 'Ethnic Minorities and the Eugenic Promise: The Transylvanian Saxon Experiment with National Renewal in Interwar Romania', *European Review of History/ Revue Européenne d'Histoire* 17/6 (2010), pp. 861–80

The Eugenic Fortress: The Transylvanian Saxon Experiment in Interwar Romania (Budapest: CEU Press, 2016)

'Pursuing the Fascist Promise: The Transylvanian Saxon "Self-Help" from Genesis to Empowerment, 1922–1935', in Robert Pyrah and Marius Turda (eds.), *Re-contextualising East Central European History: Nation, Culture and Minority Groups* (London: Legenda, 2010), pp. 55–73

Gerner, Kristian, 'Between the Holocaust and Trianon: Historical Culture in Hungary', in Davies and Szejnmann (eds.), *How the Holocaust Looks Now*, pp. 97–106

van Ginderachter, Maarten and Jon Fox (eds.), *National Indifference and the History of Nationalism in Modern Europe* (New York: Routledge, 2019)

Giustino, Cathleen M., Catherine J. Plum and Alexander Vari (eds.), *Socialist Escapes: Breaking Away from Ideology and Everyday Routine in Eastern Europe* (New York: Berghahn, 2013)

Glajar, Valentina, *The German Legacy in East-Central Europe as Recorded in Recent German-Language Literature* (Rochester, N.Y.: Camden House, 2004)

'The Presence of the Unresolved Recent Past: Herta Müller and the Securitate', in Brigid Haines and Lyn Marven (eds.), *Herta Müller* (Oxford: Oxford University Press, 2013), pp. 49–63

'"You'll Never Make a Spy out of Me": The File Story of "Fink Susanne"', in Glajar, Lewis and Petrescu (eds.), *Secret Police Files from the Eastern Bloc*, pp. 56–83

Glajar, Valentina, Alison Lewis and Corina L. Petrescu (eds.), *Secret Police Files from the Eastern Bloc: Between Surveillance and Life Writing* (Rochester: Camden House, 2016)

Glass, Christian, 'Die inszinierte Einwanderung: Stefan Jägers Triptychon "Die Einwanderung der Schwaben in das Banat" und seine Wirkungsgeschichte', in Fata (ed.), *Migration im Gedächtnis*, pp. 55–70

Glass, Hildrun, *Minderheit zwischen zwei Diktaturen: Zur Geschichte der Juden in Rumänien 1944–1949* (Munich: Oldenbourg, 2002)

Goldhagen, Daniel J., *Hitler's Willing Executioners: Ordinary Germans and the Holocaust* (New York: Vintage Books, 1997)

Goldsworthy, Vesna, *Inventing Ruritania: The Imperialism of the Imagination* (New Haven: Yale University Press, 1998)

Göllner, Carl, 'Bevölkerung: Soziale Struktur 1849–1914', in Carl Göllner (ed.), *Die Siebenbürgen Sachsen 1848–1918* (Cologne: Böhlau, 1988), pp. 37–55

Gombocz, István, '"Sich bewähren, oder bewahren?" Einführung in Leben und Schaffen des siebenbürgischen Autors Eginald Schlattner', *Monatshefte* 106/2 (2014), pp. 270–92

Górny, Maciej and Kornelia Kończal, 'The (Non-)Travelling Concept of *Les Lieux de Mémoire*', in Małgorzata Pakier and Joanna Wawrzyniak (eds.), *Memory and Change in Europe: Eastern Perspectives* (New York: Berghahn, 2016), pp. 59–76

Gorsuch, Anne E. and Diane P. Koenker (eds.), *Turizm: The Russian and East European Tourist under Capitalism and Socialism* (Ithaca, N.Y.: Cornell University Press, 2006)

Gottzmann, Carola L. and Petra Hörner, *Verheissung und Verzweiflung im Osten: Die Siedlungsgeschichte der Deutschen im Spiegel der Dichtung* (Hildesheim: Georg Olms Verlag, 1998)

Gregor, Neil, Nils Roemer and Mark Roseman (eds.), *German History from the Margins* (Bloomington: Indiana University Press, 2006)

Grewlich, Klaus W., 'Rumänien auf dem Weg nach Europa: Wirtschafts- und Finanzpolitische Perspektiven des EU-Beitritts', *Internationale Politik* 61/7 (2006), pp. 92–6

Gschwandtner, Franz, 'Ansiedlung und Landesausbau im Banat des 18. Jahrhunderts', *Transylvanian Review* 14/2 (2005), pp. 44–69

Gündisch, Konrad, 'Die "Geistliche Universität" der siebenbürgisch-sächsischen Kirchengemeinden im 15. und 16. Jahrhundert', in Leppin and Wien (eds.), *Konfessionsbildung und Konfessionskultur*, pp. 105–14

(ed.), *Generalprobe Burzenland: Neue Forschungen zur Geschichte des Deutschen Ordens in Siebenbürgen und im Banat* (Cologne: Böhlau, 2012)

Siebenbürgen und die Siebenbürger Sachsen (Munich: Langen-Müller, 1998)

Hagen, William W., *German History in Modern Times: Four Lives of the Nation* (Cambridge: Cambridge University Press, 2012)

Ordinary Prussians: Brandenburg Junkers and Villagers, 1500–1840 (New York: Cambridge University Press, 2002)

Haines, Brigid (ed.), *Herta Müller* (Cardiff: University of Wales Press, 1998)

(ed.), *Herta Müller and the Currents of European History* (Oxford: Wiley, 2020)

'"Leben wir im Detail": Herta Müller's Micro-Politics of Resistance', in Brigid Haines (ed.), *Herta Müller* (Cardiff: University of Wales Press, 1998), pp. 109–25

Haines, Brigid and Lyn Marven (eds.), *Herta Müller* (Oxford: Oxford University Press, 2013)

Halbwachs, Maurice, *On Collective Memory* (Chicago: University of Chicago Press, 1992)

Hann, Chris, *The Skeleton at the Feast: Contributions to East European Anthropology* (Canterbury, UK: Centre for Social Anthropology and Computing Monographs, 1995)

Härtel, Christian and Petra Karbus (eds.), *Das Westpaket* (Berlin: Christian Links Verlag, 2000)

Hausleitner, Mariana (ed.), *Deutsche und Juden in Bessarabien: 1814–1941* (Munich: IKGS Verlag, 2005)

Die Donauschwaben 1868–1948: Ihre Rolle im rumänischen und serbischen Banat (Stuttgart: Franz Steiner Verlag, 2014)

'Politische Bestrebungen der Schwaben im serbischen und im rumänischen Banat vor 1945', in Hausleitner (ed.), *Vom Faschismus zum Stalinismus*, pp. 41–62

(ed.), *Vom Faschismus zum Stalinismus: Deutsche und andere Minderheiten in Ostmittel- und Südosteuropa 1941–1953* (Munich: IKGS Verlag, 2008)

Hausleitner, Mariana, Brigitte Mihok and Juliane Wetzel (eds.), *Rumänien und der Holocaust: Zu den Massenverbrechen in Transnistrien 1941–1944* (Berlin: Metropol Verlag, 2001)

Hausleitner, Mariana and Harald Roth (eds.), *Der Einfluss von Faschismus und Nationalsozialismus auf Minderheiten in Ostmittel- und Südosteuropa* (Munich: IKGS Verlag, 2006)

Haynes, Rebecca, *Romanian Policy towards Germany, 1936–1940* (Basingstoke: Palgrave Macmillan, 2000)

'Saving Greater Romania: The Romanian Legionary Movement and the "New Man"', in Mark Cornwall and John Paul Newman (eds.), *Sacrifice and*

Rebirth: The Legacy of the Last Habsburg War (New York: Berghahn, 2016), pp. 174–96

Heller, Wilfried, Peter Jordan, Thede Kahl and Josef Sallanz (eds.), *Ethnizität in der Transformation: Zur Situation nationaler Minderheiten in Rumänien* (Vienna: LIT Verlag, 2006)

Heppner, Harald, 'Wien als Orientierungsraum städtischer Gestaltung im Karpatenraum', *Transylvanian Review* 14/1 (2005), pp. 69–79

Herbstritt, Georg, 'Ein feindliches Bruderland: Rumänien im Blick der DDR-Staatssicherheit', *Halbjahresschrift für südosteuropäische Geschichte, Literatur und Politik* 16/1 (2004), pp. 5–13

'Rumänische Zeitgeschichte: Vier Arbeiten über Rumänien während der kommunistischen Diktatur', *Horch und Guck: Zeitschrift zur kritischen Aufarbeitung der SED-Diktatur* 62/4 (2008), pp. 70–2

'Stasi in Siebenbürgen: Eine geheimdienstliche Regionalstudie', *Zeitschrift für Siebenbürgische Landeskunde* 29/2 (2006), pp. 187–96

Herf, Jeffrey, *Divided Memory: The Nazi Past in the Two Germanys* (Cambridge, Mass.: Harvard University Press, 1997)

Hitchins, Keith, *The Romanians, 1774–1886* (Oxford: Oxford University Press, 1996)

Hodgkin, Katherine and Susannah Radstone (eds.), *Contested Pasts: The Politics of Memory* (London: Routledge, 2003)

Holian, Anna, 'Anticommunism in the Streets: Refugee Politics in Cold War Germany', *Journal of Contemporary History* 45/1 (2010), pp. 134–61

Between National Socialism and Soviet Communism: Displaced Persons in Postwar Germany (Ann Arbor: University of Michigan Press, 2011)

Holló, László, 'The Clash of Civilisations: Der Fall Siebenbürgen', *Studia Universitatis Babes-Bolyai – Theologia Catholica Latina* 1 (2005), pp. 57–82

Hosking, Geoffrey and György Schöpflin (eds.), *Myths and Nationhood* (London: Hurst, 1997)

Hughes, Alina, 'Will There Be Conflict? Identity and Values Tensions in Transylvania's Saxon Villages', *Europolis* 4 (2008), pp. 309–28

Hughes, Michael L., '"Through No Fault of Our Own": West Germans Remember Their War Losses', *German History* 18/2 (2000), pp. 193–213

Hunyadi, Attila Gábor, 'National Economic Self-Organizational Models in Transylvania: The Confluences of the Hungarian, German and Romanian Cooperative Movements', in Attila Gábor Hunyadi (ed.), *State and Minority in Transylvania, 1918–1989: Studies on the History of the Hungarian Community* (Boulder, Co.: Atlantic Research and Publications, 2012), pp. 27–59

Iacob, Gheorghe, 'Romanians during the Emergence of Nation-States (1859–1918)', in Pop and Bolovan (eds.), *History of Romania Compendium*, pp. 501–81

Ingenhoven, Katrin, *'Ghetto' oder gelungene Integration? Untersuchung sozialräumlicher Entwicklungsprozesse in der bedeutesten Siedlungskonzentration von Aussiedlern aus*

Rumänien, der Siebenbürger-Sachsen-Siedlung in Wiehl-Drabenderhöhe (Munich: LIT Verlag, 2003)

Ioanid, Radu, *The Holocaust in Romania: The Destruction of Jews and Gypsies under the Antonescu Regime, 1940–1944* (Chicago: Ivan R. Dee, 2000)

Iordachi, Constantin, *Liberalism, Constitutional Nationalism, and Minorities: The Making of Romanian Citizenship, c. 1750–1918* (Leiden: Brill, 2019)

Iriye, Akire and Pierre-Yves Saunier (eds.), *The Palgrave Dictionary of Transnational History* (Basingstoke: Palgrave Macmillan, 2009)

Irwin-Zarecka, Iwona, *Frames of Remembrance: The Dynamics of Collective Memory* (Rutgers: Transaction Publishers, 2007)

Ittu, Gudrun-Liane, 'Viktor Orendi-Hommenau (1870–1954): Ein Siebenbürger im Dienste der deutschen Sprache und Kultur im Banat', in Kriegleder, Seidler and Tancer (eds.), *Deutsche Sprache und Kultur im Banat*, pp. 211–25

'Vom Ministerialrat, geschätzten Publizisten und Übersetzer zum mittellosen Bittsteller: Viktor Orendi-Hommenau (1870–1954) im Jahre 1944', *Germanistische Beiträge* 28 (2011), pp. 56–66

Jarausch, Konrad H., 'Critical Memory and Civil Society: The Impact of the 1960s on German Debates about the Past', in Philipp Gassert and Alan E. Steinweis (eds.), *Coping with the Nazi Past: West German Debates on Nazism and Generational Conflict, 1955–1975* (London: Berghahn, 2007), pp. 11–30

'Removing the Nazi Stain? The Quarrel of the Historians', *German Studies Review* 11/2 (1988), pp. 285–301

Jones, Sara, 'Conflicting Evidence: Hermann Kant and the Opening of the Stasi Files', *German Life and Letters* 62/2 (2009), pp. 190–205

Judson, Pieter, *Guardians of the Nations: Activists on the Language Frontiers of Imperial Austria* (Cambridge, Mass.: Harvard University Press, 2006)

The Habsburg Empire: A New History (Cambridge, Mass.: Harvard University Press, 2016)

'Nationalizing Rural Landscapes in Cisleithenia, 1880–1914', in Nancy Wingfield (ed.), *Creating the Other: Ethnic Conflict and Nationalism in Habsburg Central Europe* (New York: Berghahn, 2003), pp. 127–48

'When Is a Diaspora not a Diaspora? Rethinking Nation-Centered Narratives in Habsburg East Central Europe', in Krista O'Donnell, Renate Bridenthal and Nancy Reagin (eds.), *The Heimat Abroad: The Boundaries of Germanness* (Ann Arbor: University of Michigan, 2005), pp. 219–47

Judson, Pieter and Marsha Rozenblit (eds.), *Constructing Nationalities in East Central Europe* (New York: Berghahn, 2003)

Kallestrup, Shona, *Art and Design in Romania, 1866–1927: Local and International Aspects of the Search for National Expression* (Boulder, Co.: East European Monographs, 2006)

Kalman, Samuel, 'Faisceau Visions of Physical and Moral Transformation and the Cult of Youth in Interwar France', *European History Quarterly* 33/2 (2003), pp. 343–66

Kamusella, Tomasz, 'Central European Castles in the Air? A Reflection on the Malleable Concepts of Central Europe', *Kakanien Revisited* (July 2011), at www.kakanien-revisited.at/beitr/essay/TKamusella1.pdf

Silesia and Central European Nationalisms: The Emergence of National and Ethnic Groups in Prussian Silesia and Austrian Silesia, 1848–1918 (Lafayette, Ind.: Purdue University Press, 2007)

Kamusella, Tomasz, James Bjork, Timothy Wilson and Anna Novikov (eds.), *Creating Nationality in Central Europe, 1880–1950: Modernity, Violence and (Be) Longing in Upper Silesia* (Abingdon: Routledge, 2016)

Kansteiner, Wulf, 'Losing the War – Winning the Memory Battle: The Legacy of Nazism, World War II, and the Holocaust in the Federal Republic of Germany', in Richard Lebow, Wulf Kansteiner and Claudio Fogu (eds.), *The Politics of Memory in Postwar Europe* (Durham, N.C.: Duke University Press, 2006), pp. 102–46

'Nazis, Viewers and Statistics: Television History, Television Audience Research and Collective Memory in West Germany', *Journal of Contemporary History* 39/4 (2004), pp. 575–98

'Television Archives and the Making of Collective Memory: Nazism and World War II in Three Television Blockbusters of German Public Television', in Francis X. Blouin Jr and William G. Rosenberg (eds.), *Archives, Documentation, and Institutions of Social Memory: Essays from the Sawyer Seminar* (Ann Arbor: University of Michigan Press, 2007), pp. 368–78

Kaser, Karl, *Südosteuropäische Geschichte und Geschichtswissenschaft* (Cologne: Böhlau, 2002)

Keil, André, 'The *Preußenrenaissance* Revisited: German–German Entanglements, the Media and the Politics of History in the Late German Democratic Republic', *German History* 34/2 (2016), pp. 258–78

Keul, István, *Early Modern Religious Communities in East-Central Europe: Ethnic Diversity, Denominational Plurality, and Corporative Politics in the Principality of Transylvania (1526–1691)* (Leiden: Brill, 2009)

Kind-Kovács, Fredericke, *Written Here, Published There: How Underground Crossed the Iron Curtain* (Budapest: CEU Press, 2014)

King, Jeremy, *Budweisers into Czechs and Germans: A Local History of Bohemian Politics, 1848–1948* (Princeton: Princeton University Press, 2005)

Kiss, Csilla, 'The Misuses of Manipulation: The Failure of Transitional Justice in Post-Communist Hungary', *Europe–Asia Studies* 58/6 (2006), pp. 925–40

'We Are Not Like Us – Transitional Justice: The (Re)Construction of Post-Communist Memory', in Alice MacLachlan and Ingvild Torsen (eds.), *History and Judgement* (Vienna: IWM Junior Visiting Fellows' Conferences, 2006), at www.iwm.at/index.php?option=com_content&task=view&id=484&Itemid=27

Kissau, Kathrin, 'Ceauşescu, Dracula und Waisenhäuser? Einblicke in das Image Rumäniens in Deutschland', *Südosteuropa Mitteilungen* 48/4 (2006), pp. 44–55

Klussmann, Paul Gerhard, 'Verhör und Selbstverhör: Eginald Schlattners Roman *Rote Handschuhe*' *IDF-Publik*, 37, 8 December 2004, 6, at www.ruhr-uni-bochum.de/deutschlandforschung/PDF_Dateien/idfp37.pdf

Knigge, Volkhard and Ulrich Mählert (eds.), *Der Kommunismus im Museum: Formen der Auseinandersetzung in Deutschland und Ostmitteleuropa* (Cologne: Böhlau, 2005)

Kolstø, Pål (ed.), *Myths and Boundaries in South-Eastern Europe* (London: Hurst, 2005)

Komjathy, Anthony and Rebecca Stockwell, *German Minorities and the Third Reich: Ethnic Germans of East Central Europe between the Wars* (New York: Holmes & Meier, 1980)

König, Walter (ed.), *Siebenbürgen zwischen den beiden Weltkriegen* (Cologne: Böhlau, 1994)

Konnerth, Gerhard, 'Jubilee Address: Forty Years of Philological Studies in Sibiu', in Eric Gilder, Alexandra Mitrea and Ana-Karina Schneider (eds.), *The English Connection: Forty Years of Studies at 'Lucian Blaga' University of Sibiu* (Bucharest and Sibiu, 2010), pp. 19–29, at http://unesdoc.unesco.org /images/0019/001907/190746e.pdf

Koranyi, James, 'Reinventing the Banat: Cosmopolitanism as a German Cultural Export', *German Politics and Society* 29/3 (2011), pp. 97–114

'The Thirteen Martyrs of Arad: A Monumental Hungarian History', in Dominik Geppert and Frank Müller (eds.), *Sites of Imperial Memory: Commemorating Colonial Rule in the Nineteenth and Twentieth Centuries* (Manchester: Manchester University Press, 2015), pp. 53–69

'Voyages of Socialist Discovery: German–German Exchanges between the GDR and Romania', *Slavonic and East European Review* 92/3 (2014), pp. 479–506

Koranyi, James and Ruth Wittlinger, 'From Diaspora to Diaspora: The Case of Transylvanian Saxons in Romania and Germany', *Nationalism and Ethnic Politics* 17/1 (2011), pp. 96–115

Krenzler, Horst Günther, *Preparing for the Acquis Communautaire* (Florence: European University Institute, 1998)

Kriegleder, Wynfried, Andrea Seidler and Jozef Tancer (eds.), *Deutsche Sprache und Kultur im Banat: Studien zur Geschichte, Presse, Literatur und Theater, sprachlichen Verhältnissen, Wissenschafts-, Kultur- und Buchgeschichte, Kulturkontakten und Identitäten* (Bremen: Edition Lumière, 2015)

Kroner, Michael, 'Politische Prozesse gegen Deutsche im kommunistischen Rumänien: Versuch einer Bestandaufnahme und eines Überblicks', in Motzan and Sienerth (eds.), *Worte als Gefahr und Gefährdung*, pp. 31–49

'Zwei aufschlussreiche Zeitungsurteile über die Behandlung der Siebenbürger Sachsen im Jahre 1946: Vertreibung, Umsiedlung oder produktive Eingliederung', *Südostdeutsche Vierteljahreshefte* 53/1 (2004), pp. 31–6

Kührer-Wielach, Florian, '"Der gemeinsame Kampf gegen den Faschismus" in der rumäniendeutschen Zeitschrift *Forschungen zur Volks- und Landeskunde*: Ein Diskurs zwischen ideologischer Umziehung, gesellschaftlicher Integration und wirtschaftlicher Wertsteigerung', in Lehmann and Volkmer (eds.), *Rumäniendeutsche Erinnerungskulturen*, pp. 153–68

Siebenbürgen ohne Siebenbürger? Zentralstaatliche Integration und politischer Regionalismus nach dem Ersten Weltkrieg (Munich: De Gruyter, 2014)

Kurlander, Eric, '*Völkisch*-Nationalism and Universalism on the Margins of the Reich: A Comparison of Majority and Minority Liberalism in Germany, 1898–1933', in Gregor, Roemer and Roseman (eds.), *German History from the Margins*, pp. 84–103

Kürti, László, *The Remote Borderland: Transylvania in the Hungarian Imagination* (Albany: SUNY Press, 2001)

Kwan, Jonathan, 'Austro-German Liberalism and the Coming of the 1867 Compromise: "Politics Again in Flux"', *Austrian History Yearbook* 44 (2013), pp. 62–87

'Transylvanian Saxon Politics and Imperial Germany, 1871–1876', *Historical Journal* 61/4 (2018), pp. 991–1015

'Transylvanian Saxon Politics, Hungarian State Building and the Case of the *Allgemeiner Deutscher Schulverein* (1881–1882)', *English Historical Review* 127/526 (2012), pp. 592–624

Laczó, Ferenc and Joanna Wawrzyniak, 'Memories of 1989 in Europe between Hope, Dismay, and Neglect', *East European Politics and Societies and Cultures* 31/1 (2017), pp. 431–8

Langer, Sarah, *Zwischen Bohème und Dissidenz: Die Aktionsgruppe Banat und ihre Autoren in der rumänischen Diktatur* (Chemnitz: Institut für Europäische Studien, 2010), at www.tu-chemnitz.de/phil/europastudien/aktivitaeten/aies/veroeffentlichungen/LangerBA-Arbeit8.pdf

Lebow, Richard, Wulf Kansteiner and Claudio Fogu (eds.), *The Politics of Memory in Postwar Europe* (Durham, N.C.: Duke University Press, 2006)

Lehmann, Jürgen and Gerald Volkmer (eds.), *Rumäniendeutsche Erinnerungskulturen: Formen und Funktionen des Vergangenheitsbezuges in der rumäniendeutschen Historiografie und Literatur* (Regensburg: Verlag Friedrich Pustet, 2016)

Leiße, Olaf, Utta-Kristin Leiße, and Alexander Richter, *Beitrittsbarometer Rumänien: Grundprobleme des Landes und Einstellung Rumänischer Jugendlicher auf dem Weg in Europäische Union* (Wiesbaden: Deutscher Universitäts-Verlag, 2004)

Lengyel, Zsolt and Ulrich Wien (eds.), *Siebenbürgen in der Habsburgermonarchie: Vom Leopoldinum bis zum Ausgleich (1690–1867)* (Cologne: Böhlau, 1999)

Leppin, Volker and Wien, Ulrich A. (eds.), *Konfessionsbildung und Konfessionskultur in Siebenbürgen in der Frühen Neuzeit* (Stuttgart: Franz Steiner Verlag, 2005)

Levy, Robert, *Ana Pauker: The Rise and Fall of a Jewish Communist* (Berkeley: University of California Press, 2001)

Lewis, Simon, *Belarus – Alternative Visions: Nation, Memory and Cosmopolitanism* (Abingdon: Routledge, 2018)

Lezová, Katarína, 'The Notion of Kosovo as a Precedent and the Impact of the Hungarian Minority Issue on Slovakia's Policy towards Kosovo's Independence', *Europe–Asia Studies* 65/5 (2013), pp. 965–91

Light, Duncan, 'Gazing on Communism: Heritage Tourism and Post-Communist Identities in Germany, Hungary, and Romania', *Tourism Geographies* 2/2 (2000), pp. 157–76

  'An Unwanted Past: Contemporary Tourism and the Heritage of Communism in Romania', *International Journal of Heritage Studies* 6/2 (2000), pp. 145–60

Light, Duncan, Ion Nicolae and Bogdan Suditu, 'Toponymy and the Communist City: Street Names in Bucharest, 1948–1965', *GeoJournal* 56/2 (2002), pp. 135–44

Linden, Ronald H. and Lisa M. Pohlman, 'Now You See It, Now You Don't: Anti-EU Politics in Central and Southeast Europe', *Journal of European Integration* 25/4 (2003), pp. 311–34

Litván, György, *A Twentieth-Century Prophet: Oszkár Jászi* (Budapest: CEU Press, 2006)

Liulevicius, Vejas, *The German Myth of the East, 1800 to the Present* (Oxford: Oxford University Press, 2009)

Livezeanu, Irina, *Cultural Politics in Greater Romania: Regionalism, Nation Building, and Ethnic Struggle, 1918–1930* (Ithaca, N.Y.: Cornell University Press, 1995)

Lumans, Valdis O., *Himmler's Auxiliaries: The Volksdeutsche Mittelstelle and the German National Minorities of Europe 1933–1945* (Chapel Hill: University of North Carolina Press, 1993)

Maaz, Hans-Joachim, *Das Gestürzte Volk: Die Unglückliche Einheit* (Berlin: Argon Verlag, 1991)

Main, Izabella, 'How Is Communism Displayed? Exhibitions and Museums of Communism in Poland', in Sarkisova and Apor (eds.), *Past for the Eyes*, pp. 371–400

Manz, Stefan, *Constructing a German Diaspora: The 'Greater German Empire', 1871–1914* (New York: Routledge, 2014)

Marchetti, Christian, 'Selbstfindung und Diversität – Kleine Volkskunden in Südosteuropa', in Cornelia Eisler and Silke Göttsch-Elten (eds.), *Minderheiten im Europa der Zwischenkriegszeit: Wissenschaftliche Konzeptionen, mediale Vermittlung, politische Funktion* (Münster: Waxmann Verlag, 2017), pp. 67–98

Marin, Irina, *Contested Frontiers in the Balkans: Ottoman and Habsburg Rivalries in Eastern Europe* (London: I. B. Tauris, 2013)

Mark, James, 'Antifascism, the 1956 Revolution and the Politics of the Communist Autobiographies in Hungary 1944–2000', *Europe-Asia Studies* 58/8 (2006), pp. 1209–40

  'Containing Fascism: History in Post-Communist Baltic Occupation and Genocide Museums', in Sarkisova and Apor (eds.), *Past for the Eyes*, pp. 335–69

The Unfinished Revolution: Making Sense of the Communist Past in Central-Eastern Europe (New Haven: Yale University Press, 2010)

'What Remains? Anti-Communism, Forensic Archaeology, and the Retelling of the National Past in Lithuania and Romania', *Past & Present* 206 (2010), pp. 276–300

Mark, James, Bogdan C. Iacob, Tobias Rupprecht and Ljubica Spaskovska, *1989: A Global History of Eastern Europe* (Cambridge: Cambridge University Press, 2019)

Markel, Michael, 'Adolf Meschendörfers *Siebenbürgische Elegie*: Bausteine zu einer Rezeptionsgeschichte', in Peter Motzan and Stefan Sienerth (eds.), *Deutsche Regionalliteraturen in Rumänien, 1918–1944: Positionsbestimmungen, Forschungswege, Fallstudien* (Munich: Verlag Südostdeutsches Kulturwerk, 1997), pp. 177–222

Mârza, Daniela, 'Aspects de l'enseignement roumain confessionnel en Transylvanie', *Transylvanian Review* 15/2 (2006), pp. 36–44

Maxwell, Alexander, 'Hungaro-German Dual Nationality: Germans, Slavs, and Magyars during the 1848 Revolution', *German Studies Review* 39/1 (2016), pp. 17–39

Merten, Ulrich, *Forgotten Voices: The Expulsion of the Germans from Eastern Europe after World War II* (New Brunswick: Transaction, 2012)

Milata, Paul, *Zwischen Hitler, Stalin, und Antonescu: Rumäniendeutsche in der Waffen-SS* (Cologne: Böhlau, 2009)

Miller, Barbara, *Narratives of Guilt and Compliance in Unified Germany: Stasi Informers and Their Impact on Society* (London: Routledge, 1999)

Mitu, Sorin, *National Identity of Romanians in Transylvania* (Budapest: CEU Press, 2001)

Moeller, Robert G., 'The Politics of the Past in the 1950s: Rhetorics of Victimsation in East and West Germany', in Niven (ed.), *Germans as Victims*, pp. 26–42

War Stories: The Search for a Usable Past in the Federal Republic of Germany (Berkeley: University of California Press, 2001)

Moise, Moise (comp.), *Do Not Avenge Us: Testimonies about the Suffering of the Romanians Deported from Bessarabia to Siberia* (New York: Reflection Publishing, 2016)

Moldovean, Oana Corina, 'Eginald Schlattner: Rațiunea Turismului Literar la Roșia-Sibiu', *Studii de Știință și Cultură*, 1/12 (2008), pp. 55–60

Morar, Vasile, 'Dimensiunea etică a relației Sași–Români și Români–Sași', *Studia Hebraica* 4 (2004), pp. 196–9

Motzan, Peter, 'Risikofaktor Schriftsteller: Ein Beispiel von Repressionen und Rechtswillkür', in Motzan and Sienerth (eds.), *Worte als Gefahr und Gefährdung*, pp. 51–82

'Die vielen Wege in den Abschied: Die siebenbürgisch-deutsche Literatur in Rumänien (1919–1989): Ein sozialhistorischer Abriss', at www.siebenbuerger-sachsen-bw.de/buch/sachsen/15.htm

'Wegbegleiter und Wegbereiter: Karl Kurt Klein und die "siebenbürgische Zeitschrift" *Klingsor* (1924–1939)', in Motzan, Sienerth and Schwob (eds.), *Karl Kurt Klein*, pp. 157–80

Motzan, Peter, Stefan Sienerth and Anton Schwob (eds.), *Karl Kurt Klein: Leben – Werk – Wirkung* (Munich: Verlag Südostdeutsches Kulturwerk, 2001)

Müller, Dietmar, 'Die Siebenbürgische Frage: Neue Fragestellungen – alte Antworten', *Zeitschrift für Siebenbürgische Landeskunde* 27/1 (2004), pp. 125–32

Muresan, Alexandra, 'The Fortified Church of Biertan (Transylvania)', in Myra Shackley (ed.), *Visitor Management: Case Studies from World Heritage Sites* (Burlington, Mass.: Butterworth-Heinemann, 1998), pp. 26–45

Neumann, Victor, *The Banat of Timişoara: A European Melting Pot* (London: Scala Art and Heritage Publishers, 2019)

'Multiculturality and Interculturality: The Case of Timişoara', *Hungarian Studies* 21/1–2 (2007), pp. 3–18

Niven, Bill, *Facing the Nazi Past: United Germany and the Legacy of the Third Reich* (London: Routledge, 2002)

(ed.), *Germans as Victims: Remembering the Past in Contemporary Germany* (Basingstoke: Palgrave Macmillan, 2006)

'Introduction: German Victimhood at the Turn of the Millennium', in Niven (ed.), *Germans as Victims*, pp. 1–25

'On a Supposed Taboo: Flight and Refugees from the East in GDR Film and Television', *German Life and Letters* 65/2 (2012), pp. 216–36

Nora, Pierre (ed.), *Les Lieux de mémoire, Vols. I–III* (Paris: Gallimard, 1997)

Nowotnick, Michaela, '"95 Jahre Haft" – Kronstädter Schriftstellerprozess 1959: Darstellungsformen und Deutungsmuster der Aufarbeitung', *Halbjahresschrift für südosteuropäische Geschichte, Literatur und Politik* 21/1–2 (2012), pp. 173–81

Die Unentrinnbarkeit der Biographie: Der Roman 'Rote Handschuhe' von Eginald Schlattner als Fallstudie zur rumäniendeutschen Literatur (Cologne: Böhlau, 2016)

Oborni, Teréz, 'Between Vienna and Constantinople: Notes on the Legal Status of the Principality of Transylvania', in Gábor Kármán and Lovro Kunčević (eds.), *The European Tributary States of the Ottoman Empire in the Sixteenth and Seventeenth Centuries* (Leiden: Brill, 2013), pp. 67–89

O'Donnell, Krista, Renate Bridenthal and Nancy Reagin (eds.), *The Heimat Abroad: Boundaries of Germanness* (Ann Arbor: University of Michigan, 2005)

Ohliger, Rainer, 'Vom Vielvölkerstaat zum Nationalstaat: Migration aus und nach Rumänien', in Heinz Fassmann and Rainer Münz (eds.), *Migration in Europa: Historische Entwicklung, aktuelle Trends und politische Reaktionen* (Frankfurt am Main: Campus, 1996), pp. 285–302

Okey, Robin, *The Demise of Communist East Europe: 1989 in Context* (London: Arnold, 2004)

The Habsburg Monarchy c. 1765–1918 (Basingstoke: Macmillan, 2001)

Olick, Jeffrey K. (ed.), *The Politics of Regret: On Collective Memory and Historical Responsibility* (New York: Routledge, 2007)

De Oliveira, Claire, '"Autre est le chant des fontaines … "': Intégration et transformation de l'altérité dans l'*Élégie transylvaine* d'Adolf Meschendörfer', *Études Germaniques* 262/2 (2011), pp. 479–89

von Oppen, Karoline and Stefan Wolff, 'From the Margins to the Centre? The Discourse on Expellees and Victimhood in Germany', in Niven (ed.), *Germans as Victims*, pp. 194–209

von Oswald, Anne, Karen Schönwälder and Barbara Sonnenberger, '*Einwanderungsland Deutschland*: A New Look at Its Post-War History', in Rainer Ohliger, Karen Schönwälder and Triadafilos Triadafilopoulos (eds.), *European Encounters: Migrants, Migration, and European Societies since 1945* (London: Ashgate, 2003), pp. 19–37

Pakier, Małgorzata and Joanna Wawrzyniak (eds.), *Memory and Change in Europe: Eastern Perspectives* (New York: Berghahn, 2016)

Pakucs-Willcocks, Mária, 'Between "Faithful Subjects" and "Pernicious Nation": Greek Merchants in the Principality of Transylvania in the Seventeenth Century', *Hungarian Historical Review* 6/1 (2017), pp. 111–37

Panayi, Panikos (ed.), *Germans as Minorities during the First World War: A Global Comparative Perspective* (Farnham: Ashgate, 2014)

Passerini, Luisa, *Fascism in Popular Memory: The Cultural Experience of the Turin Working Class* (Cambridge: Cambridge University Press, 1987)

Patel, Kiran Klaus, 'Transnational Geschichte', *EGO: Europäische Geschichte Online* (2010) at http://ieg-ego.eu/de/threads/theorien-und-methoden/transnationale-geschichte

Penny, H. Glenn, 'From Migrant Knowledge to Fugitive Knowledge? German Migrants and Knowledge Production in Guatemala, 1880s–1945', *Geschichte und Gesellschaft* 43/3 (2017), pp. 381–412

'Material Connections: German Schools, Things, and Soft Power in Argentina and Chile from the 1880s through the Interwar Period', *Comparative Studies in Society and History* 59/3 (2017), pp. 519–49

Penny, H. Glenn and Stefan Rinke, 'Germans Abroad: Respatializing Historical Narrative', *Geschichte und Gesellschaft* 41/2 (2015), pp. 173–96

Péporté, Pit, Sonja Kmec, Benoît Majerus and Michael Margue, *Inventing Luxembourg: Representations of the Past, Space and Language from the Nineteenth to Twenty-First Century* (Leiden: Brill, 2010)

Pešek, Jiří, *Německé menšiny v právních normách 1938–1948: Československo ve srovnání s vybranými evropskými zeměmi*, Vol. I (Brno: Doplněk, 2006)

Petrescu, Corina L., 'Witness for the Prosecution: Eginald Schlattner in the Files of the Securitate', in Glajar, Lewis and Petrescu (eds.), *Secret Police Files from the Eastern Bloc*, pp. 84–113

Petrescu, Cristina and Dragoş Petrescu, 'Mastering vs Coming to Terms with the Past: A Critical Analysis of Post-Communist Romanian Historiography', in Sorin Antohi, Balázs Trencsényi and Péter Apor (eds.), *Narratives Unbound:*

Historical Studies in Post-Communist Eastern Europe (Budapest: CEU Press, 2007), pp. 311–408

Petritsch, Ernst D., 'Das Osmanische Reich und Siebenbürgen im Konfessionszeitalter', in Leppin and Wien (eds.), *Konfessionsbildung und Konfessionskultur*, pp. 15–24

Pettai, Vello, 'Explaining Ethnic Politics in the Baltic States: Reviewing the Triadic Nexus Model', *Journal of Baltic Studies* 37/1 (2006), pp. 124–36

Phinnemore, David (ed.), *The EU and Romania: Accession and Beyond* (London: Federal Trust for Education and Research, 2006)

Pintilescu, Corneliu, 'Problema "Naționaliști Germani" în activitatea Securității (1948–1964)', in Cosmin Budeancă and Florentin Olteanu (eds.), *Identități sociale, culturale, etnice și religioase în comunism* (Iași: Polirom, 2015), pp. 269–83

Procesul Biserica Neagră: Brașov 1958 (Brașov: Veröffentlichungen von Studium Transylvanicum, 2009)

Polak-Springer, Peter, *Recovered Territory: A German–Polish Conflict over Land and Culture, 1919–1989* (New York: Berghahn, 2015)

Polian, Pavel, *Against Their Will: The History and Geography of Forced Migrations in the USSR* (Budapest: CEU Press, 2004)

Pop, Ioan-Aurel and Ioan Bolovan (eds.), *History of Romania Compendium* (Cluj-Napoca: Romanian Culture Institute, 2006)

Popa, Dan, *Naționalitatea ca vină: deportarea etnicilor germani din România în URSS* (Bucharest: Editura Mica Valahia, 2015)

Popa, Klaus, *Akten um die deutsche Volksgruppe in Rumänien 1937–1945* (Frankfurt am Main: Peter Lang, 2005)

'Erfüllung des NS-Ungeists: Bibliografisch-biografische Porträts aus der "Deutschen Volksgruppe Rumänien" 1940–1941 (I)', *Halbjahresschrift für südosteuropäische Geschichte, Literatur und Politik* 17/1 (2005), pp. 67–76

'Erfüllung des NS-Ungeists: Biografische-bibliografisch Porträts aus der "Deutschen Volksgruppe Rumänien" 1940–1944 (II)', *Halbjahresschrift für südosteuropäische Geschichte, Literatur und Politik* 17/2 (2005), pp. 81–4

'Erfüllung des NS-Ungeists: Bibliografisch-biografische Porträts aus der "Deutschen Volksgruppe Rumänien" 1940–1944 (III)', *Halbjahresschrift für südosteuropäische Geschichte, Literatur und Politik* 18/1 (2006), pp. 86–90

'Erfüllung des NS-Ungeists: Bibliografisch-biografische Porträts aus der "Deutschen Volksgruppe Rumänien" 1940–1944 (V)', *Halbjahresschrift für südosteuropäische Geschichte, Literatur und Politik* 19/1 (2007), pp. 49–59

Portelli, Alessandro, *The Death of Luigi Trastulli and Other Stories: Form and Meaning in Oral History* (Albany: SUNY Press, 1991)

The Order Has Been Carried Out: History, Memory, and Meaning of a Nazi Massacre in Rome (Basingstoke: Palgrave Macmillan, 2007)

Priberksy, Andreas, Karin Liebhart and Sándor Kurtán, 'A Temple for the Nation: Symbolic Space of Central European Conservatism', *Cultural Studies* 16/6 (2002), pp. 797–808

Proctor, Tammy, 'Patriotic Enemies: Germans in the Americas, 1914–1920', in Panikos Panayi (ed.), *Germans as Minorities during the First World War: A Global Comparative Perspective* (Farnham: Ashgate, 2014), pp. 213–34

Protze, Helmut, 'Die Zipser Sachsen im Sprachgeographischen und Sprachhistorischen Vergleich zu den Siebenbürger Sachsen', *Zeitschrift für Siebenbürgische Landeskunde* 29/2 (2006), pp. 142–51

von Puttkamer, Joachim, Stefan Sienerth and Ulrich A. Wien (eds.), *Die Securitate in Siebenbürgen* (Cologne: Böhlau, 2014)

Radstone, Susannah (ed.), *Memory and Methodology* (Oxford: Berg, 2000)

Rădulescu, Raluca, *Das literarische Werk Hans Bergels* (Berlin: Frank und Timme, 2015)

Reid, Donald, 'Resistance and Its Discontents: Affairs, Archives, Avowals, and the Aubracs', *Journal of Modern History* 77 (2005), pp. 97–137

Reinerth, Karl M., *Zur politischen Entwicklung der Deutschen in Rumänien 1918–1928: Aus einer siebenbürgisch-sächsischen Sicht* (Thaur: Wort und Welt Verlag, 1993)

Reisch, Alfred A., *Hot Books in the Cold War: The West's CIA-Funded Secret Book Distribution Program behind the Iron Curtain* (Budapest: CEU Press, 2013)

Rock, David and Stefan Wolff (eds.), *Coming Home to Germany? The Integration of Ethnic Germans from Central and Eastern Europe in the Federal Republic* (New York: Berghahn Books, 2002)

Röder, Annemarie, *Deutsche, Schwaben, Donauschwaben: Ethnisierungsprozesse einer deutschen Minderheit in Südosteuropa* (Marburg: Deutsche Gesellschaft für Volkskunde, 1998)

'Romania 100: Nation, Identity, Global Challenge', *Journal of European Studies* 48/3–4 (2019), pp. 215–340

Roth, Harald, *Hermannstadt: Kleine Geschichte einer Stadt in Siebenbürgen* (Cologne: Böhlau, 2006)

Kleine Geschichte Siebenbürgens (Cologne: Böhlau, 2003)

Ruge, Wolfgang, 'Historiography in the German Democratic Republic: Rereading the History of National Socialism', in Reinhard Alter and Peter Monteath (eds.), *Rewriting the German Past: History and Identity in the New Germany* (Atlantic Highlands, N.J.: Humanities Press, 1997), pp. 208–21

Sălăgean, Tudor, 'Romanian Society in the Early Middle Ages (Ninth–Fourteenth Century)', in Pop and Bolovan (eds.), *History of Romania Compendium*, pp. 133–208

Sarkisova, Oksana and Péter Apor (eds.), *Past for the Eyes: East European Representations of Communism in Cinema and Museums after 1989* (Budapest: CEU Press, 2008)

Saunier, Pierre-Yves, 'Learning by Doing: Notes about the Making of *The Palgrave Dictionary of Transnational History*', *Journal of Modern European History* 6/2 (2008), pp. 159–79

Transnational History (Basingstoke: Palgrave Macmillan, 2013)

Schlarb, Cornelia, *Tradition im Wandel: Die evangelischen-lutherischen Gemeinden in Bessarabien 1814–1940* (Cologne: Böhlau, 2007)

Schlau, Wilfried (ed.), *Sozialgeschichte der baltischen Deutschen* (Cologne: Wissenschaft und Politik, 2000)

Schleichl, Sigurd Paul, 'Karl Kurt Klein (1897–1971): Aspekte eines vielfältigen germanistischen Lebenswerks', in Motzan, Sienerth and Schwob (eds.), *Karl Kurt Klein*, pp. 21–69

Schmidt, Mária, 'Das Budapester Museum "Haus des Terrors": Museum der modernen Zeitgeschichte und lebendige Gedenkstätte', in Knigge and Mählert (eds.), *Der Kommunismus im Museum*, pp. 161–9

Schmitz, Helmut, 'The Birth of the Collective from the Spirit of Empathy: From the "Historians' Dispute" to German Suffering', in Niven (ed.), *Germans as Victims*, pp. 93–108

Schödl, Günter, 'Am Rande des Reiches, am Rande der Nation: Deutsche im Königreich Ungarn (1867–1914/18)', in Schödl (ed.), *Deutsche Geschichte im Osten Europas*, pp. 349–455

  (ed.), *Deutsche Geschichte im Osten Europas: Land an der Donau* (Berlin: Siedler Verlag, 1995)

Schönhoven, Klaus, *Europa als Erinnerungsgemeinschaft* (Bonn: Friedrich-Ebert-Stiftung, 2007)

Schüller, Olga, *Für Glaube, Führer, Volk, Vater- oder Mutterland? Die Kämpfe um die deutsche Jugend im rumänischen Banat (1918–1944)* (Berlin: LIT Verlag, 2009)

Schulze, Rainer, 'Forced Migration of German Populations during and after the Second World War: History and Memory', in Jessica Reinisch and Elizabeth White (eds.), *The Disentanglement of Populations: Migration, Expulsion and Displacement in Postwar Europe, 1944–1949* (Basingstoke: Palgrave, 2011), pp. 51–70

  'The Struggle of Past and Present in Individual Identities: The Case of German Refugees and Expellees from the East', in Rock and Wolff (eds.), *Coming Home to Germany?*, pp. 38–55

Schuster, Diana, *Die Banater Autorengruppe: Selbstdarstellung und Rezeption in Rumänien und Deutschland* (Konstanz: Hartung-Gorre Verlag, 2004)

Schwellnus, Guido, 'The Adoption of Nondiscrimination and Minority Protection Rules in Romania, Hungary, and Poland', in Frank Schimmelpfennig and Ulrich Sedelmeier (eds.), *The Europeanisation of Central and Eastern Europe* (Ithaca, N.Y.: Cornell University Press, 2005), pp. 51–70

Schwob, Anton, 'Fünf Universitäten, vier Staaten und drei Sprachen: Karl Kurt Klein als Lehrer und Forscher', in Motzan, Sienerth and Schwob (eds.), *Karl Kurt Klein*, pp. 9–20

Scurtu, Ioan, 'Beiträge zur Geschichte der Deutschen Parlamentspartei 1919–1937', in König (ed.), *Siebenbürgen zwischen den beiden Weltkriegen*, pp. 55–68

Seewann, Gerhard, *Geschichte der Deutschen in Ungarn, Vol. II, 1860 bis 2006* (Marburg: Verlag Herder-Institut, 2011)

'Siebenbürger Sachse, Ungarndeutscher, Donauschwabe? Überlegungen zur Identitätsproblematik des Deutschtums in Südosteuropa', in Gerhard Seewann (ed.), *Minderheitenfragen in Südosteuropa* (Munich: Südost Institut, 1992), pp. 139–55

Sharenkova, Radostina, 'Forget-Me(-Not): Visitors and Museum Presentations about Communism before 1989', in Mihail Neamțu, Corina Doboș and Marius Stan (eds.), *History of Communism in Europe, Vol. I, Politics of Memory in Post-Communist Europe* (Bucharest: Zeta Books, 2010), pp. 65–82

Shore, Paul, *Jesuits and the Politics of Religious Pluralism in Eighteenth-Century Transylvania: Culture, Politics, and Religion, 1693–1773* (London: Routledge, 2017)

Sienerth, Stefan, 'Weltoffenheit und Provinzenge: Die siebenbürgisch-deutsche Literatur von ihren Anfängen bis zum Ausgang des 19. Jahrhunderts', in Rothe (ed.), *Die Siebenbürger Sachsen*, pp. 51–68

Șindilariu, Thomas, 'Sportpolitische Impulse aus dem "Dritten Reich" und der Strandbadbau in Siebenbürgen 1936–1939', in Hausleitner and Roth (eds.), *Der Einfluss von Faschismus*, pp. 163–82

Skey, Michael, '"There Are Times When I Feel Like a Bit of an Alien": Middling Migrants and the National Order of Things', *Nations and Nationalism* 24/3 (2018), pp. 606–23

Smith, David J., 'Framing the National Question in Central and Eastern Europe: A Quadratic Nexus?', *Global Review of Ethnopolitics* 2/1 (2002), pp. 3–16

Spariosu, Mihai, *Intercultural Conflict in and Harmony in the Central European Borderlands: The Cases of Banat and Transylvania 1848–1939* (Göttingen: V&R Unipress, 2017)

Sparwasser, Sebastian, *Identität im Spannungsfeld von Zwangsmigration und Heimkehr: Ungarndeutsche Vertriebene und die Remigration* (Vienna: New Academic Press, 2018)

Spiridon-Șerbu, Claudia, *Zensur in der rumäniendeutschen Literatur der 1970er und 1980er Jahre* (Zurich: LIT Verlag, 2018)

Stan, Lavinia, *Transitional Justice in Post-Communist Romania: The Politics of Memory* (Cambridge: Cambridge University Press, 2013)

Stan, Lavinia and Diane Vancea, 'House of Cards: The Presidency from Iliescu to Basescu', in Lavinia Stan and Diane Vancea (eds.), *Post-Communist Romania at Twenty-Five: Linking Past, Present, and Future* (Lanham, Md.: Lexington Books, 2015), pp. 193–218

Ștefan, Adelina, 'Between Limits, Lures and Excitement: Socialist Romanian Holidays Abroad during the 1960s–1980s', in Kathy Burrell and Kathrin Hörschelmann (eds.), *Mobilities in Socialist and Post-Socialist States: Societies on the Move* (London: Palgrave, 2014), pp. 87–104

Steiner, Stefan, *Reise ohne Wiederkehr: Die Deportation von Protestanten aus Kärnten 1734–1736* (Munich: Oldenbourg, 2007)

Sterbling, Anton, *'Am Anfang war das Gespräch': Reflexionen und Beiträge zur 'Aktionsgruppe Banat' und andere literatur- und kunstbezogene Arbeiten* (Hamburg: Krämer, 2008)

'Die Aussiedlung der Deutschen aus Rumänien in die Bundesrepublik Deutschland und andere Migrationsvorgänge in und aus Südosteuropa', in Edda Currle and Tanja Wunderlich (eds.), *Deutschland – ein Einwanderungsland? Rückblick, Bilanz und neue Fragen* (Stuttgart: Lucius, 2001), pp. 197–222

'Dazugehörende Fremde? Besonderheiten der Integration der Rumäniendeutschen in der Bundesrepublik Deutschland', in Christoph Köck, Aloid Moosmüller and Klaus Roth (eds.), *Zuwanderung und Integration: Kulturwissenschaftliche Zugänge und soziale Praxis* (Münster: Waxmann Verlag, 2004), pp. 109–24

Kontinuität und Wandel in Rumänien und Südosteuropa: Historisch-soziologische Analysen (Munich: Südostdeutsches Kulturwerk, 1997)

'Minderheitenprobleme und interethnische Konflikte in Siebenbürgen nach 1867', *Siebenbürgische Semesterblätter* 10/2 (1996), pp. 109–24

Stirk, Peter, 'The Idea of *Mitteleuropa*', in Peter Stirk (ed.), *Mitteleuropa: History and Prospects* (Edinburgh: Edinburgh University Press, 1994), pp. 1–35

Stoica, Cătălin Augustin, 'Once upon a Time There Was a Big Party: The Social Bases of the Romanian Communist Party (Part I)', *East European Politics and Societies* 19/4 (2005), pp. 686–716

'Once upon a Time There Was a Big Party: The Social Bases of the Romanian Communist Party (Part II)', *East European Politics and Societies* 20/3 (2006), pp. 447–82

Stollberg, Robert and Thomas Schulz, *Kirchenburgen in Siebenbürgen – Fortified Churches in Transylvania* (Cologne: Böhlau, 2007)

Strohmeyer, Arno and Norbert Spannenberger (eds.), *Frieden und Konfliktmanagement in interkulturellen Räumen: Das Osmanische Reich und die Habsburgermonarchie in der Frühen Neuzeit* (Stuttgart: Franz Steiner Verlag, 2013)

Struck, Bernhard, Kate Ferris and Jacques Revel, 'Introduction: Space and Scale in Transnational History', *International History Review* (Special Issue: 'Size Matters: Scales and Spaces in Transnational and Comparative History') 33/4 (2011), pp. 573–84

Sugar, Peter F., *Southeastern Europe under Ottoman Rule* (Seattle: University of Washington Press, 1996)

Sutherland, Claire and Elena Barabantseva (eds.), *Diaspora and Citizenship* (Abingdon: Routledge, 2011)

Swanson, John, 'Minority-Building in the German Diaspora: The Hungarian-Germans', *Austrian History Yearbook* 36 (2005), pp. 148–66

Tangible Belonging: Negotiating Germanness in Twentieth-Century Hungary (Pittsburgh: University of Pittsburgh Press, 2017)

Szabó, Zoltán Tibori, 'The Holocaust in Transylvania', in Randolph L. Braham and András Kovács (eds.), *The Holocaust in Hungary: Seventy Years Later* (Budapest: CEU Press, 2016), pp. 147–82

Szelényi, Balázs A. , *The Failure of the Central European Bourgeoisie* (Basingstoke: Palgrave Macmillan, 2006)

'From Minority to *Übermensch*: The Social Roots of Ethnic Conflict in the German Diaspora of Hungary, Romania and Slovakia', *Past & Present* 196 (2007), pp. 215–51

Ther, Philipp, 'Expellee Policy in the Soviet-Occupied Zone and the GDR: 1945–1953', in Rock and Wolff (eds.), *Coming Home to Germany?*, pp. 56–76

Thompson, Paul, 'The Voice of the Past', in Robert Perks and Alistair Thomson (eds.), *The Oral History Reader* (London: Routledge, 2012), pp. 22–8

Thorpe, Julie, *Pan-Germanism and the Austrofascist State, 1933–1938* (Manchester: Manchester University Press, 2011)

Thum, Gregor, *Uprooted: How Breslau Became Wrocław* (Princeton: Princeton University Press, 2011)

Tilkovszky, Loránt, 'Die Weimarer Republik und die Nationalitäten in Südosteuropa, mit besonderer Berücksichtigung der deutschen und ungarischen Minderheiten in Rumänien', in König (ed.), *Siebenbürgen zwischen den beiden Weltkriegen*, pp. 115–27

Tismăneanu, Vladimir, *Fantasies of Salvation: Democracy, Nationalism and Myth in Post-Communist Europe* (Princeton: Princeton University Press, 2008)

(ed.), *The Revolutions of 1989* (London: Routledge, 1999)

Stalinism for All Seasons: A Political History of Romanian Communism (Berkeley: University of California Press, 2003)

Tismăneanu, Vladimir and Marius Stan, *Romania Confronts Its Communist Past: Democracy, Memory, and Moral Justice* (Cambridge: Cambridge University Press, 2018)

Todorova, Maria, 'The Balkans: From Discovery to Invention', *Slavic Review* 53/2 (1994), pp. 453–82

Imagining the Balkans (Oxford: Oxford University Press, 1997)

Scaling the Balkans: Essays on Eastern European Entanglements (Leiden: Brill, 2019)

'The Trap of Backwardness: Modernity, Temporality, and the Study of Eastern European Nationalism', *Slavic Review* 64/1 (2005), pp. 140–64

Todorova, Maria and Zsuzsa Gille (eds.), *Post-Communist Nostalgia* (New York: Berghahn, 2010)

Tonţa, Walter, 'Stefan Jäger: Der Lebensweg eines Künstlers am Rande Mitteleuropas', in Krier (ed.), *Hommage an Stefan Jäger*, pp. 130–2

Török, Zsuzsanna, 'Planning the National Minority: Strategies of the Journal *Hitel* in Romania, 1935–1944', *Nationalism and Ethnic Politics* 7/2 (2001), pp. 57–74

Tóth, Ágnes, *Rückkehr nach Ungarn 1946–1950* (Munich: Oldenbourg, 2012)

Tracy, James D., 'The Habsburg Monarchy in Conflict with the Ottoman Empire, 1527–1593: A Clash of Civilizations', *Austrian History Yearbook* 46 (2015), pp. 1–26

Trandafoiu, Ruxandra, *Diaspora Online: Identity Politics and Romanian Migrants* (New York: Berghahn, 2013)

Traşcă, Ottmar and Remus Gabriel Anghel (eds.), *Un veac frământat: Germanii din România după 1918* (Cluj: Institutului pentru Studierea Problemelor Minorităţilor Naţionale, 2018)

de Trégomain, Pierre, 'Constructing Authenticity: Commemorative Strategy of the Transylvanian Saxons in West Germany's Early Years', in Mareike König and Rainer Ohliger (eds.), *Enlarging European Memory: Migration Movements in Historical Perspective* (Ostfildern: Jan Thorbecke Verlag, 2006), pp. 99–111

'Versperrte Wahrnehmung: Die Auseinandersetzung der evangelischen Kirche A.B. In Rumänien mit dem Nationalsozialismus 1944–1948', in Hausleitner and Roth (eds.), *Der Einfluss von Faschismus*, pp. 331–50

Trencsényi, Balázs and Michal Kopeček (eds.), *Discourses of Collective Identity in Central and Southeast Europe (1770–1945): Late Enlightenment – Emergence of the Modern 'National Idea', Vol. I* (Budapest: CEU Press, 2006)

Turda, Marius, 'Controlling the National Body: Ideas of Racial Purification in Romania, 1918–1944', in Christian Promitzer, Sevasti Trubeta and Marius Turda (eds.), *Health, Hygiene and Eugenics in Southeastern Europe to 1945* (Budapest: CEU Press, 2011), pp. 325–50

'The Nation as Object: Race, Blood and Biopolitics in Interwar Romania', *Slavic Review* 66/3 (2007), pp. 413–41

Ursprung, Daniel, *Herrschaftslegitimation zwischen Tradition und Innovation: Repräsentation und Inszenierung von Herrschaft in der rumänischen Geschichte in der Vormoderne und bei Ceauşescu* (Heidelberg: Studium Transylvanicum, 2007)

Verdery, Katherine, *My Life as a Spy: Investigations in a Secret Police File* (Durham, N.C.: Duke University Press, 2018)

National Ideology under Socialism: Identity and Cultural Politics in Ceauşescu's Romania (Berkeley: University of California Press, 1991)

Transylvanian Villagers: Three Centuries of Political, Economic, and Ethnic Change (Berkeley: University of California Press, 1983)

Verona, Sergiu, *Military Occupation and Diplomacy: Soviet Troops in Romania, 1944–1958* (Durham, N.C.: Duke University Press, 1992)

Volkmer, Gerald, *Die Siebenbürgische Frage (1878–1900)* (Cologne: Böhlau, 2004)

Vukov, Nikolai, 'The "Unmemorable" and the "Unforgettable": "Museumizing" the Socialist Past in Post-1989 Bulgaria', in Sarkisova and Apor (eds.), *Past for the Eyes*, pp. 307–34

Vultur, Smaranda (ed.), *Germanii dîn Banat: prin povestirile lor* (Bucharest: Paideia, 2000)

Istorie trăită, istorie povestită: deportarea în Bărăgan, 1951–1956 (Timişoara: Editura Amarcord, 1997)

Wawrzyniak, Joanna, *Veterans, Victims, and Memory: The Politics of the Second World War in Communist Poland* (Frankfurt am Main: Peter Lang Edition, 2015)

Weber, Annemarie, *Rumäniendeutsche? Diskurse zur Gruppenidentität einer Minderheit (1944–1971)* (Cologne: Böhlau, 2010)

Weber, Georg, Renate Weber-Schlenther, Armin Nassehi, Oliver Sill and Georg Kneer (eds.), *Die Deportation der Siebenbürger Sachsen in die Sowjetunion 1945–1949: Die Deportation als historisches Geschehen, Vol. I* (Cologne: Böhlau, 1995)

(eds.), *Die Deportation der Siebenbürger Sachsen in die Sowjetunion 1945–1949: Die Deportation als biographisches Ereignis und literarisches Thema, Vol. II* (Cologne: Böhlau, 1995)

(eds.), *Die Deportation der Siebenbürger Sachsen in die Sowjetunion 1945–1949: Quellen und Bilder, Vol. III* (Cologne: Böhlau, 1995)

Weber, Petru, 'The Public Memory of the Holocaust in Postwar Romania', *Studia Hebraica* 4 (2004), pp. 341–8

Weiß, Peter Ulrich, *Kulturarbeit als diplomatischer Zankapfel: Die kulturellen Auslandsbeziehungen im Dreiecksverhältnis der beiden deutschen Staaten und Rumäniens von 1950 bis 1972* (Munich: R. Oldenbourg Verlag, 2010)

White, John J., 'A Romanian German in Germany: The Challenge of Ethnic and Ideological Identity in Herta Müller's Literary Work', in Rock and Wolff (eds.), *Coming Home to Germany?*, pp. 171–87

Wien, Ulrich A., *Kirchenleitung über dem Abgrund: Bischof Friedrich Müller vor den Herausforderungen durch Minderheitenexistenz, Nationalsozialismus und Kommunismus* (Cologne: Böhlau, 1998)

Windisch-Middendorf, Renate, *Der Mann ohne Vaterland: Hans Bergel – Leben und Werk* (Berlin: Frank & Timme, 2010)

Wingfield, Nancy, *Flag Wars and Stone Saints: How the Bohemian Lands Became Czech* (Cambridge, Mass.: Harvard University Press, 2007)

Winter, Jay, *Sites of Memory, Sites of Mourning: The Great War in European Cultural History* (Cambridge: Cambridge University Press, 1995)

Wolf, Josef, 'Selbstrepräsentation und kulturpolitische Neuorientierung der Banater Schwaben 1918–1925', in Engel and Tonţa (eds.), *Die Banater Schwaben nach dem Ersten Weltkrieg*, pp. 79–139

Wolff, Larry, *Inventing Eastern Europe: The Map of Civilisation on the Mind of the Enlightenment* (Stanford: Stanford University Press, 1994)

Wolff, Stefan, 'The Politics of Homeland: Irredentism and Recognition in the Policies of German Federal Governments and Expellee Organizations toward Ethnic German Minorities in Central and Eastern Europe, 1949–1999', in Krista O'Donnell, Renate Bridenthal and Nancy Reagin (eds.), *The Heimat Abroad: Boundaries of Germanness* (Ann Arbor: University of Michigan, 2005), pp. 287–313

Wolff, Stefan and Karl Cordell, 'Ethnic Germans in Poland and the Czech Republic: A Comparative Evaluation', *Nationalities Papers: The Journal of Nationalism and Ethnicity* 33/2 (2005), pp. 255–76

Wöll, Alexander and Harald Wydra (eds.), *Democracy and Myth in Russia and Eastern Europe* (London: Routledge, 2008)

Wood, Steve, 'German Expellee Organisations in the Enlarged EU', *German Politics* 14/4 (2005), pp. 487–97

Yoder, Jennifer A., 'Truth without Reconciliation: An Appraisal of the Enquete Commission on the SED Dictatorship in Germany', *German Politics* 8/3 (1999), pp. 59–80

Zach, Krista, Joachim Bahlcke and Konrad G. Gündisch, *Konfessionelle Pluralität, Stände und Nation: Ausgewählte Abhandlungen zur südosteuropäischen Religions- und Gesellschaftsgeschichte* (Berlin: LIT Verlag, 2004)

Zach, Krista and Cornelius R. Zach (eds.), *Deutsche und Rumänen in der Erinnerungsliteratur: Memorialistik als Geschichtsquelle* (Munich: IKGS Verlag, 2005)

Zahra, Tara, *The Great Departure: Mass Migration from Eastern Europe and the Making of the Free World* (New York: Norton, 2016)

  Kidnapped Souls: National Indifference and the Battle for Children in the Bohemian Lands, 1900–1948 (Ithaca, N.Y.: Cornell University Press, 2008)

  'Travel Agents on Trial: Policing Mobility in Late Imperial Austria', *Past & Present* 223 (2014), pp. 161–93

de Zayas, Alfred, *Nemesis at Potsdam. The Anglo-Americans and the Expulsion of the Germans: Background, Execution, Consequences* (London: Routledge, 1977)

Zierden, Josef, 'Deutsche Frösche: Zur "Diktatur des Dorfes" bei Herta Müller', *Text + Kritik* 155 (2002), pp. 30–8

Zimmermann, Harald, 'Die deutsche Südostsiedlung im Mittelalter', in Schödl (ed.), *Deutsche Geschichte im Osten Europas*, pp. 11–88

Zinner, Tibor, *A magyarországi németek kitelepítése* (Budapest: Magyar Hivatalos Közlönykiadó, 2004)

Index

For EU product safety concerns, contact us at Calle de José Abascal, 56–1°,
28003 Madrid, Spain or eugpsr@cambridge.org.

www.ingramcontent.com/pod-product-compliance
Ingram Content Group UK Ltd.
Pitfield, Milton Keynes, MK11 3LW, UK
UKHW020359140625
459647UK00020B/2558